HKPropel ≫ Accessing your HKPropel digital product is easy!

If it's your first time using HKPropel:

1. Visit HKPropel.HumanKinetics.com.
2. Click the "New user? Register here" link on the opening screen to register for an one-time-use access code.
3. Follow the onscreen prompts to create your HKPropel account. Use a **valid emai** to ensure you receive important system updates and to help us find your account
4. Enter the access code exactly as shown below, including hyphens. You will not need to re-enter this access code on subsequent visits, and this access code cannot be redeemed by any other user.
5. After your first visit, simply log in to HKPropel.HumanKinetics.com to access your digital product.

If you already have an HKPropel account:

1. Visit HKPropel.HumanKinetics.com and log in with your username (email address) and password.
2. Once you are logged in, click the arrow next to your name in the top right corner and then click **My Account**.
3. Under the "Add Access Code" heading, enter the access code exactly as shown below, including hyphens, and click the **Add** button.
4. Once your code is redeemed, navigate to your Library on the Dashboard to access your digital content.

> **Product:** Dimensions of Leisure for Life 2nd Edition HKPropel Access
>
> **Student access code:** IWWL-GK18-FA5W-7566

INSTRUCTORS: *If you received this textbook as a desk copy, you should use the access instructions provided by your sales rep. instead of the student access code above.*

NOTE TO STUDENTS: If your instructor uses HKPropel to assign work to your class, you will need to enter a **class enrollment token** in HKPropel on the **My Account** page. This token will be provided **by your instructor at no cost to you,** but it is required **in addition** to the unique access code that is printed above.

Helpful tips:
You may reset your password from the log in screen at any time if you forget it.

Your license to this digital product will expire **1 year** after the date you redeem the access code. You can check the expiration dates of all your HKPropel products at any time in **My Account**.

If you purchased a used book, you may purchase a new access code by visiting US.HumanKinetics.com and searching for "Dimensions of Leisure for Life HKPropel Access."

For assistance, contact us via email at HKPropelCustSer@hkusa.com.   10-2021

Mary Sara Wells, PhD

University of Utah

Mary Parr, PhD

Kent State University

EDITORS

HUMAN KINETICS

Library of Congress Cataloging-in-Publication Data

Names: Tapps, Tyler Nicholas, editor. | Wells, Mary Sara, editor. | Parr, Mary, 1962- editor.

Title: Dimensions of leisure for life / Tyler Tapps, Mary Sara Wells, Mary Parr, editors.

Description: Second edition. | Champaign, IL : Human Kinetics, 2022. | Includes bibliographical references and index.

Identifiers: LCCN 2021022741 (print) | LCCN 2021022742 (ebook) | ISBN 9781492598497 (paperback) | ISBN 9781492598503 (epub) | ISBN 9781492598510 (pdf)

Subjects: LCSH: Leisure. | Recreation.

Classification: LCC GV14 .D56 2022 (print) | LCC GV14 (ebook) | DDC 790.1--dc23

LC record available at https://lccn.loc.gov/2021022741

LC ebook record available at https://lccn.loc.gov/2021022742

ISBN: 978-1-4925-9849-7 (print)

Senior Acquisitions Editor: Amy N. Tocco; **Copyeditor:** Janet Kiefer; **Indexer:** Rebecca L. McCorkle; **Permissions Manager:** Dalene Reeder; **Graphic Designer:** Julie L. Denzer; **Cover Designer:** Keri Evans; **Cover Design Specialist:** Susan Rothermel Allen; **Photograph (cover):** wundervisuals / Getty Images; **Photo Asset Manager:** Laura Fitch; **Photo Production Manager:** Jason Allen; **Senior Art Manager:** Kelly Hendren; **Illustrations:** © Human Kinetics, unless otherwise noted; **Printer:** Premier Print Group

Printed in the United States of America   10 9 8 7 6 5 4 3 2 1

Human Kinetics
1607 N. Market Street
Champaign, IL 61820
USA

United States and International
Website: **US.HumanKinetics.com**
Email: info@hkusa.com
Phone: 1-800-747-4457

Canada
Website: **Canada.HumanKinetics.com**
Email: info@hkcanada.com

E8083

Tell us what you think!
Human Kinetics would love to hear what we can do to improve the customer experience. Use this QR code to take our brief survey.

Contents

(5) Leisure and Well-Being   63
Colleen Hood, Cynthia Carruthers

PART III   Dimensions of Leisure in Society

(6) Leisure History and Heritage   83
Lee J. deLisle

PART IV   Leisure in Your World

(15) Leisure and Geography   **209**

Augustus W. Hallmon, Mariela Fernandez

(16) Leisure Across the Life Span   **227**

Mary Sara Wells

(17) Charting Your Course   **241**

Paul A. Schlag

Preface

Leisure exists in many contexts and in many forms. This book addresses multiple ways leisure affects lives and even our larger society. Now, more than ever, most people seek leisure rather than define it, but the more we understand the dimensions of leisure that contribute to our quality of life and that of our communities, the more likely we are to appreciate it.

Leisure is often perceived as less important within the larger scope of life. Earning a living, pursuing an education, and raising a family often take precedence over meaningful leisure. When you are asked to board an airplane "at your leisure," the suggestion is that you can do so whenever you are ready, no rush! To some people, leisure means doing nothing, but to others, leisure means doing a lot of things. When we consider all the public, not-for-profit, and commercial providers of leisure opportunities around the world, leisure can be viewed as a serious, important aspect of our lives.

Leisure has probably played a role in everyone's life to some extent. From social development and connecting with friends to participating in activities you think are fun, everybody has a context for leisure. You know what you like and do not like, and you learn what you enjoy and do not enjoy. Sometimes people take leisure for granted, and that is not a negative thing. As people move beyond formal schooling, leisure sometimes becomes more elusive when careers, intimate partnerships, and other commitments (such as parenthood) become priorities. Therefore, understanding more about the value of leisure and its many opportunities may be useful throughout your life. Well-being and quality of life are not trivial issues. Ironically, students spend years preparing for careers that may change multiple times during their lives. Leisure education, on the other hand, can affect quality of life issues that last a lifetime.

Clearly your life is different from the lives of your parents and certainly much different from the lives of your grandparents; the instantaneous world of communication that you know did not exist for them. Society is different, and the values that are held have changed and will continue to change as diversity, equity, and inclusion are acknowledged and embraced. This book is meant to examine leisure through an academic approach and allow you to link the concepts presented here to your life while considering the personal as well as the societal and professional career aspects of each concept.

The title of this book is *Dimensions of Leisure for Life*. Dimensions refer to the scope and importance of leisure for individuals as well as society. You can easily consider your personal take on leisure, but the social impact of leisure—related to economics, community health, technology, and inclusion, for example—is not as often considered.

The authors of this book explore many of these dimensions. A unique aspect of the notion of leisure is that it emanates from scholarly disciplines, as you will note in the chapters about culture, history, politics, health, economics, and the natural environment. The authors represent different areas of expertise related to these disciplines as they are applied to leisure.

Many books about leisure were written in the 20th century, with most focusing on the past 60 years, when predictions of a leisure society (which has never come to fruition) emerged. Some of these books have focused on how recreation and leisure can improve the health and education of different populations. According to noted leisure sociologist Geoffrey Godbey, the early focus was not necessarily on the intellectual aspects of leisure but rather on its moral importance. Another approach to leisure has focused on the social problem of dealing with free time in an industrialized world. This view largely examines leisure in relationship to work as a social phenomenon. Also, this book addresses the generational needs and social issues surrounding each generation and their impact on leisure pursuits.

This book is designed to lead you through the meanings of leisure, the vastness of the ideas, and the benefits as well as the negative implications of leisure. Not all leisure activities are good, and we hope this book will highlight the value of leisure as well as some of the concerns that leisure raises. For example, some outdoor leisure activities can have long-lasting negative environmental effects. In addition to presenting academic content, the book includes a number of activities designed to connect theories and concepts to your own personal leisure pursuits and careers in the various leisure services industries. We have tried to show the potential fun of experiential learning through and about leisure.

This book guides you through a study of leisure as a multidisciplinary field from both an individual and a societal perspective. The authors use social science methods and current research to study leisure behavior and its practical applications. Relevant career opportunities within the broad scope of the "leisure services" delivery system are also presented. The text emphasizes inclusivity and prepares students and professionals to incorporate inclusive practices into their work.

Part I examines the broad dimensions of leisure and its related industries. It looks at leisure as a social science and analyses its societal value. Part II discusses how individual dimensions of leisure affect a person's quality of life, physical and mental health, and level of physical activity. Part III details how recreation history informs contemporary leisure studies. It uncovers the intersection of leisure and society, family life, technology, natural resources, economics, and public policy. Part IV presents the study of leisure from a consumer perspective. Awareness of local options as well as age, gender, sexual orientation, race, ethnicity, religion, and socioeconomic status; geographic distribution of leisure spaces; and stage of development all influence an individual's leisure choices and level of involvement in leisure activities.

Throughout the text, you will consider the role that recreation and leisure play in your life. You are encouraged to seek out the resources that are available, learn to recognize and challenge the obstacles to participation, and commit to a leisure plan that will enhance personal growth. In addition, learning outcomes and review questions in each chapter help you set learning goals and retain key information. Vocabulary terms allow you to identify important content.

This new edition has been updated with current research and applications within the field and contains the following features to help you connect theoretical concepts to practical applications:

- On the Job sidebars in each chapter help you better understand common issues in the recreation and leisure workforce.
- Self-Exploration sidebars throughout the chapters provide opportunities for you to reflect on the role of leisure in your life.
- A new chapter on leisure and family life discusses the impact of leisure on family structures and how to create valuable leisure experiences for all family members.
- The chapter on technology has been updated to reflect the rapid pace of digital advancement in leisure and its effect on individual equality and privacy.

Student Resources in HK*Propel*

New to this edition are several additional resources delivered online through HK*Propel*. These help to bring the content to life and further student comprehension. The resources include chapter overviews, assignments, web links, key term flashcards, and chapter quizzes (available only if assigned by the instructor).

To access these resources, see the card at the front of the print book for your unique HK*Propel* access code. For ebook users, reference the HK*Propel* access code instructions on the page immediately following the book cover.

Instructor Resources in HK*Propel*

A variety of instructor resources are available online within the instructor pack in HK*Propel*:

- Presentation package—The presentation package includes nearly 300 slides that cover the key points from the text. Instructors can easily add new slides to the presentation package to suit their needs.
- Instructor guide—The instructor guide includes chapter overviews, activities, case studies, and movie recommendations.
- Test package—The test package contains a bank of more than 450 questions in multiple-choice, true-or-false, multiple response, matching, fill-in-the-blank, and essay and short-answer format. The files may be downloaded for integration with a learning management system or printed as paper-based tests. Instructors may also create their own customized quizzes or tests from the test bank questions to assign to students directly through HK*Propel*. Multiple-choice, true-or-false, multiple response, and matching questions are automatically graded, and student scores can be easily reviewed by instructors in the platform.

- Chapter quizzes—Ready-made chapter quizzes allow instructors to assess student comprehension of the most important concepts in each chapter. Each quiz contains 10 questions, drawn from the larger test package. Each quiz may be downloaded or assigned to students within HK*Propel*. The chapter quizzes are automatically graded with scores available for review in the platform.

Instructor ancillaries are free to adopting instructors, including an ebook version of the text that allows instructors to add highlights, annotations, and bookmarks. Please contact your sales manager for details about how to access instructor resources in HK*Propel*.

We hope that after you read this book you will recognize that leisure can be examined from numerous perspectives. The more we understand the dimensions of leisure that contribute to quality of life for us and those in our communities, the more likely we are to appreciate them. Making leisure scholarly does not take the enjoyment from it. We hope that you will have some fun with this book, and we hope some of the ideas in this book will help you further understand your own behavior and why leisure should be given its due in our society.

Dimensions of Leisure

Importance of Leisure to Individuals and Society

Mary Parr

Kent State University

Tyler Tapps

Northwest Missouri State University

Mary Sara Wells

University of Utah

VOCABULARY TERMS

benefits

commercial recreation

enjoyment

gig economy

leisure

leisure education

leisure industry

not-for-profit organizations

park

parks and natural
  resources

play

recreation

sports

sport tourism

state of being or state
  of mind

tourists

work

work ethic

LEARNING OUTCOMES

After reading this chapter, you will be able to

- distinguish among leisure, recreation, play, and related concepts;
- identify the definition of leisure that is most meaningful for you;
- list at least five benefits of recreation and leisure;
- explain the relationship between quality of life and leisure; and
- describe the differences among the three major sectors of the leisure industry.

"Are you alive?" This is a question I typically ask my students on the first day of class. The question is usually met with some skeptical looks and a tentative "ye-e-ss," and I quickly follow up with "How do you know?" And the obvious responses come forth: "My heart is beating," "I'm breathing. . . ." This leads to the question: "Is there more to you than a beating heart and functioning lungs?" Of course there is. Which brings us to the central question addressed in this book: What are the roles of leisure, recreation, and play in living a meaningful life?

Leisure, recreation, and play can be viewed as rights, privileges, healthy experiences, services, and commodities. The world would be a dreary place if people did not have places to play and if organizations such as governments did not set aside space to be used for recreation and the public good. In this chapter, the terms associated with leisure, recreation, and play are discussed; the chapter also discusses the leisure industry, which provides opportunities for recreation. The contributions that leisure and recreation make to the quality of life of individuals and communities and the myriad **benefits** that can be gained will also be discussed. Regardless of whether leisure is planned or spontaneous, social or solitary, and passive or active, it has the potential to greatly enrich our lives.

What would it mean to live a life without recreation and leisure? What would the world be like without it? What would your life look like? We may not always recognize it, but when we view life without it, we are able to see the multitude of ways it touches our lives. If no one had leisure or free time, people would labor all day in the paid workforce. Stay-at-home parents would devote every waking second of their lives to house cleaning and taking care of children. Children would study and do chores at home, with no time to play. People would never retire from their jobs. Technology would be used strictly for work and not for social networking.

More importantly, if people had free time but no recreation places or opportunities, their lives would be diminished. If no park, recreation, sport, arts, or outdoor opportunities existed in the United States, people would have no places to relax outside their homes. Children would have no playgrounds. We would have no intramurals, no youth sports, and no baseball, softball, and other team leagues. Older adults would have no senior centers in which to congregate. Where would families go on vacation when they wanted an opportunity to see the natural wonders of the country? Private individuals with wealth would own the land and keep the general public out. Musicians would have no place to play. Art would not be available to the public. Fitness equipment manufacturers would not exist, nor would movie theaters, bookstores, shopping malls, or sports complexes. Without recreation and leisure, our world would be a radically different place.

Fortunately, most people value their leisure and have access to a variety of recreation opportunities in their communities and throughout the United States. Many people take these opportunities for granted, but without them, adults' and children's quality of life would be greatly diminished. The **leisure industry** is huge not only in the United States but throughout the world. Recreation, parks, tourism, sports, and other leisure opportunities are ubiquitous. However, the meanings of these opportunities and the values they provide require further exploration.

Descriptions and Definitions

After thinking about and discussing the topic of leisure, students often conclude that leisure is different for everybody. One person's exercise regimen is their nirvana, while to another it is pure work; one person's me time is supported by another's obligation. While leisure may be defined, experienced, or understood in multiple ways, it is not true that every individual has a unique understanding of the concept. In order to understand leisure and its components, common understandings are needed

---

Self-Exploration

Think about what leisure opportunities you have had during the past month. Would you say you had too little, too much, or just the right amount of leisure time? What would you do if you had more time for leisure? Is having leisure a priority in your life? What are the priorities in your life?

What are your favorite things to do during your leisure? What are the primary leisure activities of your parents or grandparents? Are your preferred leisure activities like or unlike theirs? What would you say were the primary leisure activities of other students at your university during the past month? Are your leisure preferences like or unlike theirs?

through definitions. Note that *understandings* is plural because there is no single meaning of the terms associated with leisure and recreation. Recognizing the ways that scholars have used the words in research as well how these words have been described in daily lives may be useful. Such understandings allow researchers to measure phenomena, such as the amount of free time people have, or the economic value of an activity, such as sport tourism, and help us determine whether opportunities meet the expectations of participants. The following terms are discussed next to establish some common understandings: *leisure, recreation, parks and natural resources, tourism, commercial recreation, sports, play,* and *work.*

Leisure

Leisure is probably the most nebulous of these ideas and has been subject to many interpretations related primarily to the use of free time, participation in recreational activities, and state of mind. Leisure is often associated with social and cultural contexts of life as well. Obviously, leisure is not understood in the same way by everyone nor can the concept be limited to a single definition. In the postmodern 21st century, the approaches to and applications of leisure are expanding, as you will read about in all the chapters of this book. Some individuals view leisure as a period of time they call free or unobligated time.

Free or unobligated time can be measured, but determining when you are at leisure is difficult. If you are on spring break but have nowhere to travel like your friends do, is that free time really leisure for you? You may have unobligated time between classes. Do you perceive that time as leisure? Unemployed persons may have an abundance of free time but wouldn't consider themselves to be living a life of leisure. Older adults may see an abundance of free time as burdensome, with more hours to fill than meaningful activities to fill them. When some people think of leisure they think of doing nothing, which in a work-oriented society puts leisure in a negative light. Doing nothing is often equated with wasting time; time that could be put to more productive use. Yet even with busy, work-oriented lives come enjoyable, meaningful experiences with family and friends. On the flip side, thinking of leisure as

kali9/Getty Images/Getty Images

For many people, leisure activities double as social experiences.

free time in our increasingly busy lives leads many to conclude they don't have any.

Some people see leisure as earned activities that generally occur outside paid or unpaid work activities. It's the idea that you probably heard as a child: "You can go out and play once your homework is done." The activities undertaken in leisure are generally associated with recreation and are pursued mainly for **enjoyment** or fun. **Recreation** activities can be categorized into groups that share important characteristics, such as competitive sports, cooperative games, outdoor endeavors, cultural pursuits, and socializing. Leisure described as recreational activity is usually measured by the distribution and frequency of participation in specific activities. But thinking of leisure in terms of a set of specific activities also has its limitations. There is no universal list of activities that all would agree are leisure activities; what is enjoyable and meaningful for some may be boring or anxiety-producing for others.

Other people conceive of leisure as an attitude, a psychological construction, or a state of being related to personal experiences. The amount of free time can be counted quantitatively as can the number of activities a person pursues. A psychological experience or state of mind, however, has distinct qualitative connotations; it is freely chosen, not compulsory, and is done for its own sake (i.e., intrinsic motivation) and not as a means to another goal (i.e., extrinsic motivation). The concept of perceived freedom is among the best-known psychological conceptualizations of leisure. In this concept, leisure exists when people perceive themselves as freely choosing an activity that is simultaneously enjoyable and intrinsically motivated (Neulinger, 1981). Another psychological concept of leisure is optimal arousal (Ellis, 1973), where activities are stimulating enough to maintain interest; neither overstimulating to cause anxiety nor understimulating to cause boredom. In leisure, most people attempt to achieve balance and pleasant psychological states like the simple notion of enjoyment or having fun (Mannell & Kleiber, 1997). Leisure can also be characterized as a state of mind related to spiritual and psychological understandings. For example, leisure has been described as "a mental and spiritual attitude" independent of time or work (Pieper, 1963, p. 40). Leisure might also elicit a sense of calm or silence, which many people find in wilderness experiences. Regardless, all definitions of leisure as a state of mind refer to relative freedom and enjoyment on some level.

The definition of leisure as a psychological construct, a **state of being** or **state of mind**, is perhaps the most favored, but it has its drawbacks. Even when you're engaged in a recreation activity, you may feel guilty (e.g., because a huge project assignment is due and you are not working on it) or anxious about the future (e.g., worrying about that same assignment) and may never really experience leisure as a state of mind. In addition, leisure as a psychological experience that occurs during freely chosen activities in one's free time can lead to an overemphasis on the *individual* aspect of leisure. That is, our state of mind, ability to choose activities, and ability to create free time in our schedules are entirely up to us. Everyone can have leisure if they learn to make better choices—let go of the guilt, carve out me time, and do something fun!

Learning to make good leisure choices is an important aspect of living a meaningful life, but we must also consider the social and cultural influences that affect freedom in leisure. Laws limit participation in certain activities, such as hunting, gambling, or the consumption of alcoholic beverages and access to bars. Cultural norms or social stigma can also limit freedom of choice and expression. For example, one's religious beliefs, societal gender and sexual stereotypes, or racial and ethnic stereotypes may influence what are deemed and unacceptable activities.

Leisure, understood from the perspective of critical theory, takes into account systems of power that operate to limit freedom of choice for some while enhancing it for others. Your local recreation center staff have the power to make decisions about which programs and services to offer, and residents have the option to choose among the offerings or choose not to participate. However, the recreation center's decisions may actually limit freedom of choice by assuming needs and wants based on a demographic profile, for example, that urban, male youth want opportunities to play traditional sports such as football and basketball. A critical perspective suggests that limiting options in this way exercises power to reinforce certain activities as culturally appropriate while keeping other types of activities out of bounds (Hallmon, 2020).

Although it is a slippery idea, leisure can come from any experience in which motives are more important than the activity itself or the time spent pursuing an activity. Thus, the experience of leisure generally includes relative freedom to choose what you want to do (e.g., running, reading a book, watching TV, taking a walk, updating your social media). The idea of relative freedom is carefully used because no activity can be completely free—we all have obligations to our own well-being as well as the well-being of others. Nevertheless, leisure is undertaken because it is enjoyable and makes a person feel good physically and mentally. In other words, leisure experiences generally offer some element of satisfaction. Leisure experience may be more likely to occur during free time, but as a state of mind, leisure is not limited to a specific time or activity.

Recreation

The terms *leisure* and *recreation* are frequently used interchangeably, especially when leisure is defined as activity done for fun. Sometimes what people say they do for leisure is the same as what they say they do for recreation. However, others do not view the words as synonymous. Recreation is undertaken because of conscious or unconscious end results. These ends might include benefits such as relaxation, stress relief, or creative expression. Recreation can also be viewed as a means to an end. For example, a person might take a walk to see the beauty of wildflowers. Generally, recreation is associated with activities that are voluntary, organized, socially redeeming, and fun and that occur during free time. Recreation most often involves participation in an activity, whether a physical activity such as basketball or hiking or a passive activity such as picnicking or seeing a movie. It is typically considered beneficial to society as a whole, and thus the U.S. government, as well as state and local governments, fund recreation opportunities in communities and in undeveloped natural areas.

Recreation experiences usually include more than just participation in the activity itself. Researchers have called this notion a multiphasic experience (Stewart, 1998). On the simplest level you might anticipate or plan a recreation activity, such as going to the beach or attending a concert; participate in the actual activity; and then remember and reflect on some aspect of the experience, such as someone you met or a beautiful sunset.

BJI / Blue Jean Images/Getty Images

Recreation refers to the enjoyable activities that people do during their free time. Make the most of your free time by getting out there and doing something you love!

Recreation activities are available to people in a variety of ways. These activities are most often associated with parks and natural resources, tourism and commercial recreation, and sports. Recreation also occurs through cultural activities and performing arts, volunteer opportunities and community service, and numerous unstructured activities such as family gatherings, special interest clubs, and social networking.

Parks and natural resources refer to outdoor, nature-based areas used for recreation activity. A **park** is typically defined as a natural or near-natural green or open space that is bounded in some way and has the purpose of natural resource conservation and preservation, human use, or both. Outdoor spaces for recreation include urban parks and greenways, state parks, and national areas such as national parks, national forests, Bureau of Land Management lands, and Army Corps of Engineers recreation areas.

Tourism is travel for mainly recreational or leisure purposes. **Tourists** are generally defined as people who travel to and stay in places outside their usual environment for the purpose of leisure rather than permanent residence or remuneration. **Commercial recreation** refers to market-driven, private-sector recreation activities for which a fee is charged by a profit-oriented enterprise. Many recreation opportunities fall into this category, such as country clubs, ski operations, restaurants, movie theaters, and health clubs.

Sports include a range of recreational and entertainment activities that involve rules, physical prowess, and contests between individuals or teams—generally with an uncertain outcome. However, the word *sport* is sometimes used to describe any type of competition regardless of physical prerequisites. Examples of these types of competition are NASCAR, poker, chess, or esports. Sports can also be work performed by professional athletes to entertain spectators during their leisure.

Play

Some people use the term **play** interchangeably with *recreation* or *leisure*. Play is usually associated more with children than with adults, although play is

All sentient beings, including animals, children, and adults, have the propensity to play. Play is also a great mood lifter and stress reliever.

DGLimages/iStock/Getty Images

commonly used in a variety of contexts. Characteristics of play include spontaneity, purposelessness, and the creation of an imaginary world. Play is almost always pleasurable and self-expressive and can range from disorganized activity to structured involvement. Many adults like to be spontaneous and find a sense of play a refreshing break from the structure of everyday living. Regardless, play refers to spontaneous and expressive activity done for its own sake with little obvious, direct extrinsic value. When play serves as a means to socialize children or to relieve stress, it certainly has instrumental value as well.

Theories of play have been proposed since the late 19th century. Before scientific research was conducted concerning play, people were assumed to play when the spirit moved them. However, play has been examined from several dimensions.

- A biological theory suggested that play was an innate need that must be met and was genetically required for survival.
- A Freudian analysis of play suggested that society legitimizes certain play behaviors as a way to deal with internal conflicts. For example, instead of attacking someone out of frustration, a person might kick or hit a ball.
- Developmental psychologists theorized that play was essential to defining the self and that a child, for example, might be socialized into society through play.
- Sociologists examined play as a way to maintain the values of society.

Most discussions of play today blend these ideas and suggest that we need to play in order to function well and interact with our environment at an optimal level (Ellis, 1973). People express who they are and interact socially through play. Contemporary psychologists have addressed the critical need for children to play, and parents and paraprofessionals in the field have been listening. Health officials have suggested that growing levels of childhood obesity and the epidemic level of adult-onset diabetes could be related to lack of play in contemporary life.

Work

For most people, the distinction among leisure, recreation, and play is seldom considered. The greatest juxtaposition to these notions of free time and enjoyment is work. In contemporary Western society, people learn that work and leisure form distinct spheres in their lives, although not everyone works

in traditional, economically productive ways. For example, volunteering in the community is usually called *volunteer work,* and raising children is typically seen as another form of unpaid work. Therefore, work should be defined as activity undertaken for economic gain or a socially redeeming value.

During the 19th and early 20th centuries, factory laborers commonly worked 60 to 100 hours per week, which left little time for rest and relaxation or, even more importantly, less time to exercise control over how they spent their time and energy. Labor unions consistently campaigned for shorter workweeks, and "Eight hours for work, eight hours for rest, eight hours for what we will!" was immortalized in a song written by I.G. Blanchard in the mid-1860s and became a union tagline. After much struggle, the Fair Labor Standards Act of 1938 set the maximum workweek at 44 hours, and the current standard workweek of 40 hours was adopted in 1940. Technological advances have increased productivity and efficiency; we can produce more in less time, but rather than claiming the unused time for what we will, most Americans simply work more. With advances in communication technology (cell phones, broadband Internet) and market globalization, many workers are expected to be available 24 hours a day, 7 days a week.

Work, in contrast to leisure, recreation, and play, implies greater obligation and thus less freedom—that is, someone else has considerable control over our time, activities, and self-expression. Schedules, tasks, acceptable behaviors, and perhaps even what we wear are set by someone else. Our work obligations are scheduled first, then other obligations and recreation are scheduled around our work, whether it's a daily work shift, weekly days off, or yearly vacation time. However, for many people, work has greater meaning than just putting in one's time for a monetary reward. In other words, work can be more than a means to an end. Many people build their identities around work (e.g., being a nurse, a pilot, a social worker, a professor). Others have a great deal of social interaction during their work. Perhaps individuals could find the same meanings outside work, but work is a central aspect of what society believes people should do to be productive citizens. However, if the meaningfulness of work is uncertain and people only work because of the income and benefits (e.g., health insurance, retirement contributions), leisure may be a more important aspect of their lives.

Importance of Leisure and Recreation for Individuals and Society

The mission of the National Recreation and Park Association (the largest citizen and professional organization in the United States that advocates for the value of recreation) is "to advance parks, recreation and environmental conservation efforts that enhance the quality of life for all people" (NRPA, n.d.). Their aim is to affect communities through conservation and preservation of open spaces, improve health and wellness through parks and recreation, and ensure all people have access to its benefits. A key component of their efforts is enhancement of quality of life.

Quality of life can be defined as the degree to which a person enjoys the important possibilities of life (Global Development Research Center, n.d.). These possibilities reflect the interaction of personal and environmental factors. Enjoyment includes feeling satisfied and achieving something important. The three major life domains associated with quality of life are being, belonging, and becoming.

- *Being* addresses who you are and includes physical aspects such as health, nutrition, exercise, and appearance; psychological aspects related to adjustment and cognition; and personal standards of conduct and values related to one's spiritual beliefs.

- *Belonging* addresses a person's fit or physical belonging in an environment, such as at home, in the workplace, or at school. Social belonging includes acceptance by intimate others, work colleagues, fellow students, friends, and neighbors. Community belonging connotes access to resources such as adequate income, health services, employment, education and recreation services, and community activities.

- *Becoming* refers to purposeful activities aimed at personal achievement including practical day-to-day actions, such as paid work or volunteer activities; leisure, including activities for relaxation and stress reduction; and growth opportunities that improve or maintain knowledge and skills.

As evident from these examples, recreation and leisure opportunities are central components of quality of life. They are certainly not the only components,

but they are integral to creating quality of life. It is important to note that conditions such as poverty, homelessness, and social exclusion experienced by marginalized groups present unique challenges for living a quality, meaningful life. Participatory action research conducted by Iwasaki and Hopper (2017) as part of a community-based youth engagement project for high-risk youth revealed that constructive, leisure-like pursuits helped facilitate participants' sense of joyful, composed, connected, discovered, and empowered lives. The ways that leisure and recreation contribute to this quality of life, however, are not always evident to people until they stop to consider the benefits that leisure and recreation offer.

Individual Benefits

Imagine that you have just finished a leisure activity, such as walking on a trail, making a gift for a family member, or attending a concert. The satisfaction and exhilaration that result are part of the leisure experience. The value of a leisure or recreation experience is connected to its meanings and motives. Recreation and leisure experiences can be planned or spontaneous, social or solitary, and passive or active. Many of these benefits can be considered private goods; that is, the benefit accrues to the individual.

Some of the common individual benefits of leisure are physiological (physical) and psychological (mental) health. The physiological benefits of recreation are usually embodied in regular exercise and physical activity that often occur in free time. Many of the benefits of physical activity have been documented scientifically. For example, regular physical activity reduces our risk for heart attack, colon cancer, diabetes, and high blood pressure and may reduce the risk for stroke. Regular physical activity helps us control our weight; contributes to healthy bones, muscles, and joints; reduces falls among older adults; helps to relieve the pain of arthritis; and is associated with fewer hospitalizations, physician visits, and medications. Moreover, physical activity need not be strenuous to be beneficial. For example, guidelines from the U.S. government suggest that adults of all ages need to do two types of physical activity each week to improve health:

1. About 2 hours and 30 minutes (150 minutes) to 5 hours (300 minutes) of moderate-intensity aerobic activity, such as brisk walking, every week or 75 to 150 minutes of vigorous-intensity aerobic physical activity

Self-Exploration

The following issues define aspects of quality of life. What would you say are the important dimensions that define your quality of life? How does leisure relate to these questions?

- Do you consider yourself physically healthy?
- Do you eat a healthy diet?
- Do you get enough sleep each night?
- Do you exercise regularly (e.g., walking, fitness activities, strenuous sports)?
- Are you generally positive (i.e., in a good mood) about your life?
- Are you a person of high morals (i.e., a clear understanding of right and wrong)?
- Are you usually free of worry and stress?
- Do you feel emotionally close to your family and friends?
- Do you know how to access services in your university or community (e.g., medical, social)?
- Do you have enough money to do what you want to do?
- Do you have leisure interests?
- Are you satisfied with your leisure?
- Are you able to cope with the changes that occur (and will occur) in your life?

2. Muscle-strengthening activities on 2 or more days per week that work all major muscle groups including legs, hips, back, abdomen, chest, shoulders, and arms (U.S. Department of Health and Human Services, 2018)

Given the amount of scientific evidence about how leisure-time physical activity contributes to health, many leisure activities have great potential to contribute to our quality of life.

Many of the physiological benefits of leisure activities reduce our feelings of stress. Leisure can result in mental and physical relaxation and improve mood. Kim and Brown (2018) examined the relationship between leisure, stress, and healthy behaviors among college students. They found that participating in intrinsically motivated leisure activities was associated with lower levels of perceived stress and less engagement in unhealthy behaviors such as smoking, alcohol consumption, and poor eating habits. Furthermore, lower perceived stress and higher engagement in healthy behaviors had a positive impact on students' GPAs. Numerous studies have documented the public health benefits of urban green spaces, such as stress reduction and mental relaxation, increased physical activity, social cohesion, and even a boost to the immune system (Braubach et al., 2017). Other psychological benefits of leisure are enhanced self-competence, improved sense of self-worth, enhanced self-identity, and a better ability to relate to others.

Broader Social Benefits

Recreation provides benefits beyond those focused on individuals. These are considered public goods—that is, the benefits are shared by members of the community, regardless of whether a given individual participates. The most common type of benefits is economic. For example, communities that provide activities and accommodations for tourists receive an economic benefit as a result of recreation. The economic impact of travel, particularly emerging activities like sport tourism, can be huge. Property values adjacent to parks, open spaces, and certain recreation amenities tend to be higher. Leisure and recreation may make us healthier and less likely to miss work because of illness, which benefits the economy. According to the National Recreation and Park Association, spending by local parks and recreation agencies contributed $166 billion in economic activity supporting more than 1.1 million jobs paying $50.8 billion in salaries, wages, and benefits in 2017 (NRPA, 2020).

Recreation and leisure can benefit the environment. Parks and recreation play a role in preserving green space and the biological diversity of areas. In addition to preservation and protection of natural areas, parks and recreation contribute to conservation and sustainability of natural resources. You can read more about this topic in chapter 10.

Another way geographically defined communities (e.g., your hometown) benefit from recreation and leisure is in the development of a sense of belonging and connection to community life. Researchers have noted that access to neighborhood green spaces can promote the development of social relationships and cohesion. Social cohesion is characterized by trust, solidarity, and overall connection to neighbors (Jennings, Larson, & Yun, 2016). For example, many cities and towns sponsor community-wide festivals to celebrate a particular ethnic heritage. Participants are invited to share an emotional connection to the community's ethnic heritage through music, food, dance, crafts, and ethnic traditions. Communities also benefit from recreation or leisure when people develop pride in their community by rallying around the local sport team or celebrating historical events. Furthermore, green spaces increase neighborhood satisfaction, thereby enhancing a sense of place and place attachment (Jennings et al., 2016).

The benefits we have discussed are sometimes difficult to measure. The value of recreation and leisure often lies within how they *prevent* problems like obesity, community decay, and environmental destruction. Prevention, however, is difficult to assess. For example, it would be unethical to teach only half the children in a community to swim and then determine over the years how many people drowned who had not received the lessons. This case is extreme, but the point is that calculating the direct value of leisure in terms of statistics takes a long time and is not easy. Nevertheless, many agencies, organizations, and businesses promote and facilitate leisure experiences on the theory that they provide benefits.

Value of a Leisure Ethic

With the myriad benefits of leisure and the plethora of opportunities within the leisure industries, leisure seems like it should be a top priority for all individuals and communities. However, some people do not see the value of leisure, and many people do not believe they have enough opportuni-

A recreation experience includes anticipating the activity, doing the activity, and recalling the memories. Facebook, Instagram, and social media stories are popular ways to preserve memories or experiences.

Hinterhaus Productions/DigitalVision/Getty Images

ties for recreation. A number of explanations can be considered, including the domination of the work ethic and trivialization of enjoyment, perceptions of work and time, technology, and the invisibility of leisure education.

The **work ethic** is still alive and well in society. When getting to know someone new, one of the first questions we ask is "What do you do?" People are more likely to be valued for what they do, which usually includes gainful employment. Some of these work ideas are shaped by lingering puritanism and the traditional way work has been valued over leisure, especially in the United States. Much of what students study in colleges and universities relates directly to job and career readiness, but gainful employment is only one aspect of life. Living a satisfying, meaningful life also includes our personal relationships, like being a spouse or friend, and our commitments to what we enjoy doing outside the workplace, such as church work, sports fandom, or walking in the woods.

Related to this work ethic is the devaluing of enjoyment. Based on the definitions already discussed, leisure is signified by the relative freedom to choose what you enjoy. Few opportunities are available in life for the purpose of having fun or finding enjoyment. People need to laugh, to be creative, to be passionate about living. Leisure and recreation provide those intangible intrinsic opportunities, but they sometimes get lost in the busy task- and goal-oriented lives most people live. What greater feeling is there than to be happy because of involvement in enjoyable personal activities and social relationships?

Given perceptions of use of time and its relationship to work, many people think they have limited leisure. Time, interestingly, is the most equally distributed resource. Everyone has 24 hours a day—no more and no less. Although average paid work hours have remained fairly constant in terms of the standard 40-hour workweek, exceeding the standard is the norm in some occupations. For example, professionals and managers are usually expected to work more hours than other workers, even though working more does not necessarily mean increased earnings. In some occupations, people are rewarded for their long work hours, whereas most other workers must increase their work hours simply to hold on to their present lifestyles.

Work schedules, once dominated by 8-hour shifts, are more flexible and varied. According to a Gallup report, more than one third of U.S. workers participate in the **gig economy**, an alternative work arrangement characterized by independent, short-term working relationships, or *gigs* (Gallup, 2018). In addition, even within traditional work arrangements, hours are not uniform across various population segments. For example, in 2018, employed women worked an average of 41.1 hours per week, while men worked an average of 43.5 hours per week, but 84 percent of women spent an average of 2.6 hours on household activities, while 69 percent of men spent an average of 2 hours on household activities (Bureau of Labor Statistics, 2020). Many women participate in the paid workforce but continue to shoulder disproportionate responsibilities for unpaid work, such as housework and child care. As people work longer hours (whether in paid or unpaid work and whether they earn more or not), they surrender more of their time. Most people want leisure time, but often it feels like a scarce resource.

Ironically, technology compromises people's perceptions about leisure. Although various forms of technology liberate people from some of the drudgery of work, technology is often expected to save time so that more work can be done. Furthermore, various uses of technology can constitute leisure, such as electronic game playing and interacting with social media. You can read more about leisure's relationship to technology in chapter 9.

People's perceptions that they don't have enough leisure may be due to their lack of skills in using their free time. **Leisure education** has not found great enthusiasm in society. Furthermore, some people think of leisure education as an oxymoron—the two words seem contradictory. Nevertheless, leisure education could be a way to contribute to better living for all. The main aim of leisure education can be helping individuals, families, communities, and societies to achieve a suitable quality of life and good health by using leisure time intelligently and by developing and cultivating physical, emotional, spiritual, mental, and social aspects related to the aims of education in the country and its cultural heritage (Sivan, 2019). Therefore, helping children, youth, and adults make the right choices during leisure is critical to their enjoyment as well as for maintaining social civilities. In addition, leisure education may have the potential to help mitigate social problems. Perhaps if individuals were aware of and had access to interesting leisure options, they might not smoke or drink as much, or crime levels might decrease.

Self-Exploration

Given what you've read so far in this chapter, think further about what leisure means to you. Which definition of leisure makes the most sense to you? If you had to choose between having more leisure time or more money, which would you choose? Do you have more or less leisure than adults you know, such as your parents? Do you have more or less leisure than your classmates and friends? What type of career do you hope to have? How will it allow, or not allow, opportunities for leisure? If your friends were to describe your leisure life, what would they say about you?

Another way to think about education for leisure is contextually. The value and meaning of particular recreation and leisure activities, and of free time in general, are learned. Some forms of leisure involve skills whereas others do not. People generally prefer doing leisure activities in which they feel competent. Thus, learning specific skills cannot be disassociated from appreciation and enjoyment in experiences. The context of leisure education certainly has connections to active learning and experiential education that contribute to quality of life.

Areas of the Leisure Industry

Although leisure and recreation can occur without any equipment, programs, services, facilities, or spaces, most people at leisure use these elements, which comprise the leisure industry. The idea of an industry that includes many activity providers has its roots at the beginning of the 20th century. At that time, leisure was becoming a commodity that people wanted, and entrepreneurs recognized that they could make money by providing leisure activities. Thus, the leisure industry emerged, consisting of public and private enterprises that sought to provide positive structured and planned leisure opportunities to ensure that people used their leisure time appropriately and to create a positive economic impact. Citizens began to recognize that the positive outcomes of leisure could best be achieved by providing structured leisure opportunities for individuals, families, and communities.

The leisure industries that evolved in industrialized countries in the 20th century were based on the idea that people's demand for leisure creates a supply of opportunities. Similarly, a supply of activities requires that demand be created. Thus, many private, public, sports-oriented, and tourism-based opportunities, referred to as leisure industries, were initiated for people seeking ways to consume, experience, and enjoy leisure. The leisure industry is represented in each of the three primary economic sectors:

1. Public or governmental recreation agencies
2. Private, not-for-profit organizations
3. Commercial, private, for-profit sectors

Regardless of the economic sector, organizations representing the leisure industry provide leisure experiences through sports, recreation, arts, the outdoors, and tourism opportunities. However their philosophies, objectives, facilities, financing, and membership may differ based on their economic sector. The primary distinguishing characteristic among public, private nonprofit and commercial leisure organizations is their funding source. Public agencies are a function of government and thus receive tax revenue. Private nonprofit agencies are nongovernmental and rely primarily on donations, membership and service fees, and grants for their funding. Commercial agencies rely solely on fees for services—that is, the customer pays to play.

Public or Governmental Recreation Agencies

Public recreation agencies are theoretically available to all citizens of a community, state, region, or nation because they are owned by the public rather than private citizens. Public recreation and the involvement of governments in leisure services stem from a concern for citizens' health and welfare and the wise use of natural resources. Governments based on democratic principles (i.e., a democracy) generally assume some responsibility for providing elements that contribute to quality of life for all citizens, and public spaces and recreation opportunities are part of that obligation.

Two primary functions are evident in the provision of leisure opportunities from a public governmental perspective (Henderson et al., 2001). The first is management of land and natural

On the Job

Creating Experiences

Professional opportunities in the leisure industry are vast and varied. They can encompass working for professional sports teams or guiding services or in areas such as national parks, municipal recreation centers, amusement parks, restaurants, hotels, local gyms, and so many more. What ties many of them together, however, is creating experiences for participants and guests. While each of these professions requires a unique set of hard skills, they all require the ability to create spaces for people to experience their unobligated time in a way that that is meaningful. This can involve numerous skills, such as customer service, leadership, and experience design. Those who excel at creating experiences rather than merely organizing events change how customers are involved so that they can become transformed in some way as a result of their participation. This will likely increase satisfaction, making it more likely that they will return. Creating experiences is truly one of the attributes of a quality leisure professional.

resources typically by providing opportunities for outdoor recreation while at the same time ensuring that the resources are not exploited. National and state governments have focused primarily on resource-oriented outdoor recreation (e.g., national parks, state parks, national wilderness areas, etc.), whereas local governments have provided both resources and opportunities for leisure activity (e.g., municipal recreation centers, aquatic centers, city parks, etc.).

The second function of public leisure providers is to deliver services in the form of activity instruction, competition, special events, and performances for community residents. In many areas, this role is changing to brokering or facilitating recreation opportunities rather than directly providing services

Jeff Kravitz/FilmMagic/Getty Images

Festivals and concerts are a growing part of the leisure industry. Cheering for your favorite band with a huge crowd is a great way to blow off steam for a few hours . . . or days.

because so many more opportunities in the not-for-profit and private sectors now exist in many areas.

Private, Not-for-Profit Organizations

Not-for-profit organizations are sometimes called nonprofit, voluntary, third sector, independent sector, or nongovernmental organizations and are voluntary associations that usually focus on a particular issue, activity, or population. Not-for-profit organizations are limited in their scope based on the mission of the particular organization. The Y (formerly known as the YMCA) focuses on youth development, healthy living, and social responsibility. The mission of the Y is accomplished by a variety of recreation activities, such as fitness instruction and facilities, outdoor education and camping opportunities, social clubs, child care, family nights, support groups, and volunteering.

The not-for-profit sector often fills gaps between the public sector and the private sector (Moiseichik & Moss, 2016). Local groups often identify needs within their communities before governments can react. These organizations address community needs by offering membership (e.g., The Y, Girl Scouts/Girl Guides, sports leagues) or by providing service or advocacy (e.g., environmental groups such as the Sierra Club, health-related organizations such as the Muscular Dystrophy Association, or religious groups). Some nongovernmental organizations operate solely to provide recreation, sport, and leisure opportunities. Other not-for-profit groups exist for many reasons, among which are providing leisure and recreation as a means to address other goals.

Although religious organizations are not necessarily associated with nongovernmental organizations, they are more like this sector than the other sectors. It would be remiss not to acknowledge the contributions that religious organizations such as churches, synagogues, mosques, and temples make to leisure by offering activities such as sports leagues, youth camps, and retreat centers. Regardless of an organization's purpose, many organizations use recreation to get people involved with one another, often for a specific cause.

Commercial, Private, For-Profit Agencies

Private commercial organizations are aimed at satisfying, and often creating, a demand for recreation services and are focused on appealing to participants (customers) who purchase a product or service. Private leisure industries may be the fastest-growing sector in the leisure industry because of the commodification of leisure and the market-driven nature of the world's economy. New markets, services, and products appear almost daily. The consumption of goods and services in the United States includes a number of private recreation opportunities.

These businesses provide many opportunities for investment and profit making for entrepreneurs. Because of the competitive nature of this sector, these industries are always focused on improving their services to attract participants. Satisfied customers will return to leisure experiences they have enjoyed and will tell their friends about good leisure experiences. The more positive experiences that people have, the more they are likely to seek (i.e., buy) those experiences in the future. You can read more about the economic impact of leisure services in chapter 11.

Tourism and Sport Industries

Various opportunities for tourism as well as sport occur across all economic sectors. Although travel for trade and religious purposes dates to ancient times, tourism is a relatively recent idea. Tourism is an outgrowth of people's desire to relax, to have new and different experiences away from their daily routines, to visit other environments, and to learn about other cultures. Not all tourism possibilities come from the private sector, but the number of such opportunities continues to grow.

The tourism industry faces challenges for the future. One is the influence of tourism on the destination's social system and culture. Although tourism can be a huge boost to economically depressed areas, it also carries issues related to pollution, infrastructure costs, social problems, and potential seasonal unemployment. Tourism also can have a negative impact on the environment. If the environment degrades, many forms of tourism change. Sustainable tourism is an aspect that moves from a strictly socioeconomic focus toward preserving resources for the future (Crossley, Rood, Brayley, Price-Howard, & Holdnak, 2018). Organizations focused on sustainable tourism attempt to limit consumption of natural resources at a higher rate than they can be replaced. Ecotourism is a related area that connects tourism to the environment. Despite the potential drawbacks, however, tourism is increasing in popularity globally. Sustainable tourism can be maximized when all leisure industries work together to provide quality recreation opportunities.

Sports comprise a big leisure business whether done for recreation in local communities or for spectators in college, national, or international competitions.

Another area that often cuts across all sectors is sports. Sports can be provided by public recreation agencies (e.g., municipal recreation leagues), nongovernmental organizations (e.g., Little League), or for-profit companies (e.g., private sports facilities that charge admission fees to spectators). Sports offer a means for participation as well as a venue for spectators and can range from international sporting events such as the Olympics to local sporting events like high school football games.

Sport tourism is a fast-growing area within the leisure industry. Many people travel to, watch, or participate in athletic events in nearby communities as well as around the world (e.g., the Olympics). Sports are an increasingly popular tourism product that can take place in urban or nonurban settings, indoors or outdoors, in all types of climatic conditions, and in all seasons. Sport tourism can contribute to economic development, positive image and identity, and tourism promotion and marketing and includes four primary domains:

1. Active sport tourism, wherein people travel to participate in a sport (e.g., running a marathon in a destination city, such as Boston)

2. Event sport tourism, wherein people travel to watch a sport (e.g., attending a college football game)

3. Nostalgic sport tourism, in which people visit sports museums and famous sports venues and take part in sports-themed cruises (e.g., going to Cooperstown, New York, to visit the National Baseball Hall of Fame and Museum)

4. Youth sport tourism, which coincides with the increase in youth club sports and travel teams and represents a $17 billion industry with expected continued growth (Sports Events Media Group, 2019)

Esports

Esports, or electronic sports, involve individuals or teams of players who compete in video game competitions. Participation in esports has increased substantially since about 2010, with an estimated 100 million players worldwide. As of 2016, esports research has primarily focused on the factors that influence participation (Seo, 2016). Although information about player engagement is available, a scarce amount of research has investigated the factors that underlie expertise in esports. Esports consist of several categories, some of which include multiplayer online battle arenas, multiplayer online role-playing, real-time strategy, and first-person shooter. A common theme among these categories is that performance is typically carried out in a team-based environment, where a player's avatar is placed in a virtual environment with the goal of eliminating their competitors or achieving an objective (e.g., capturing the flag). Players must combine their perceptual–cognitive abilities (e.g., anticipation, visual search behavior, pattern recall, and decision making) and domain-specific skills (e.g., keyboard and mouse or controller movements) to achieve successful performance.

In recent years, esports and video gaming have ranked among the fastest growing forms of recreation and competitive play utilizing the Internet driven by new broadcasting technology (Pluss et al., 2019). Other names for esports are cybersports, gaming, competitive gaming, and virtual sports. Esports recreational offerings through campus recreation and club sports are increasing (Brock 2017). As of 2018, there were more than 150 esports studies published across the following disciplines:

- Media studies
- Recreation and leisure
- Informatics
- Business
- Sport science
- Sociology
- Law
- Cognitive science

Summary

It is a wonderful life when leisure is meaningful to individuals and available in communities. A world without leisure and recreation opportunities would be a very dreary place. Leisure is important, and this book addresses many dimensions of leisure and quality of life. Several key ideas can frame our thoughts about leisure.

First, leisure is a part of life; it extends from the play of children to activities that help us age well. The basis of support for leisure opportunities is the theory that leisure can be a creative and constructive force in the lives of individuals, social groups, communities, and the global society.

Second, leisure is culturally situated; it involves individual and collective manifestations that vary from country to country as well as within the diversity of a single country. Therefore, all understanding about leisure is evolving and contextual. An intriguing aspect of leisure is that it has various meanings that are important to all people at some level. We hope this book helps you to explore what is important and enjoyable to you.

Third, opportunities for leisure are numerous. However, action is needed by individuals as well as policy makers to communicate the personal, economic, social, and environmental potential of leisure and to ensure that people have a variety of opportunities for expression of leisure.

Learning Activities

1. List 20 activities you enjoy. You do not need to share the list with anyone, so be honest. Next, go through your list and mark the items as follows:
   - *Social interaction.* Mark each activity as *A* (an activity done alone), *P* (an activity done with people), and *AP* (an activity that can be done alone or with people).
   - *Cost.* Put a dollar symbol ($) by any activity that you have to pay for every time it is done.
   - *Activity level.* Write *PA* for every activity that is physically active (e.g., jogging) and *RE* for every activity that is relaxing or passive (e.g., watching television).
   - *Planning level.* Write *PL* for an activity that requires some amount of planning and *SP* for an activity that is spontaneous.
   - *Time duration.* Write the number of minutes that you usually spend when you do this activity. For example, walking the dog might be 20 minutes and watching TV might be 180 minutes.

- *Time passage.* Indicate the last time you did this activity with *Y* (yesterday), *PW* (during the past week), *PM* (during the past month), *PY* (during the past year), or *MY* (many years ago).
- *Work or leisure.* Mark each item as *W* (you consider the activity work) or *L* (you consider the activity to be leisure).

Do you see any patterns in what you do? What did you learn about yourself and your leisure?

2. Answer yes or no to the following questions:
   - Do you feel continually rushed and pressed for time? *y*
   - Has it been a while since you did anything fun? *y*
   - Has it been a while since you had time for relaxation? *y*
   - Are you neglecting your health in any way? *y*
   - Do you feel dissatisfied or discontent with the past semester? *y*
   - Is there a relationship in your life that needs attention? *y*
   - Are you studying more and enjoying it less? *y*
   - Do you believe something is missing in your life? *y*

   If you answered yes to any of these questions, you are a candidate for more leisure and you might think about how leisure and recreation could benefit you.

3. Some people would like to live a more leisurely life. A leisurely life is not the same as a life of leisure. The following six points describe possible components of a leisurely life. Identify which of the following, if any, you would like to make a part of your leisurely life. After you have identified something that might be important, think about one thing that you could do to achieve this goal.
   - Working and living under control and not always at a frantic pace ✓
   - Working at a moderate pace by putting order and planning into your life
   - Enjoying life as you go rather than waiting for something big to happen (like a new job, marriage, winning the lottery)
   - Allowing balance in your life ✓
   - Taking care of yourself by eating well, exercising regularly, getting enough sleep, and avoiding stressful situations ✓
   - Seeing life as a glass half full; anticipating the future as bright while living in the present ✓

Review Questions

1. How do values determine what you do with your leisure? How do societal values affect the relevance of leisure?
2. What are the primary sectors that provide leisure services? Give examples of all of the ones you have participated in.
3. Why is it important to develop definitions and descriptions of leisure, recreation, and play?
4. Which of the definitions of leisure fits most closely with your personal views?
5. What benefits do you seek most often in your leisure?
6. What might be some negative impacts of leisure?
7. What needs to happen if leisure is to have a greater value in American society?
8. If you were given a choice between having more time for leisure or more money for leisure, which would you choose? In this hypothetical question, you cannot have both!
9. Why do people need to be educated about leisure?

Go to HK*Propel* to access additional learning content.

Leisure Through a Social Science Lens

Erik Rabinowitz
Appalachian State University

J. Joy James
Appalachian State University

Daniel Theriault
Appalachian State University

VOCABULARY TERMS

anthropology
cross-cultural
deviance
economics
epistemology
ethnography
flow

interpretivism
macroeconomics
methodology
microeconomics
ontology
positivism
postmodernism

postpositivism
psychology
sensation seeking
social sciences
sociology

LEARNING OUTCOMES

After reading this chapter, you will be able to

- define social science;
- define how social science helps us understand leisure and leisure behaviors;
- discuss leisure from a psychological, sociological, anthropological, and geographical perspective; and
- provide examples of how each helps us better understand human leisure behaviors.

Have you ever watched a hamster running in its wheel endlessly day in and day out or the sloth that has all the time in the world to move about? Imagine you are like this hamster, every day rushing to each location, and your life is all work and no play. In American society, some people work all possible hours in a week, not unlike that hamster in the wheel. Other people are like the sloth, with more free time than they know how to use. Retirees, children, and underemployed or unemployed people may have around two thirds of their time available for leisure (O'Sullivan, 2013). The average time spent in leisure activities for those who are unemployed or over the age of 64 is approximately 7 hours per day (Bureau of Labor Statistics, 2018). How do the hamster and sloth metaphor relate to leisure and social science? The disparity in time is what makes studying the social sciences and leisure fascinating.

The **social sciences** are about people, how they act individually and in a group. This chapter discusses areas of study at both levels. Individually, people's lives—their food, employment opportunities, health, and leisure activities—are shaped by environmental, social, psychological, and biological factors. Examination of these areas will help us understand the impact leisure has on our lives individually and as a society. For example, the psychological basis for why we choose certain leisure activities over others will be explored. We use psychological theories every day without even being aware; for example, we drive past the doughnut shop and may have a biological response of our mouths drooling. Similarly, when we see reminders of our favorite recreation and leisure activities, we may feel compelled to do them. A whitewater kayaker, for example, might have this response when passing a roaring river. This response may be amplified if the kayaker passes the river and notices four of their good friends out kayaking; this is a sociological behavior elaborated on later in the chapter. Our biological systems and the role of our genetic makeup versus the role of nature, or the product of our environment, also may play a significant role in our leisure choices. Imagine if no leisure activities existed: The impact on our society could be detrimental from an individual,

How they apply to leisure behavior

Lilly Roadstones/Stone/Getty Images

What happens when your life becomes all work and no play?

a social, and even an economic perspective. Some countries are completely dependent on leisure for their economic survival. As a group, we are living through a major transformation in society, and the traditions that hold it together often revolve around leisure participation. Certainly you have heard the phrase "money makes the world go around," but maybe the quote should be "leisure makes the world go around"; without leisure, people probably would be very disinterested in making money.

In this chapter, we examine what it means to be a social scientist and how social science helps us in our daily lives. Social science draws from numerous disciplines of study. This chapter examines some of the major fields of social science as well as the application of theories from these fields to leisure behavior. The final sections discuss the benefit social science has on leisure and society as a whole.

We Are All Social Scientists

Every day you draw from sociology, political science, economics, anthropology, geography, history, psychology, and other related disciplines providing an integrated view of your world. This interdisciplinary understanding helps you to make connections between, and think critically about, issues both past and present.

To understand social science, we must first understand how we come to truth or our "assumptions about knowledge and how it is attained" (Samdahl, 1999, p. 119). The folk tale of the blind men and the elephant illustrates this point well (and points out the fallacy of learning by experience only). In this story, the blind men surround the elephant at different points. Each firmly believes in the truth of what he can touch and perceive. The man at the trunk believes the elephant is elongated and quite flexible like a snake. The man at the tail perceives the elephant as a string and possibly as quite smelly. The man touching the tusk believes the elephant is smooth and pointy, maybe a spear. The man touching the elephant's ears and feeling air move thinks the elephant is a fan. Each draws on previous experiences and values to frame his sensory experience and then puts it forward as truth. Each has his own idea of what the elephant is and believes he has the truth. The men are not wrong, nor are they completely right. What is the truth or reality of the elephant?

Social science provides us a way to learn about things. Growing out of skepticism and created to test speculations, social science offers a systematic way to discover truth. "The goal of social research is to discover, understand, and communicate truth about people in society" (Henderson, 1991, p. 9). The goal of social scientific theory is in discovering patterns in social life (Babbie, 2002).

One could think of social science research as a puzzle. The researcher is akin to a puzzle solver (Henderson, 1991). By piecing together the social puzzle, the researcher attempts to discover, explain, and predict social patterns. Unfortunately, the researcher is working without a specific picture to determine how the puzzle pieces fit together. The picture that the researcher does have is based on observations, experience, paradigm, and previous research.

Benefits of Social Science

Social science's intent is to discover patterns of social life. The presumption that there is one way of knowing is a bit arrogant. Each of the social science disciplines offers explanations, descriptions, or theories related to the human condition. Through understanding these disciplines and their research, practitioners can work on solutions to the challenges and issues facing their constituencies.

Social science provides information to inform policy making and management decisions on the personal, community, national, and global levels. Communities benefit from social science through initiatives that improve management information (through technological advances), allocation or budgetary efficiency, and institutional change. For example, information on products and quality of sports equipment can improve consumer choices as well as policy for implementing youth sport programs (Smith, 1998). Social science, whether prompted by curiosity of the researcher or by public need, can reveal patterns of behavior and provide potential solutions. For example, one of the most famous industrial history experiments took place at Western Electric's factory in the Hawthorne suburb of Chicago in the late 1920s and early 1930s. The National Research Council was studying human relations, and the researchers changed the lighting and ventilation of work areas to see whether worker performance would improve. It was determined, however, that the greatest effect resulted from the workers being watched. This was later titled the Hawthorne effect, which "refers to an increase in performance caused by the special attention given to employees, rather than tangible changes in the work" (Lussier, 2005, p. 13). This discovery changed how managers motivate their employees.

For many years, it was thought recreation was good for you or would enhance human development, but this was anecdotal evidence. To garner resources (e.g., money, facilities, or employees) for an organ-ization or agency, benefits of recreation needed to be determined empirically (i.e., determined through research methods of observation and experimentation). The recreation field turned to social science (e.g., psychology, sociology, and economics) to help generate evidence of both economic and noneconomic benefits of leisure. For example, researchers investigating the benefits of participation in outdoor adventure programs suggested that participants improve their self-concept (Burton, 1981; Ewert, 1982; Moote & Wodarski, 1997), whereas other researchers indicated that self-confidence and personal development were outcomes (Holland, Powell, Thomsen, & Monz, 2018; Kaplan, 1984; Nye, 1976). These findings can be used to demonstrate benefits of programs such as Outward Bound or National Outdoor Leadership School.

Social science research has been used to determine pricing for programs, crowding capacity in natural areas or parks, and ways to garner financial resources for youth-at-risk programs. Beyond our field, social science offers insight into potential partnerships and collaborations. For instance,

Adie Bush/Cultura/Getty Images

Researchers have determined that outdoor adventure programs help improve participants' self-confidence.

On the Job

Applying Social Science Research

One skill that can be beneficial to leisure professionals is the ability to interpret and apply social science research to their jobs. While trial and error can be one method of determining what will work in a parks, recreation, or tourism program, it is not necessarily the most efficient. If we look at research that has been conducted using social science theories or models, we can get an estimate of what variables might affect our goals in positive ways. This gives us a leg up as professionals when we implement them into our programs as a means of accomplishing our mission. For example, one thing we learn about flow in this chapter is that we should try to match challenge and ability as a means of creating optimal experiences. From a programmatic perspective, therefore, we would know to create climbing routes of varying challenges so that we can direct participants to the right one in order to optimize their experiences. Learning more about other social science research can similarly help in innumerable ways by helping leisure professionals better target experience improvements with what is likely to work, rather than merely guessing at methods that may not actually have an impact.

education research demonstrates that playing chess can improve academic performance of students by increasing concentration and raising test scores (Root, 2008). An urban recreation center that works with at-risk youth can use this information to create a chess club, partner with schools, garner resources, and ultimately affect students' academic performance. The ability to demonstrate leisure's benefits beyond casual observations requires good methodology from social science. Although most of us know from personal experience that leisure is beneficial to our quality of life, social science will help us know empirically where, how, when, and for whom this is true.

There are only 108 waking hours in a week. If a person spends 60 hours working, they also spend 48 hours doing something else (besides sleeping). If the person spends 18 hours on personal care and daily chores, this leaves roughly 30 hours for leisure time. According to social scientists, without those 30 hours of leisure, the person will most likely be unhappy (psychology), alone (sociology), and a workaholic (anthropology) but financially okay (economics); however, what is the point of having money if you do not have time to spend it? U.S. trends over the last 80 years have shown that our work hours have decreased, and leisure time has increased. At the beginning of the 20th century, a workweek averaged 50 to 60 hours, and since that time the standard workweek has declined to 35 to 40 hours, thereby increasing other time, including leisure time, from 53 hours to 70 hours. With this knowledge from social science, recreation practitioners can provide programs and help people understand their choices in both work and leisure.

The human condition is like a puzzle with some missing pieces. We can see the picture as a whole but not always the nuances that provide information. By investigating the missing pieces of the social puzzle, the researcher attempts to discover, explain, and predict social patterns. Think back to the blind men and the elephant. Think of the puzzle as the elephant and the blind men as social scientists. Each man experiences the elephant from a different perspective (i.e., psychologically, economically, sociologically, or anthropologically) and offers explanations that are accurate. If the blind men share their knowledge, they all can better understand the phenomenon of the elephant. Like the elephant in the puzzle, the human subject is neither quantifiable nor qualifiable. Social sciences offer the ability to move beyond our blindness and use knowledge from a systematic approach to better understand the human condition.

Social Science Perspectives

The paradigm or worldview that a researcher has determines how they will put together the puzzle. To understand how each blind man approaches the truth, one must investigate their paradigms from three perspectives. The first perspective is **ontology**: What is the blind man's belief of reality? Is truth universal or are there multiple realities? The second perspective is **epistemology**, the blind man's beliefs about how to get information or how the blind man believes the puzzle should be put together. The third perspective is **methodology**. This consists of the procedures and techniques that are used to collect information to help put the puzzle together. These three perspectives determine the blind man's paradigm.

Paradigm is at the heart of how the social scientist strategizes putting the puzzle pieces together. In social science there are many paradigms, such as positivism, postpositivism, interpretivism, postmodernism, and critical theory (see table 2.1).

The paradigm of **positivism** offers that there is one elephant (or truth). When one is attempting to solve a puzzle, objectivity is of utmost importance. The scientific method involves inquiry by gathering evidence through observation, measurement, or empirical data to discover the truth. We are all familiar with this paradigm at an early age—think back to your elementary school science fair. You determined a topic to investigate and then came up with a research question. You conducted a review or literature search for what was known about the phenomenon. Then you picked a methodology to conduct your experiment. The results were gathered, and an analysis was conducted. Then you were the expert on this research and presented it at the school science fair!

TABLE 2.1 Social Science Perspectives

Term	Definition	Example	In recreation
Ontology	A set of concepts and categories in a subject area or domain that shows their properties and the relations between them	A scientist established different categories to divide existing things in an effort to better understand and how they fit together.	Breakdown of recreation into indoor and outdoor; then a breakdown of outdoor recreation into fishing, hunting, etc.
Epistemology	The investigation of what distinguishes justified truth from untruth	Fabricated news stories cannot be truth because they are not factual.	Needs assessment to check practitioner perceptions of local issues
Methodology	The strategy underlying the use of specific research methods	Grounded theory would suggest the use of interviews.	Using questionnaires to complete visitor surveys
Positivism	The search for universal laws through the scientific method	Searching for underlying principles to explain why apples fall from trees.	That going to sleep-away camp is good for kids
Postpositivism	Recognizes that all observation is fallible and that all theory is revisable	It was once believed the Earth was flat, but today we believe it is round.	Change of definitions of leisure from free time to many definitions being recognized as legitimate
Interpretivism	The integration of human interest and meaning into a study	I had a nightmare last night and I think I forgot to do some of my homework.	Why basketball is my favorite sport
Postmodernism	Emphasizes the ambiguity, fragmentation, particularity, and discontinuity of knowledge claims	Being skeptical of grand narratives such as "leisure is always a force for good in society."	Inclusion of online shopping as a form of recreation, rather than limiting it to brick-and-mortar agencies
Critical theory	Questions the systems of oppression behind everyday thought and action	The absence of female employees might be due to sexism.	Female rafting guides encountering sexist assumptions about their career choice

A person using **postpositivism** when viewing the elephant would suggest although there is one truth, we cannot prove it, but we can show it is false. This paradigm recognizes that you cannot separate the knower and the known; in other words, the knowledge that the blind man had of a snake informed his interpretation of the elephant's trunk. This realization of our own bias opens the doors for other research methods. A postpositivistic researcher would continue to use the scientific method but has less faith in the method than the positivists. So the postpositivist might use some or all of the blind men to confirm the reality of the elephant. In this paradigm, the researcher is still the expert but also recognizes their own shortcomings.

Using the paradigm of **interpretivism**, the social scientist would agree that all the blind men are viewing their own reality or truth of what is an elephant. There are many realities, which implies that objectivity of positivism is not practical. "The researcher should try to understand the contextual realities and subjective meanings that shape people's interactions with their world" (Samdahl, 1999, p. 14). In the interpretivist paradigm, the participant, rather than the researcher, is viewed as the expert on the phenomenon that is being researched (Samdahl, 1999). This view allows the researcher to put the puzzle together by considering how people define their experience. The interpretivist researcher is trained to conduct research whereby an understanding of the phenomenon emerges from the people being studied.

The scientist using the **postmodernism** paradigm would question the reality of the elephant. This point of view illustrates there is really no answer to the question, only various points of view (as in the case of the blind men and the elephant). Therefore, all the images of the elephant are equally true (Babbie, 2002). This paradigm is skeptical of grand theories that try to explain everything.

A researcher using a critical theory paradigm might question the assumptions and systems of oppression (e.g., racism, sexism, ableism) that brought these blind men and this elephant together. For example, critical scholars might ask: Why are only blind men present? Or, why is it assumed that the blind men are unable to come together and understand that they are, in fact, touching an elephant? Critical theorists' goal is to shine a light on systems of oppression to facilitate awareness of how these forces shape everyday existence (Crotty, 1997). This work is important because oppression often masquerades as normal or natural (Bonilla-Silva, 2003). Awareness of the ways oppression hides within the status quo creates the possibility of ongoing social action (Friere, 2010) to move us toward justice, freedom, or perhaps love (hooks, 2001).

There are other paradigms of social science (e.g., constructivist, participatory)—more than we can discuss in this chapter. What is important is each paradigm has its own assumptions, values, methods, and criticisms. Each of the social science disciplines (e.g., psychology, sociology, economics, anthropology, geography) can encompass all the paradigms discussed. Thus, there are many perspectives with which to view the elephant, and one must understand the assumptions that the individual makes when conducting investigations.

Connecting the Social Sciences to Leisure

In this section we will be discussing elements (e.g., theories, concepts, frameworks, and methodologies) of how different social science disciplines connect with leisure. Examining these discipline approaches to understanding the human experience will help us understand how leisure enriches lives and is essential to human existence.

Psychological Concepts and Leisure Application

One of the major fields of study influencing social science is psychology. **Psychology** is the study of the way the human mind works and how it influences behavior. We all use the principles of psychology daily without realizing it. When we reward ourselves with a night at the movies for doing something good, we are using psychology's learning principle of positive reinforcement. When we get nervous right before we drop in from the top of a skateboard ramp, we are activating our autonomic nervous system. When we tell ourselves to calm down, work harder, or give up, we are using psychological cognitive approaches. These examples illustrate psychology as the study of humans' thoughts, emotions, and behavior.

Psychology can be used to examine leisure behaviors. For example, why does one person choose to jump out of a plane whereas another says, "Look at that idiot jumping out of a perfectly good plane!" One of the psychological theories at play in these scenarios is the theory of sensation seeking. **Sensation seeking** is "the need for varied, novel and complex sensations and the willingness to take physical and social risks for the sake of such experiences" (Zuckerman, 1983, p. 10). According to the theory of sensation seeking, four subcomponents make up how much a person desires sensation-seeking attributes and opportunities:

Self-Exploration

Are you a sensation seeker? How would you rate yourself? Go online and search for Zuckerman's 1983 Sensation Seeking Scale test and take a quick questionnaire to see how you score.

That nervous feeling you get right before participating in a challenging activity is a sign your body's autonomic nervous system is gearing up. This is an example of a psychological principle you unconsciously use on yourself.

Anion/fotolia.com

1. Thrill and adventure seeking, which relate to the willingness to take physical risks and participate in high-risk sports
2. Experience seeking, which relates to the need for new and exciting experiences
3. Disinhibition, which relates to a willingness to take social risks and engage in health risk behaviors (e.g., binge drinking or having unprotected sex)
4. Boredom susceptibility, which relates to intolerance for monotony and repetitive activities

Have you ever participated in a leisure activity, such as snowboarding, playing the guitar, or meditating, where you lost all sense of time; your ability and the challenge were perfectly matched; you became totally unaware of your surroundings; or you just seemed to get into the rhythm of things, on the ball, in the zone, or in the groove? This is called the flow theory. The nine factors of **flow** are these:

1. The challenge level and skill level are matched.
2. A high degree of concentration is present.
3. Self-consciousness is lost.
4. Sense of time is distorted.
5. Successes and failures are apparent.
6. Clear and obtainable goals are present.
7. The person has a sense of personal control.
8. The experience is intrinsically rewarding.
9. The person becomes absorbed in the activity.

Not all of these factors are needed for flow to be experienced. An expert skier who skis on a bunny hill is likely to be bored, whereas a beginner on a black diamond hill is likely to feel anxiety. The optimal situation for flow is when the person is in the middle, matching their skill level with the challenge. The borrowing and merging of psychological theories and leisure are too expansive to discuss in this text; however, you can almost take any major theory of psychology and use the theory to better understand leisure behaviors.

The psychological perspective of leisure shows us that leisure is a time for building purpose in our lives, is individually determined, and should have beneficial results. Some of the psychological benefits of leisure might include, but are not limited to, increases in self-actualization, self-identity,

Self-Exploration

Can you remember a time you were in flow? What made that situation ideal for flow, and could you replicate those conditions to put yourself in flow? How does the person next to you answer these questions?

self-esteem, or self-concept; personal enjoyment and growth; reduction of anxiety and depression; enhanced feelings of spirituality; and improvements in overall psychological well-being. Additionally, it is well documented that as a result of leisure engagement, people make significant gains in informational knowledge, visual learning, problem solving, creativity, and recognition memory.

Sociological Concepts and Leisure Application

Cliques, team sports, social clubs, parties, social networking sites, and religious holidays are all components of **sociology**, which is the systematic study of social behavior and human groups. For example, sociologists study things such as race or ethnicity, social class, gender roles, family, deviance, and crime. **Deviance** consists of actions or behaviors that differ from cultural norms. Many people participate in leisure pursuits that society may deem socially inappropriate or deviant. Bondage, graffiti, and entering in the Cannabis Cup (a festival held in the Netherlands focused on marijuana) are just a few of these types of leisure pursuits that may be deemed deviant. The culture a person inhabits can determine whether a leisure activity is considered deviant. For instance, in Amsterdam the Cannabis Cup is not considered socially deviant because it is part of the social norms; this is an example of what social scientists call **cross-cultural** differences. Another instance is whistling loudly during a music concert in the United States to show your appreciation; in Europe, whistling shows disapproval, like booing. A sociologist looking at leisure from a gender perspective may find that many women today are not allowed to participate in many leisure and recreation pursuits, like some Islamic women who are limited by the prevailing culture in which they live. Or sometimes women are just treated differently: Coed intramural basketball may have modified rules, such as a woman receives three points per basket whereas a man receives the traditional

two points (Steinbach, 2013). Not until 1974 were girls even allowed to play in Little League baseball (Little League of America, 2003). American society has gained speed in the push for equal treatment for women. This sociological trend is an example of how society can flourish and nurture leisure opportunities; for example, girls can now play in Little League. One of the most important examples of a law affecting society in regard to equal treatment for men and women is Title IX of the Education Amendments of 1972 (sometimes called the Equal Opportunity in Education Act), which protects against discrimination on the basis of sex.

For leisure to flourish, society must encourage and support it. This is where sociology becomes a significant player in our understanding of the benefits of leisure to our society. Some of the sociological benefits resulting when a family has common or shared leisure activities are improved family bonding, increases in marital and family satisfaction, and stability. People who work for companies that offer leisure opportunities for their employees (e.g., Google and Microsoft) are more likely to have high job satisfaction and to enjoy their work; the companies benefit through reduced health care costs, fewer on-the-job accidents, and a lower rate of employee turnover. Communities that provide citizens with many leisure opportunities show increases in quality-of-life assessments, higher community involvement and satisfaction, and lower crime rates than communities that offer fewer leisure opportunities.

Economic Concepts and Leisure Application

Economics examines the production, distribution, and consumption of goods and services. How many of us work all week so we can play on the weekend? Imagine if you added up all the money you spent in the last year on leisure activities. The economic impact of leisure can be substantial; in some areas the economy is partially or even completely dependent on tourism and the offering of leisure escapes. In North Dakota, which has over 600,000 residents, the fifth largest economic producer in the state is the leisure industry (North Dakota Department of Commerce Tourism Division, 2018)!

Most economists examine economics through two major theories: microeconomics and macroeconomics. **Microeconomics** looks at how individuals, families, organizations, and states make decisions to spend their money, whereas macroeconomics looks at the total of economic activity (growth, inflation, and unemployment) of a national or regional economy as a whole. From a leisure perspective, microeconomics looks at the relationship between a person's economic state of affairs and their leisure choices. If an unemployed worker has $100 left after paying all their monthly bills and chooses to take the kids miniature golfing, this is a microeconomic issue. Leisure and macroeconomics examine the growth of leisure needs and demands on the economic system. For example, if unemployment is high then available time for leisure activities may also be high, but money for expenditures on leisure is low; this is a macroeconomic scenario. The economy of some countries is dependent on tourism, and leisure is directly connected to this; in Jamaica, one in every four jobs is related to the tourism industry (Bartlett, 2018). People do not think about the economic impact leisure has on our society, but could you imagine if all the leisure opportunities in a country like Jamaica were nonexistent? Although poverty exists in this country now, what would it be without tourism? The COVID-19 pandemic highlighted the global impact of tourism; in May 2020, there were "67 million fewer international tourist arrivals, 80 US$ billion lost in exports and 100% destinations with travel restrictions" (World Tourism Organization, 2020, p. 1). The pandemic affected not only people's ability to travel but also their livelihoods, causing a reenvisioning of travel.

Imagine how economics plays a role from the perspective of recreation and leisure providers. Every day they are presented an economics-based question. For example, if an amusement park has long lines, the managers are forced to reflect on numerous questions. Should they raise the price of admission? Should they expand the park? Even if they decide to do nothing, what impact will that decision have? Although economic considerations should not be the only criteria used to answer these questions, economics has a significant influence on the decisions.

Anthropological Concepts and Leisure Application

Are you curious about why sports fans paint their faces, why people follow bands around the country, or why people play at all? This is the type of curiosity that would inspire an anthropologist to investigate. The field of anthropology is the study of humankind. Everything in culture and society—traditions, values, leisure, language, beliefs, economics, and more—can be investigated. Anthropologists want to understand humans' impact on society and on other humans. The fanatical sports devotee and the band groupie are of interest to anthropologists, as is the way humans play. The anthropologist's paradigm is to study and learn directly from people through ethnographic methods. Anthropology prioritizes understanding people from their unique perspectives, which is quite a different perspective from other social sciences.

In studying and describing all aspects of people, many anthropologists use the method of ethnography. "Rather than *studying people*, ethnography means *learning from people*" (Spradley, 1980, p. 3). Although leisure studies have benefited from many social science fields (e.g., psychology, social psychology, economics), the contribution of anthropology to the field has been small (Chick, 1998). What has been studied in the leisure field has come from ethnographies describing cultures' games, sports, and recreation. It has been suggested that leisure ethnography will help us to understand the nature and distribution of leisure as well as its validity as a concept in other cultures (Chick, 1998). Using ethnographic methods and cultural theory, one researcher studied how regular participation in pickup basketball develops values and community (McLaughlin, 2008). This study helps us understand informal recreation activity participation and the nuances that are involved within the community of participants. Cross-cultural understanding of leisure can be found through ethnography of anthropology. Why is this important? From a social science perspective, anthropology offers descriptions of society and culture that can provide insight into benefits and challenges of leisure for a pluralistic society.

Geography Concepts and Leisure Application

Have you ever visited a national, state, or local park and thought about how important it is to set aside lands for this experience? In using these lands, we must balance our desire for positive leisure experiences and our need to protect the lands for future generations. Geography is the study of the Earth and its features and of the distribution of life on the Earth, including human life and the effects of human activity. Geography has not always been considered a social science, and many geographers do not consider themselves social scientists. But with the improvements and accessibility of geographic information system technology, interesting social science issues are being examined. For example, figure 2.1 is a map of the population within 350 miles of Adirondack Park. Access to this map allows the park managers to watch for changes in population growth and urban sprawl and make informed decisions on all sorts of things, like resource management, accessibility, and staffing needs.

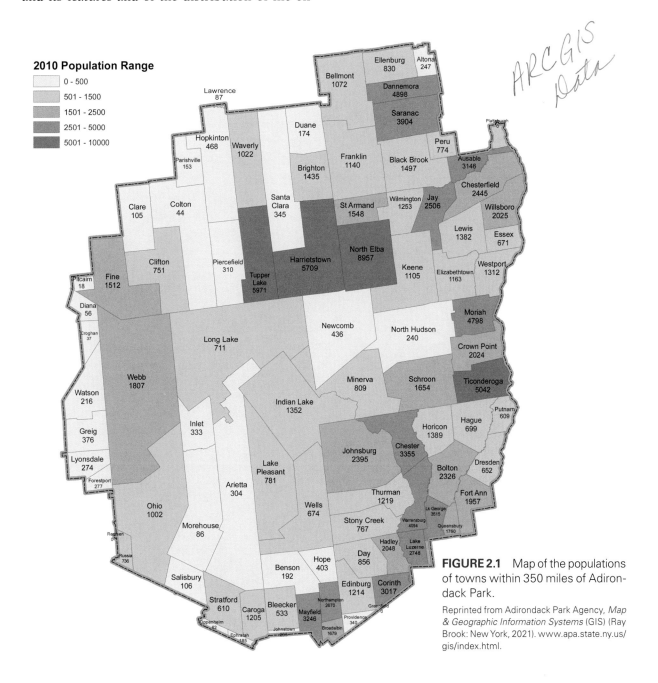

FIGURE 2.1 Map of the populations of towns within 350 miles of Adirondack Park.

Reprinted from Adirondack Park Agency, *Map & Geographic Information Systems* (GIS) (Ray Brook: New York, 2021). www.apa.state.ny.us/gis/index.html.

Summary

The value of studying people is paramount to recreation professionals. Through social science we can begin to understand how employment opportunities, culture, health, and leisure choices are shaped by environmental, social, psychological, and biological factors. That is, social science helps us understand the human equation. This chapter provides context on social science and its impact on leisure behaviors.

The social sciences are about people: how they act individually and in a group. Social science encompasses disciplines such as psychology, sociology, economics, anthropology, and geography. All of these disciplines can provide insight into leisure behaviors. Also important to social science is the understanding of the paradigm or worldview of the researcher. The major paradigms discussed are positivism, postpositivism, interpretivism, postmodernism, and critical theory. Ontology, epistemology, and methodology are the determinants of a social scientist's paradigm (or worldview). These perspectives determine how research is conducted within the paradigm.

Social science draws from numerous disciplines of study. Psychology, the study of individual human behavior, can offer insight into why a person participates in a recreational activity. Sociology, the study of two or more human behaviors, can provide insight into group behavior, such as at a sporting event (e.g., when fans do the wave). Economics, which examines the production, distribution, and consumption of goods and services, is at the heart of pricing recreational activities, which are the basis of the tourism industry for some countries. Anthropology, the study of humankind and cultures, can best inform a national park or heritage site of the culture being preserved. Geography, the study of Earth's lands, inhabitants, and features, provides data for natural resource and land management decisions.

Social science provides tangible benefits for leisure and society. Social science research informs policy making and management decisions. Communities benefit from social science through initiatives that improve quality of life through technological advances, allocation or budgetary efficiency, and institutional change. Social science provides empirical evidence to substantiate the provision of fiscal resources, staffing, and facilities for recreation.

Learning Activities

1. Choose any recreation or leisure activity and find literature on how the activity is being examined through a social science lens. Look for the psychological, social, economic, anthropological, and geographical issues, benefits, and constraints.

2. Put on your imaginary lab coats and be a social scientist. With the advent of social networking websites (like Facebook, Twitter, and Instagram), leisure interactions have changed. Using one of the major areas of social science, examine the benefits, constraints, and negative aspects of leisure participation. Write a two-page report and be ready to discuss your findings and thoughts. Here are some questions to think about before beginning this assignment: How would scientists in your area of social science approach this problem? How might they examine this issue? What do you suspect the results of their study might be? How has leisure changed as a result of these social networking sites? What are examples from the area of social science you have chosen?

3. Attend a social event. Examine how each field of the social sciences interacts with, explains, or plays a role in the success or failure of the event. Write a one-page paper, providing examples of how each of the following fields was important: psychology, sociology, economics, anthropology, and geography.

4. Form a group with four fellow students. Each student picks an article that addresses the benefits of leisure through each field of social science: psychology, sociology, economics, anthropology, and geography. After each student writes a one-page summary of the benefits, hold a roundtable discussion of all members' findings. Find common themes in everyone's findings and note how these themes were examined in their field. *Benefits of Leisure* (Driver, Brown, & Peterson, 1991) is a good starting place for finding literature to review.

5. Select one of the social science perspectives discussed in this chapter and locate one additional theory that can be used to understand leisure. Then use that theory to explore the potential benefits and limitations of your favorite leisure activity.

Review Questions

1. In social science there are many paradigms, such as positivism, postpositivism, interpretivism, and postmodernism. Explain each.

2. One of the major fields of study that influences social science is psychology. Explain this influence through a leisure example.

3. What might a sociologist who looks at leisure from a gender perspective find with regard to women and recreation pursuits? Explain and support your answer.

4. Explain micro- and macroeconomics as they apply to leisure.

5. How do ethnographies help social science?

6. Discuss the benefits of leisure from a psychological, social, economics, anthropology, and geography lens.

Go to HK*Propel* to access additional learning content.

Leisure as Part of Your Lifestyle

Leisure and Quality of Life

Ariel Rodríguez

Springfield College

VOCABULARY TERMS

autonomy	prevention	social embeddedness
competence	quality of life	social network
coping	relatedness	social support
neighborhood	sacralization	spiritual health
physical health	social climate	transcendence

LEARNING OUTCOMES

After reading this chapter, you will be able to

- describe how leisure affects your quality of life;
- explain the relationship between leisure and other key aspects of life;
- identify leisure resources that may improve your quality of life; and
- list strategies to enhance your quality of life through leisure.

Imagine you have been studying for your exam for what feels like a lifetime. You know that your exam will be in less than an hour, but you cannot help but think about what you will do afterward. You think about texting your friends to see whether you can get a group to grab some food at the union. Perhaps you are in the mood to go to the student recreation center and get in a cardio workout. You quickly text your friends and ask them to meet you after your exam, and they quickly reply that they will. Although you are tired from studying and stressed about the exam, you cannot help but smile as you look forward to relaxing and meeting up with your friends after the exam.

Throughout this chapter, we introduce several frameworks to help explain how leisure affects quality of life. The subsequent discussion focuses on the meanings derived from leisure activities throughout those parts of life that contribute most to our quality of life.

What Is Quality of Life?

To understand how leisure influences quality of life, it is important to first understand the meaning of quality of life. According to the World Health Organization (n.d.), **quality of life** is "an individual's perception of their position in life in the context of the culture and value systems in which they live and in relation to their goals, expectations, standards, and concerns" (para. 2). In other words, quality of life is the personal determination of the worth or value of some aspect of a person's life. In general, research suggests the most important aspects of life that contribute to one's quality of life include their health, productivity (e.g., employment, volunteering, school), material well-being, social support, safety, community, spiritual beliefs, and leisure (Cummins, 1996; Iwasaki, 2007; WHO, n.d.). Lastly, quality of life is not a destination, just like being happy is not a destination. It is a journey that traverses our entire life, and at each point in our life, different aspects of our life are more important than others.

Steve Prezant/Image Source/Getty Images

Engaging in meaningful activities with people who provide strong social support is an important contribution to the quality of a person's life.

The Connection Between Leisure and Quality of Life

Leisure activities provide a context where we can gain and enhance deeper meanings in our lives (Iwasaki, 2007). These meanings become major pathways through which quality of life is improved. Meanings derived through leisure activities that help promote quality of life include, for example, the development of positive emotions and identities, the fulfillment of important life needs, the maintenance of our spiritual balance, the enhancement of our social and cultural connection with others, the ability to cope with and transcend difficult life situations, and the promotion of positive human development across our life span (Brajša-Žganec, Merkaš, & Šverko, 2011; Caldwell, 2005; Iwasaki, 2007). Let us explore how meanings derived through leisure activities interact with some of the most important aspects of our lives.

Personal Health

Think about the last time you were not feeling well. Perhaps you had a headache from stress or maybe you went to the gym after a long hiatus and pushed yourself a little too far. When people do not feel well, they are less inclined to do everyday activities, including engaging in leisure activities that promote meaning in their lives.

From a holistic model, health refers to physical, mental, and social well-being in addition to the absence of disease, illness, and disability (Larson, 1991). Consistent with the holistic model's perspective of health, at least three ways in which leisure influences health and well-being have been identified: prevention, coping, and transcendence. Each of the concepts has unique implications (Caldwell, 2005). For instance, **prevention** refers to the ability of leisure to prevent illnesses. **Coping** refers to the ability of leisure to help people cope with negative daily stresses, whereas **transcendence** refers to the ability of leisure to help a person overcome a traumatic life event. Let us explore these further in the subsequent sections.

Physical Well-Being

Physical well-being refers to a person's subjective perception of their **physical health** over time and objectively the condition of their body and its ability to prevent illnesses. Many things contribute to a person's physical health, including what we eat and drink, the amount of regular physical activity

we integrate into our daily life, and the amount and quality of rest we have. When a person incorporates leisure in a way that reduces or eliminates risk behavior and poor health choices and provides opportunities for expression that meet physiological and psychological needs, leisure helps reduce and even prevent illnesses.

Incorporating physical activities such as playing basketball, working out, or swimming helps prevent illness. There is strong scientific evidence that regular participation in physical activities can help promote joint functioning, muscle strength, and appropriate body weight (Kahn et al., 2002; Miilunpalo, 2001; Wankel & Berger, 1991). There is also evidence that being physically active can prevent chronic diseases, reduce the number of illnesses a person experiences, and even extend a person's life span (Pedersen & Clemmensen, 1997; Reis & Gibbs, 2012; Schnohr, Scharling, & Jensen, 2003).

Leisure provides a context for us to improve our quality of life not only when we participate in physical activities, but also when we engage in deeper meaning making through these physical activities. For instance, when we participate in leisure activities that are physically demanding, such as walking, we are likely to promote our physical well-being. However, going for a walk alone at home on a treadmill, as one might have had to do during the COVID-19 pandemic, walking with teammates as part of a fundraiser event, and walking as part of a spiritual hike like *El Camino de Santiago* are likely to yield different meanings that differently contribute to quality of life. While they all may directly promote physical health and reduce illnesses, walking in a fundraiser with teammates or as part of a spiritual hike may also promote social connections, positive emotions, and positive identification with a cause that is larger than oneself, all of which affect quality of life.

Mental Well-Being

Mental well-being refers to being emotionally and cognitively healthy. Leisure activities and their settings can help you maintain emotional stability and cognitive well-being. In fact, many of the same activities that help improve physical health may also help reduce anxiety, tension, and depression (Biddle, Fox, Boutcher, & Faulkner, 2000; Mutrie, 2000). Physical activity as an adjunct therapy has also been effective in the treatment of disorders like schizophrenia, developmental disorders, somatoform disorders, substance abuse disorders, smoking

Self-Exploration

Think about what activities or hobbies have helped you to relax and relieve stress throughout your life. Are they still a part of your life? Through life transitions and life challenges, we can often look to these activities to help bring a sense of balance to our lives. What are you doing today to maintain these activities in your life?

cessation, and sleep apnea (Fox, Boutcher, Faulkner, & Biddle, 2000).

The meanings experienced through engagement in leisure activities have the potential to enhance or diminish a person's mental health. When a leisure activity helps to promote positive emotions, positive identities, and self-esteem, it is more likely to improve one's quality of life. For example, engaging in cultural music, art, and traditional ceremonies and festivals was found to promote a strong sense of pride and self-esteem in Indigenous people, which subsequently promoted their quality of life (Iwasaki, 2007). However, as described through Csikszentmihalyi's (1990) flow theory, high-performance expectations, such in an athletic activity or a musical performance, without the appropriate skills can cause anxiety instead of pleasure. Likewise, a person who has played and beaten a specific video game many times may become bored because the challenge is so low relative to their skill level.

Coping

The stresses of everyday life, such as those experienced from work or school, may be emotionally and psychologically taxing. These stresses may make you irritable, decrease your ability to concentrate, increase the frequency of headaches, and increase your muscular tension. Prolonged exposure to stress may cause depression, digestive issues, and cardiovascular illnesses. Therefore, the management of stress is critical for a healthy life.

As a form of coping, leisure can be an important buffer against stress from daily life (Coleman & Iso-Ahola, 1993; Heintzman, 2015; Iso-Ahola & Park, 1996; Iwasaki, 2001). "As stress levels increase, leisure coping strategies appear to act as a buffer against the negative impact of stress to help people maintain good physical health" (Iwasaki, 2003, p. 106). When engagement in a leisure activity is perceived to be self-determined and promotes social support, it serves as a coping strategy that may help buffer negative life stresses (Coleman & Iso-Ahola, 1993).

A task is self-determined when it fulfills your needs for autonomy, competence, and relatedness.

Autonomy refers to choice, such as when you want to participate in an activity or have a specific experience. **Competence** generally refers to whether you are knowledgeable enough to get what you want from an activity or experience. **Relatedness** refers to the desire to feel connected to others, such as loving or caring for others along with being loved and cared for (Deci & Ryan, 2000; Ryan & Deci, 2000).

Transcendence

Some events can cause a severe amount of stress. These traumatic events may involve life-threatening situations, such as being assaulted or losing a loved one. These events are often so horrifying to the person that memories of the event make a person feel they are reliving the event. Such flashbacks may bring back the same feelings of helplessness and fear once experienced during the event.

As a form of transcendence, "someone uses leisure to find new meaning to life and becomes reborn in a way that allows for a fuller realization of one's potential" (Caldwell, 2005, p. 15). In other words, leisure is a way to deal with extreme negative life events (e.g., natural disaster or loss of a loved one). More specifically, "leisure is a resource for the self-protective effects of emotion-focused and problem-focused coping, and [this] experience may be the foundation for adjustment and personal growth following a negative life event" (Kleiber, Hutchinson, & Williams, 2002, p. 225). Leisure activities may buffer the impact of negative life events by distracting us from our problems, generating optimism about the future, and aiding in the reconstruction of a life story that is continuous with the past (Kleiber et al.). For instance, during the deadly outbreak of COVID-19 in Italy, people found strength and solidarity through their collective voluntary actions (Finley, 2020). By volunteering, their focus shifted from the pandemic to how they could help those in need, which promoted optimism among the volunteers.

Spirituality

Spirituality provides a space where individuals can engage with religious and other spiritual beliefs.

People who are spiritually healthy are said to believe in something greater than themselves, have strong spiritual beliefs and values, and be filled with love, happiness, and peace (Hawks, 1994). Moreover, they have greater access to spiritual resources, such as a faith community during challenging times, that help them better cope (Heintzman, 2015). **Spiritual health** is marked by "a high level of faith, hope, and commitment in relation to a well-defined worldview or belief system that provides a sense of meaning and purpose to existence" (Hawks, 1994, p. 6). At least three factors contribute to spiritual health: having a worldview that provides meaning and purpose to life, feeling connected to others, and maintaining a strong commitment to and personal faith in one's worldview (Hawks, 1994).

Leisure experiences have been known to promote spiritual health. For example, camping and other outdoor activities in nature and in the wilderness are often associated with spiritual values. Additionally, many people participate in spiritual activities, such as going to a spiritual or religious facility, during their leisure time. One model that theorizes the relationship between leisure and spiritual health is the model of leisure and spiritual well-being (Heintzman, 2002).

The model of leisure and spiritual well-being theorizes that there is a homeostatic level of spiritual well-being that is unique to each person. There are times when people feel alienated from their spiritual energy and consciously or unconsciously suppress their spiritual self. During these times, a person may need assistance to get their spiritual level back to normal. Two techniques identified in the model are sacralization and resacralization. **Sacralization** is the process of sensitizing a person to their spiritual self; resacralization involves sensitizing a person who was sensitized previously but has consciously or unconsciously moved from their spiritual self. Many leisure activities, such as meditation, rhythmic breathing techniques, creative visualization, and relaxation exercises, can assist with sacralization and resacralization. Conversely, there are times when people get spiritual energy boosts, moments

We can connect with nature in many ways, such as camping, hiking, fishing, and hunting. Many people who have hectic lives use their time in nature to simply relax and get in touch with their true selves.

Nattrass/iStock/Getty Images

in their life when their spiritual energy is higher than normal, and they become off-centered. Having elevated levels of spiritual energy may occur because of a spiritual emergency or a time in life when one's personal growth at a spiritual level becomes overwhelming or even chaotic. The model recommends using grounding techniques to get spiritual levels back to normal. Some leisure activities that help ground people include gardening, tai chi, and walking (Heintzman, 2002).

Leisure and Work

Due in part to increases in the cost of higher education, many students are turning to part-time and full-time jobs to help pay for their education. With their roles as students and employees, students have a dwindling amount of time for leisure activities. This dualistic nature of work and leisure is part of the foundation of the United States. To understand this conflict, one needs to look no further than the inauguration speech by President Barack Obama. While discussing historical elements of the United States, he stated: "Our journey has never been one of shortcuts or settling for less. It has not been the path for the fainthearted—for those who prefer leisure over work" (CNN, 2009). In his speech, Obama echoed a common belief in the United States that work signifies achievement, whereas leisure signifies laziness or nonproductivity, but as you have seen throughout this chapter, leisure is much more than time away from work; it is a powerful mechanism through which deeper meanings are gained and enhanced that promote our quality of life. Let us explore the relationship between work and leisure a bit further.

Spillover and Compensation Theory

Two traditional theories used to predict the relationship between work and leisure time are spillover and compensation theory. Spillover theory states that people participate in activities in their leisure time similar to their work, and thus worklike activities spill over into leisure activities. For instance, people who are computer savvy and work as computer programmers may have a higher likelihood of playing video games during their free time than playing basketball or volleyball.

Alternatively, compensation theory purports that people participate in leisure activities that are fundamentally dissimilar from those found in their work—activities that help people meet their needs not met at work. Of the two theoretical frameworks, spillover tends to have more support than compensation theory in predicting the relationship between work and leisure (Mannell & Reid, 1999). However, due to the limited amount of leisure-related meaning making explored in these earlier frameworks, their capacity to explain the intersection between work, leisure, and quality of life is limited. Let us explore alternative concepts that help to shed light on this relationship.

Serious Leisure

While spillover and compensation theory assume leisure and work are dualistic, serious leisure suggests leisure can resemble work. According to Stebbins (1999) serious leisure is "the systematic pursuit of an amateur, hobbyist, or volunteer activity that participants find so substantial and interesting that, in the typical case, they launch themselves on a career centered on acquiring and expressing its special skills, knowledge, and experience" (p. 69).

There are six distinctive qualities of serious leisure: perseverance, career-related results, generation of knowledge, achievement of intrinsic rewards, identification, and unique ethos. People who engage in serious leisure pursuits have had to persevere. There may have been difficult times when they contemplated giving up their pursuit but instead continued. These people wish to find a career in their leisure pursuit, and for many people, this is a turning point at which their level of involvement increases. People who have serious leisure pursuits make genuine efforts to obtain more knowledge and skills concerning their leisure pursuit. This may come in many forms. For example, an amateur woodworker may begin to buy magazines focused on furniture building, or a gardener might take classes about different plants. For these people, the leisure pursuit is self-gratifying; they engage in it because they love it. Moreover, they identify strongly with their leisure pursuit and engage in what is termed a *unique ethos*: a special culture that is based around the leisure pursuit. An example of this is the culture that revolves around online games, such as *Final Fantasy XIV*. In the game, a unique language has developed that is consistent with online gaming but unique to the game. If an outsider were to read an online conversation between players, they would have difficulties understanding the language.

Serious leisure provides a context for participants to improve their quality of life. Research suggests engaging in serious leisure leads to experiencing joy and a sense of usefulness (Cassie & Halpenny, 2003)

There are many instances in which people transform leisure activities into careers. The key is that when you started this activity, you did it for leisure purposes.

and helps fulfill personal growth while increasing levels of happiness (Kim, Heo, Lee, & Kim, 2015). In a sample of students, it was found that participants of serious leisure were more likely to have high levels of leisure satisfaction and satisfaction with their life (Liu & Yu, 2015). Among older adults, serious leisure participation may also provide an opportunity to give back to the community, maintain an active body and mind, and develop social contacts and friendships (Misener, Doherty, & Hamm-Kerwin, 2010), all of which promote one's quality of life.

Self-Exploration

Think about the leisure activities you enjoy the most. Which would you consider doing as a career? What do you think would be your biggest challenge in pursuing a career in your favorite leisure activity?

Unemployment

The COVID-19 pandemic and the subsequent economic downturn in the United States increased the number of unemployed Americans by more than 14 million in 3 months, from 6.2 million in February 2020 to 20.5 million in May 2020 (Kocchar, 2020). When individuals are jobless but actively seeking work, leisure can help buffer the stresses of their joblessness. Researchers have found that leisure provides a source of well-being for unemployed young adults, including those in minority ethnic and racial groups (Melamed, Meir, & Samson, 1995). For instance, it has been found that unemployed young adults who participated in leisure activities that were more challenging and active had higher levels of psychological well-being than those who did not (Haworth & Ducker, 1991). How people use their leisure influences the wellness outcomes people derive from leisure. Another example comes from a study of the mental health of unemployed men (Kilpatrick & Trew, 1985). Unemployed men who spent their leisure time doing passive activities, such as watching television, had the poorest psychological well-being. Unemployed men who were active, such as through volunteering and actively pursuing leisure interests outside the home, had higher levels of psychological well-being.

Materialism

Money is necessary to purchase food and clothes, keep a roof over our head, have access to transportation, enjoy certain leisure activities, and live a comfortable life. However, money increases the quality of your life only to a certain point. Once you have enough money to meet daily necessities, in general, making more money no longer significantly affects your quality of life. Along these lines, living a life largely identified by the pursuit of wealth and possessions, or materialism, is associated with lower levels of quality of life. Materialism is characterized as an extrinsic goal pursuit that is more commonly associated with lower levels of quality of life. This contrasts with intrinsic goal pursuits, such as caring for one's community and maintaining close relationships, which tend to promote higher levels of quality of life (Hudders & Pandelaere, 2012).

From a leisure perspective, materialism serves as a cautionary tale. If we find ourselves consuming leisure products or even engaging in leisure pursuits for social recognition, for the sake of acquiring more goods, or for other extrinsic goals, it is likely not to contribute positively to our quality of life.

Social Support

Going to college is often a major transition for students. Many students leave their homes and relocate to their university. As part of the relocation, students often leave behind the social support that they have had throughout their lives. For instance, some friends from your high school may attend your new university, but many other friends simply move on.

Although your family might still be there for you, they may be miles away. You are on your own to do your laundry, pay bills, clean your apartment, and do all the other chores that we often take for granted when we live at home. In other words, your social support has changed. This stripping of a person's social support often makes the first year of college quite difficult. Yet, all is not gloom; in your first year at a university, you also meet new friends, perhaps while engaging in student activities provided by your college or as part of a student club. You may also visit your family a few times and even begin to make deep connections with new leisure places you experience.

Spending time with people, in particular those who care about you, such as your family, friends, and significant others, has consistently been associated with better physical health, mental health, and quality of life throughout the life span (Bovier, Chamot, & Perneger, 2004; Cummins, 1996; Langford, Bowsher, Maloney, & Lillis, 1997). For instance, social support helps decrease depression, increase personal competence during stressful life events, and influence positive affect, sense of stability, recognition of self-worth, and life satisfaction (Langford et al.). Think about your friends in college. How often have they stepped up to the plate when you needed someone to hang out with, grab a quick bite with, or simply talk to? If you answered, "very often," this is a good indicator that you have strong social support. A study of undergraduate students found that the very happiest students were highly social and had stronger romantic and other social relationships more often than did less happy students (Diener & Seligman, 2002).

Social support has been defined as "the assistance and protection given to others, especially to individuals" (Langford et al., 1997, p. 95). Assistance can come in many forms, such as lending money or providing a person with a place to call home. Social

---

Self-Exploration

Think about the people in your life you interact with. Some of them are just passing through your life, whereas others make a deeper impact. Whom do you reach out to when you want to grab a bite or go to the gym? Whom do you reach out to when you feel bored? Whom do you reach out to when you feel anxious or are experiencing a difficult life moment? Was your answer to these questions no one, one person, or different people? What are you actively doing to help strengthen your relationship with others who play a deeper role in your life?

support may include providing someone with emotional support after a breakup, following a bad exam, or when they need some encouragement. Protection refers to what one may envision a shield doing for a knight; a person may protect another by shielding them from threats, such as life stresses.

Necessary Components for Social Support

At least three components are necessary to foster social support: social networks, social embeddedness, and social climate (Langford et al., 1997). To understand a social network, envision a car traveling along a road. The road represents the social network: It provides a path for social support to function. Having large social networks, such as having an interstate highway system, to continue the analogy, does not necessarily mean that you have a greater amount of social support, but smaller social networks would limit your social support; only so many cars can fit on a small strip of road.

Social embeddedness refers to the connectedness people have to others within their social network—the depth and strength of relational ties between people in a social network (Langford et al., 1997). Imagine two separate roads, one with a sheet of ice over it and the other without. Lower levels of social embeddedness are more like a road with ice, where cars or people slip in and out of the road or network with little keeping them together. Social embeddedness is necessary for strong social support to develop.

Social climate refers to the personality of people in a social network (Langford et al., 1997). In keeping with the driving analogy, it is the difference between driving on a road with courteous drivers or drivers who conduct themselves in dangerous and inappropriate ways on the road. Social networks with more "courteous drivers" tend to foster more positive social support.

Leisure and Social Support

It has been well documented that leisure participation is often social and organized around groups of family members or friends (Coleman, 1993; Coleman & Iso-Ahola, 1993; Godbey, Caldwell, Floyd, & Payne, 2005). As such, an important role of leisure activities and programs is to provide people an opportunity to develop companionship and friendships (Coleman & Iso-Ahola, 1993). These

Self-Exploration

Think about your first year of college. Did you feel alienated and out of place at first? Did it take long to form a social support network away from your family and hometown friends?

opportunities can promote social support because they increase people's social networks in a safe and fun environment. For example, researchers have found that people who are more involved in sport and recreation activities develop larger networks of friends, receive more social support, and are more likely to socialize with other people (Coleman & Iso-Ahola). Given that leisure participation involves some form of active involvement by participants, this may promote social embeddedness. Moreover, many leisure activities naturally provide a social climate that promotes an exchange of assistance or helpfulness and protection and are integral to social support. For instance, sport-based activities such as team basketball, softball, soccer, football, and volleyball have rules and regulations that encourage group and team unity. It is by playing together that teams have advantages. As the saying goes, "There is no *I* in *team*."

Neighborhoods and Communities

Researchers have defined community as "an area in which individuals and groups regularly interact to integrate various attributes, opportunities and services for the fulfillment of subsistence needs and the establishment of a sense of community" (Allen, 1990, p. 184) and neighborhood as "the area immediately adjacent to a resident dwelling" (p. 186). In other words, our neighborhood is where we live, whereas our community is where we primarily interact with other people. The spaces in which we live and regularly interact influence our quality of life (Allen; Baker & Palmer, 2006; Sirgy & Cornwell, 2002). Moreover, they affect our capacity to gain deeper meanings from leisure activities. For instance, if you are unsatisfied with the recreation facilities near your home, the lack of lighting in your neighborhood, or the crime level where you spend most of your day, your capacity to engage in leisure activities in your neighborhood and community will be diminished, which limits opportunities to derive deeper meanings that affect your quality of life.

Recreation Programs and Facilities

The recreation programs and facilities near the neighborhood where we live or within the community where we engage are important contributors to quality of life. Three sectors provide recreation facilities and programs: public, nonprofit, and private. Public recreation facilities span most imaginable leisure activities. At the local level, such as cities, townships, counties, and special districts, this may include traditional parks, skate parks, dog parks, playgrounds, museums, fitness centers, convention centers, aquatic facilities, or hiking trails. Most public programming occurs at the local level of government. At the state and federal levels, facilities primarily focus on outdoor recreation and tourism-oriented activities as one might find in our national parks, such as Yellowstone and the Grand Canyon. In fact, in 2019, there were more than 327 million recreation visitors to national parks across the United States (National Park Service, 2020).

The nonprofit and private sectors provide several programs and facilities for recreation. We can join the local Y and work out in the gym or volunteer in the local 4-H to increase our participation and pride in our community. We can attend a private dinner with a loved one, go to a health spa to relax, or take a trip to Disney World with our family. We can even engage in private online communities through online games.

Strategies for Enhancing Quality of Life Through Leisure

As discussed throughout this chapter, in order to enhance quality of life through leisure, the following strategies may be pursued:

- Engage in self-determined leisure activities that promote your health, both physically and mentally, and enrich your social support system.
- If you are spiritually inclined, be conscious of your spiritual balance and use leisure activities to balance your spirituality.
- Use leisure activities strategically to help you cope or transcend difficult life situations, such as being unemployed.
- Be cautious of engaging in leisure activities solely for extrinsic purposes.
- Explore the many recreation programs and facilities offered where you live and primarily engage with others.

Summary

Leisure activities provide a context where we can gain and enhance deeper meanings in our life. These meanings become major pathways through which our quality of life is improved. Meanings are derived through leisure activities that help promote quality of life. Examples include the development of positive emotions and identities, the fulfillment of important life needs, the maintenance of our spiritual balance, the enhancement of our social and cultural connection with others, the ability to cope with and transcend difficult life situations, and the promotion of positive human development across our life span. Throughout this chapter, we explored how meanings derived through leisure activities interact with some of the most important aspects of our life, namely our health, spirituality, work, social support system, and communities and neighborhoods. We learned how leisure affects health and how it can help us cope and transcend difficult life events, such as being unemployed. We also discussed how leisure can promote spiritual health and help individuals stay balanced spiritually. The importance of social support and how leisure can promote social support was also discussed. Lastly, we reviewed how leisure opportunities within communities and neighborhoods can promote quality of life.

Learning Activities

1. Create a video post. In this video you will have up to three minutes to present a compelling argument for how leisure affects quality of life. Arguments should be supported with convincing details and examples.

2. Discuss with at least three other people in your class the changes they are making in their lives based on what they have learned from the chapter. The intent is to apply the new understanding you have about leisure and its role and function in your life and lifestyle.

3. Describe the last time you volunteered (if you have not volunteered, find someone close to you who has and ask them the following questions). Describe the volunteering experience: Where did it take place? What was the cause? With whom did you volunteer? Describe how this volunteering experience made you feel. Was it a meaningful experience? What would have made this experience more meaningful to you? How might a volunteering experience, such as the one you had, positively influence the physical, mental, and spiritual health of a person who is unemployed?

4. Complete an activity journal or diary that contains work, leisure, school, and social activities and involvements for seven days. Each day, document how the activities in each category contribute to your quality of life, including your physical, mental, and spiritual health. After seven days, decide whether there are any activities that you would like to discontinue, activities that you would like to do more of, and activities that you would like to include in your daily life and why.

Review Questions

1. Describe the mechanism by which leisure influences quality of life.
2. Describe the competing relationships between leisure and work.
3. Will making a great deal of money automatically lead to better quality of life? Explain.
4. What leisure activities should you do if your spiritual energy is too high? Too low?
5. What strategies should you implement to enhance your quality of life through leisure?

Go to HK*Propel* to access additional learning content.

Leisure, Health, and Physical Activity

Jason N. Bocarro

North Carolina State University

Michael A. Kanters

North Carolina State University

VOCABULARY TERMS

health   **leisure-time physical activity**

LEARNING OUTCOMES

After reading this chapter, you will be able to

- identify some of the major trends and statistics relating to physical inactivity and the consequences of these trends;
- understand how the leisure services field can facilitate active living and positively contribute to addressing this public health issue; and
- understand how leisure behavior can contribute to personal health and wellness.

Have you ever wondered why most online exercise subscriptions remain unused or underused? Why do so many people sign up for gym memberships and never go to the gym? Why do the people who do go to the gym watch TV or stream videos when they work out? Although most people in Western society believe that physical activity has health benefits, many do not find exercise to be fun and either look for distractions to make it more palatable or simply never get around to it. There is a disconnect between knowledge and action.

Looking to a purely medical solution to this problem discounts the potential contribution of the parks and recreation profession. We are trained to understand what motivates people to engage in leisure experiences. We are the so-called experts in creating leisure experiences that are both enjoyable and meaningful for participants. By acting as integral partners in solving the crisis of physical inactivity, obesity, and health in our society, parks and recreation professionals are more likely to find solutions that people will accept.

Parks and recreation services have the potential to improve everyone's health and physical activity levels. Furthermore, services and programs offered by the parks and recreation profession attract a wide and diverse segment of the population. This is why many public health professionals and policy makers interested in increasing the physical activity level of Americans look to the parks and recreation profession. For example, during the COVID-19 pandemic, an overwhelming majority of adults in the United States (83%) felt that their local parks, trails, and open spaces were essential for people's mental and physical health (NRPA, 2020).

The potential for leisure amenities and programs to help people become more physically active (i.e., to engage in active recreation), and thus healthier, is great. Sports programs, parks, trails and greenways, and outdoor adventure activities are just some examples of how the leisure services industry enhances all people's personal health and wellness.

This chapter begins by outlining recent physical activity trends and some of the health and economic ramifications that have occurred because of inactivity. The chapter describes how leisure activities, leisure services, and leisure professionals can play an integral role in addressing this public health crisis. We end by sharing some real-life examples of how recreation and leisure professionals are imple-

menting health strategies and making a difference in their communities.

Physical Activity Trends

Obesity and the associated health costs have become a major worldwide concern. According to the World Health Organization (WHO, 2018b), rates of obesity for both children and adults have reached pandemic levels. According to projections by WHO, there are 1.9 billion overweight and 650 million obese adults worldwide. Globally, overweight and obesity, along with associated health issues, are now on the rise in low- and middle-income countries. In the United States, the Centers for Disease Control and Prevention (CDC) reports that 65 percent of adults and 16 percent of children and adolescents are overweight or obese. The worldwide prevalence of overweight and obesity has doubled since 1980 (Global Burden of Disease Collaborative Network, 2017), resulting in nearly a third of the world's population being classified as overweight and obese.

One of the primary reasons for these higher rates of obesity is increasingly sedentary lifestyles. As figure 4.1 shows, sedentary living and physical inactivity across all age, social, ethnic, and economic categories have reached epidemic proportions in the United States. Studies have shown that obesity, diabetes, and other diseases linked to physical inactivity can increase the risk of severe illnesses. For example, the COVID-19 pandemic has shown that the benefits of physical activity can mitigate the most common preexisting chronic conditions that increase risk of severe COVID-19 infections and mortality (Sallis, Adlakha, Oyeyemi, & Salvo, 2020).

Trends regarding sedentary living and obesity have attracted much media and political attention because sedentary living substantially increases the risk of significant diseases including heart attacks, breast and colon cancer, osteoporosis, stroke, and numerous other life-threatening illnesses (see Calle & Kaaks, 2004; Dempsey et al., 2020). As figure 4.2 shows, this can have a profound economic cost.

The percentage of overweight adults, adolescents, and children has increased so significantly that the CDC and numerous other U.S. federal, state, and local agencies have identified the reduction of obesity as one of the nation's top health priorities. The field of parks and recreation can make a major, positive contribution in addressing this public health challenge.

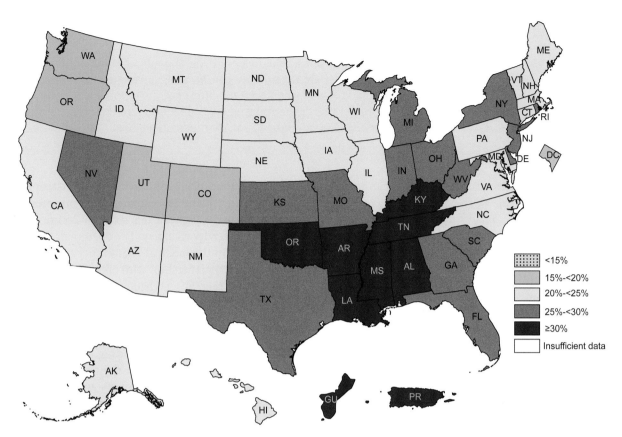

FIGURE 4.1 Prevalence of self-reported physical inactivity among U.S. adults by state and territory, BRFSS, 2015-2018.

Reprinted from Center for Disease Control and Prevention, *Physical Activity: Adult Physical Inactivity Prevalence Maps* (2021). www.cdc.gov/physical activity/data/inactivity-prevalence-maps/index.html#overall

As obesity increases, so does the use of health-care services (36 percent increase in annual costs to the individual).

ESTIMATES OF COST TO THE NATION RANGE FROM $1.7 TRILLION PER YEAR:

- $480.7 billion in direct costs
- $1.24 trillion in lost productivity
- Indirect quality of life costs, lost human potential, premature loss of life, and other nonmeasurable, noneconomic consequences (Waters & Graf, 2018)

FIGURE 4.2 Economic consequences of obesity.

What Is Health?

The World Health Organization defines health as "a complete state of physical, mental and social well-being, and not merely the absence of disease or infirmity" (World Health Organization, 2018a). Thus, it is important to recognize that the dimensions of health include physical, social, emotional, and psychological aspects. WHO recognizes that governments have a responsibility for the health of their people that can be fulfilled by the provision of adequate health and social measures. Increasing physical activity is a key component of improving people's health.

Benefits of Regular Physical Activity

- Reduce the risk of premature death
- Improve aerobic endurance and muscular strength

Self-Exploration

Think about what you did last week. How much physical activity did you engage in? How would you categorize your physical activity (e.g., moderate, vigorous)? Review the CDC guidelines for physical activity online (you can find these by searching at www.cdc.gov) and then evaluate whether your physical activity in the past week met these guidelines. Then determine whether you need more physical activity in your life. What specific changes could you make to satisfy these guidelines?

- Favorably affect risk factors for cardiovascular disease
- Decrease blood pressure in adolescents with borderline hypertension
- Increase physical fitness in obese children
- Decrease degree of overweight in obese children
- Increase of self-esteem and self-concept
- Reduce anxiety and stress

As the list indicates, physical activity carries numerous benefits. Most people are at least aware of some of these benefits. However, as was the case with previous public health challenges (like smoking and AIDS) and more recently with the COVID-19 pandemic, translating knowledge into action requires a coordinated effort by a variety of agencies and policy initiatives. Parks and recreation is considered a profession that can play a pivotal role.

Parks and Recreation: Making a Difference

The role of parks and recreation in helping people to become physically active has seemed obvious since the recreation movement began well over a century ago (Bocarro et al., 2009). However, that role has become more pronounced since the emergence of some key political reports and research. For example, every 10 years, the U.S. Department of Health and Human Services initiates a health promotion and disease prevention plan for the country called *Healthy People*. The core principles of *Healthy People 2030* state that health and well-being of the population and communities are essential to a fully functioning, equitable society and that health promotion must be shared by organizations across the private, public, and nonprofit sectors (Office of Disease Prevention and Health Promotion, n.d.).

Healthy People 2020 emphasized that the design of communities and the presence of parks, trails, and other public recreational facilities affect people's abilities to reach the recommended 30 minutes of moderate-intensity physical activity or 20 minutes of vigorous activity each day. The document specifically called on the medical community to develop nontraditional partnerships with organizations such as parks and recreation. *Healthy People 2030* (U.S. Department of Health and Human Services, n.d.) continues to emphasize that the neighborhoods people live in have a major impact on health and well-being. For example, providing opportunities for people to walk and bike in their communities through the addition of greenways and trails and sidewalk connectivity can help improve overall health and quality of life. Community parks and recreation departments play a critical role in planning for, building, and maintaining these attributes that not only make communities more attractive but facilitate a more active lifestyle.

Other landmark reports have pointed to the importance of parks and recreation in increasing physical activity. A review of environmental and policy approaches for increasing physical activity found that creating and enhancing access to places for physical activity and providing informational outreach can increase by 25 percent the number of people who exercise three times or more per week (Task Force on Community Preventive Services, 2002). In a national survey of city managers in the United States, 89 percent indicated that the primary governmental agency responsible for helping to address the obesity problem is parks and recreation (International City/County Management Association, 2005).

As parks and recreation professionals design programs and interventions to address levels of physical inactivity within their communities, it is important to be aware of some of the following trends.

People 12 to 21 Years Old

- Fifty percent do not engage in regular, vigorous physical activity.

- Fourteen percent report no recent physical activity.
- Inactivity is more prevalent among females (14 percent) than males (7 percent).
- Inactivity is more prevalent among Black females (21 percent) than White females (12 percent).
- People in urban areas tend to be less overweight or obese than those in rural areas, putting them less at risk for the health risks associated with overweight or obesity (e.g., stroke, high blood pressure, diabetes, and so on).
- Physical activity declines with age.
- Enrollment in physical education classes is declining.
- Funding for after-school and community-based programs continues to be a challenge.
- Approximately 80 percent of physical activity occurs outside of school (in community-based programs).

Adults (22 and Older)

- Six of 10 adults do not engage in the recommended amount of activity.
- One of four adults report no physical activity at all.
- Physical inactivity is more prevalent among women than men.
- Physical inactivity is more prevalent among Black and Hispanic adults than Whites.
- Physical inactivity is more prevalent among older adults than younger adults.
- Physical inactivity is related to affluence. Less affluent people are less active; more affluent people are more active.

Parks and recreation professionals must consider statistics such as these. For example, understanding why certain segments of the population (e.g., people from rural communities, Black Americans and Hispanics) are less physically active is an important determinant to consider before programmatic, environmental, or policy changes are adopted or resource allocations are made.

Leisure and Life Stress

For more than two decades, stress has been identified as a significant health issue. In 1983, *Time* magazine declared that stress was "the epidemic of the 80s" (Wallis, Mehrtens, & Thompson, 1983). Since then our lives have been further influenced by social media, cell phones, text messaging, 24-hour news from around the world, a global economy, self-managed retirement plans, changing expectations in the home and at work, and a growing list of things we can't control, like climate change, terrorism, pandemics, and the ever-changing causes of cancer. (See chapter 5 for more in-depth discussion of coping with stressors.)

Most leisure researchers acknowledge that leisure activities can have both positive and detrimental effects, but there is a growing consensus that leisure can act as a protective factor against negative events that occur and can contribute to a person's general state of resiliency (Weybright, Caldwell, & Weaver, 2019). Efforts to understand why some people stay healthy and others become ill when negative life events occur indicate that people with a higher degree of resiliency or balance between risk and protective factors tend to be healthier. It also seems evident that leisure is a general protective factor, and the specific outcomes of leisure participation can also be protective. Common leisure-related protective factors include these (Weybright et al.):

- Benefits of personally meaningful or intrinsically interesting activity

---

Self-Exploration

Look at the Self-Exploration sidebar on page 52 and consider your current levels of physical activity. Now think back to your childhood and the community in which you lived. Describe your patterns of **leisure-time physical activity** and the community resources that facilitated your activity levels. How much did your leisure-time physical activity depend on the resources provided by your community's parks and recreation services (i.e., parks and open spaces, swimming pools, community centers, sport facilities, walking trails)? What improvements would you recommend for your childhood community to better facilitate an active leisure lifestyle for its residents?

- Social support, friendships, and social acceptance
- Competence and self-efficacy
- Experiences of challenge and being totally absorbed in an activity
- Feelings of self-determination and control over one's life
- Feeling relaxed, disengaging from stress, and being distracted from negative life events through leisure
- Continuity in life after experiencing disability

It seems clear that leisure activities can be therapeutic and can decrease the negative health effects of stressful life events. How leisure contributes to stress-related coping responses at different ages and across various ethnic and socioeconomic groups is unclear; however, it does seem evident that leisure in and of itself does not yield the desired outcomes. The environment in which leisure occurs and the leisure choices people make can either maximize or minimize the protective nature of leisure. It also seems clear that people need help to maximize the benefits of leisure activities (Caldwell, 2005). Leisure education at an early age can help children develop a repertoire of healthy leisure activities and avoid the many potential negative outcomes of physical inactivity.

Therefore, a community's resources for leisure-time physical activity affect people's amount of activity. Well-designed parks and recreation facilities and programs can help shape behavior patterns in the following ways, which provide greater stress-buffering properties:

- Activities can foster social interaction and friendships.
- Developmental sport and leisure activity programs that incorporate well-designed skill acquisition properties can help people develop a repertoire of leisure skills, fostering feelings of competency and self-efficacy.
- Aesthetically pleasing and nature-based outdoor spaces can provide opportunities for relaxing, which fosters disengagement from stressful environments or negative life events.

Community parks and recreation facilities and services provide an endless array of benefits. Not only do they help make our communities better places to live, but if designed well, these facilities and services can also provide protective factors against life's many negative and stressful events.

Promoting Lifelong Physical Health Through Recreation and Leisure

The importance of theories as well as the notion of theory guiding practice has long been debated. A simple explanation of the importance of theories is that they have been empirically tested and provide some understanding of outcomes given specific circumstances. These theories can then help us use available resources to effect specific outcomes. In the case of physical activity promotion, the leisure repertoire theory is useful in understanding why people do or don't engage in certain leisure activities.

Leisure researchers highlight the importance of involving people in a variety of leisure activities at a young age (see figure 4.3). The leisure repertoire theory suggests that people who develop a wide spectrum of activities during childhood are more likely to continue to participate in activities as they get older because of their broader leisure repertoire (and more activities to draw from). Thus, a person's leisure repertoire usually consists of activities in which they participate on a regular basis and do well.

When applying this theory, one can see that an important predictor of lifelong participation in leisure activities does not appear to be the volume of leisure involvement as a child but rather the number of different leisure activities that young people are taught (Roberts & Brodie, 1992). As adults we become more conservative about our leisure lifestyle and tend to make leisure choices from our own repertoire of skilled activities (Iso-Ahola, Jackson, & Dunn, 1994; Roberts, 1999). For example, adults in their 30s and 40s tend to have more family and work commitments and therefore less leisure time. Thus, they are more likely to engage in leisure activities that are accessible and that they have enjoyed previously in their lives (see figure 4.4). Consequently, the greater the repertoire of choices, the more likely people will remain committed leisure participants when moving from adolescence to adulthood.

Organized sport is one of the most popular leisure-time activities for children and adolescents, with more than 45 million children participating in organized youth sports in the United States

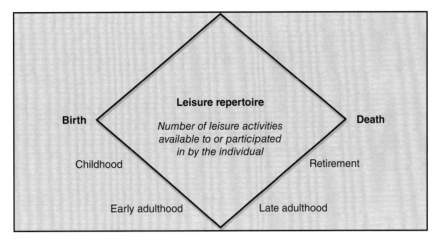

FIGURE 4.3 Leisure repertoire model.

Adapted from Iso-Ahola, Jackson, & Dunn (1994).

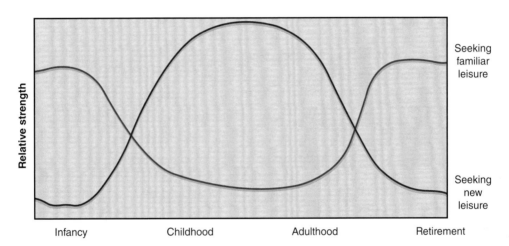

FIGURE 4.4 Tendencies to seek familiar and new forms of leisure.

Adapted from Iso-Ahola, Jackson, & Dunn (1994).

On the Job

Promoting Physical Activity in the Workforce

Many major corporations are beginning to realize that a healthy workforce means a more productive workforce, and a more productive workforce means higher profits. This has led to many employers offering physical health and fitness programs as one of the benefits of employment. This could include a range of options such as providing discounts at local gyms, having onsite facilities and equipment, or even hiring instructors for classes during lunch and break times. This is a unique opportunity for leisure professionals who want to work in a corporate environment or for leisure businesses that can offer partnerships with these organizations. Providing such services gives leisure professionals the opportunity to help improve the physical health and well-being of their clients and makes them an integral part of the corporate environment.

(Merkel, 2013). Studies measuring physical activity have generally shown that organized sport has been successful in reducing bouts of sedentary behavior among children and adolescents (e.g., Van Hoye et al., 2013; Marques, Ekelund, & Sardinha, 2016). Furthermore, physical activity that children get during sport participation did not occur during nonplaying days and was generally replaced with low-intensity and sedentary activities, suggesting that children are unlikely to compensate for missed physical activity resulting from sports (Wickel & Eisenmann, 2007).

However, sport opportunities have been compromised across the United States. The decentralized location of participation opportunities (Bunds et al., 2018), coupled with an increasing pay-to-play youth sport delivery model, has limited sport opportunities to only those who have the ability to pay for and transport their children to and from games and practices, especially in rural and low-income communities (Edwards, Bocarro, & Kanters, 2013). Furthermore, only 58 percent of youth ages 6 to 17 participated in sports in 2017, and participation rates were much lower for girls, racial and ethnic minorities, youth from households of low socioeconomic status, and youth with disabilities (U.S. Department of Health & Human Services, 2019). Therefore, any discussion examining the benefits of physical activity needs to consider issues of cost, access, and equity.

The ultimate purpose of physically active leisure programs is to promote active lifestyles and lifelong participation in physical activity (Vanreusel & Scheerder, 2016). By age 16, most adolescents have adopted a pattern of leisure activities that will form the foundation of their adult leisure lifestyle (Roberts, 1999). For example, in a study of men and women, the main characteristic of adults who had become committed to sport was that they had participated in several (usually three or more) games or activities during their lives (Roberts & Brodie, 1992).

Therefore, researchers and policy makers have begun to examine the long-term ramifications of youth involvement. These results have suggested that enjoyable participation in activities during childhood and adolescence can result in a leisure-for-life philosophy. Young adults are not likely to participate in sport if they have not participated in the past (Perkins, Jacobs, Barber, & Eccles, 2004, Telama et al., 2006). Thus, youth are more likely to continue participation in an activity if they begin participating at a young age. Longitudinal studies have shown that children who were involved in organized sport were more likely to be healthier as adults and engaged in higher levels of physical activity than nonparticipants (Logan et al., 2020).

Examining Factors That Influence Behavior

Many policy makers and practitioners have struggled with how to create interventions that make people healthier. In the past, strategies have focused on trying to make individual people healthier or more physically active and have not accounted for other important factors that may reinforce both healthy and unhealthy behaviors. For example, a parks and recreation department may successfully educate a teenager about the benefits of engaging in physically active leisure programs. However, if that teenager's peer group or family thinks that these programs are a waste of time or if the programs are situated in an area that is perceived as unsafe, the department's efforts will have limited success.

One model that has guided the design of interventions is the social ecological model (McLeroy, Bibeau, Steckler, & Glanz, 1988). The social ecological model recognizes that multiple levels influence people's health and well-being. The model has five levels:

1. Interpersonal and individual factors
2. Interpersonal processes
3. Institutional (organizational) factors
4. Community factors
5. Public policy

The following sections discuss each of these in more detail.

Intrapersonal and Individual Factors

Interpersonal and individual factors primarily focus on individual characteristics such as psychological, developmental, and biological variables. Intervention strategies at this level tend to focus on educating people to change individual behavior, influencing their attitudes, and challenging their beliefs. There are numerous examples of parks and recreation programs attempting to persuade an individual to change their behavior. On college campuses, campus recreation programs try to convince faculty and students to change their behavior and become more physically active by using their facilities. In

Viktorcvetkovic/E+/Getty Images

How can we think about different levels of the socioecological model so we can get people to be more physically active outdoors?

2009, the National Hockey League established the Hockey Is for Everyone program, which focused part of its efforts on persuading people from less affluent communities that hockey could be a viable, healthy, and enjoyable leisure activity.

Interpersonal Processes

Interpersonal processes relate to primary social groups such as a person's family, friends, and peers. Intervention strategies focus on educating family members and peers and involving them in helping people change their behaviors. Examples are providing parents with information about recreation programs to encourage the parents to support their children's physical activity.

Institutional (Organizational) Factors

Institutional factors examine the policies, practices, and physical environment of an organization (typically the workplace or school) and how the organization supports healthy behavior change.

For example, Moore Square Middle School in Wake County, North Carolina, decided that the interscholastic, highly competitive sport model was excluding many children from participating in sport. Furthermore, they felt that the interscholastic sport model often limited children to traditional sports such as basketball, football, and cheerleading. The school decided to implement an intramural sport program, giving every child at the school the opportunity to participate in a wide assortment of sports. Other examples of institutional factors include company incentives for employees to work out, time devoted to recess and physical education, and facilities provided within an organization to encourage physical activity.

Community Factors

Community factors involve the relationships among different organizations and social networks within a defined area. This may involve coordination of efforts among members of a community (schools, citizen groups, and community leaders).

For example, the CDC recommends that schools and communities form partnerships so that school facilities can be used for recreation programs and physical activity opportunities after school hours, thereby increasing daily physical activity opportunities among adolescents. Schools have been recommended as a safe and accessible place for physical activity to occur within the community (American Academy of Pediatrics, 2006), and numerous communities across the country have established partnerships for the construction and joint use of school facilities. For example, all school grounds in Berkeley, California, are open to the public, and in Pitt County, North Carolina, local public school facilities are kept open to allow community use of school facilities through their schools and recreation program (Spengler, Young, & Linton, 2007). Other examples are coalitions and community groups formed to create green spaces, safe recreation areas, and parks within communities (see Hardison Moody et al., 2020).

Public Policy

Public policy focuses on laws and policies at local, state, and national levels that promote physical activity. This includes physical education curricular legislation and government funding of facilities to promote physical activity patterns. For example, many local and state governments have the power to make communities healthier by implementing laws and policies that support more walking- and biking-friendly streets. When communities adopt this type of policy, they change how streets are designed and built so that residents of all ages and abilities can travel easily and safely along community streets, whether they are walking, biking, or riding the bus. ChangeLab Solutions (www.changelabsolutions.org) is an organization that has been established to help communities, advocates, and leaders navigate the complex world of policy as well as provide fact sheets, tool kits, training, and technical assistance to explain legal issues related to creating healthier communities.

Previously, many strategies focused primarily on intrapersonal and interpersonal factors. However, focusing physical activity intervention strategies on intrapersonal factors and interpersonal processes can have limited or even no impact. For example, data may show that a particular strategy increases the population's knowledge about the benefits of physical activity, increases people's willingness to engage in physical activity (intrapersonal factors), and increases the level of support a person receives from their social support system (interpersonal processes), but that will have limited impact if a person's economic situation prohibits them from being physically active or their community has no safe environments in which citizens can be physically active. Research has shown that interventions designed to affect multiple levels of the social ecological model are much more effective at bringing about behavioral change within a community. Although it is rare for any one intervention to put into practice every level of the social ecological model, the more levels that a program or initiative contains the more effective the change will be.

The social ecological approach may be particularly prevalent when we work with underserved or specific populations with unique issues (e.g., lower income residents, people living in rural areas, certain minority populations, older adults, people with disabilities). Thus, the social ecological framework recognizes that different factors influence a person's ability to change their physical activity behavior. The model strongly supports the notion that everyone lives within an environment influenced by social systems that influence healthy behavior patterns.

Strategies and Examples of Enhancing Physical Health Through Leisure

In the last few years, the National Recreation and Park Association has engaged in several physical activity initiatives. The number of studies examining the impact of parks and recreation facilities on people's physical activity levels has also increased. The following section shows three examples of research being put into action. The initiatives discussed here are strongly guided and influenced by the social ecological model.

North Carolina Senior Games

Engaging seniors and elderly adults in regular physical activity can have several benefits (Payne, Orsega-Smith, Spangler, & Godbey, 1999). Studies during the COVID-19 pandemic showed that older adults who continued to be physically active had fewer symptoms of depression and better overall mental health (e.g., Callow et al., 2020). However, the CDC has shown that only a third of persons aged 65 years and older participate in regular, sustained physical activity. The North Carolina Senior Games (NCSG) was designed to encourage year-round participation in local communities for people aged 55 years and older. It consists of local games run by local organizations, all under the NCSG umbrella.

In 2019, tens of thousands of participants participated in sports and arts programs at 52 local games programs that serve all 100 counties in North Carolina. Nearly all local games programs are offered in collaboration with local parks and recreation departments. In addition, the state championship for Senior Games serves more than 3,000 individuals across the state and is hosted by multiple recreation departments and their staffs throughout North Carolina. In 2020, the COVID-19 pandemic halted local games programs to keep participants safe. However, NCSG provided a virtual championship for sports and arts participants that made a significant impact on those who participated and allowed them to remain physically active through virtual competitions.

The NCSG program emphasizes educating people about the benefits of senior games (intrapersonal level) and often works through local resources like senior centers to engage senior peer groups (inter-

personal level). This is important, because research has shown that many older adults participate in physical activity programs that are available through local community organizations (Orsega-Smith, Payne, & Godbey, 2003). Furthermore, many older adults like to participate in group-based physical activity programs (King, 2001). NCSG is successful in highlighting a third dimension of the social ecological model—the community (having a local infrastructure to support this change). Physical activity for these older participants is encouraged and maintained through NCSG, which is a locally based community organization. Research has shown the importance of providing supportive environments in which people can be physically active, such as community settings, facilities, and programs (Sallis, Bauman, & Pratt, 1998). The results of research focused on NCSG have been encouraging. Researchers who compared the attitudes of NCSG participants with the CDC's measures found that NCSG participants reported feeling healthier and engaged in more daily physical activity (Cardenas, Henderson, & Wilson, 2009).

Morsa Images/E+/Getty Images

Physical activity during sport participation is generally an expected outcome, but it is not always realized.

Youth Sport Programs That Encourage Physical Activity

Youth sport has the potential to increase physical activity among children and play a major role in improving their health. Although it seems obvious that participation in youth sport would enhance children's health, the outcomes associated with youth sport participation are often contradictory. The book *The Last Child in the Woods* indicates that the increase in child obesity has "coincided with the greatest increase in organized sports for children in history" (Louv, 2005, p. 47).

Critics of sport question whether sport is addressing the public health challenge posed by obesity. There may be several reasons for the apparent positive association between child obesity and organized youth sport opportunities. One is that fewer options are available for students who are not advanced athletes (Koplan, Liverman, & Kraak, 2005), particularly given the increasing cost of sports. A recent systematic review suggested that interpersonal and intrapersonal constraints (no longer having fun, lack of enjoyment, lack of interest) were more predictive of children dropping out of sport than structural constraints (e.g., time, cost, and access; Crane & Temple, 2015). For whatever reason, participation in youth sport has declined significantly among both boys and girls during middle school years (see Hedstrom & Gould, 2004; Zarrett, Veliz, & Sabo, 2020). Following are other reasons for declining participation in youth sport:

- Students want to participate in other activities (Seefeldt, Ewing, & Walk, 1992).
- The distance from children's homes to their schools has increased. Because local school systems are building bigger schools on the outskirts of communities, where land is cheaper, students are faced with longer commuting times. Freeman and Quigg (2009) reported parents were typically very supportive of their children's out-of-school activities but spend a considerable amount of time transporting to and from activities.
- Children have an increasingly negative attitude toward physical activity as they get older (Trudeau & Shepherd, 2005).
- Teenagers' preoccupation with technology has increased; recent statistics show that 95 percent of teenagers (ages 12-17) have access to a smartphone, 84 percent own a game console (e.g., an Xbox or PlayStation), and 45 percent say they are now online on a near constant basis (Pew Research Center, 2018).

A growing body of research that has examined declining physical activity patterns in youth has led to calls for schools to introduce (or reintroduce) intramural programs (see Bocarro, Kanters, Casper, & Forrester, 2008; Koplan et al., 2005). The primary motivation for implementing intramural programs is to reengineer sporting opportunities around children's motives for participating in sport. For example, when asked why they participate in sport, children rate wanting to win as eighth, behind factors such as to have fun, to stay in shape, to learn and improve skills, and to play as part of a team (Seefeldt et al., 1992).

Although interscholastic competitive sport programs have strong roots within North American culture, they often serve only the most elite youth athletes—kids who make the school team. These programs also require participants to give up a significant portion of their free time to practice, travel, and participate in games, and in some cases the programs preclude participation in other sports. In other cases, students in certain grades are excluded from participation altogether (e.g., sixth-grade students in North Carolina are not allowed to try out for school teams). Recall our earlier discussion about the leisure repertoire theory, and about the ramifications of excluding children from sport and leisure opportunities at a time when they are open to engaging in new activities that may provide a platform for lifetime involvement.

The intramural school sport philosophy incorporates the social ecological model in several ways. First, it provides more children with a diverse array of activities, considering some of the factors identified previously (intrapersonal level). Intramurals are often socially oriented, and mixed-gender participation is allowed (interpersonal level). This is important, given that a school social climate that supports girls' sports has been a critical variable in influencing girls' levels of physical activity (Barr-Anderson et al., 2007; Birnbaum et al., 2005). Finally, intramural school sport programs provide an ecological context for shaping physical activity participation at the organizational or institutional level.

Parks, Greenways, and Trails

Parks, trails, and greenways are community resources that have tremendous potential to contribute to people's overall health. Research shows that having access to these resources increases a person's physical activity levels (regardless of a person's income, age, race, or gender). That is because parks, greenways, and trails are typically free and accessible to all residents. Furthermore, these outdoor environments often make unique contributions that cannot be achieved in indoor settings such as gyms or at home (Shores & West, 2008). At the interpersonal level, research has shown that youth living in communities with parks and playgrounds tend to be more physically active than those living in communities with fewer parks (Davidson & Lawson, 2006). At the intrapersonal level, low-income youth who had access to supervised parks were found to be significantly more active than those without such access (Farley et al., 2007). Despite the potential of parks to contribute to people's health, some caveats must be discussed. Pinckney, Outley, Brown, and Tehiault (2018) provide an excellent discussion on how many public spaces (such as parks and trails) are not perceived as safe spaces for Black youth and adults. Furthermore, as issues of health equity have been raised, more scrutiny as to the location of urban green space has shown that green community resources such as parks are often unequally distributed, further increasing health inequity (Jennings, Browning, & Rigolon, 2019).

Thomas Barwick/DigitalVision/Getty Images

Having access to greenways and trails has been shown to encourage more physical activity and is a desirable amenity for most people.

However, it is important to consider other factors within the social ecological model. For example, at the community level, proximity to parks, greenways, and trails as well as perceived neighborhood walkability is associated with higher use and rates of physical activity. Conversely, parks that have low ratings of maintenance, have high rates of physical incivilities (e.g., empty beer bottles, evidence of drug use), and are located near industrial sites are linked to lower use and lower levels of physical activity.

The NCSG; youth sport programs; and parks, trails, and greenways are just three examples of physical activity initiatives. However, the number of physical activity initiatives continues to increase as community leaders begin to see the role and value of parks and recreation in addressing public health challenges posed by more sedentary lifestyles.

Physical activity initiatives have other tangential benefits. As we have seen, having access to parks, trails, greenways, and other recreation programs can help people maintain higher levels of physical activity, which decreases both individual and societal health costs. Think about where you would like to live when you graduate from college. Many community leaders have started to ask themselves what makes their community attractive, knowing that some of the most educated people want access to physical activity opportunities for their families because of the health benefits described here.

Summary

Over the past decade, obesity in children and adults across all sectors of our population has become one of the top health priorities in the United States. Parks and recreation programs and leisure services have great potential to affect the health of the population. The dimensions of health extend beyond physical characteristics and include social, emotional, and psychological aspects. Although numerous factors affect individual responses to stress, leisure activities can both directly and indirectly moderate negative stress responses. Indeed, the engagement, challenging, or relaxing characteristics of leisure activities can directly minimize stress responses. It is important to engage people as early as possible in leisure activities—research shows that children who develop a wide spectrum of activities are more likely to continue to participate in activities as they get older relative to more inactive children. The social ecological model has helped policy makers, researchers, and practitioners develop strategies to improve individual health behaviors through parks and recreation programs and leisure services.

Learning Activities

1. Select a community that you are familiar with and have access to (avoid large cities). Summarize that community's parks and recreation resources from the perspective of facilitating physical activity. What recommendations would you make for improvements? Submit a PowerPoint presentation with recorded audio and a brief (two-page) summary report.

2. Interview some people from different backgrounds, races, ethnicities, and cultures. How would you describe the leisure-time physical activity patterns of your subjects? Do cultural differences affect variations in leisure-time physical activity patterns? (Write your answers on a maximum of two pages.)

Review Questions

1. What are the current trends in physical activity and health across the United States? Is there cause for concern?

2. How do leisure services facilitate active living and make a major contribution in addressing public health issues?

3. How do leisure and community leisure services moderate the negative relationship between stress and health?

4. How can leisure behavior contribute to personal health and wellness?

Go to HK*Propel* to access additional learning content.

Leisure and Well-Being

Colleen Hood

Brock University

Cynthia Carruthers

University of Nevada at Las Vegas

VOCABULARY TERMS

distress

emotion-focused coping

eudaemonic or psychologi-
cal well-being

gratifications

habituation

hedonic or subjective
well-being

hedonists

intentional activity

intrinsic motivation

mental health

person–activity fit

pleasures

positive mental health

problem-focused coping

savoring

virtues

well-being

LEARNING OUTCOMES

After reading this chapter, you will be able to

- describe the essential dimensions of well-being;
- identify and discuss three strategies for managing distress;
- describe the three principal determinants of happiness;
- compare and contrast the contributions of pleasurable experiences and the gratifications to well-being;
- identify the critical qualities of leisure that link the leisure experience to well-being; and
- describe the five strategies for enhancing the value of leisure in supporting well-being.

Imagine that you have a day off from your studies. It is spring and the sun is shining and warm. You and a friend decide to hike out to the cliffs by the ocean. You start off with high expectations; you are excited about getting outside, about being physically active, and about doing something fun with your friend. As you reach the trailhead, you decide to leave your worries behind. You step out of the car onto the trail with an open and clear mind and become very aware of the sounds of the birds, insects, and rustling branches—and the quiet of being away from the city. In the distance you can hear the rumbling of the ocean. As you begin to walk, you are aware of warming up and you can feel your blood pumping through your body. It reminds you of the many times you went hiking and camping with your family and how special the outdoors is to you. You notice the smells of damp earth and decay and they remind you of the renewal that comes with spring. You notice that your friend is struggling a bit with the slope and the pace and go back to offer assistance. You slow down and point out the various signs of spring to him as you are working your way up the slope. As you move forward, you feel your mood improving and a smile start to spread across your face. You know the climb to the cliffs will be difficult, but you look forward to the challenge and know that you will feel great after. You feel alive and excited and can't wait to see the ocean, smell the sea air, and hear the sound of the waves crashing against the shore.

In the preceding story, you are engaged in a leisure experience that supports well-being. This chapter introduces a number of concepts that link leisure involvement to well-being and creating a good life. Leisure involvement can either be supportive of well-being or detrimental to well-being; this chapter invites you to examine your own leisure practices and to be purposeful about your leisure choices and experiences.

In the scenario described, you have made a number of choices that help the experience contribute to your well-being. You were intentional in leaving behind your worries and in being fully present in the current experience. You chose a leisure experience that has been important to you in the past and that you have enjoyed before. You chose a leisure experience that is physically demanding yet within your capabilities. You focused on the sounds, smells, and bodily sensations that accompanied the experience. You were aware of the challenges ahead but felt confident in your ability to manage those challenges. You wanted to support your friend and to help him see the **pleasures** in the experience as well. You anticipated enjoyment and happiness in both the journey and the destination.

In the last 30 to 40 years, there has been a growing interest in what is necessary to live a good life. This interest in the good life has resulted in a dramatic increase in the number of researchers who are examining what is required to create a life of happiness, meaning, and fulfillment, and this interest has spread to a number of disciplines that have traditionally focused on problem resolution (such as medicine, psychology, and other allied health professions). The positive psychology movement from 1989 to the present has certainly put the issue of understanding well-being in the foreground of psychological research (Seligman, 2019). This movement emphasizes the importance of understanding human strengths, capacities, and happiness as avenues through which to help citizens create better lives for themselves. This movement has influenced many other fields in terms of the ways they approach working with people and has made the notion of strengths-based practice one of interest to many professions whose practitioners work with people, including recreation and leisure studies (Hood & Carruthers, 2012; Stebbins, 2018), social work (Pulla & Francis, 2014), psychology and counseling (Ruini, 2017), and medicine (Kubzansky et al., 2018).

Leisure professionals have traditionally been interested in the value of leisure for people in terms of health, social involvement, and personal and community well-being. Leisure has many benefits, but some members of the public do not recognize the value of leisure in building a life of meaning. Given that leisure is seen as a discretionary experience that occurs in free time, people often bypass leisure in order to accomplish tasks of daily living and work. However, we must not underestimate the importance of leisure in creating a balanced, healthy life that supports overall well-being (Carruthers & Hood, 2004; Parsons, Houge Mackenzie, Filep, & Brymer, 2019). This chapter explores the relationship between leisure, mental health, and well-being and provides an overview of the concept of well-being; the relationships among stress, coping, and well-being; and the relationship between leisure and well-being, including leisure choices that both undermine and support well-being. The chapter

Thomas Barwick/DigitalVision/Getty Images

Filling your life with joy is an important step in creating a good life.

ends with a discussion of strategies that can be used to increase the value of leisure in supporting well-being and building the best possible life.

Understanding Well-Being and Mental Health

Well-being has been studied from a number of different perspectives, including philosophy, psychology, geography, sociology, and political science. As a result of the breadth of interest, the term well-being has many definitions, and many factors have been found to affect well-being. In a philosophical sense, well-being refers to how well a person's life is going. In a medical sense, well-being refers to the status of a person's physiological being. In an economic sense, well-being refers to how satisfied a person is in terms of income, financial stability, and material goods. In a psychological sense, well-being refers to the degree to which a person experiences positive emotion and

fulfillment (Disabato, Goodman, Kashdan, Short, & Jarden, 2016; Seligman, 2011).

In much of the psychological literature related to well-being, the concept has been examined or defined as either **hedonic or subjective well-being** (relatively more positive emotion than negative, coupled with an overall evaluation that life is good) or **eudaemonic or psychological well-being** (personal growth and fulfillment of potential). However, there

Self-Exploration

How would you define well-being? What are the things that support your well-being? What challenges your well-being? Which of these factors are under your control? What actions do you take in your leisure to enhance your personal well-being? Well-being is a very personal concept and to a large degree within your control.

are a number of contemporary researchers who now argue for a blended approach to understanding well-being—one that incorporates aspects of both hedonic and eudaemonic definitions into one overarching concept (Dodge, Daly, Huyton, & Sanders, 2012; Taylor, 2015; Vitterso, 2013). Vitterso, for example, stated that well-being must be understood as more than feeling good, it must include the pursuit of meaningful goals (virtues). Shah and Marks (2004) also supported the notion of an integration of both perspectives, stating that "well-being is more than just happiness. As well as feeling satisfied and happy, well-being means developing as a person, being fulfilled, and making a contribution to the community" (p. 2). It is clear that, while there are a number of terms used to describe well-being, most of these related concepts incorporate some focus on feeling good, functioning well, growth and development, and ability to manage challenge and difficulty. The CDC (2018) concurs, stating that "at minimum, well-being includes the presence of positive emotions and moods (e.g., contentment, happiness), the absence of negative emotions (e.g., depression, anxiety), satisfaction with life, fulfillment and positive functioning" (2018, n.p.).

Extensive contemporary psychological theory development and research is clarifying the relationship between mental health and well-being. What has traditionally been called **mental health** is now more holistically being called well-being (Thompson, 2018). In 2004, the World Health Organization (WHO) suggested that good mental health is "a state of well-being in which the individual realizes his or her own abilities, can cope with the normal stresses of life, can work productively and fruitfully, and is able to make a contribution to his or her community" (p. 12). Srivastava (2011) defined **positive mental health** as "a state of well-being whereby individuals recognize their abilities, are able to cope with the normal stresses of life, work productively and fruitfully, and make a contribution to their communities" (p. 75). Clearly these two definitions of mental health have a focus on functioning well (eudaimonic well-being). Interestingly, Vaillant (2012), in his examination of various definitions of positive mental health, incorporated a greater focus on both positive emotion (hedonic well-being) and functioning well (eudaimonic well-being). He identified positive functioning, maturity, social intelligence, subjective well-being, and resilience as

On the Job

Campus Recreation and Student Well-Being

One popular area of employment in the field of recreation and leisure studies is campus recreation. Historically, campus recreation has been characterized as an organization that provides fitness equipment, intramurals, and other opportunities for students to enhance their physical engagement and fitness. However, there is increasing awareness that student well-being, which includes physical, cognitive, social, and psychological well-being, is a necessary area of focus for campus recreation. More recently, campus recreation organizations have expanded their services to embrace the notion that student well-being applies to more than just physical health. While maintaining their original services, many have also begun to provide additional opportunities that target emotional well-being, such as classes on guided meditation, trauma-informed yoga, and labyrinths. Although these are important contributions to overall well-being, campus recreation can also play a vital role in educating students about the value of leisure for health and well-being beyond providing opportunities for recreation engagement. Campus recreation services can provide leisure education opportunities that encourage students to be independent and purposeful in their leisure choices. Campus recreation services can assist students in selecting leisure experiences that are a good fit for the individual and that tap into unique aspects of personality, strengths, and interests. Campus recreation services can help students learn the skills necessary to maximize the value of leisure for overall well-being, including focusing on and savoring positive emotion, being fully present, and creating a balanced lifestyle. Campus recreation services can support students to learn and experience the value of leisure in developing a meaningful life through such things as being of service, creating social relationships around valued leisure engagements, and developing personal awareness of their guiding values and principles. These possibilities for campus recreation services help address students' needs in maintaining overall well-being and highlight the connection between leisure and overall health.

key components used to determine levels of mental health. In this chapter, we will use the term *well-being* to refer to this blended conception of subjective and psychological well-being. Additionally, we will describe the many contributions of leisure to positive mental health through the framework of well-being enhancement.

Some of the factors that influence well-being include your cultural background and connection, physical and social environment, socioeconomic status, family status and structure, age, and gender. Interestingly, these factors often influence the experience of leisure as well (Allison & Schneider, 2000). Although these factors may have a significant effect on well-being, they are often not within our direct control. However, we may be able to control other factors. In fact, many researchers suggest that well-being is often a result of the choices we make (Fredrickson, 2009; Ryan & Deci, 2010). For example, the experience of more positive emotion than negative emotion on a daily basis directly affects your sense of well-being and is influenced by several factors. The way you focus your attention on the events of daily life influences how much positive emotion you feel. This focus of attention is something that you can actively address and modify by practicing activities that highlight the positive events in life, such as gratitude exercises, and by monitoring your focus and directing your attention toward the positive. Positive emotion is often generated by participating in physical activity, so choosing physically active leisure is a way to increase the amount of positive emotion you experience. Exercising personal control and autonomy, seeking contexts in which you can feel competent, creating and sustaining a social world that is rich and fulfilling, maintaining moderate levels of physical activity, and engaging in experiences that develop and express your true self are all examples of ways to improve your well-being and are a result of personal lifestyle choices (Chirkov, Ryan, & Sheldon, 2011). These modifiable factors are also directly related to leisure involvement and can be supported and enhanced through leisure engagement (Sirgy, Uysal, & Kruger, 2017; Walker, Kleiber, & Mannell, 2019).

Creating a life that is rich with positive emotion, fulfillment, and expression of personal capacities has many significant benefits. People who experience more positive emotion than negative tend to be more resilient to challenges in life—they

bounce back more quickly in the face of adversity (Fredrickson, 2009). They tend to be more optimistic and believe that even when they experience difficulties, they are much less likely to give up in the face of difficulties. These people tend to look for the good in situations and people and seek out and focus their attention on the aspects of life that support their hopeful, optimistic perspective (Carver & Scheier, 2002). People who have fulfilling lives tend to live longer and live better—they get sick less often, and when they do get sick, they recover more quickly (Fredrickson, 2009). Their neural complexity and adaptability are greater than those of people who do not have rich and fulfilling lives; thus, positive people are more flexible in problem solving and maintain cognitive function longer as they age (Phillips, 2017). Positive emotion also affects social connectedness and relationship satisfaction; people who experience lives that are rich also have strong relationships with family, friends, and partners (Fredrickson, 2013; Gustavson, Roysamb, Borren, Torvik, & Karevold, 2016). It seems obvious that a focus on building a life of meaning and well-being, including positive emotion and the cultivation and expression of strengths, creates a positive spiral of capacities and resources that support ongoing engagement and satisfaction with life. Positive emotion, fulfillment, and the expression of one's capacities and strengths can all be cultivated through leisure, contributing directly to well-being and positive mental health.

Stress and Well-Being: The Important Role of Coping

No matter how happy and fulfilled people are, it is inevitable that they will experience stress at some point. In fact, to avoid stress is to avoid life. Not all stress is negative, and, in fact, stress can support development in important ways. This form of stress, called *eustress* (Selye, 1975), arises from positive events, such as marriage, the birth of a baby, starting a new job, or going away to university for the first time. Eustress also encompasses those events that are perceived as challenging but in which the challenge is perceived as manageable. The types of experiences that generate eustress vary by individual, but the outcomes tend to be similar—increased motivation, improved performance, and increased excitement and engagement.

fstop123/E+/Getty Images

Well-being is supported by engagement in expressive activities like music that allow you to develop yourself fully.

Not all stress results in enhanced performance, however. When stress leads to negative outcomes, it is referred to as *distress* and is often based on how we perceive the situation. Among its many other benefits, well-being creates a greater capacity for dealing with the challenges and hardships of life (Carruthers & Hood, 2007). If people want to improve their well-being, they can do so by constructively engaging their emotions and building a life of meaning (Ben-Shahar, 2007). People who are experiencing positive emotion and developing their strengths are less likely to interpret situations as stressful, and they are more likely to believe that they have the resources necessary to meet life's challenges (Carruthers & Hood, 2005). They are also more likely to have a repertoire of coping skills upon which to draw, as well as the ability to know when and how to use these skills.

When people believe that they do not have the ability to deal with the challenges of their lives, the resulting negative stress, called **distress**, can have many negative physical and emotional con-

sequences (Davis, Eshelman, & McKay, 2019). Distress is created by a perception or appraisal of threat (Hood & Carruthers, 2002). That perception creates a physiological stress response that is called *fight or flight* (Frydenberg, 2002). This evolutionary response protected our ancestors from disasters and dangers by preparing them to run from or fight immediate environmental threats (Davis et al., 2019). However, in contemporary society, people cannot always fight or run from the stressors, nor would running or fighting serve as an effective coping strategy. However, the physiological response to threat remains the same today. If people do not have the contemporary coping skills necessary to deal with the stressors in their lives, their bodies are stuck in the chronic stress state, which has negative consequences for physical and mental health (Davis et al.). If people are able to successfully adapt or respond to a stressor so that it is no longer perceived as threatening, the flight-or-fight response is turned off. Their bodies return to a relaxed state, ready for the next challenge.

Managing Stress to Enhance Well-Being

The stressors in one's life can be managed in three ways (Hood & Carruthers, 2002). First, people can target the thoughts or perceptions of threat that trigger the fight-or-flight response and the related feelings. Second, people can take action to address directly the environmental challenges. Third, people can pursue activities that reduce the physiological stress response. People cannot be simultaneously physiologically stressed and relaxed.

Emotion-Focused Coping

One's perceptions or thoughts are the primary source of distress (Lazarus & Folkman, 1984). People who experience chronic distress may have distorted and irrational thoughts (Burns, 2020). Some people are genetically predisposed to overreact to stress (Lykken & Tellegen, 1996). Emotion-focused coping strategies target the thoughts and feelings associated with distress (Gruszczynska, 2013). When people use emotion-focused coping strategies, they might examine the ways in which their irrational thoughts contribute to their negative emotions (Lazarus & Folkman, 1984). For example, a young woman who is anxious about going to college parties may be afraid that she will make a social blunder and others will judge her harshly. She can recognize and challenge that negative self-talk and replace it with rational, constructive thoughts or just realize that her distorted thoughts are not reality and let them go. She can learn to keep situations in perspective and not overreact emotionally to life events. Emotion regulation strategies can also be used to enhance positive emotion, which can dampen the stress response (Gruszczynska, 2013).

Another example of emotion-focused coping is distraction (Lazarus & Folkman, 1984). Distraction is the process of diverting attention away from one issue and focusing attention on another. If a person is not thinking about a potential threat, the physiological stress response will be turned off, resulting in the relaxation response. When people believe there is nothing that they can do to change the situation, it does little good to think about it. In fact, the distress created by thinking about it can result in physical and emotional harm (Davis et al., 2019). Under these circumstances, it may be helpful to turn one's mind to an enjoyable, engaging leisure activity (Kleiber, Hutchinson, & Williams, 2002; Lyubomirsky, 2008). Leisure experiences that are personally meaningful, challenging, and enjoyable are optimal experiences for disengaging from everyday routines and worries (Hood & Carruthers, 2002). To reap the reward of this coping response and turn off the physiological stress response, it is important to immerse oneself in the leisure experience as completely as possible.

A final example of emotion-focused coping is acceptance (Lazarus & Folkman, 1984). Like distraction, this coping strategy is used when people believe that there is little that they can do or should do to change a situation. Many things in life are out of our control; it is simply not within our power to change them. Worrying and fretting about them will just create chronic stress and undermine our physical and mental health. Acceptance of a situation is experiencing it for what it really is, without defense or distortion, and letting it be (Kabat-Zinn, 1990). Mindfulness meditation is a leisure activity through which acceptance can be cultivated. The focus of mindfulness meditation is to see and accept things as they are, moment by moment.

Problem-Focused Coping

A second strategy for coping is problem-focused coping. Problem-focused coping involves taking action to directly address the challenges of life. For example, problem-focused coping strategies for the stress associated with taking a final exam might include joining a study group, setting aside two hours a day to study, and getting a good night's sleep before the exam. Problem-based coping requires a realistic assessment of actions that can be taken to improve a situation and the willingness to act. The development of one's personal strengths and resources contributes to one's ability to cope with life's demands (Carruthers & Hood, 2002; Hood & Carruthers, 2002). Enhancing or developing resources can be seen as a proactive approach to coping. The cultivation of physical resources, such as health, fitness, and energy, can contribute to one's coping capacity. The development of emotional resources, such as a belief in one's own competence, worth, and purpose, can contribute to one's coping capacity. Engagement in optimally challenging, meaningful leisure can enhance these emotional resources (Iwasaki, 2008). The creation and maintenance of social resources, such as social connections and support, can also contribute to one's coping repertoire. Leisure is an important area for the cultivation of these social networks (Iwasaki).

Relaxation

A third strategy for coping is to pursue activities that facilitate the relaxation response. Relaxation allows for physiological and emotional recuperation from stress (Davis et al., 2019), and leisure is an important path to attaining a relaxed state. Leisure can serve as a context for engaging in personal reflection, gaining a sense of perspective and appreciation, and living in the moment (Kleiber & McGuire, 2016). Engaging in physical leisure activities decreases anxiety and depression (Lyubomirsky, 2008). Experiencing nature through activities such as walking in nature preserves and hiking in the wilderness has a restorative effect (Hartig, Mitchell, DeVries, & Frumkin, 2014). Involvement in leisure activities that are nontaxing and enjoyable, such as watching television or listening to music, also induces the relaxation response. After immersing ourselves in optimally challenging activities that require our full concentration, we often feel refreshed. The full attention required to engage in the activity helps us disengage from our ruminations and distress (Lyubomirsky, 2008). Finally, activities such as meditation, yoga, and tai chi can directly reduce the physiological stress response (Olson, 2006).

Leisure-Based Coping

A fourth strategy for coping includes three specific forms of coping that are leisure based: leisure palliative coping, leisure mood enhancement, and leisure companionship (Iwasaki & Mannell, 2000). Leisure palliative coping might include activities like running, cycling, or hiking that give us temporary relief from stress and an opportunity to regroup and gain perspective. Leisure mood enhancement activities might include watching a funny movie or playing a game with friends. Leisure companionship would include any activities that involve social interaction that facilitates a supportive social network of friends. With each of these leisure coping strategies, the activities we select to cope with stress will likely reduce stress but may not necessarily improve our health and well-being. Leisure mood enhancement activities could include excessive alcohol consump-

An important way of getting the most out of life is taking time now and then to appreciate the good things in life.

10'000 Hours/ DigitalVision/Getty Images

tion or drug use. Leisure companionship might include promiscuous sexual activity, and leisure palliative coping might include engaging in reckless or dangerous activities.

Leisure involvement clearly can support a person's ability to cope with stress (Hutchinson, Bland, & Kleiber, 2008). Certain qualities of the leisure experience are particularly important for supporting well-being and building a life of meaning and purpose. These qualities support both the experience of happiness and positive emotion and the development and expression of one's full potential (Carruthers & Hood, 2007).

Participating in Meaningful Leisure to Enhance Well-Being

In examining the connection between leisure experience, coping, and well-being, we must consider some of the essential defining qualities of the experience. When most people think of leisure, they think of experiences like relaxing at the beach, talking on the phone, or watching TV. Recreation activities are viewed by most people as those activities that seem to be recreation, such as sports, crafts, hobbies, and games. These activities are a form of leisure but do not represent the full range of leisure experiences. Many leisure researchers have suggested that the quality of the experience and the perception of the participant determine whether the experience is leisure and whether it has value and benefit to the participant. Thus, it is not the activity that is most important in defining an experience as leisure or recreation but rather the participant's subjective assessment of the activity (Walker et al., 2019).

The defining qualities of leisure that are most closely related to well-being are positive emotion or pleasure, perception of freedom and control, intrinsic motivation, and change in level of engagement from the activities and experiences that surround leisure. The positive emotion associated with leisure, either in anticipation, experience, or recollection, creates a direct link to well-being. The freedom inherent in leisure allows the participant to choose and modify the situation to create the most rewarding and meaningful experiences possible. This sense of freedom and control over your own experience often allows you to appreciate those experiences and craft the experiences in such a way as to bring about the greatest pleasure and benefit. Intrinsic motivation, or the desire to

participate in an activity for the rewards inherent in that experience, supports well-being and reinforces the importance of the person–activity fit. Activities that feel right are those that have the greatest value and tend to occur frequently in leisure experiences.

Leisure involvement is often experienced in contrast to other daily experiences. This contrast may occur in terms of level of engagement, such as shifting from studying to going for a run. The contrast may involve a shift from an individual experience to a social experience, or it may involve a shift in sense of obligation, such as taking a break from studying to call a friend or family member. Regardless of the nature of the shift, leisure is often experienced in contrast to what was going on before and what will happen after the leisure interlude (Kleiber & McGuire, 2016). Interestingly, engaging leisure experience can lead to a disengagement from daily life concerns while simultaneously fostering a full immersion in the present moment. The capacity for leisure to support disengagement from daily life concerns and engagement in personally meaningful, pleasurable activities is an important way that leisure supports well-being (Hutchinson & Kleiber, 2005; Kleiber & McGuire, 2016; Stebbins, 2015).

Determinants of Happiness

Many scholars have worked to understand what determines happiness and well-being. They have found that there are three principal determinants of happiness: genetics, circumstantial factors, and intentional activities (Sheldon & Lyubomirsky, 2004). The significant role of leisure in the construction of enduring happiness is discussed within this framework.

Genetics

The first principal determinant of happiness is genetics and inherited tendencies. There is much evidence that people differ in their genetically determined ranges of happiness (Lykken & Tellegen, 1996). Most of us know people who are perpetually happy, with little change from day to day. Although these people experience the same challenges and disappointments as everyone else, they return relatively quickly to a state of happiness. We also know people who are unhappy, with little change from day to day. Their perpetual unhappiness often exists despite apparent good fortune. The genetic set point, by its very nature, is resistant to change. However, recent research suggests that one's genetic predispositions and environment interact (Klein, 2006). For example, a stressful family home may trigger depression in a child with a genetic predisposition for depression, whereas the depression gene may not be expressed if the child is in a loving, stress-free home. The key to well-being is to operate at the most optimal levels of one's own genetic range (Lykken & Tellegen, 1996; Lyubomirsky, 2008).

Circumstantial Factors

The second principal determinant of happiness involves circumstantial factors, such as health, possessions, socioeconomic status, or geographic location. One's life circumstances account for approximately 10 percent of one's happiness level. Although changes in life circumstances can temporarily boost happiness levels, the impact of these factors typically fades over time (Lyubomirsky, 2012). For example, getting an A on an exam, buying a new cell phone, or getting a new roommate may give you an immediate boost in happiness, but it tends to be relatively short lived. You will soon drift back to your set point of happiness.

This lessening of effects seems to be due to the fact that people quickly grow habituated to or dissatisfied with their new circumstances (Lyubomirsky, 2012). **Habituation** occurs when we become accustomed to the new circumstances and our nervous systems no longer register the experience as novel or worthy of notice (Seligman, 2002). New circumstances might affect happiness levels immediately and dramatically, but due to habituation, they have few long-term effects. A good example of the impact of circumstantial factors on happiness is the research on lottery winners by Brickman, Coates, and Janoff-Bulman (1978). Their study found that lottery winners were no happier one year later than they had been before winning. This relationship is also demonstrated in the face of negative life events;

people who acquired a spinal cord injury that required the use of a wheelchair were also found to return to their preinjury levels of happiness over time (Allman, 1990).

Ironically, people often live their lives believing that external circumstances will bring happiness (Seligman, 2002). They pursue money, large homes, fancy cars, prestigious jobs, and beauty with the belief that once they obtain these things, they will be happy. Yet there is much evidence that the pursuit of money and material possessions often contributes to unhappiness (Lyubomirsky, 2008).

Intentional Activities

Although changing our genetic makeup is impossible and changing our external circumstances tends to have little effect on long-term happiness, we still have the power to change our happiness levels (Lykken, 1999). The third principal element that determines well-being or happiness is **intentional activity** (Lyubomirsky, 2008). Intentional activities, defined as effortful, goal-oriented endeavors, account for approximately 40 percent of a person's happiness level (Lyubomirsky). Interestingly, the effects of these intentional activities are much less likely to fade over time and thus result in lasting changes to happiness. People can incorporate many types of activities into their lives to increase their happiness level; however, the activities that increase one person's happiness may have little impact on the happiness of another. The selection of intentional activities is very individualized. Leisure provides a rich source of activities through which people can intentionally cultivate well-being (Carruthers & Hood, 2004).

There are two general types of intentional activities that can increase one's level of happiness or well-being (Ben-Shahar, 2007). The first is engagement in activities that bring positive emotion, such as joy, excitement, humor, pleasure, contentment, satisfaction, and relaxation, into one's day-to-day life. People who are experiencing well-being feel happy more often than they feel sad (Carruthers & Hood, 2004). Oftentimes people in our society get so caught up in creating a positive future for themselves that they do not enjoy the process or journey (Ben-Shahar, 2007). Enjoying the present moments of one's life is an essential component of happiness (Csikszentmihalyi, 1990).

Happiness in the present can be created through involvement in pleasurable activities (Seligman, 2002). These activities often have a strong sensory

Self-Exploration

What kinds of things do you do each day to make your life happier and more fulfilling? What practices add the most happiness to your day? What do you do to bring more pleasure into your life? What leisure activities, if any, do you engage in that help you grow as a person and develop skills and capacities? In what ways do you see yourself making a contribution to the world through your leisure, if any? When you think about your life, what kinds of choices do you consciously make that support your happiness and fulfillment?

component to them. For example, pleasure may be obtained by eating a piece of decadent chocolate cake, taking a warm bubble bath, or cuddling with your partner in front of a fireplace. Pleasurable activities may be sought because they are arousing, such as riding a roller coaster or bungee jumping, or soothing, such as sitting on a beach or listening to music. These types of activities are important to well-being. However, many people do not intentionally build such activities into their lives. To get the full happiness boost from pleasurable activities, people must be fully present for those moments. People also should have a variety of happy habits (Lykken, 1999). Doing the same pleasurable activity repeatedly leads to habituation; an activity that is done too often loses its pleasurable impact.

The second general type of intentional activity that can increase one's level of happiness or well-being is engagement in meaningful experiences that result in the cultivation of one's full potential (Ben-Shahar, 2007; Hood & Carruthers, 2007). Clear distinctions have been made among leading a pleasant life, a good life, and a meaningful life (Seligman, 2002). A pleasant life is one in which people experience pleasure regularly in their day-to-day lives. They savor and mindfully live those momentary delights. However, these pleasurable experiences do not alone constitute a good life. A good life is one in which people cultivate and invest their signature strengths and virtues in their relationships, leisure, and work. This investment of the best of self in challenging, meaningful activity or **gratifications** increases a person's capacity for growth and feelings of competence, satisfaction, and well-being. Last, a meaningful life is one in which people use their "signature strengths in the service of something larger" than themselves (Seligman, 2002, p. 249). Authentic happiness is ultimately constructed by investment in meaningful activity through which people can realize their full potential as human beings. Although experiencing positive

emotion is important, most of us want more from life than just to feel good (Ben-Shahar, 2007; Seligman, 2002). The evolution of self occurs through engaging in ongoing self-discovery, creating contexts and opportunities for self-development, and making meaning in our lives (Fava & Ruini, 2003).

Although leisure is not the only life domain in which people can cultivate their signature strengths and create a meaningful life, it is an important one (Carruthers & Hood, 2007). Leisure offers many opportunities to seek out optimal challenges and realize one's full physical, emotional, social, intellectual, and spiritual potential. When people engage in activities that are totally engrossing and stretch their capabilities, they often experience an enjoyment that draws them back to the activity over and over again. The challenges inherent in the activity demand the participant's full attention to be successful; the person is immersed in the activity and experiences a feeling of flow (Csikszentmihalyi, 1990). People experiencing flow activities are unlikely to habituate. To continue to be optimally challenged, they must seek out increasingly complex or engaging opportunities. Rock climbers traverse a higher mountain. Artists investigate other media or subjects. Travelers explore new landscapes.

Leisure Choices That Undermine Well-Being

Just as fire can warm a home or burn it down, leisure can enhance well-being or undermine it. By definition, leisure is behavior that is chosen because it will result in pleasure, enjoyment, or satisfaction (Neulinger, 1981; Walker et al., 2019). However, people who pursue pleasure at the expense of challenging and meaningful activity, take leisure behaviors to an extreme, or regularly disengage from their lives through leisure may be undermining their well-being (Csikszentmihalyi, 1990; Seligman, 2002). The term *purple recreation* refers to a type of leisure that challenges societal norms and is detrimental to the participant, to others, or to the community (Curtis, 1988).

Humans are genetically programmed to seek positive emotion and to avoid negative emotion (Klein, 2006). When we desire something, neurotransmitters that energize and drive us are released (Nettle, 2005). When we satisfy our desires, neurotransmitters that cause the sensation of pleasure are released, spurring us to future pursuit of the next best experience (Klein, 2006). This genetic programming causes us to pursue sensory pleasure and strive for excellence (Nettle, 2005).

People have a finite amount of time and energy. Pleasurable activities can contribute to well-being but if overdone can undermine engagement in the meaningful experiences that result in the cultivation of one's full potential. Watching television, for example, can reduce physiological stress. However, Americans spend the majority of their leisure time watching television (Russell, 2020). Television viewing is associated with less involvement in physical and social activities, both of which contribute to long term well-being (Layard, 2005).

Hedonists take the pursuit of pleasure and the avoidance of pain to an extreme. They believe that happiness "is reducible to a succession of pleasurable experiences" (Ben-Shahar, 2007, p. 20). They seek immediate gratification with little concern for future well-being or sometimes find pleasure in doing nothing rather than in engaging in positive experiences (Ben-Shahar, 2007). If something that these people desire requires hard work, effort, sacrifice, or overcoming difficulties, they will often avoid it (Seligman, 2002). Unfortunately, the happiness that results from the pursuit of challenging and meaningful goals escapes the hedonist. After all, the best moments in life "usually occur when a person's body or mind is stretched to its limits in a

---

Self-Exploration

Thinking about the past few months: Have you overindulged in a leisure activity that you usually enjoy? How did you feel after you overindulged? How was your enjoyment of the experience affected by overdoing it? Did your overindulgence in one activity take time away from an activity that might have been more meaningful?

---

voluntary effort to accomplish something difficult and worthwhile" (Csikszentmihalyi, 1990, p. 3).

Overindulgence in pleasurable leisure experiences poses other threats to well-being. Ideally, people are able to balance the desire for happiness in the present with a commitment to the cultivation of a meaningful, satisfying life (Ben-Shahar, 2007). However, some people lose the ability to maintain the balance. They begin to compulsively pursue experiences with little regard for the long-term consequences (Goldstein, 2005; Klein, 2006). They lose their ability to control their behaviors, regardless of the negative consequences. The same neurotransmitter systems that cause humans to seek pleasure and avoid pain are engaged. These compulsive experiences, many of which could be considered purple recreation, can significantly harm a person's physical, emotional, social, intellectual, and spiritual well-being as well as the well-being of their community.

Strategies for Enhancing Well-Being and Mental Health Through Leisure

The defining qualities of leisure make it an ideal context and experience through which to enhance well-being and to develop capacities associated with living a life of meaning. Given that leisure is freely chosen, supports a sense of autonomy and competence, generates pleasure and positive emotion, and is motivated by a desire for the experience alone, leisure is an essential domain for engagement in intentional activities that support well-being (Carruthers & Hood, 2004, 2007; Hood & Carruthers, 2007).

However, not all leisure experiences are equal in their capacity to support well-being nor do all people possess the ability to gain the greatest benefit of leisure. Five broad approaches to gaining the greatest benefit from leisure experiences have been identified: savoring leisure, authentic leisure, leisure gratifications, mindful leisure, and virtuous leisure (Hood & Carruthers, 2007).

Savoring Leisure

One critical approach for enhancing the value of leisure in creating a life of well-being is savoring leisure. **Savoring** leisure is defined as "paying attention to the positive aspects of, and emotions

Simonkr/E+/Getty Images

When you're feeling stressed, a simple change in scenery can help you refocus and feel calmer.

associated with, leisure involvement and purposefully seeking leisure experiences that give rise to positive emotions" (Hood & Carruthers, 2007, pp. 310-311). The premise of savoring leisure is that we often participate in activities without paying much attention to the actual participation. Hood and Carruthers (2007) suggested that many of the benefits associated with leisure involvement are based on the assumption that leisure engagement is pleasant and enjoyable, and learning to savor leisure experiences can help us become more aware of the positive aspects of those experiences.

Savoring leisure experience is linked directly to well-being through the cultivation of positive emotion (Livingstone & Srivastava, 2012; Salces-Cubero, Ramirez-Fernandez, & Ortega-Martinez, 2019; Smith, Harrison, Kurtz, & Bryant, 2014; Smith & Hollinger-Smith, 2015). Strategies or practices associated with savoring leisure include these: (1) purposefully selecting experiences that will generate positive emotion (such as nature, music, art, good conversation); (2) purposefully discovering a set of experiences that generate positive emotion and building them into daily life in novel and interesting ways to avoid habituation (Bao & Lyubomirsky, 2014); (3) paying conscious attention to the positive aspects and outcomes associated with an experience (Bryant & Veroff, 2007); (4) recreating those positive

emotions and experiences through reminiscing and storytelling (Quoidbach, Berry, Hansenne, & Mikolajczak, 2010; Smith et al., 2014); and (5) selecting experiences that require active engagement (mind, body, or emotion; Ben-Shahar, 2007; Fredrickson, 2000; Lykken, 1999; Lyubomirsky, 2008; Seligman, 2002; Sheldon & Lyubomirsky, 2004). Passive activities or casual leisure experiences can be powerful in generating positive emotions, but a balance of active and passive leisure is needed to create a life of well-being (Hutchinson & Kleiber, 2005). Regardless of the nature of involvement, the positive emotions associated with leisure involvement are central and necessary for our well-being.

Authentic Leisure

A second important approach for enhancing the value of leisure in supporting a life of well-being is consciously and purposefully selecting leisure experiences that feel right. Researchers have identified the importance of person–activity fit in their discussion of the role of intentional activities in enhancing happiness (Sheldon & Lyubomirsky, 2004). They stated that "not all activities will help a particular person become happier. People have enduring strengths, interests, values, and inclinations, which predispose them to benefit more from some activities than others" (p. 138). In fact, one researcher stated that "if there's any 'secret' to becoming happier, the secret is in establishing which happiness strategies suit you best" (Lyubomirsky, 2008, p. 70). She suggested that as we attempt to determine which activities suit us best, we can evaluate them in terms of the degree to which the activity feels natural, is enjoyable, has inherent value for us, does not involve guilt or obligation, and is not done because of the requirements and expectations of the situation.

The notion of person–activity fit is woven into the conception of authentic leisure (Hood & Carruthers, 2007). Authenticity has been described as experiencing and expressing oneself in ways that are consistent and true to the inner experience (Harter, 2002) and is based on self-knowledge and action that is congruent with that knowledge (Jongman-Sereno & Leary, 2018). Schlegel and Hicks (2011) reviewed the literature linking authenticity (the true self) with various measures of well-being and found that the research demonstrated a significant relationship between expression of the true self and increased self-esteem, increased positive affect, decreased negative affect, and increased relational quality and durability. There is clear evidence that authenticity is directly linked to both hedonic and eudaemonic well-being (Schlegel, Hirsch, & Smith, 2013).

Authentic leisure is a blend of person–activity fit and authenticity, and it is proposed that leisure is an ideal context in which to construct and engage in authentic experience. Leisure is a potent context in which to both come to know your preferences, capacities, and interests and to express those essential aspects of the self in meaningful engagements (Fenton, 2018; Hartman & Anderson, 2018; Hixon, 2013; Layland, Hill, & Nelson, 2019). The relative freedom inherent in leisure choices allows people to experiment with experience to learn about themselves (Kleiber & McGuire, 2016; Marcia, 1966; Marcia & Josselson, 2012) and then to purposefully select and engage in experiences that allow them to express important aspects of the self (Carruthers & Hood, 2007).

An additional strategy for engaging in authentic leisure that builds more happiness into life is finding or creating a social world around authentic leisure experiences (Carruthers & Hood, 2007). Leisure has an important role in identity development and expression (Duerden, Widmer, Taniguchi, & McCoy, 2009; Kleiber & McGuire, 2016), and it has been suggested that engagement in social worlds that

are created around leisure experiences is central to human development and well-being. For example, if a person becomes interested in taekwondo and finds that this leisure activity fits with their needs, interests, and capacities, then participation in taekwondo can support their happiness and well-being. As the person becomes more experienced and involved in the activity, they will learn the language, etiquette, and culture of taekwondo enthusiasts and will soon begin to identify through this involvement. The sense of attachment to and engagement in a social world related to a preferred, meaningful activity creates a set of reciprocal relationships, a sense of belonging, and a unique identity associated with the social world surrounding the activity (Elkington & Stebbins, 2014). All of these qualities are associated with greater well-being.

Leisure Gratifications

Participation in leisure experiences that give rise to positive emotion and that feel right set the stage for engagement in activities that require investment of attention and result in an ongoing upward spiral of skill and capacity development. These types of activities are referred to as leisure gratifications by Hood and Carruthers (2007) and are very similar in nature to the concept of flow developed by Csikszentmihalyi (1990). Leisure gratifications are defined as "leisure experiences that are optimally challenging and engaging, and that lead to sustained personal effort and commitment to the experience" (Hood & Carruthers, 2007, p. 314). This conception of leisure is based on the premise that people want to be happy and they want to develop themselves in meaningful ways (Seligman, 2002).

People can engage in a set of strategies designed to enhance the possibility of experiencing leisure gratifications. Probably one of the most important decisions about activity engagement is to select activities that are a good fit with interests and capacities and that afford degrees of skilled performance; thus, as skills increase, greater challenge can be undertaken to avoid boredom. These types of skill-based activities also allow for early skill development without experiencing anxiety and frustration. As skills increase, greater and greater challenge is undertaken to achieve the sense of flow and full engagement that is so rewarding for most people (Csikszentmihalyi, 1990, 2014).

Matching one's goals for engagement with the possibilities presented by the activity is an important

SHODOgraphy/iStock/Getty Images

Push your limits; never stop challenging yourself.

way to manage the level of engagement. For example, if you are participating in an activity where your skills exceed the demands of the activity, boredom is likely. As a result, you can either modify the way you engage in the activity, to increase the challenge, or you can modify your reasons for engagement (e.g., social connection rather than competition). If the demands of your chosen activity exceed your skills, then anxiety may result. In this situation, you can either modify the activity so the demands are not so great or change your goals for involvement (e.g., enjoyment, laughter, and personal improvement, rather than demonstration of acquired skills).

Leisure gratifications fulfill an important role in supporting personal development and capacity development (Freire, Tavares, Silva, & Teixeira, 2016; Riva, 2014; Riva, Rainisio, & Boffi, 2014). Engagement in these kinds of experiences also produces significant feelings of satisfaction, pleasure, and fulfillment (Carr, 2019; Elkington, 2011). These two dimensions of experience, positive emotion and self-development, are the cornerstones of well-being.

Mindful Leisure

A conscious and direct focus on the positive aspects of an experience reflects the approach called savoring leisure. Mindful leisure takes this conscious engagement in an experience and broadens it to include attention to the entirety of the current experience coupled with a simultaneous disengagement from daily life concerns (Brown & Ryan, 2003). Thus, although savoring leisure involves narrowing attention to the positive aspects of the experience, mindful leisure involves focusing one's full attention on the current experience and not attending to worries about the future or other issues of concern. Mindfulness practices and interventions have been shown to directly affect well-being (Davis & Hayes, 2011). Mindfulness can be helpful in reducing distress, depressive symptoms, ruminative thinking, pain perception, and anxiety, and it can also directly increase well-being, including increasing empathy for others, self-compassion, positive emotion, and satisfaction with life (Chiesa & Serretti, 2009;

Garland & Howard, 2013; Krygier et al., 2013; Vollestad, Nielson, & Nielson, 2012).

Becoming more mindful in leisure requires us to increase our capacity to attend to the present moment. We can learn to pay attention to the present moment by slowing our thought processes through such activities as breathing exercises, mental imagery, yoga, and relaxation techniques (Fredrickson, 2000; Fredrickson, Coffey, Pek, Cohn, & Finkel, 2008). These allow us to quiet our minds and physiological responses so we can be fully present in the current experience. In addition, full engagement can be supported by examining the habits of thought that interfere with being fully present in the moment. Examining negative self-talk habits, ruminations, and worry can be extremely helpful in disengaging from those thoughts and engaging fully in the current experience. Finally, full engagement can be supported by selecting leisure activities that are personally meaningful and optimally challenging (Sheldon & Lyubomirsky, 2004). These types of activities are often so engaging that they result in a momentary disengagement from the concerns of daily life. Thus, mindful leisure can be experienced through purposeful engagement in experiences that build capacity for mindful involvement in the present (controlling anxiety and enhancing relaxation) as well as through purposeful engagement in leisure experiences that are so fully absorbing that they don't allow daily concerns and anxieties to affect the experience.

Virtuous Leisure

The term *virtuous* comes from the work of Seligman (2002), who discussed the importance of "using one's strengths and virtues in the service of something much larger than you are" (p. 263). Virtues are characteristics that are viewed as universally good and that support individual and collective well-being. It has been suggested that life has the greatest meaning when a person has many opportunities to use personal strengths and virtues in the service of something greater than that person. Thus, virtuous leisure was defined as "the capacity to engage in leisure experiences that develop and/or mobilize personal strengths, capacities, interests, and abilities in the service of something larger than oneself" (Hood & Carruthers, 2007, p. 316).

Experiences that would be considered virtuous leisure include obvious leisure engagements such as volunteering or less obvious forms of engagement such as helping a neighbor, teaching others a skill that you possess, or planting a beautiful garden that brings others pleasure. Finding contexts in which a person can use their strengths in service is central to engaging in virtuous leisure. Experiencing these acts of service and reflecting on the positive outcomes is also necessary. Interestingly, the research associated with volunteering clearly demonstrates that the greatest benefit occurs for the person providing the service rather than the person receiving the assistance (Borgonovi, 2008; Kahana, Bhatta, Lovegreen, Kahana, & Midlarsky, 2013; Pillavin & Siegl, 2016). Finally, finding opportunities to be of service in the community can help us develop reciprocal interdependent relationships with other community members and allow us to feel connected to and needed by our community (Morrow-Howell et al., 2014; Townsend et al., 2014).

Summary

Leisure has some direct and powerful connections to building a life of meaning and well-being. However, not all leisure has the same benefit, and some leisure experiences may be detrimental to well-being. The freedom of the leisure context and experience sets the stage for the possibility of engaging in leisure in such a way as to maximize its benefits. However, for many people, this type of leisure engagement requires effort and knowledge and must be purposeful. Leisure services professionals can help citizens engage in leisure that is personally meaningful, that allows for engagement and disengagement, that is pleasurable, and that allows participants to develop and express their best selves while feeling connected and important to their communities, families, and friends. These supports may include educational opportunities to learn about the potent connection between leisure engagement and well-being, opportunities to experience various types of leisure and the resultant effects on feelings of well-being, or the creation of communities and places where enriched opportunities for leisure experiences are part of the daily fabric of life.

Learning Activities

1. Play the Tim McGraw song "Live Like You Were Dying." Discuss the message of the song as it relates to leisure, relationships, and well-being (e.g., positive emotion, personal growth, and meaning).

2. Locate a volunteer opportunity in your community in which you are interested (e.g., community cleanup, political rally, charity event, marathon support, soup kitchen). Volunteer at the event and really pitch in. Write a brief paper reflecting on your reactions to the virtuous leisure experience. Share your reactions with your classmates.

Review Questions

1. Provide an example of a stressful situation from your own life and explain how you drew from more than one type of strategy to manage the stressor. How successful were you in managing the stress?

2. How does each of the two types of intentional activities contribute to overall well-being?

3. Describe a personally meaningful leisure experience in which you have recently engaged. Thinking about the five broad strategies identified to increase the value of leisure for well-being, identify strategies that you could use to increase the value of that experience.

Go to HK*Propel* to access additional learning content.

PART

III

Dimensions of Leisure in Society

Leisure History and Heritage

Lee J. deLisle

Southern Connecticut State University

VOCABULARY TERMS

arête	**Dark Ages**	**Pax Romana**
blood sports	**Enlightenment**	**playground movement**
bread and circuses	**evolution**	**Renaissance**
civilization	**festivals**	*schole*
creation	**Industrial Revolution**	**threats to survival**

LEARNING OUTCOMES

After reading this chapter, you will be able to

- understand the role of leisure in human evolutionary development;
- describe and give examples of the relationship between leisure and threats to survival;
- identify sociological and technological practices that expand leisure opportunities;
- describe the relationship between leisure and work;
- discuss the influence of ancient cultures on our contemporary understanding and use of leisure;
- describe political, religious, and economic influences on leisure behaviors and
- identify the stages of development in the formation of recreational services in the United States.

Almost 1 million years ago, a group of hominids sat around a fire in a cave in what is now Iraq. Their home had light and heat, there were animal skins spread on the floor for comfort, and the group lived together peacefully while struggling against the forces of nature that challenged their very existence. After finishing their meal, they split the long bones of the animal they had hunted that day and enjoyed the sweet marrow within each bone. This simple pleasure, dessert, is an indication that they had some time to enjoy this leisure activity. As each subsequent generation of humans evolved, additional leisure activities such as art, storytelling, dance, religion, and sport contributed to their group culture and the development of the human race.

Social realities such as ritual and religion, slavery, technology, economic development, and the enhancement of the human intellect through play and formal education all contributed to our present understanding of what it means to be human. Equally important in human development are the influences of war, greed, corruption, superstition, and social and physical disease on the quality of life experienced in past epochs and the subsequent rate of human development. In this chapter we examine the emergence of Western civilization through an understanding of the role of leisure in this unending human drama.

Understanding Leisure From a Historical Perspective

Leisure can be described in many ways, both objectively and subjectively, depending on context and intent. To understand the status of leisure activity in contemporary society, it is very helpful to understand its importance in the history of past civilizations. To study leisure from a historical perspective, we need a common point of reference. For the purpose of this chapter, *leisure* is best defined as "free or unobligated time." This value-neutral concept can be understood across temporal and cultural boundaries.

JohnnyGreig/E+/Getty Images

Leisure provides time to explore other cultures or expand your personal culture.

The influential book *Leisure: The Basis of Culture* positions leisure as the most critical element in the formation and continuation of personal and communal culture (Pieper, 1963). Contemplation, celebration, and community, according to this book, are based in our use of leisure. How we experience leisure defines who we are as individuals and as a society. What we do with our leisure says something about our interests, our character, and our understanding of what it means to be fully human. Free time, constructively used, advances societies, enhances individual lives, and produces cultural development over time.

The relationship of leisure to personal and communal cultural development in past epochs can be seen as the interplay between activities needed for survival and time free from threat. This relationship between leisure and **threats to survival** is germane to our understanding of history but is also observable in contemporary societies. Despite all the technological advances in our modern world, we still face threats to survival. The most obvious examples are floods, hurricanes, disease, and other natural forces that are beyond our control. Unfortunately, human activity such as war, military occupation, terrorism, and other threats continue to constrain individual and communal leisure.

The amount and quality of leisure are inversely related to the level of threat to survival that is experienced by an individual or community. As threats increase, leisure tends to decrease. As we individually and communally master or overcome these threats, we have more free time at our disposal, allowing for creative and cooperative behaviors that enhance our quality of life and deepen the cultural foundations of society.

This chapter takes us on a journey from prehistoric times to our modern understanding of leisure and recreational services. We will begin in your own backyard.

Imagine that in the course of digging a garden in your backyard you unearth what turns out to be a human settlement that is determined to be more than 10,000 years old. As you sift through the remnants of this prehistoric site, you discover artifacts in the firepit that, with a little bit of insight and creative thinking, could help you understand the amount of leisure that this group might have enjoyed. We know that leisure is needed for creative activity.

The Primacy of Leisure

A number of **creation** stories have been preserved from ancient civilizations. Creation myths attempt to explain the origins of the world in ways that are relevant and understandable to a certain group of people. Many stories also emphasize the role of rest in relationship to work. Consider the creation story of the book of Genesis in the Judeo-Christian tradition.

> And on the seventh day God finished his work which he had done, and he rested on the seventh day from all his work which he had done. So God blessed the seventh day and hallowed it, because on it God rested from all his work which he had done in creation. (Book of Genesis 2:1-3 RSV)

According to this story, God worked to create all the elements of the cosmos in six days and on the seventh day rested. It should be noted that humans (man) arrived on the scene on the sixth day. If we subscribe to the existence of days as presented in the story, then the first full day on Earth for man was the Sabbath, a day of rest, a day of leisure. The idea of the original condition of human existence to be one of leisure is significant in our understanding of later religious practices that attempt to address issues related to the use of free time. At this point in our study of human evolution, we understand that leisure was considered by some to be the natural and original or primal state of human existence. This is sometimes referred to as the *primacy of leisure.*

Importance of Fire and Its Effect on the Division of Labor

There is evidence that approximately 1.2 million years ago, prehumans learned to control fire. Controlling fire allowed humans to master their environment to a much greater degree by using fire as protection against attacks from wild animals, as a means to cook and preserve food, and to provide heat and light to extend the day. These extra hours provided time for tool making and for basic communication between group members. It was a time to reflect on the events of the day and plan the next day's hunt or a move to a new camp. This leisure brought greater organization and stability to the group, contributing to communal well-being, reducing threats to survival, and allowing for the creation of forms of self-expression such as language, art, music, and dance.

Along with the development of tools and language and the controlled use of fire was the emerging ability of humans to plan and organize tasks. The fastest, strongest men became warriors and hunters, finding food for cooking and storage and protecting the settlement. Others stayed closer to the camp and foraged for edible plants and roots and maintained the communal living amenities. Job responsibilities became more specialized. This division of labor allowed for periods of work and periods of rest—leisure was on the increase. One result of this increase in free time was the celebration of festivals. **Festivals** marked special times in the ancient lunar calendar, times that were sacred, or *sacro* (set apart), from the rest of the year (deLisle, 2009). Festivals also commemorated past events, oftentimes spiritual or religious, providing a cyclical understanding of time, an enormous advance in ancient culture. One insightful book on human festivity tells us that what makes a festival time special is the cessation of normal daily activities to allow for access to something extraordinary, even otherworldly (Pieper, 1999).

Agricultural Alternatives

As humans sought to infuse their existence with meaning through creation stories, the development of taboos and requisite punishments, and the nascent emergence of creative activities, there remained some very basic concerns about survival. Hunter-gatherers were required to follow their source of

food, animal herds, as they migrated according to the seasonal food supply. For the humans, there were certainly times of starvation and death due to a lack of food provided by animals. Other natural factors, including competition from other human groups, forced these clans to defend themselves or die.

Early humans gradually found that certain plants and fruits were edible. As this process developed over the centuries, there was a shift from hunter-gatherer strategies to a dependency on agriculture. This was not a universal and complete change, because we still today find hunter-gatherer societies in remote places in the world. Life for these early farmers revolved around the activities needed for effective farming, with work becoming cyclical, based on the planting, growing, and harvesting seasons. This shift represents a major milestone in human development because it affected both the work and leisure patterns of society. There was a time for each needed activity and time for rest, recuperation, and celebration.

The formation of communities led to the growth of technology, more sophisticated means of communication, an increase in creative and artistic endeavors, and a sense of prosperity for those communities that were well managed and benefited from their efforts to progress. With the relative stability of community living, many threats to survival were reduced or altered, creating more leisure. However, other threats arose, including barbaric behaviors.

The greatest threat to survival came from the actions of neighboring communities that used force to attack and conquer others. It is a cycle that continues into the 21st century. In ancient times, war often resulted in the taking of property and the bondage of slavery for the defeated group. This was not a slavery based on race or ethnicity but one based on the rules of war in ancient civilizations. Slave labor, regardless of our modern feelings about it, supported civilizations that have produced some of the most valued contributions to Western civilization. Democratic governance, architecture, science, the arts, philosophy, and religion all benefited from the additional leisure realized by free men as a result of the enforced labor of conquered civilizations.

Rise of Civilization

By 4000 BCE, farming, building, and trading communities were spread across the Middle East. There remained some groups who wandered as hunters and herders, but the majority had settled into the stability of agricultural and commercial life. The Fertile Crescent, or Fertile Triangle, situated between the Tigris and Euphrates rivers (a region called Mesopotamia, "the land between the rivers") was a focal point of civilization for 3,500 years. This area, which is today the country of Iraq, was the most sophisticated and powerful nation in the ancient world. Mesopotamia is remembered for many positive contributions to the advancement of civilization, including the first written code of laws, the Code of Hammurabi, and the first public park, the Hanging Gardens of Babylon. As is the case in all settled areas, Mesopotamia was the site of repetitive warfare; the region was invaded and ruled by the Sumerians, Akkadians, Babylonians, Assyrians, and Chaldeans during those 3,500 years. Each group assimilated the cultural practices of their subjects and introduced new elements to the advancement of civilization.

Advancements during this time included the development of a numbering system, calendars, techniques for measurement, irrigation, currency, and written contracts for business transactions. Aesthetic advancements included arts and crafts, reading and writing, sculpture, and ornate architectural features such as columns, arches, and domes. Governmental structures became more sophisticated, and commercial organizations were formed to share their expertise. Efforts were made to make life more enjoyable for free men, including the staging of festivals and celebrations that satisfied the religious needs of the community and brought a welcome break from the ordinary demands of daily life. Hunting was pursued as a leisure activity, as were competitive sport activities that prepared men for war and provided amusement for participants and spectators. The first truly organized state or kingdom familiar to us is that of Egypt.

Leisure in the Land of the Pharaohs

Egypt, a confederacy of cities along the Nile River, is a great example of how civilization and culture are closely related to leisure. Egypt benefited from a strategic location both militarily and economically, the existence of a religious system that helped to control behaviors through a belief in the rewards of an afterlife, personal and communal wealth, and slave labor that freed citizens from much of the hard work of the kingdom. All of these positive factors reduced threats to survival, thereby increasing leisure.

The amount of leisure available to the population was inversely proportional to one's place in society (figure 6.1). The leisure class had great land holdings and grew wealthy from agricultural enterprises. Peasants labored daily for the benefit of the upper

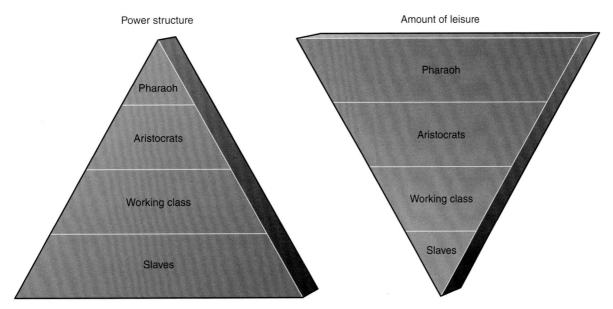

FIGURE 6.1 The pyramid, an icon of Egyptian culture, also represents the hierarchical structure of Egyptian society and the amount of leisure available to each group.

classes. When the Nile flooded, however, it was festival time, a religious occasion when all work paused long enough for everyone to celebrate with feasts, games, and rituals. The dynasties of Egypt are critical to our understanding of Western civilization because we see the positive effect of stability and order on the advancement of culture.

Emergence of Greece

By 1000 BCE, the Greeks were developing an alphabet, were sailing to foreign shores for trade and colonization, and had a class system in society that provided much leisure for the wealthy citizens. Women were not a part of society in terms of rights and privileges but ranked a little higher than the working class or slaves. Slavery was important in the development of the leisure class of ancient Greece. The practice was highly accepted, and no guilt was associated with the keeping of slaves.

The Greeks are best identified through the cultural developments brought by their position in the ancient world. Philosophy, mathematics, logic, government, the arts, music, theater, literature, sport, and so many other aspects of a thriving society were developed to work toward the ideal of perfection. Deeply embedded in the ideals of heroism, satire, education, political awareness, and aesthetics was the need for and use of leisure. Most Greek men spent time in the *gymnasia,* a community building that allowed for physical activity, sports, and education. For adult males it was the right use of leisure—to improve the mind, keep fit, and engage in social dialogue. It is interesting to note that the Greek word for leisure, *schole,* is the root for our word *school.* This reminds us that the Greeks dedicated their leisure to self-improvement rather than merely amusement. Leisure was used to better the human condition, to contribute to one's community, to bring about intellectual and physical stimulation and learning, and to improve on the art of living.

The Greek ideal of *arête* suggested that all pursuits, including recreational activities, be performed excellently, with complete mastery. *Arête* was the pursuit of perfection; it combined noble actions with noble thoughts. This concept of unity of mind and action to achieve perfection found its way into the very foundation of the Greek code of living. There is no real English translation of *arête* except for "proud and valorous behavior"—our classical sense of sportsmanship would illustrate a portion of this concept. The Olympic ideals were founded on the sense of *arête*—human perfection and nobility (Shivers & deLisle, 1997).

Caput Mundi: The Glory of Rome

The Roman era begins with the arrival of the Etruscans to central Italy. The citizens of Rome, who numbered close to 1 million during the pre-Christian era, established their city and its surrounding environs as the capital of the entire known Western world. Rome was truly the head of the world: *caput mundi.* Rome became the strongest military power in the Western world. The conquests that resulted from this power led to an increase in wealth for some and a greater gap between rich and poor. A new leisure class arose. The wealthy and the urban middle class enjoyed a good lifestyle, whereas the peasants and slaves suffered. So many slaves were available that the wages of citizen workers declined. The well-to-do no longer performed manual labor or lived the simple life of their ancestors. Although there was decadence and a distinct level of brutality, there was also great development of the arts and sciences.

Leisure Activities in Imperial Rome

Romans set aside time for games, races, gladiatorial contests, and other amusements. Public festivals and entertainment were numerous and varied for both rich and poor. Gladiatorial combats, theatrical performances, horse racing, and acrobatics were some of the events held to entertain the people. History, poetry, oratory, and the didactic essay were integral parts of Roman literature. Architecture, sculpture, and painting flourished. Roman architecture formed a style of its own.

Romans enjoyed feasts, public entertainment, and the public baths. The Roman baths were recreational centers built on a grand scale. Often covering hundreds of acres, these facilities offered bathing pools of varying temperatures, saunas, restaurants, rooms for massage, and sexual partners of all ages and persuasions. These pleasure palaces were a sign of the sophistication of Roman culture as well as a contributing factor to Rome's eventual downfall. Several theories about the fall of Rome attribute its decline to the misuse of leisure. The early Christians would not attend the blood sports or the baths and were thereby viewed as a threat to the order of the empire, resulting in their execution by the Romans.

Photo courtesy of Lee deLisle

The Colosseum or Amphitheater of Flavius in Rome was the site of gladiatorial battles and other blood sports, holding more than 55,000 spectators and offering free entertainment for all.

Leisure and the Politics of Social Control

Throngs of foreigners came to Rome. The rulers, politicians, and policy makers saw the inherent danger of a large population of underpaid, overworked nonresidents in their midst. To maintain the **Pax Romana**, the relative peace experienced in Rome, the leaders controlled the citizens' behavior through planned special events intended to entertain, educate, inspire, and distract the masses. **Bread and circuses** is the term used to describe the strategy of the ruling class to control the lower classes by offering them a ration of food each week and the spectacles of the amphitheaters like the Colosseum, the circuses, and racetracks of Rome. The **blood sports** of ancient Rome provide us with some understanding of the lack of respect for human life that characterized Roman culture.

Rome was in decline for several hundred years, effectively losing its influence by the fourth century CE. The reasons for this decline have been the

Self-Exploration

Consider your own leisure activities; can you see the influence of Roman leisure in your own choice of recreational activities?

subject of hundreds of books and research articles. What can be said with some confidence is that the use of leisure by the ruling class and the masses certainly contributed to the moral and cultural devolution of this great society.

Medieval Period: Castles, Churches, and the Peasant Culture

The thousand years between the fall of the Roman Empire (455) and the Renaissance (1455) are referred to as the medieval period or the Middle Ages. The downfall of the Roman Empire in the West brought the scourge of barbarism to Europe. This time is also referred to as the **Dark Ages**, because the European continent was subject to endless war, constant migration, food shortages, poor living conditions, and diseases such as the bubonic plague of 1347 to 1350, which produced more death and destruction than any preceding war or natural disaster. About 25 percent of the population of Europe was destroyed in this 3-year period at a rate of 1,000 deaths per day (Deaux, 1969). The disease, commonly seen as a punishment from God, was spread through fleas that transmitted the disease from the burgeoning rat population in urban areas to unsuspecting residents. The disease caused red, swollen circles called *buboes* and damaged the respiratory systems of the victims. If untreated, people died within 4 to 7 days of contracting the disease. Children attempted to reconcile this horror through games and songs. The game ring-around-the-rosy was based on their experience of the plague. The original song was this:

Ring around of roses

. . . describing the red swollen circles on the skin;

A pocket full of posies

. . . many people carried flowers in their pockets and would then press them to their nose to mask the smell of dead bodies;

Achoo, Achoo, (or ashes, ashes) we all fall down

. . . because the disease compromised the respiratory system, the momentary cessation of the heart during a sneeze could cause an afflicted person to die on the spot. The ashes referred to the burning of bodies, because there were too many for traditional burials.

The Dark Ages, filled with fear, disease, warfare, and very difficult living conditions, challenged the human spirit and threatened the continued cultural development of the human race. Considering the relationship between threats to survival and the amount and quality of free time available, it is no wonder that cultural advancements all but ceased during this difficult period.

One saving grace during these difficult times was the rise of institutional Christianity and the birth of Islam on the Arabian Peninsula and subsequent formation of an Islamic empire. Organized religion supported literacy and, in the case of Islam, retained and disseminated the scientific knowledge of the previous 2,000 years. Islamic scholars collected and protected the classical works of knowledge and became a ready source for translation when reason replaced superstition. The monastic system of early Christianity led to the development of the great universities of Western Europe, fostering the reengagement of the populace with learning and scientific advancement.

The plague was a catalyst for change in Europe. Economic, social, governmental, and ecclesial practices, accepted and endured for centuries, were no longer held to be valid or effective means of making sense of life's experiences. The plague set the stage for economic and social change that would be realized during the following two centuries.

Feudalism, the prevalent economic system of the time, and town autonomy permitted the emergence of the European fledgling nation-states. Banking, accounting, and public finance were invented. Trade, travel, and industry augmented economic development.

Leisure in the Middle Ages

Leisure, as in past times, was determined by wealth and class and was controlled to some degree by the Christian Church. Peasants' work was relieved by the Sabbath, church festivals, holidays, and aristocratic largesse. At one point, the Roman Church provided over 185 holy days or saint's days, creating leisure opportunities for the overworked peasantry. Sports, gambling, music, dance, and drinking were favorite pastimes for men. Women socialized in groups in the home. Children, when not working for their families, enjoyed simple games, rhymes, and stories. Protestant sects also had an impact on leisure, usually by restricting the types of activities that were allowed during free time.

Aristocrats benefited from the peasant labor and enjoyed riding, hunting, reading, and great feasts. On feast days the aristocrats invested in parades and heraldry, providing entertainment for the peasants while reinforcing aristocratic control over the social structure of the community.

Fairs and Trading

Another respite from the hard labor of peasant life was fairs and markets that visited locales to sell or barter crafts and goods. Fairs were held on a regular basis near urban areas, allowing the citizens a break from their business and exposure to new ideas and products that were brought to town by the traveling merchants. Fairs were a time for lavish display booths. Dancing bears, wrestling contests, stage shows, mountebanks selling the latest snake oil, and an occasional hanging or other form of public punishment contributed to the leisure amusement of travelers.

Renaissance: A Resurgence of Classical Values

The **Renaissance** marked the rebirth of the classical values of ancient Greece and Rome. People were conscious of a changing world around them and reveled in the idea that they were part of this evolution. The old anchors of feudalism and dedication to religion were slowly giving way to the emerging nation-states and the revival of interest in ancient Roman legal and literary studies. The center of this intellectual movement on the Italian peninsula between 1350 and 1525 was the city of Florence.

The Renaissance was an age of spectacles, filled with the mock combat of festival sports, the pomp and circumstance of processions, and the uproar of great citywide celebrations. Almost any occasion—a saint's day, the arrival of visiting nobility, the anniversary of a great battle, even the political reverses of some feared or hated prince—was reason enough for crowds to fill the streets with revelry. When there were no opportunities to celebrate, the people found outlet in hunts, ball games, horse races, boxing matches, snowball fights, racket games, gambling, dancing, musical entertainments, and banquets. The energy and enthusiasm of the Renaissance found expression in a wide variety of sports and games. Schoolmasters considered physical activity an essential part of the curriculum. Exercise was deemed a necessity for both young and old. The forerunners to tennis, baseball, and bowling were very popular. Physical activity was both utilitarian and enjoyable. It provided for the sound body in which a sound mind could exist, and it was fun.

The mature Renaissance gave way to an even more rationally oriented philosophy. Scientific

Photo courtesy of Lee deLisle

This mural on the wall of a palazzo in Tivoli, Italy, extols the virtues of reading, education, and fine arts for men and women of social means.

evidence and the Enlightenment were the underlying bases for the emergence of a humanist, romantic, secular philosophy that counteracted stoicism, asceticism, and religiosity. The **Enlightenment** was an 18th-century philosophical movement that freed people's minds from dependence on the supernatural and otherworldly rewards. Religious rule was replaced by an insistence on human reason rather than divine law, natural rights instead of supernaturalism, the scientific method rather than faith-based truths, social contracts and personal liberty rather than authoritarian mandate, and a humanitarian and democratic belief rather than aristocratic rule.

This was a time for learning based on scientific inquiry. The humanist-oriented concept that the human, not God, is the measure of all things played a great part in the recovery of leisure as an important aspect of human life.

Industrial Revolution

The **Industrial Revolution** was the movement toward centralized workplaces—factories that brought together large numbers of skilled and unskilled workers and great technological innovations in the production of goods. Factory work caused a previously unimagined segmentation of leisure. A farmer or craftsman working at home could take a break when needed, stop for lunch, and enjoy the company of family while completing their work tasks. Factory work settings broke the basic fabric of life, because free time was controlled by the employer in terms of both the amount of time available daily or weekly and the physical location of the worker. Leisure became segmented by gender, age, time of day, and day of the week. Leisure was further segmented by economic status, because the factory worker's life was similar to a form of economic slavery. Workers' rights were not considered, and eventually women and children (as young as nine years of age) entered the factory setting to contribute to the economic well-being of the family. Education for the young was an afterthought, and many social problems arose from the lack of supervision of children during the long workday of the parents. This problem led to the intervention of churches and philanthropic organizations and governmental agencies that addressed social issues by providing recreational services in urban settings.

The effects of the Enlightenment and the Industrial Revolution, a heightened awareness and reliance on science and reason, and the emergence of a large middle class produced inventions and discoveries and new cultural paradigms at an unprecedented pace. Distant unknown lands beckoned, and those with the financial ability sought to explore new worlds. The settling of North America by the Spanish, Dutch, English, and French created new opportunities for religious and economic advancement. With this new adventure came many of the problems of the Old World. Social problems arising from the difficulties of living and working in newly found cities were addressed in some respects by the development of private and public philanthropic services, including the provision of spaces and programs to meet the leisure needs of a new world.

The course of human history has seen several notable, major shifts in the basic character of social and communal living. Early humans, hunter-gathers, slowly embraced an agrarian lifestyle that allowed for the formation of societies and nation states. Peasants and their rulers embraced the system of feudalism until the lower classes sought more autonomy from aristocratic controls. From the guilds and cottage industries of Europe and the growth of the new colonies in America came a technological and industrial revolution that continues to affect our lives today.

Origins and Development of Recreational Services in the United States

With parents working up to 18 hours a day in factories, children were often left to fend for themselves in new cities along the East Coast of the United States. Churches and social leaders sought to remedy this situation initially by providing safe places for children to play, to literally get them off the streets. A philanthropic church-based effort to provide safe places for urban children to recreate, called the **playground movement**, began in the late 1800s. In 1868, the first outdoor playground was established in Boston under the guidance of the First Church of Boston. It was situated next to a public school and was associated with a vacation program. Nearby Brookline, Massachusetts, purchased land for the expressed desire of creating playgrounds in 1871.

This was followed by the designation of meadows in Chicago as a play area in 1876. Tennis courts, baseball diamonds, and other facilities were added in later years. In 1898, New York City opened 31 playgrounds under the supervision of the Board of Education.

By 1900, only a few U.S. cities provided public playgrounds. Today nearly all cities have recreational areas available, some with highly organized programs supervised by professional practitioners.

Along with the growth of social service–based recreational programming, there was, despite the efforts of the churches, an enormous increase in commercial amusements and recreation in early America. Drinking, theater performances, professional and amateur sports, and travel all captivated the imagination of the urban populations. Leisure activity, as was the case in so many other previous cultures, was delineated by class and wealth. Spectator sports ranged from loosely organized professional sports to the emergence of college sports and amateur events. Betting was common, and drinking was a part of the experience. Participative activities included athletic clubs, lawn sports such as tennis or croquet, bicycling, skating, and outdoor pursuits like hiking, fishing, camping, and visiting parks and natural sites. The health movement of the 19th century emphasized the value of outdoor experiences, particularly the seashore and natural spas, as restorative experiences for stressed-out city dwellers. Examples such as the Muscular Christianity movement of the 19th century emphasized the importance of active physical activity over passive entertainment. This focus on exercise and sport influenced other organizations, such as the YMCA, to include recreational sports as a part of their programs. Early support of recreational sports eventually led to the development of new sports such as basketball and volleyball.

By the early 20th century, a thriving leisure-based economy had emerged, fueled by government-sponsored recreation sites, commercial amusements, and

©Library of Congress

Factory work greatly enhanced economic growth in the United States but did so at great cost to individuals and families.

travel experiences. Labor unions fought to reduce the workweek to five days per week and eight hours per day, providing workers with increasing opportunities to participate in leisure activity. By 1940, the revision of the Fair Labor Standards Act reduced the work week to 40 hours. State and federal legislation imposed restrictions upon the number of hours children can work. White-collar and professional workers have enjoyed similar reductions in hours.

Labor-saving devices, competitive decreases in the cost of entertainment, better and faster transportation, and improved communication all served to expand leisure and its opportunities. Much of this wealth has been reinvested and consumed in the processes of further production; much has been wasted in wars and other enterprises that produced few social values; and much has been expended on social betterment, education, and recreational experience.

A recognition of the importance of leisure and recreational activities in terms of human and social value gained general acceptance. As work receded from its preeminent place in Western culture, religious leaders reconsidered the place of leisure in human life. The churches incorporated leisure into their philosophy and theology. The Puritan tradition, which viewed work as the antithesis of leisure, had been largely dispelled. Churches often support leisure and recreational activities, adopting techniques developed by practitioners in the field of recreational service. Methodists encouraged the camp meeting movement, which became permanent settlements in places like Oak Bluff on Martha's Vineyard and Ocean Grove, New Jersey. Chautauqua, originally a place to train Sunday school teachers in upstate New York, became the site for educational summer experiences that were the model of wholesome recreation for individuals and families. Catholic youth centers and Jewish community centers grew from the identified need to provide wholesome recreational opportunities for their respective communities.

During the 20th century, diverse entities began to address the need for professional preparation of recreational service providers, which led to the joining of these diverse groups of park and nature enthusiasts, sports leaders, youth social service providers, and recreation business leaders to eventually form the leading association for recreation professionals in the United States, the National Recreation and Park Association.

Heritage of the National Recreation and Park Association

A natural outcome of the development of parks and play spaces was the formation of an organization of individuals whose profession was supervising and maintaining public parklands. The first such meeting took place in Boston in 1898, marking the beginning of the New England Association of Park Superintendents. In 1904, the group was expanded and was referred to as the American Association of Park Superintendents. In 1921, the group promoted itself to the lofty title of the American Institute of Park Executives.

In a parallel development, the Playground Association of America was founded in Washington, DC, in 1906. This group was based on a social service model focusing on the provision of recreational services and programs. By 1911, the group saw the need to change its name to the Playground and Recreation Association of America. In 1926, a training school for recreational leadership was established to train executives in the profession of recreational management. In 1930, the name was again changed to the National Recreation Association. These newly trained professionals formed their own group, the Society of Recreation Workers of America, in 1938 and experienced growth in specific areas of recreational services including state, industrial, armed forces, rural, and hospital settings as well as a branch dedicated to professional education.

A merger of interests and organizations took place in 1965 with the formation of the National Recreation and Park Association. This association is the leading advocate for the promotion of recreational services and park-related activities in the United States. Annual conferences held in major cities throughout the United States provide more than 8,000 professionals with the opportunity for continuing education, professional development, and access to new equipment, programming ideas, and technologies. For a more extensive review of the development of the recreation and parks movement in the United States, visit the Joseph Lee Memorial Library and archives online at www.NRPA.org.

Recreational activity is now universally recognized as one of the basic needs of human life. When a need is deemed significant to society, government, as well as private and philanthropic enterprise, takes

On the Job

Heritage Sites

Some of the unusual types of parks, recreation, and tourism services that can be used to provide an understanding of how leisure has been viewed historically are heritage sites. These locations throughout the world provide an understanding of the cultural and natural heritage of the area. Professionals who work in these locations are not only serving in the current leisure industry by providing access to visitors from all over the world, but they are also a conduit for understanding the cultures of the past. Many of the professionals who work as tour guides or in interpretive centers in these locations have a deep understanding of the cultures that originated in these areas, including who the people were, how they interacted with each other and their surroundings, and how they played. Whether it is through petroglyphs, relics of toys, ancient ceremonies passed down through generations, or structures such as the Colosseum in Rome or the Great Pyramid of Egypt, we are able to learn much about the historical nature of leisure from professionals who serve these sites. Heritage sites showcase one of many diverse work environments you can seek as a leisure professional.

responsibility to meet that need for the mutual benefit and welfare of all concerned. Recreational activity is such an important aspect of life that modern society would suffer an inestimable loss without it.

Leisure, Recreation, and Quality of Life

From the social service foundations of recreational services in the late 19th century, we now recognize parks and recreation as an integral part of many communities providing year-round activities and special events that contribute to our quality of life. Since the 1950s, recreational services have grown in importance. Several trends since World War II have shaped the recreational services profession, including a growing concern for the protection of the natural environment; a stronger emphasis on the role of recreational activities in combating poverty and racial tension; additional recreational programming for girls and women; specialized disciplines within the profession to address the needs of military groups (morale, welfare, and recreation); programs for individuals with differing abilities; dedicated facilities and programs for the elderly; and the constant adjustment of the profession to the economic realities of the time (McClean, Hurd, & Rogers, 2005). Although all admit that recreational services are not the answer to the world's problems, recreational professionals continue to improve the quality of life of individuals and communities.

Increased expectations for quality leisure experiences and well-planned services create the need for professionally prepared individuals to address the social, physical, environmental, and economic requirements of the recreational industry. These services can be loosely grouped into three categories:

1. Governmentally based services, such as national and state parks, municipal parks and recreation departments, and other tax-based entities

2. Nonprofit organizations such as the Boys & Girls Clubs of America, scouting organizations, and faith-based organizations with a social imperative to improve the quality of life for citizens

3. Commercial enterprises that seek to provide recreational experiences combined with a private profit motive

During the past 40 years, recreational service provision in the public and nonprofit sectors has adopted many practices of the commercial approach to recreation. Community recreation departments have accepted the importance of marketing both the message of the benefits of recreation and the specific programs offered in their communities. Self-sufficiency typified by an entrepreneurial approach to service provision has allowed programs to grow despite governmental budget reductions. A majority of recreational programs now include a fee to cover some or all of the costs of operating a program or facility. There has been much debate over this, because public-based recreation must continue to provide services to all citizens while operating in a financially responsible manner. Private commercial enterprises have become more involved in providing recreational programs and services to local communities. The growth of the consumer mentality has coincided with the commodification or commercialization of recreational experiences for many families.

Recreational activity involves one third of our time, one third of our money, and one third of our land. It has become a major force in contemporary society. Recreational service providers in the 21st century are confronted by the same social and economic challenges that are present in the larger society. The statement that the future is not what it used to be illustrates the challenges ahead. Geopolitical upheavals such as war, occupation, and terrorism have made the future seem not quite as secure as it seemed several decades ago. The economic system based on the free market economy has faltered to the point of creating a lack of confidence in the current practices of large financial institutions. Although these challenges may be perceived as threats to survival, the average person continues to seek out meaningful expression through leisure activities. Variables including the environment, technology, demography, changing value systems, economics, health, and work versus free time have been identified as important factors in determining the future path of leisure services (Godbey, 1997). Leisure service providers in the current environment must become more agile and innovative. They must seek out cooperative relationships with competitors, make greater use of outsourced or contractual collaborators, analyze the product of their efforts in terms of benefits provided to the individual and the community, and become both entrepreneurial and "interpreneurial" by identifying and sharing common goals (Godbey, 1997). Service providers will need to provide customized services that meet the ever-changing needs of an increasingly diverse customer base. All of this will need to be accomplished while adapting to and incorporating new technologies that shape both the interests of the public and the means of delivering leisure services. Recreational professionals must shape the future of this long-standing relationship between leisure and human development.

Summary

Leisure and recreational activities both define and contribute to the advancement of human culture. Leisure and its use have added great value to life. The roots of education, the arts, and commercial entertainment are found in the perceived value of leisure and the activities associated with its use. Political and religious ideologies were formed and supported through the control of leisure.

Ancient tribes and civilizations were confronted with threats to their survival that limited the amount and quality of leisure made available to them. History tells us that when people had the luxury of leisure, they often made great strides in cultural and technological advancement.

Leisure contributed to the establishment of the greatest civilizations on Earth. The Egyptians, Greeks, and Romans, through their use of leisure, created the foundations of Western civilization. Theater, the arts, philosophy, science, politics and government, sports, and amusements all emanated from the use or misuse of leisure.

When the machinations of war and internecine strife were in the forefront, leisure was reduced, and civilization's advancement came to a halt. Peace and security are critical to human advancement and the realization of the benefits of leisure opportunities. As rationalism replaced superstition and humans created stable systems of government and land distribution, leisure reemerged, bringing an enlightened populace to new heights of discovery. At that time, the threats to quality living became economic rather than natural phenomena, yet war continues to limit our potential as individuals and communities. Threats to survival, and their impact on leisure and cultural advancement, will continue to challenge the status quo and the potential for the future.

The last quarter of the 20th century in the United States was an age of massive human leisure. In no epoch of the past has there ever been such a distribution of free time. The development of civilization, with organization, division of labor, mechanization, mass production, and automation, brought leisure within the grasp of all. The 21st century promises to be one of rapid change, adaptation, and continual discovery, as we pursue our personal and communal visions of human excellence.

Recreational service, mirroring the evolution of human culture, has evolved from a private and personally directed leisure experience to a highly complex, governmentally administered organization. Public, commercial, and voluntary institutions work side-by-side to provide essential opportunities for all members of a community.

But like the societies of the ancient world, there are obvious differences in the interests and activities of the various groups within any community. Western societies are constantly challenged by the possibilities that leisure presents. Are we to embrace the *schole* of ancient Greece and use our free time for contemplation of all that is good, to better ourselves and our communities through education and community service? Or are we to embrace only the bread and circuses of ancient Rome, with an emphasis on passive entertainment, conformity, and the devolution of social and moral standards?

We each must confront the challenge of leisure as we seek to define ourselves and our relationship to our communities. For those entering the recreational services profession, the challenge is to lead, to serve, and to inspire.

Learning Activity

If leisure is the basis of culture, you can analyze your personal culture by recording and analyzing your leisure activities. To do this, construct a spreadsheet to record all your daily activities for a 7-day period. The chart will include a cell for each of the 24 hours for all 7 days. Indicate what you do for each hour (e.g., sleep, attend classes, shop, engage in computer time, do homework, participate in various social or recreational activities). Classify activities as obligatory or discretionary. Summarize your findings, identifying quantitative information like your average hours of sleep, screen time, work, and school for the week (numerical descriptions) and qualitative observations about your activities. You can further examine your leisure activity by creating a second chart to track all of your discretionary (nonessential) purchases for the same week. Identify what you have learned about your behaviors through this exercise.

Review Questions

1. Explain why leisure is considered to be the basis of culture. Give three examples of how leisure shapes personal and communal culture.

2. Why do we consider leisure to be free time?

3. How do threats to survival affect leisure? Compare one ancient threat to survival to a contemporary threat from your own life experiences.

4. Identify some prehistoric activities that may have enhanced leisure for early humans.

5. What was *schole* and how does it help us to understand ancient Greek leisure activity?

6. Give two examples of the Greek idea of *arête* in modern society.

7. What role did slaves play in the accumulation of leisure in ancient societies?

8. How did the Pax Romana contribute to leisure in ancient Rome?

9. How was leisure used by the Roman rulers as a form of social control?

10. What were blood sports all about? Provide a 21st-century example of our continued fascination with this type of entertainment.

11. What was so dark about the Dark Ages? How did this period affect leisure?

12. *Renaissance* means "rebirth"; what was reborn during this era? How did this affect leisure?

13. How did the Enlightenment improve people's ways of thinking?

14. How did the Industrial Revolution permanently alter our way of life relative to leisure?

15. Identify the major transitional points in the development of the recreational movement in the United States.

16. What are the three categories of organizations that typically provide recreational services? Provide one example of each.

17. Why is it important for students of the 21st century to understand the leisure attitudes and practices of past civilizations?

18. How can this knowledge of the past help you to maximize your own leisure?

Go to HK*Propel* to access additional learning content.

Contemporary Leisure

Brett Lashua

University College London

VOCABULARY TERMS

contemporary leisure   **culture wars**   **paradigm**
critical theory   **functionalism**   **technology**
cultural hegemony   **generations**

LEARNING OUTCOMES

At the end of this chapter, you will

- understand different ways of viewing contemporary leisure;
- consider the centrality of technology for your generation;
- have a greater sociological understanding of leisure and culture;
- develop different definitions of popular culture; and
- explore the politics of popular leisure and recent culture wars.

This chapter explores contemporary leisure through a focus on popular culture. The word *contemporary* means "existing or happening now" (Cambridge Dictionary, 2020). In order to develop understandings of what is happening now and how we arrived at this existing moment, the chapter also looks at contemporary leisure through historical and sociological theoretical lenses. This helps place contemporary leisure in context, to illustrate how leisure is made meaningful or meaningfully constructed. It also allows insights into a crucial question: how does social change occur? Exploring contemporary leisure through sociological, historical, and popular cultural views can help us to answer this question.

This chapter first explores the impact of technological innovations on **generations** before turning to definitions of popular culture. Here, the chapter initially wrestles with sociological theories of culture and then dismantles different meanings of the word *popular*. Finally, the many debates and questions raised throughout the chapter about technology, generations, popular culture, and contemporary leisure are brought together through a consideration of the culture wars, or recent debates over the values,

beliefs, and practices that increasingly play out in popular leisure and social media. By the end of the chapter, you should be able to look at contemporary leisure and recognize varying ways that it represents or *signifies* important social issues, shared values, and vital conflicts over changes in contemporary society.

As a kind of thought experiment to try to defamiliarize the familiar and see the world with fresh eyes, consider what your daily leisure would be like without contemporary technologies. Can you imagine life without the Internet, smartphones, tablets, laptops, and other digital devices? What would you

Westend61/Getty Images

Technology has changed the way we communicate and has shaped our leisure.

CHAPTER 7 • Contemporary Leisure | 101

do in the absence of media streaming? How would you interact and stay connected with friends and family without social media? Perhaps it is difficult to imagine your leisure—and even your identity or sense of self—without these technologies.

Generations

However commonplace they may seem now, recent technological innovations have transformed contemporary leisure for an entire generation—Generation Z (those born from 1996-2010). This is a generation of digital natives, having grown up with digital technologies and not knowing what life was like before the Internet and online connectivity were enmeshed in almost every aspect of people's lives.

In many ways, each generation—and its popular leisure—is shaped by the technologies that come to characterize it. For example, while rock 'n' roll has become a defining feature of leisure for the post–World War II baby boomer generation (those born between 1945-1964), a number of key technological innovations facilitated the rise of rock 'n' roll (Peterson, 1990):

- The invention of transistors allowed production of portable record players and radios.
- Vinyl records were less brittle than shellac records and therefore easier to distribute widely across the country.
- Beginning in the 1950s, television made it possible for regional musicians such as Elvis Presley to be seen and heard by larger national audiences.

In sum, these technologies had social impacts; they facilitated a new identity category—the teenager—characterized by the consumption of the new leisure products of popular culture. Rock 'n' roll and vinyl records became emblematic of the baby boomer generation.

Consider this extension of the example: Later generations of teenagers (Generation X, born between 1965-1979; Generation Y, born between 1980-1995; and Generation Z) have been characterized by the technologies that shaped their leisure—portable cassette players (du Gay et al., 1997) for Generation X, the iPod and digital MP3 files (Bull, 2005) for Generation Y, and streaming services (Lashua, 2011) for Generation Z. By tuning in to technological changes and contemporary trends, we can read popular culture to learn about leisure, youthful identities, society, and generational change—for example, for Generation Z, leisure has become increasingly globalized, interconnected, immediate, and commercialized.

In order to understand contemporary leisure, it is important to understand generational changes. For example, when computers and early versions of the Internet became increasingly available in the 1990s, some theorists considered a new identity category then, too: the global cybercitizen, or netizen (Rheingold, 1993). In current social media environments facilitated by smartphones, mobile connectivity, and user-generated content and on social media platforms such as YouTube, Facebook, Instagram, Twitter, Snapchat, TikTok, and others, it could be argued that a new category of leisure identity for Generation Z is the "prosumer"—consumers who

---

On the Job

Technology Across Generations

One of the challenges leisure professionals face is adapting to changing **technology** for participants across generations. Technology can change how we provide services in many positive ways, such as the creative methods many used in the COVID-19 pandemic. Parks, recreation, and tourism organizations were able to maintain services by offering remote fitness classes, museum tours, contactless delivery for restaurants, and even videos of animals such as penguins at zoos. Forced creativity enabled organizations to find different opportunities to grow as professionals, some of which were expected to continue beyond the pandemic. However, while the convenience of technology has helped in these situations, it is important to realize that technology does not provide equal access to all. In addition to limitations based on income level, adults from different generations may have differing abilities to access services based on an understanding of how these new technologies work. Thus, it is important for professionals to find methods of maintaining communication with participants across generations to understand their needs in adapting services through technology so that they are still able to engage in services as much as possible.

produce online content. In essence, contemporary technologies shape what we do, who we are, and how we relate to and differ from other generations.

Ways of Seeing, Ways of Knowing

When considering changing technologies, generations, and contemporary leisure practices, history is useful where it allows us to understand change. By inviting you to think about social and technological changes, this chapter asks you to consider how different theories and paradigms (Kuhn, 1962) or ways of seeing shape our understanding of contemporary leisure and popular culture. A **paradigm** is a set of "scientific theories, experimental practices, training methods and forms of professional organization and publication" that "cluster together" to characterize and define how we see the world (Hamilton, 1997, p. 78). In other words, a paradigm is a worldview that shapes what we choose to see as meaningful, the kinds of questions we are able to ask about the world, and dominant and alternative approaches to knowledge production.

For example, in the 19th century, many viewed society (and culture) as ordered naturally, as in biological and physical sciences. This idea was challenged in the early 20th century by a new paradigm that argued that our social worlds are not natural or given but constructed through ideas and actions. There are many, often conflicting, paradigms; however, an important point is to recognize the ways that any paradigm shapes what we are able to see and understand as real, meaningful, valuable, and legitimate knowledge. The next section begins to explore popular culture through two different paradigms by examining the words *popular* and *culture*. This is important in developing a framework, or worldview, of what constitutes contemporary leisure and how it may be understood in a changing world.

Defining *Popular* and *Culture*: Historical and Sociological Views

Both *popular* and *culture* are complex terms. When attempting to define popular culture, or what Sharpe and Lashua (2008) described as "popular leisure," it is useful to decouple these terms to try to make sense of each word independently. According to the cultural theorist Raymond Williams (1983, p. 87), "culture is one of the two or three most complicated words in the English language." Although he didn't specify what the other words were, it is not difficult to imagine that *popular* and *leisure* are just as difficult to define as *culture*. Each definition draws from particular paradigms, or ways of seeing, and each definition has its own set of advantages and disadvantages; therefore, it is necessary to take these into account, too.

Defining Culture

Scholars have defined culture in a number of ways. One tradition has defined culture as "the best that has been thought and said in a society. It is the great ideas, as represented in classical works of literature, painting, music, and philosophy" and thus associated with "high culture" (Hall, 1997, p. 2). In this sense, being cultured was seen as "a general process of intellectual, spiritual and aesthetic development" (Williams, 1983, p. 90); that is, refined, or somehow better. Many leisure activities continue to bear the impression of this view, although—as discussed later in the chapter—this conceptualization has been heavily critiqued as limited and elitist.

Another, less-exclusive view is that of culture composed of "widely-distributed forms of popular music, publishing, art, design and literature, or the activities of leisure-time or entertainment, which make up a majority of the lives of 'ordinary people'" (Hall, 1997, p. 2). Such activities can be seen as mass culture or popular culture, yet again these draw considerations of high versus low culture and the positive or negative values associated with each. On one hand, this view moves the ideas of culture away from the domain of the elite, as again in the words of Williams, "culture is ordinary" (1958, p. 75); yet, on the other hand, here we begin to encounter the challenges of the unpacking of the values associated with the word *popular* and its powerful connotations

---

Self-Exploration

What does the word *culture* mean to you? Jot down five words that you think of when you hear the word *culture*. Then browse the online culture or arts and entertainment section of a major news outlet. Note the keywords and activities presented. What similarities or differences do you notice between your view of culture and what you see on these websites?

of mass consumerism—to be dealt with later in the chapter.

A third conceptualization from sociological and anthropological traditions considers culture as a way of life that is learned and transmitted across generations. For sociologists, "culture is made up of all of the ideas, beliefs, behaviors, and products common to, and defining, a group's way of life" (Stolley, 2005, p. 41). This definition of culture "allows us to speak of such practices as the seaside holiday, the celebration of Christmas, and youth subcultures, as examples of culture. These are usually referred to as lived cultures or practices" (Storey, 2018, p. 2). This concept clearly connects important ideas to leisure and what leisure represents (e.g., family, religion, or rebelliousness).

The definition of culture as a way of life centralizes the social construction of meaning. While there are numerous theoretical views of the construction of cultural meanings, the next part of the chapter will focus on two key worldviews: functionalism and critical theory.

Functionalism

Characterized by a search for "patterns of normative expectations and guidelines governing acceptable behavior" (Giddens & Sutton, 2017, p. 83), functionalism was part of the foundations of sociological thinking at the end of the 19th century and remained dominant through the 1960s. Shared social expectations and accepted behaviors were seen as parts of the functioning of society in which particular social structures or institutions, such as schools and families as well as recreation and leisure services, were important parts of a cohesive society. This view—also called structural functionalism—was championed by early sociologists including August Comte (1865/2009) and Émile Durkheim (1893/1984) and later by American sociologists such as Talcott Parsons (1937). In a functionalist framework, society is seen as a complex system of parts that ideally work together to promote solidarity and stability—that is, a fully functioning society. Another way of characterizing functionalism is to view society like a body, with a number of organs that must work together in order to keep the body healthy and stable (Giddens, 1984). In addition to schools and families, such organs include religion, government, and social class; media and sports can be viewed as emergent social structures, too.

Functionalism centralizes common, shared cultural activities that create and sustain solidarity and produce collective cultural norms, values, and expectations that endure over time. For example, some sports, such as baseball, reinforce widely held values such as fair play and teamwork as well as patriotic or nationalistic values within the United States. So, too, the kinds of books that young people read or should not read in schools form an important way that young people are socialized through cultural activities (Lashua, 2016).

Functionalist views usefully point out the role of culture in shaping collective beliefs, shared identities, and societal norms. These are deeply embedded in recreation and leisure services and research—for example, the rational recreation movement of the 20th century (Stormann, 1991) sought to improve society by improving citizens' pastimes physically, socially, and morally and by replacing amusements seen as cheap or crude (see Bailey, 2014). Functionalist perspectives of contemporary leisure and culture are evident in many recreation programs for young people, particularly those deemed at risk. Here, the metaphor of an organ that needs to function well for the health of a larger body can be seen clearly: youth leisure programs should produce good citizens, which will in turn help produce a good society.

The idea of leisure, media, and sports—culture—as parts of a wider structural social machinery that requires its parts to function well in order to have a functioning society has been critiqued and challenged. After all, not everyone would agree about what ideas or behaviors constitute a functioning society, particularly one that is rife with social inequality. What kinds of activities count in this view, and who gets to say so? Indeed, functionalism was critiqued for failing to consider conflicts created by differences of class, race, gender, sexuality, age, and other markers and also for focusing too much attention on consensus and social cohesion at the expense of conflict, individual agency, and free choice. What may be seen as the development of a functioning society for some may be seen as sharply oppressive, unequal, and unjust for others.

In this sense, cultural activities in recreation, leisure, and sports are not necessarily always good or beneficial at a macrosocietal level, as many are part of the reproduction of structural inequalities. For example, marginalized young people deemed at risk may reject or resist social norms and values that are oppressive or exclusive. The arena of culture becomes one of the key sites where functionalism fails most in its inability to account for conflict and the need for social change. Seeing culture in this way requires a different worldview—a paradigm shift—to focus on culture and difference through critical theory.

Critical Theory

Critiques of functionalism emerged in the 1920s, often as a response to the incredible rise of mass consumer culture and debates that arose about the perceived value, or harm, that mass culture—and thus mass leisure—was having in modern capitalist and democratic societies. One group of scholars that emerged during these years at the Institute of Social Research in Frankfurt (known as the Frankfort School) sought to understand the role of culture and cultural change in mass culture that increasingly characterized industrialized societies and social institutions such as the family, education, work, and leisure. While not a singular body of thought, the Frankfurt School developed varying strands of what became known, collectively, as critical theory.

Critical theory (Horkheimer, 1937) seeks to understand how dominant ruling ideologies (the ideas of those in power) conceal oppressive social relations and help to preserve the status quo. Consumerism, especially the consumption of mass leisure goods and services, and the ways that consumer societies reproduce dominant social relations, became an explicit early focus of critical theory.

Critical theorists of the Frankfurt School were highly skeptical of popular culture such as music and cinema (Adorno, 1941; Benjamin, 1936/1968). These activities were distractions from the everyday social, political, and economic realities of working-class people and thus part of the means by which the ruling classes continued to exert control over the masses, thereby preserving elite interests and tastes (Skeldon, 2017).

Critical theory differed from functionalism in a number of ways. Primarily, in attempting to grapple with questions of why societies change, it addressed questions of power, conflict, and inequalities that were largely glossed over in the way that functionalism treated culture. The critical theoretical turn toward cultural conflict also led to increased attention to cultural texts as *signifiers* in the production of cultural meanings. As important signifiers, or signs, cultural texts such as music, films, comics, magazines, advertisements, and commercials were seen as important sites in the production, consumption, and representation of cultural meanings and also the construction of identities, communities, and cultures (Hall, 1997). This means that popular culture—especially leisure—is an important site to study contemporary societies and social change. In further view of social change, popular culture was also seen as an important site for resistance to challenge dominant views and cultural values.

Although attentive to the social, economic, and political forces in people's lives, critical theory was criticized for treating people as easily manipulated masses or cultural dupes without the ability to shape or change their own worlds. The degree of effects that media have in people's lives and dispositions remains hotly debated. Some have argued, for example, that playing violent video games or watching violent films causes violence or that listening to sexually overt or violent music can lead to teenagers being troubled; this is why parental advisory stickers that warn of explicit content are widely used. Yet the idea of media effects has been largely debunked (Barker & Petley, 1997). Although popular culture and mass media are influential, they cannot make anyone do anything. The idea that people are passive masses unaware that they are being manipulated strips popular culture of its potential meaningfulness in people's individual, everyday lives. As Williams cautioned, there is no such thing as masses, "only ways of seeing people as masses" (1960, p. 319). Here, finally, it is necessary to turn to the other half of the term *popular culture* and begin to unpack the varying meanings and uses of the word *popular*.

Defining Popular

This part of the chapter draws from Storey's (2018) six definitions of the word *popular* in *popular culture*. Not only do these definitions sit at the heart of this chapter in helping to make sense of contemporary leisure, but they also showcase where the preceding sociological views of culture play out.

Storey's First Definition: Widely Favored and Well Liked

One "obvious starting point" for Storey (2018, p. 5) is with a quantitative definition. Here popular is defined as "widely-favored and well-liked by many people" (p. 5). In contemporary leisure, this definition can be seen in things such as audience figures for sport or recreation participation; the popularity of new trends, fads, or games (e.g., number of items sold or number of people participating); in music (e.g., number of digital downloads); in cinema (e.g., number of tickets sold); or on social media (e.g., number of likes).

The rising popularity of esports (i.e., competitive video gaming) may be seen as an outstanding example; competitions include popular games as *League of Legends*, *Overwatch*, and *Super Smash Bros*. Audiences for esports reached 474 million people in 2021 (Gough, 2021) and generated revenues over $1 billion (Gough, 2020). For comparison, Major League Baseball and Minor League Baseball had a combined audience of 110 million people in 2019 (Major League Baseball, 2019). While these are indeed large figures, the question remains: Does this mean esports are popular? Many do not consider them to be real sports and wouldn't think so. Popularity depends on more than numbers.

A problem with this definition is the difficulty of "agree[ing] on a figure over which something becomes popular culture, and below which it is just culture" (Storey, 2018, pp. 5-6). How many likes must a YouTube video have to be considered popular? How many participants must a cultural activity have—for example, dressing or performing in drag (see Skeldon, 2017)—for it to be viewed as popular? If the number is too small, this definition risks including too much, or if it's too large,

Esports attract increasingly large audiences.

Pedro Pavante/Riot Games via Getty Images

it risks excluding too much (e.g., books that were not best sellers but are today considered classics). The number of social media users globally—3.96 billion people in July 2020 (Kemp, 2020)—tells us that social media is widely favored but not why or how it is used meaningfully in people's lives. Finally, this simple, quantitative measure ignores issues, highlighted previously, of which parts of culture count as *popular* culture and who gets to say so. This draws us back to issues of contemporary leisure and popular culture as questions of good versus bad culture or high versus low culture.

Storey's Second Definition: High Versus Low Culture

Indeed, most of the activities that are generally perceived as popular culture are often characterized—hierarchically—as low culture. For Storey's second definition, popular culture is frequently defined as inferior or "the culture that is left over after we have decided what is high culture. . . texts and practices that fail to meet the required standards to qualify as high culture" (2018, p. 6). Mitchell and Reid-Walsh (2002) described this as the junk food perspective, where popular culture is likened to sugary treats—tasty but not nutritious; neither good for you nor worthy of serious academic attention (Sharpe & Lashua, 2008). Again, a key question here that draws us back to matters of power and conflict (rather than functionalist notions of consensus and shared tastes) is who determines what counts as high culture? The cultural elites?

In addition, this definition is weak when considering how cultural change occurs. Some practices that were once seen as low culture—Shakespearean theater, for example—have since become associated with high culture and elite tastes. In music, many popular groups have moved into the spheres of high culture by being enshrined in museums, knighted by Britain's queen, and otherwise honored with awards conferring the status of national treasures. Yet many of these musicians and their popular music were previously seen as among the lowest forms of consumer culture pandering to the masses and teenager sensibilities.

Alternately, some pursuits once associated with high culture and cultural elites can become mainstream and be viewed as popular pastimes. One only needs to think again of Shakespeare, whose plays have been frequently reimagined as Hollywood films, becoming nonelite, popular fare once more:

> ## Self-Exploration
>
> Can you think of examples of leisure pastimes you enjoy that were once seen as low culture but are now viewed as high culture? What about the inverse—do you participate in leisure activities that were once seen as high culture but are no longer viewed as elite? Why do you think perceptions of these activities have changed?

Romeo + Juliet (Luhrman, 1996), *Gnomeo & Juliet* (Asbury, 2011), *10 Things I Hate About You* (Junger, 1999), *Strange Magic* (Rydstrom, 2015), and *My Own Private Idaho* (van Zant, 1996). In sum, the distinctions of high and low culture are very blurry and change over time, making this definition of popular not particularly useful.

Storey's Third Definition: Mass Produced for Mass Consumption

A third definition of popular from Storey (2018) that is useful when considering contemporary leisure focuses on mass culture that has been "mass produced for mass consumption" (p. 34). Drawn from both functionalism and the Frankfurt School theorists, this definition considers popular culture as "hopelessly commercial" (Storey, 2018, p. 8). In this view of popular culture, "Its audience is a mass of non-discriminating consumers. The culture itself is formulaic, manipulative (to the political right or left, depending on who is doing the analysis). It is a culture that is consumed with brain-numbed and brain-numbing passivity" (Storey, 2018, p. 8). Amongst critiques of consumer leisure cultures (Coalter, 2000; Roberts, 2006), here also are echoes of the generic lumping together of groups of people into supposedly docile and easily controlled masses (as noted previously), without individual free choice and agency.

This definition also presumes that mass-produced and mass-consumed leisure cannot be highly valued (in the sense that many may place a lot of value in such pursuits). Numerous examples of fan cultures center on mass-produced and mass-consumed toys, comics, pop music, films, TV series, sport paraphernalia, or other collectible items, through which many people construct a strong sense of social identity and community (Jenkins, 2012; Lamerichs, 2011). In short, the idea of popular culture as mass-produced consumerism is a weak definition, as noted previously in view of culture, where it fails to consider the diverse ways that people use and make meaning from the products that they consume. Critiques of mass culture as alienating and dehumanizing succeed, to an extent, on a macro level of social organization (Grindstaff, 2008) but are less persuasive on a micro level of analysis of individuals, friends, and families in their local, everyday, and interpersonal relations.

Storey's Fourth Definition: Authentic

As a fourth definition, Storey (2018, p. 9) offers yet another set of meanings with popular being somehow understood as an authentic culture that is "of the people" or a genuine folk culture. This ideal of culture "actually made by the people for themselves" (Williams, 1983, p. 237) differs from earlier definitions in which popular culture is somehow imposed on people (i.e., masses) from above (e.g., by elites or corporate forces) (Storey, 2018). Here again is a distinction raised by the Frankfurt School of critical theorists about authenticity when considering culture that is mass produced for mass consumption (Adorno, 1941; Benjamin, 1936/1968; Witkin, 2000); that is, mass-consumed leisure cannot be genuine or authentic if it does not originate from the people—which in this case refers to the working classes. This characterization, however, is highly problematic. One problem is that it takes on an overly romantic view of working-class cultures and their authentically folksy organic pastimes that are also somehow a kind of protest against capitalism or commercialization (Storey, 2018). Such views also risk overromanticizing the past as a better, simpler, or somehow more authentic time.

Further problems emerge when considering popular culture as both authenticity and being of the people. What is authentic? Which people make this culture? These are thickets of complicated ideas and historical developments. First, seemingly authentic pastimes (such as baseball) are often borrowed or iterative versions of activities that originated elsewhere and have traveled, changing along the way (Hise, 2010). Popular music serves as perhaps the best case in point here. Rock 'n' roll emerged in the United States in the early 1950s at the confluence of different cultural crossroads and African American styles but quickly became associated with, and then representative of, predominantly White middle-class teenagers from the baby boomer generation (see Lashua, 2019). There is nothing innately authentic about rock 'n' roll, yet it is often constructed mythologically as an authentic element of 1950s teenage popular culture.

This points quickly to a second problem, where claims of cultures that originate from the people invite sharp questioning, as notions of the people are often exclusive and restrictive: "who qualifies for inclusion in the category 'the people'?" asked Storey (2018, p. 9). Taking baseball again as an example of a popular activity that was once seen as an authentic pastime, for many years the game was exclusive of African Americans and other minority people. Even today, the sport continues to exclude female players and coaches, especially at the professional level; it wasn't until 2020 that the San Francisco Giants hired Alyssa Nakken as the first female coach in Major League Baseball history. Other contemporary leisure activities that may appear open or welcome to all people remain exclusionary: They operate in exclusive areas or neighborhoods, have expensive admission costs, or they are otherwise prohibitive based on long-established traditions or norms about who belongs. The emergence of video game culture provides another good case, where technological industries and hypermasculine gaming communities (Delamere & Shaw, 2008) drew widespread attention for sexism and harassment directed toward women in the 2014 #GamerGate scandal (see Mortensen, 2018). In sum, from a critical theoretical viewpoint, pastimes that are purportedly of the people are often only inclusive of some people, but not others. From this perspective, popular culture becomes something else: a battleground.

Storey's Fifth Definition: Cultural Hegemony

Storey's (2018) fifth definition of popular may be the most important. Here Storey engages with the idea of popular culture as a contested terrain and a site of struggle over cultural meanings and practices between subordinate groups (i.e., resistance) and the interests and forces (i.e., incorporation) of dominant groups. Along with these two terms—*resistance* and *incorporation*—it is necessary to introduce a third: *cultural hegemony*.

Drawing from the ideas of the Italian theorist Antonio Gramsci (1891-1937), Storey (2018, p. 10) explains **cultural hegemony** as "the way in which dominant groups in society, through a process of 'intellectual and moral leadership', seek to win the consent of subordinate groups in society." That is, a ruling or elite class of people and their way of life usually do not remain in a dominant social position through force. Rather, there is a *negotiation* between dominant and subordinate groups. This negotiation often plays out in leisure as attempts to define, maintain, and delineate class distinctions of high and low culture. Furthermore, cultural hegemony

> can also be used to explore and explain conflicts involving ethnicity, "race," gender, generation, sexuality, disability, etc.—all are at different moments engaged in forms of cultural struggle against the homogenizing forces of incorporation of the official or dominant culture. (Storey, 2018, p. 11)

Here the term *incorporation* refers to the ways that a cultural form that is initially seen as new, resistant, or revolutionary is brought into the mainstream and normalized through processes of commodification. It is marketed and sold as a new or edgy consumer product, but it is largely unchanged. Skateboarding could be seen as a prime example here. Skateboarding developed as a radical do-it-yourself, anticon-

sumerist youth subculture in the early 1970s (made possible in part due to the technological innovation of urethane wheels) that was resistant to mainstream or dominant society (Borden, 2001). As the subculture grew and was perceived as a potential threat to dominant sports and the social values those sports represented, skating's signs, symbols, and artifacts (fashions, hairstyles, lifestyles, skate parks, and skateboarding equipment) were incorporated and turned into consumer products.

Cultural hegemony involves the *negotiation* between the forces of incorporation and resistance; therefore, it is important to note that in this process, neither side wins. For example, on one hand, skateboarding has developed as a cool and widely accepted lifestyle sport (Wheaton, 2004); on the other hand, it is no longer a resistant threat to mainstream sports, because it is now part of vast commercial sport industries and sport institutions, with codified rules, professional competitions, and leagues. This conversion is a process termed *sportification* (D'Orazio, 2020; see Thorpe and Wheaton [2011] for a discussion of incorporation and the X

Sean Justice/The Image Bank RF/Getty Images

Are extreme sports a form of cultural resistance, or are they now mainstream?

Games). Other definitions of popular as discussed previously can be seen at work here, too—for example, skateboarding as well-liked, as high versus low culture, as mass produced for mass consumption, as authentic, or of the people—but none of these previous definitions adequately contextualizes popular culture as well as hegemony in relation to critical questions of social transformation. That is, in adopting new cultural forms by commodifying them, dominant groups (and their ideas) must change. As new, innovative, or resistant cultural practices are commodified, they often grow and become more "popular" but must also change in ways that make them less threatening to mainstream values and conventions. In this manner, signs of resistant leisure activities (e.g., tattoos; see Thompson, 2019) become mainstream. Rather than challenging the dominant order of things, they become part of it, albeit in a safer manifestation. Additional examples abound where contemporary leisure practices that were once viewed as underground, alternative, or counterhegemonic are now widely accepted and relatively tamed, such as bicycle motocross (BMX), surfing, or mixed martial arts. In sum, it is important to understand contemporary leisure as a contested terrain of hegemonic struggle and negotiation or a battleground between varying forces of incorporation and resistance (Sharpe, 2017).

As Storey (2018) noted, cultural hegemony is an important way to understand social transformation not only in terms of class, but also gender, race, sexualities, (dis)abilities, age, and generations. After all, younger generations often try to differentiate themselves and change the world through contemporary, popular leisure practices that resist older generations and established practices. Yet, as with previous definitions, as a way to explain popular culture, hegemony theory is not above critique. Its view of dominance and resistance has been seen as too binary, setting up simplistic power blocs that are too rigid and totalizing; things are not often so simple or directional as (top-down) dominance and (bottom-up) resistance (Sharpe, 2017).

Storey's Sixth Definition: Postmodern

As a final characterization, Storey describes popular culture as informed by debates around postmodernism. In briefest terms, "postmodern culture is a culture that no longer recognizes the distinction between high and popular culture" and is characterized by a "blurring of the distinction between 'authentic' and 'commercial' culture" (Storey, 2018, p. 12). Postmodernism emerged in the 1970s as one way to explain social changes due to the declining influences of social institutions that were formally seen as stable and true (Lyotard, 1984), such as shifting ideas around families, gender, sexualities, and communities. Other characteristics of postmodern popular culture are the blending of old and new styles (e.g., retro being considered cool in fashion, music, or art); the repurposing and remaking of urban spaces (e.g., the use of former factories or warehouses, which are prime examples of modernity, for nightclubs, restaurants, or other consumer leisure spaces); and the swirling of vast amounts of media.

Furthermore, along with blurred postmodern distinctions of high and low culture, globalization has brought about the increased blurring of work and leisure, blending of local and global cultures (e.g., in popular music or in food cultures), and an increasingly fluid sense of self-identity. As a set of ideas, postmodernism also questions traditional views of popular culture as capable of being explained by singular grand narratives, such as capitalism or democracy. While some celebrate the freedom of postmodern ideas to use culture as a bank of resources that can be selected or mixed in new and creative ways beyond the rigidity of fixed ideas (indeed, remix culture is a great example of postmodernism), others lamented the loss of former certainties and despaired the "final victory of commerce over culture" (Storey, 2018, p. 12). When hip-hop is used to sell luxury products or luxury lifestyles are hailed as environmental protests, or when celebrities are more influential than politicians but almost anyone can become a celebrity influencer via social media, these are characteristics of postmodern culture. Postmodernism remains an apt way of characterizing contemporary leisure, even if it is also frustrating in what it offers to make sense of complex leisure and popular cultural worlds.

Self-Exploration

Make a list of five of your favorite contemporary leisure activities. Then try to decide which of Storey's (2018) definitions of popular culture most aptly characterize your choices. Add to your list by considering the favorable and unfavorable critiques of each definition.

Culture Wars and the Politics of Popular Leisure

Popular culture and the contemporary leisure pastimes that are subsumed within it are powerful arenas of social relations, and thus also conflict. Furthermore, the two sociological views that have been outlined previously (functionalism and critical theory—including subsequent theoretical turns toward critical feminism and critical race theory) remain very much in play in explanations of contemporary leisure and are characteristic of the social divides that have become known as culture wars.

The phrase *culture wars* refers to the polarization of societal views on change, values, morality, and lifestyles. Originally described by Hunter (1991) during the 1990s, culture wars in the United States centered on debates over freedoms regarding issues such as gun laws, religion and the state, abortion, parenting, free speech and censorship, drug use, LGBTQ+ (lesbian, gay, bisexual, transgender, questioning, and other sexual orientations and gender identities) rights, and privacy. These debates played out in discussions of controversial popular media (such as hip-hop music, video games, television series, and cinema) concerning the kind of society Americans had and the kind of society they ideally wanted (Hartman, 2019).

In the 21st century, culture wars have continued, with expanded debates about race and equality, sexism and sexual harassment, social class and inequality, sexual equality, transgender rights, climate change. While the culture wars have widely played out on TV series and in popular music, they have increasingly taken form online via forums and discussion boards and social media platforms such as Facebook, Instagram, and Twitter.

As spheres of public debate, the culture wars are useful examples that help to showcase a number of varying threads about contemporary leisure running through this chapter. First, they highlight the generational inflections of contemporary leisure, with older generations generally less progressive than younger ones. Second, the culture wars are highly indicative of the increasing role of digital technologies in shaping contemporary leisure and generational lifestyle politics. Third, they broadly represent the different ways of looking at leisure and popular culture through historical and sociological lenses (i.e., paradigms). These views spotlight where leisure pastimes are viewed as good for a functional society (for cohesion and collective values), whereas critical views argue that analyses of leisure and cultural practices reveal where society is inequitable and where changes should occur. Fourth, the complicated meanings of both parts of the term *popular culture* show that contemporary leisure and popular culture matter as sites of contested meanings and values. In sum, considering contemporary leisure is not so much about counting how many or which activities are currently happening or trendy now, but rather attempting to engage with questions of why and how contemporary leisure matters as part of people's differing ways of life.

Summary

This chapter began by asking you to consider life without technology such as smartphones, social media, and the Internet. It then asked you to ponder differences between generations and the technologies that have characterized them. One point of this thought experiment was to begin to consider social change and the ways that changes in recreation and leisure have illustrated or signified broader cultural questions and societal worldviews.

Accordingly, the chapter framed two sociological paradigms—functionalism and critical theory—to contextualize culture and make sense of contemporary leisure in society. These two views of culture were then linked to Storey's (2018) six definitions of the term *popular*, particularly as a contested terrain between dominant and subordinate cultural groups in society. In this sense, contemporary leisure is a key site in struggles over the meanings, values, and legitimacy that can be seen in the culture wars over what counts as best for society and who gets to say so. More importantly, studying contemporary leisure offers crucial insights beyond what is exciting or happening now, highlighting ways that we can identify how the world has or has not changed and asking what kinds of social transformations we might wish to see next.

Learning Activities

1. Watch a film or read a book (I recommend science fiction or young adult fiction). Try to identify the sociological worldview that frames the film or book (functionalism or critical theory). For example, Suzanne Collins' *The Hunger Games* is a series of books and films about leisure, social control, and resistance in a dystopian society.

2. Record an interview with someone much older than you and ask about their generation, the technological innovations, and the kinds of popular culture they enjoyed as a teenager. Listen to the interview later and construct an analysis of why popular culture mattered to your interviewee and consider how things have changed.

3. Spend some time on Twitter. Identify threads you think are examples of culture wars, with debates about the values and transformational potential of popular culture and contemporary leisure. Identify and discuss whether functionalism or critical theory are illustrated in the threads.

4. Contemporary leisure is often politically partisan, and activism is a long-standing arena of leisure. Research a contemporary movement (e.g., for environmental sustainability, for racial justice, for gender equity, for LGBTQ+ rights) and discuss how this movement aligns with some of the ideas in this chapter about sociological worldviews, popular culture, technology, generations, and social change.

5. If the world has changed for you and your generation's leisure, how do you think it will change for the next generation?

Review Questions

1. Is there one device, gadget, or online platform that you think most defines your generation? Why does it matter to you?

2. Why do you think the word *culture* still seems to signify elite or high status leisure?

3. How do functionalist and critical theory worldviews differ?

4. Using one example (such as attending a concert or watching Netflix), work through each of Storey's six definitions of what *popular* may mean. Which definition do you think is the strongest?

5. To what extent do you think that culture wars are a battleground between generations about shared values and social change?

Go to HK*Propel* to access additional learning content.

Leisure and Family Life

Camilla J. Hodge

Brigham Young University

Karen K. Melton

Baylor University

VOCABULARY TERMS

activity factors

balance activities

core activities

families

family circumstances

family connection experiences

family factors

family relationships

family structure

growth connection experiences

joint activities

maintenance connection experiences

novelty

parallel activities

social connection

social interaction

social isolation

time

LEARNING OUTCOMES

After reading this chapter, you will be able to

- explain why leisure has become the primary context for family time;
- define and describe families using inclusive language and concepts;
- explain how leisure can be used to increase the health and well-being of individuals, families, and societies; and
- create connection experiences in your own family activities.

Think back to one of the most memorable and meaningful recreation activities or other leisure experiences you shared with a family member. What did you do together? Where were you? What made that experience memorable or meaningful? How did you feel during that experience, and how do you feel when you remember it? What if there was a way to make the recreation activities you share with family members more positive, memorable, and meaningful? This chapter provides you with the knowledge to create family leisure experiences that improve your life. We will first take a look at the history of family life in the United States and leisure's role in family life. Second, we will consider different types of family structures, circumstances, and relationships so we can define families inclusively. Third, we will explain the connection between families, leisure, and the health and well-being of individuals, families, and communities. Finally, we will explain how you can design high-quality recreation activities that support social connection and improve quality of life.

Families in Society

Today, leisure is crucial to how we do family life, but it hasn't always been that way. Before the Industrial Revolution in the United States (c. 1760-1840), roughly 90 percent of the population lived and worked on a farm or a plantation (Mintz & Kellogg, 1988). This meant many families were part of largely self-sustaining systems or communities. They built their own houses, grew and made their own food, constructed their own furniture, and manufactured their own clothing—which included first spinning wool, making cloth, and then sewing clothing items (Mintz & Kellogg, 1988). Because of this labor-intensive process to survive, every family member (even children as young as six or seven years old) was expected to be productive and contribute to farming, animal care, or other tasks necessary for living. This also meant that prior to the industrial era, work—not leisure—was the context in which families spent most of their time together.

Ariel Skelley/Digital Vision/Getty Images

In the 21st century, families spent large portions of their days separated from each other, making shared leisure experiences highly relevant to family relationships.

Leisure as a part of family life became more common after the Industrial Revolution. The shift to employment outside of the home in the late 19th century and the introduction of compulsory education until a specific age in the early 20th century meant family members were typically spending a large portion of their days separated from each other. This model of family life persists. Today, children are often enrolled in schools and after-school programs that occur away from home, and adult family members (like parents) are typically paid for labor completed for an organization or corporation that exists outside of the home. The money parents earn then allows them to purchase goods and services that enable their families to survive and even thrive.

Part of what helps families thrive in modern society takes place not in work time but in leisure time. Today, leisure plays an important role in establishing and maintaining family relationships (Kleiber, Walker, & Mannell, 2011; Orthner, Barnett-Morris, & Mancini, 1994). The shift in family time use from work-centered activities to leisure activities can also be seen in the change in cultural norms of the United States. In the context of many contemporary families, time spent in leisure and recreation is central to strengthening family relationships (Aron & Aron, 1986; Kleiber et al., 2011; Orthner & Mancini, 1991).

The History of Families Is Complex

It is all too easy to oversimplify the social and economic contexts of families from the 18th to 20th centuries. Oversimplifying families' contexts during these periods can leave us with the false impression that all families' experiences were homogenous—that families' day-to-day lives and life stories were all the same. This is untrue.

Careful reading of history clearly shows us that families varied broadly in their structure, race and ethnicity, economics, culture, and what they valued. Realizing and remembering this is essential to being able to accurately understand families' leisure, because intended or not, families' leisure is a product of the interaction between all these factors. Here, we highlight three factors that have influenced and continue to influence families' leisure: (1) historical events; (2) race, ethnicity, and culture; and (3) economics.

Historical Events

Although we have mentioned only the Industrial Revolution as an influence on family life, many other historical events have greatly shaped family life as well. As you read over the time line shown in figure 8.1, choose two events to focus on and think about the following questions:

- What would family life (including leisure) have looked like in the time periods before and after these events?

- How would different families be affected differently by each event? Are there any families that would be more affected than others?

- What are some events not listed in this time line that have affected family life? Identify at least two.

Race, Ethnicity, and Culture

Family life may be different between different races, ethnicities, and cultures. For example, consider the different holiday celebrations in the month of December: winter solstice, Hanukkah, Christmas, and Kwanzaa. Each holiday is celebrated for different reasons by different cultural groups, and even

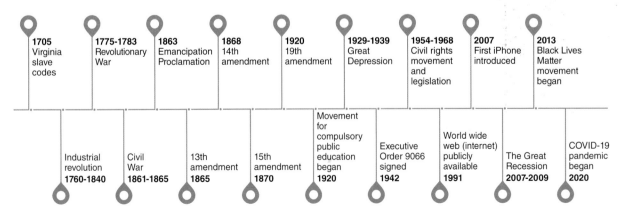

FIGURE 8.1 How have U.S. historical events affected family life and leisure?

within these cultural groups, the ways in which families celebrate the same holiday are likely to differ. Also consider the way history interacts with race, ethnicity, and culture to restrict access to leisure and influence whether families feel safe or welcome in specific leisure spaces.

Economics

Leisure became most common for families with higher incomes after the Industrial Revolution. Families with lower incomes had fewer opportunities for leisure because of limited time outside of work and limited individual and family and community resources. In modern society, we continue to see disparities in access to leisure time and opportunities based on income or social class. To better understand these disparities, please consider the following:

- Which of the historical events included in figure 8.1 most likely had significant effects on families' financial well-being?
- Are there families who were likely more financially affected than others? Who were they, and why would they have been more affected than other families?
- What have been your own experiences with access to leisure opportunities?

Time use trends in the United States provide additional evidence for this change. For example, from 1965 to 2012, parents' time together and their time with their children increased continually and dramatically (Dotti Sani & Treas, 2016; Genadek, Flood, & Roman, 2016). Importantly, through statistical analyses, researchers were able to show that these increases in time together were attributed to parents actually spending more leisure time with their families rather than social changes such as having fewer children (Genadek et al., 2016). Other research has demonstrated that fathers' time with their children has tripled since 1965 (Livingston & Parker, 2019).

However, the amount of family time is not our major concern. When families around the world were expected to shelter in place because of the COVID-19 pandemic, the model of work and school being separate from family life was disrupted. Many parents worked at home or had no work at all, and children continued their education at home. Under these conditions, the amount of family time increased exponentially—families were together all the time! For some families, spending more time together had a positive effect on their health and relationships. For other families, however, the increased time together was not beneficial. Parents' stress increased, and children's hyperactivity, emotional symptoms, and behavioral problems also increased (Spinelli, Lionetti, Pastore, & Fasolo, 2020). For still other families, more time together had even more serious consequences. The United Nations estimated that three months of quarantine resulted in a 20 percent rise in domestic violence that in some cases led to deaths. These statistics suggest that simply increasing the quantity of time families spend together is not an effective way to support the health and well-being of individuals and families. Instead, it is the quality of family time that most influences the health and well-being of individuals and families.

At this point, the major takeaway is: Because of socio-historical influences, family time use has changed from a work context to a leisure context. Overall, the shift in family time contexts from work to leisure means some of the functions families fulfill in society have also changed. In the next section, we identify some of these new family functions and how they can potentially support greater health and well-being.

Family Functions That Support Health and Well-Being in Society

As we discussed in the previous section, work is no longer the primary context in which families spend their time. Instead, leisure has become the primary context for families' shared time. Families serve as a center for social connection, identity, and developing a sense of belonging (Bogenschneider et al., 2012; Melton et al., 2018). One of the most pressing public health concerns in our society is social connectedness or a lack thereof (Holt-Lunstad, Robles, & Sbarra, 2017). More than one fourth of the population in the United States lives alone, and some 20 to 43 percent of adults 60 years old and older report feeling lonely frequently or intensely (Holt-Lunstad et al., 2017). Feeling lonely, or socially isolated, can lead to increased illness and even increased likelihood of death. Thus, feeling socially connected is perhaps one of the greatest opportunities to increase the health and well-being of individuals, families, and societies. The time families share together in leisure is one tool that can be used to increase social connections (and subsequently health and well-being) across the life span—but only when family time is high quality. That means high-quality leisure experiences for families that support positive social relationships may be the key pieces of supporting health and well-being.

Who Are Families?

Today, families are as different as their preferences in leisure activities. Therefore, before we learn more about high-quality family leisure experiences, we should consider what it means to be family—especially because the word *family* may bring to mind very different images for one person than for another (Melton et al., 2018).

SolStock/E+/Getty Images

What do you think of when you think of the word *family*?

Dynamic cultural, historical, and social forces contribute to the way we think of family (Melton et al., 2018). Family can perhaps be defined best by the type of relationship or circumstances between two or more people (Melton et al., 2018)—and those relationships and circumstances are incredibly diverse. For that reason, we will use the following definition as we continue discussing leisure in families in this chapter: "Family represents the social relationships between or among at least two people related by birth, marriage, adoption, or . . . ties of affection" (Melton et al., 2018, p. 406).

Overlooked Family Structures, Circumstances, and Relationships

As we noted in the first section of this chapter, families' leisure experiences are likely to differ greatly because of social, cultural, and historical effects. Unfortunately, what is known about those differences in leisure experiences from a research standpoint is extremely limited. When one of the authors of this chapter reviewed the last 25 years of family leisure research, she found that the vast majority of research studied predominantly White, middle-class families in which two married parents are present (Hodge et al., 2015, 2017). She also found the relationships between parents and their adolescent children were most commonly included in research. This research finding is one indicator of a pervasive and persistent cultural bias in which White, two-parent, heterosexual, nuclear families, and their middle-class values are held as a standard to which all other families are compared (Moras, Shehan, & Berardo, 2018). Families that meet this cultural standard have historically held a privileged status in society. As a result, families falling outside of the cultural expectation have consistently been underserved by leisure experience providers. Table 8.1 summarizes family structures, family circumstances, and family relationships that are often overlooked. Table 8.1 also provides examples of noninclusive leisure experience design.

TABLE 8.1   Diversity in Family Structures, Circumstances, and Relationships

	Family structures	Family circumstances	Family relationships
Definition	The term *family structure* is used to describe how members of a household are organized. It encompasses marital status, living arrangements, and whether household members are biologically related (Pasley & Petren, 2015).	We use the term *family circumstances* to describe the life conditions, traditions, cultures, or situations of families. Family circumstances are likely to affect daily family life and family leisure.	Family relationships are the named associations or connections between or among at least two people. An individual likely has multiple family relationships, and the number of their family relationships may change across the life span.
Examples (regardless of sexual orientation or gender identity)	• One-parent families • Two-parent families • Single-parent-plus-partner families • Grandparent families (i.e., grandparents raising grandchildren) • Multigenerational families • Adoptive families	• Immigrant families • Military families • Childless couples • Multilingual families	• Grandparents and grandchildren • Siblings • Cousins • Fictive kin (families built on close social ties rather than blood relations or marriage) • Pets
Noninclusive examples	Using language or images that describe or promote a leisure experience that center on White, middle-class, two-parent norms. Such language or images would likely make some families feel unwelcome or unrepresented.	Providing leisure resource materials only in English when a large portion of the population speaks another language. This creates inequitable access (i.e., barriers) to leisure experiences.	Describing a community event as family friendly and only providing activities that would appeal to parents and young children. This excludes other important family relationships from the leisure experience.

Self-Exploration

Everyone has assumptions that are based on their own experiences. Although some assumptions generally hold true, others can be incorrect, flawed, or problematic (Reiss, 2012). Our personal family experiences can lead us to make assumptions about who families are, what family life is like, and what leisure experiences can or should look like in families. To reflect on this, answer the following questions:

- What assumptions do you have about families, family life, and leisure? For example, one assumption about family leisure might be that family leisure has a positive effect on all family members, but that may not be true.
- Where did those assumptions come from (your personal experience, media, etc.)?
- Are your assumptions true for all families?
- How might you find evidence that supports or disproves your assumptions?

As is indicated in table 8.1, pets can also be family members. Popular culture in Westernized societies now include pets as family members. Evidence of this trend includes the introduction of terms like *cat mom* or *dog mom* (to describe the parent–child relationship between a human and their animal) as well as building and interior design trends that create designated spaces for pets (e.g., dog parks, cat patios, or rooms designated just for dogs).

Using Leisure to Increase Families' Health

With an inclusive definition of family, we can start to identify and describe the ways family leisure can support individuals', families', and communities' health. **Social isolation** is a serious public health concern. Social isolation, also known as loneliness, is also a growing social concern, and some 40 percent of people in the United States report feeling isolated and say that their relationships are not meaningful (*Cigna*, 2018). These feelings of loneliness have almost the same negative impact on health as smoking 15 cigarettes a day or having alcohol use disorder (Holt-Lunstad, Smith, Baker, Harris, & Stephenson, 2015). Loneliness is also twice as harmful as obesity on your mental and physical health (Holt-Lunstad et al., 2015). This means loneliness is a big issue in the United States.

Scientists have suggested that building social connections may be the answer to this big issue (Holt-Lunstad et al., 2017). We further suggest that shared leisure experiences, especially those that occur in families, could be used as a prevention tool that protects against social isolation and loneliness

across the life span. These protective family experiences are called family connection experiences. **Family connection experiences** can occur as a result of activities that sustain or maintain the bond between two or more family members or activities that establish, augment, alter, or grow the bond between two or more family members.

To better understand the concept of connection experiences, let's consider that families are a system (Broderick, 1993). The word *system* may seem a little weird, but consider a car as an analogy. A car is a system that can run for a long time on a full tank of gas, but eventually the gas will run out and the car will also need other, more intensive upkeep. This principle is similar for families, except instead of needing a tank of gas, let's think of the activities a family does together as their main energy source. It is not so much the activity itself that provides energy, but rather the activity provides the opportunity for connection, and the connection is the true source of energy in relationships. At times, families may need only gas in their tank to keep them going. In relationships, we call these **maintenance connection experiences**. At other times, families need other, more specialized, or more intensive experiences (analogous to an oil change or tune-up)—these are **growth connection experiences**. We suggest maintenance connection experiences and growth connection experiences are likely to (1) occur in leisure for families, (2) reduce loneliness and social isolation, and (3) increase social connection and ultimately improve the health and well-being of individuals, families, and societies.

In the next sections, we will first define health in the context of social connection. Second, we will describe some research that has documented how types of connection experiences in family leisure are connected to positive family relationships that support the health of individuals, families, and societies.

Defining Health in the Context of Social Connection

The World Health Organization (WHO, n.d.) defines health as "a state of complete physical, mental, and *social well-being* [emphasis added] and not merely the absence of disease or infirmity." WHO has identified social support networks as a factor directly associated with health (Holt-Lunstad et al., 2017). This means that being socially healthy is more than simply not feeling lonely. Instead, health as it relates to social connection speaks to the social relationships we have and the quality of those social relationships.

In a TED Talk that now has more than 38 million views, Dr. Robert Waldinger, director of the 75-year-long Harvard Study of Adult Development, said "Good relationships keep us happier and healthier" (Waldinger, 2015). Good relationships predicted better physical health, improved cognitive functioning, longer life, and greater happiness among 724 men and their partners who were enrolled in the study. And it wasn't just the number of relationships that predicted these outcomes—the quality of those relationships was vital to increased health and happiness. Therefore, high-quality social connections are essential to health and happiness across the life span.

Family Leisure Experiences That Build Social Connection

If social connection is essential to health and happiness across the life span, then what is it about shared leisure that can help people grow or maintain high-quality relationships? Arthur and Elaine Aron, two of the leading experts on interpersonal relationships, have said social connection is built on shared experience and shared enjoyment (Aron & Aron, 1986). Likewise, some notable social psychologists (i.e., scientists who study people's behaviors in social groups) have said "leisure is a major social space for the development and maintenance of relationships" (Kleiber et al., 2011, p. 393). In other words, leisure might be, in modern society, the best place to create connection experiences for families. This means leisure is perhaps the primary context for connection experiences that shape the way relationships are formed, maintained, and expanded across the life span.

The potential for family leisure to create connection experiences that reduce feelings of social isolation or loneliness is high. In fact, one of the leading causes of loneliness is dissatisfaction with one's family, social, and community life (Bialik, 2018). Family leisure has been linked to increased life and relationship satisfaction (Agate, Zabriskie, Agate, & Poff, 2009; Orthner & Mancini, 1991). Greater amounts of family leisure—and especially greater satisfaction with family leisure—is associated with increased quality of life in families (Hodge et al., 2017). Thus, family leisure can be used not only to treat existing problems like social isolation but also to amplify good things like quality of life, subjective well-being, or essentially, happiness. Leisure has also been shown to create opportunities for different types of interaction in families, and family interaction (including conflict) has been linked to increased relationship satisfaction for married partners (Orthner, 1975). Likewise, leisure has been linked to family stability. In one study, married partners who participated in recreation activities together were more likely to still be married five years later (Hill, 1988). Overall, family leisure can be an important tool for improving relationships and life satisfaction, which affects the physical, social, and mental health of individuals, families, and communities.

Creating Maintenance and Growth Connection Experiences in Family Leisure

Although it may seem like some of the best moments or experiences in life just happen, Chip and Dan Heath, authors of *The Power of Moments*, argue that we can actually design or create these moments of connection intentionally. We happen to agree, and so to help you think about how you can design and create maintenance and growth connection experiences in your own family relationships, consider the following elements to intentionally design a connection experience (Melton, Hodge, & Duerden, 2020):

1. *Family factors.* Think about what you and the family member(s) involved in the leisure or recreation activity need and bring into the leisure experience. Are you both or all feeling a little bored and wanting to try something

new? What do you and your family members like to do (or not like to do)? We call these **family factors.**

2. *Activity factors.* Think about how an activity may or may not meet that need, and how you and your family members can shape that activity. We call these **activity factors.**

3. *Time.* Think about all the stages of the activity: before, during, and after. What can you do before the activity to build excitement or anticipation? What can you do after the activity to reinforce the connection experience? This is the element of **time.**

In this chapter, we will focus on the activity factors that influence the development of maintenance or growth connection experiences. Activity factors are the identifiable physical and social elements that interact during the family activity to create an experience (Melton, 2017). Two subcategories of activity factors that greatly influence connection experiences are environmental factors and interpersonal factors.

Environmental Factors

When thinking about designing either maintenance or growth leisure-based connection experiences for families, **novelty** is perhaps the most important feature of the physical elements to consider. Novelty is the level of complexity that results when the physical and social elements of the activity are unfamiliar. Connection experiences can have varying levels of novelty. Shared recreation activities that are routine and familiar are great for maintaining relationships because they provide a sense of continuity and stability (Zabriskie & McCormick, 2001). Activities that are done less frequently or take place in a new or unfamiliar location are great for growing relationships because they create opportunities for change and development (Zabriskie & McCormick, 2001). Moreover, when an activity is novel, families may experience shared struggle that can increase their sense of connection (Aron & Aron, 1986; Heath & Heath, 2017).

The idea of novelty in shared family leisure isn't new. In 2001, two researchers published a paper that

---

On the Job

Beginner Classes for Families: Family Leisure Education

We know from research on optimal experiences and flow theory (Csikszentmihalyi, 1990) that too much novelty can result in unpleasant leisure experiences characterized by high anxiety. For families who are new to camping, for example, the learning curve associated with new outdoor skills can make the novelty of the activity too high to support their well-being. As a leisure professional, it is important for you to keep this in mind when developing leisure experiences. In fact, it may be a career in and of itself to help families manage novelty in their leisure.

For example, the Arizona State Parks Family Campout program (https://azstateparks.com/family-camp/) was designed especially for families interested in camping who need to reduce the challenge and novelty of the experience. Program leaders facilitate a weekend experience for families (typically parents with children) who have little or no experience camping. Professional guides introduce families to outdoor adventures in a structured environment. Here is one participant's story:

> I am a single mother of three boys. And my boys begged me to take them camping. So, I bought a tent, and we traveled to the closest state park. It took us 2 hours to put together our tent—I was frustrated, and the poles were bent. It rained that night, and everything was wet. I was miserable. I thought, "This is it . . . I am never camping again!" . . . Then one day, a colleague shared about their experience at the Family Campout Program. We had to bring our food, clothes, and sleeping bags, but they provided the rest of the outdoor equipment. We spent two full days and one night full of fun activities, like hiking, mountain biking, listening to speakers, campfire with smores, playing with critters, and stargazing with telescopes. The best part was getting to meet a whole bunch of other beginner families who were learning to enjoy the great outdoors. We had so much fun! I finally realized why my children enjoyed camping. We completed the program three more times that year. Now, I feel like I have graduated "camping school," and we camp eight times a year with friends we have made along the way.

This is just one example of how practitioners and professionals can use knowledge of family leisure in the real world.

first introduced the idea of novelty as an important factor when thinking about family leisure. Dr. Ramon Zabriskie and Dr. Bryan McCormick published the core and balance model of family leisure functioning. In this model, they linked **core activities** with increased emotional closeness, known as cohesion, in families. They also linked **balance activities** with increased adaptability, or the ability to respond to change, in families. This model has been the foundation for years of family leisure research and recreation programming!

To determine how novel the activity environment is, ask yourself the following questions:

- Is this an activity we are familiar with, that we do together regularly? Or is it something we do only once or twice a year? Or is this a brand-new activity? If it is a brand new activity, how can we make sure we do not feel overwhelmed?
- Is the location where we will be doing the activity familiar? How familiar is the location (do we come here regularly)? Is it a scenic location?

These types of questions can help you start to identify where novelty may be present in an activity.

Interpersonal Factors

When thinking about designing either maintenance or growth leisure-based connection experiences for families, we should also consider the number and type of interactions between family members. **Social interactions** are the verbal and nonverbal communications between family members during a recreation activity (Melton, 2017). Connection experiences can have low and high levels of social interaction. Shared family activities that have few to no social interactions (e.g., watching movies) are great for the maintenance of relationships. Activities that have high levels of social interactions are great for growing relationships. Connection generally occurs through positive social interactions, though some scholars have even suggested conflict in family leisure can be a part of overall healthy and positive relationships (Orthner & Mancini, 1991). Until recently, most family leisure scholars have focused on verbal communication as being

the key mechanism for connection; however, other nonverbal forms of interaction, such as touch, have an important role to play as well (Melton, Larson, & Boccia, 2019).

In 1975, Dr. Dennis Orthner introduced three important concepts that have guided our understanding of how different recreation activities create different patterns of social interaction in family leisure. He studied leisure in married couples at different life stages and described their leisure as (1) **joint activities**, (2) **parallel activities**, or (3) individual activities. Certain recreation activities require interaction. For example, collaborative board games require that team members (such as couples) talk to each other and work together to succeed. These types of recreation activities are joint activities. Other recreation activities, like watching a movie, don't necessarily require the couples to interact. These are parallel activities. Recreation activities in which only one person is participating are individual. Research suggests that joint activities are perhaps the most important for couple relationships.

You and your family members can increase or decrease the social interactions to create either maintenance or growth connection experiences by thinking about the following:

- *Talking, touching, and eye contact.* Positive forms of talking, touching, and eye contact are associated with creating connections with others. How can you appropriately promote these interactions during family leisure?
- *Disclosure.* While it is great to talk to each other during an activity, it can be even better when you or your family members disclose new information about yourselves. Disclosure requires some vulnerability, so when appropriate, consider ways that you and your family members can reflect and share about their experience.
- *Responsiveness.* Responsiveness is when family members pay attention to what others are thinking and feeling and respond. Responsiveness can be exhibited by comments such as "good job" or "thanks for sharing"; it also comes in the form of high-fives

Social interaction can take many forms. For example, couples can interact during leisure by talking to each other, making eye contact, and touching each other.

and hugs (Heath & Heath, 2017). How can you and your family member(s) be responsive to one another during a family activity?

Summary

Social connection, especially the relationships you have with your family, affects your health and well-being across the life span. Leisure is the primary context in which families spend time together in modern society, and high-quality leisure experiences can result in family connection experiences. Intentionally designing leisure experiences that either maintain or grow the relationships people have with their families can act as a buffer against illness and early death.

Based on time use data in the United States, most people engage in passive, low-engagement leisure like watching movies or shows on television or streaming services. Families need a mix of predictable and novel leisure experiences to have and maintain healthy relationships. Likewise, families need shared leisure experiences that require a high level of social interaction for optimal relationship maintenance and growth. Family relationships and circumstances are diverse, yet all can benefit from high-quality leisure that results in connection experiences. You, as a person with family relationships or as a recreation practitioner, can use experience design tools in conjunction with the domains of family, activity, and time to meet families' needs through leisure.

Learning Activities

1. List five activities that you did with your family as a child (ages 5-12), five activities that you did with your family as an adolescent (ages 13-18), and five activities that you do with your family now. Have the activities stayed the same over time? Why or why not?

2. Compare your lists with a class peer or in a small group. What activities are the same? What activities are different? Why do you think some activities are the same and some activities are different?

Review Questions

1. Many social, cultural, historical, and even economic factors affect what families do for leisure. Identify at least three factors that have affected family leisure and discuss *how* these factors have affected family leisure.

2. In small groups, share with each other family relationships in your life that have been greatly affected by shared leisure experiences. Discuss the following:
   - How has leisure affected your relationships (positively or negatively)?
   - How have your relationships supported or undermined your health and well-being?
   - How might you change your leisure experiences in this relationship to promote connection?

3. Develop a plan to increase the number and quality of the family connection experiences you have with one of your family members. Come to class prepared to share your plan with others.

Go to HK*Propel* to access additional learning content.

An Introduction to Digital Leisure

Callie Spencer Schultz
Western Carolina University

Janet K. L. McKeown
Vancouver Island University

Callie Spencer Schultz
Western Carolina University

Janet K. L. McKeown
Vancouver Island University

VOCABULARY TERMS

digital leisure

digital technology

geosocial networking
  applications

immaterial labor

nomophobia

self-tracking

social media

LEARNING OUTCOMES

After reading this chapter, you will be able to

- define digital leisure, digital technology, and social media;
- identify ways digital technologies influence the relationships we have with ourselves, our bodies, and our leisure;
- consider how digital leisure can foster social connections;
- understand how power relations can influence digital leisure; and
- consider the connections between digital leisure and surveillance.

"Life is digital" (Lupton, 2015, p. 1). Think about this statement for just a moment. It is powerful, thrilling, devastating, and hopeful all at once. Lupton's assertion here is that life today cannot be understood without "the recognition that computer software and hardware devices not only underpin but actively constitute selfhood, embodiment, social life, social relations, and social institutions" (p. 2). Digital technologies are integral threads in the fabric that makes us human! Digital technologies are attached to almost every aspect of our being, including our physical bodies, our social lives, our sex lives, our school, our marriages, our work, and politics. Examples of each of these include, respectively, Apple watches, Instagram, online porn, personal school profiles, wedding registry sites, LinkedIn, and social media promotion of political candidates and issues. These aspects are all intertwined with leisure.

Indeed, as Kumm, Holt, and Kleiber (2016) have noted, "Nearly every realm of human existence is now profoundly affected by technology" (p. 161). But what do we mean by technology? In a contemporary context, when people say "technology," they are not commonly using that terminology to refer to the toothbrush, hammer, refrigerator, AvaLung filtration devices, or flushable toilet. Instead, when people use this language in a contemporary context, they are most often referring to any number of digital technologies. Therefore, we begin by briefly clarifying three key terms (defined in the glossary): digital technology, social media, and digital leisure. In order for technology to be **digital technology**, it must do something with data (generate, process, store, etc.). Some of the most prevalent digital technologies today are social media sites and services. When defining **social media**, is important to note the user-generated (rather than editor-created) nature of content (boyd, 2014). Finally, **digital leisure** (see Silk et al, 2016) has physical, psychological, and temporal components and can be understood as "time spent engaged in digital practices and spaces while in a leisurely state of mind" (Schultz & McKeown, 2018, p. 233). Importantly, digital leisure practices and spaces are also intertwined with work in ways that physical leisure spaces are not. This is often done through surveillance that allows compa-

AndreyPopov/Getty Images/Getty Images

Digital technologies are attached to almost every aspect of our being, tracking how and when we eat, sleep, workout, and even have sex.

nies to benefit monetarily from your digital leisure time (i.e., by tracking your data and selling it for profit). The very fact of this capitalist surveillance blurs the lines between work and leisure in digital leisure spaces.

Most of us are guilty of mindless consumption of digital technology (e.g., scrolling through your phone when you're bored). In this chapter, we guide you through an exploration of the relationships between digital technologies and leisure with the hopes that you can begin to think more intentionally and critically about your own engagement in digital leisure. We want to make it clear that we do not wish to make digital technology and its related personal and government use seem like a controlling big brother or boogeyman; it is much more complex than that. There are, indeed, many benefits of digital technologies, many of which we all experienced during the COVID-19 pandemic. What we do believe is that digital technologies are increasingly acting to blur traditional dichotomies such as work–leisure, natural–built, and even human–technology. Importantly, the popular idea that the online realm is fake or pretend and offline is real life no longer holds true (if it ever did). For example, time spent in an online gaming community may shape a person's identity, community, and feelings of belonging in real life. As emerging recreation and leisure practitioners, you will need to engage increasingly with digital technologies as you work in the field. Therefore, in this chapter, we aim to provide a brief introduction to several critical big topics surrounding digital technologies and leisure. In fact, there is an entire emerging subfield called digital leisure studies dedicated to the study of the intersections of leisure and digital technologies (Redhead, 2016; Schultz & McKeown, 2018). Because this field and this topic are morphing and reinventing themselves at an alarmingly fast pace, we have organized the information in this chapter as a series of questions exploring the various intersections between digital technologies and leisure. The answers provided capture some of the current research related to these questions but are not all encompassing. Rather they are intended to provide an entry point into each of these topics. We encourage you to continue to think about these questions and new answers to them as you read this chapter and begin your career:

- What role do digital technologies play in leisure time?

- What role do digital technologies play in shaping my identity?
- Should I be creeped out about the fact that digital technologies are merging with my body? What are the implications of digital technology use for my health and well-being?
- How do digital technologies affect my social life?
- Are digital leisure spaces equitable?
- To what extent am I being watched by big brother during my leisure time? Should I care?
- Can I opt out and live a whole, happy, healthy human life? What real options do I have?

The Role of Digital Technologies in Leisure Time

As noted in the introduction, various aspects of social life have become increasingly digitized since the advent of mass social media sites and services such as Facebook. This digitization of social life extends into and shapes the ways people spend their leisure time as well as the ways people engage in leisure spaces. For example, based on data presented by the American Bureau of Labor Time Use Statistics (2020) (figure 9.1), the leisure activities that take up the greatest amount of free time (which totals 5 hours and 11 minutes per day) include watching TV (2 hours and 49 minutes) and socializing and communicating (38 minutes). These trends are also reflected in other countries. For example, Canadians appear to be spending an increasing amount of their free time at home online—approximately 24.5 hours a week (or 3.5 hours a day) (Media Technology Monitor, 2017). The ways leisure has been digitized is further evidenced by the global growth of social media sites such as Facebook (2.7 billion users) and Twitter (330 million active users; 77% are in countries outside the United States), as well as video sites such as YouTube (2 billion users in 70 countries and in 76 languages). While we recognize that not all digital time is leisure time, we believe these statistics indicate a global trend in leisure preferences toward spending leisure time engaged in digital leisure practices and spaces (Schultz & McKeown, 2018). Complete to the self-exploration activity on the next page to assess your own digital leisure time.

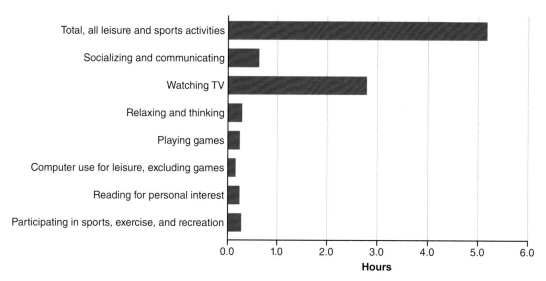

FIGURE 9.1 American Bureau of Labor 2019 Time Use Survey results for people aged 15 years and older.
Reprinted from U.S. Bureau of Labor Statistics, *Graphic for Economic News Releases* (Washington, DC, 2020).

When we look at the pervasiveness of digital technologies in leisure time and spaces and the growth of digital leisure, there are two potential answers to the question of how digital technologies shape our leisure time. While some scholars argue that digital technologies have given us more leisure time by making some of our jobs easier and less time consuming or by adding leisure to our workday (e.g., using social media during the workday), a growing number of leisure scholars argue that digital technologies are making our leisure time obsolete. The argument here is that when we are using digital technologies during our leisure time or when participating in digital leisure, we are actually doing work in the form of producing web content and data that will then be sold for a profit. The labor produced while using social media sites is called **immaterial labor**, which is "labour that produces immaterial products such as information, knowledges, ideas, images, relationships, and affects" (Hardt & Negri, 2004, p. 65). Rose and Spencer (2016) explain that "immaterial labour not only produces capital in the form of goods, but also produces social and cultural capital and its structures spill over into other forms of labour" (p. 813). They argue that there are two different types of immaterial labor produced by users within social media sites like Facebook. The first is immaterial labor in the form of the data produced as Facebook surveils every action you take on the site. From likes to your profile to your posts to your ad views, your information becomes Facebook's intellectual property; Facebook mines that data and sells

Self-Exploration

Create a log to track your time spent using digital technologies for 24 hours (this includes all things with a screen). Track what you are doing during that time and how it makes you feel. The log should include the following:

Activity:

Start time:

End time:

Description (What was I doing? How did I feel? How did I present myself? Who was I interacting with?):

How many total hours did you spend using digital technologies? What percent of your time *awake* were you using digital technologies? How much of your leisure time was digital leisure? Did you have any epiphanies after tracking your time, activities, and feelings?

On the Job

Using Digital Technologies to Encourage People to Get Outside

At this point in your career, you have heard of campaigns aimed at getting people off their screens, outside, and physically active. For example, Richard Louv's 2005 book, *Last Child in the Woods*, has been cited in efforts to get children off screens and into nature as a solution to nature deficit disorder. However, what would happen if instead of working to get participants off phones and into nature, we figured out ways to use digital technologies to get folks into nature more? This is the current trend in the industry, and employers are looking for employees with ideas for how to accomplish this very goal. There are several examples of creative solutions including star identification apps in use at summer camps, the AllTrails app educating people about local trails, and formal partnerships. For example, the U.S. National Park Foundation teamed up with augmented reality game *Pokémon Go* to get more folks into national parks by playing the game. While increased social media use (and resulting notoriety of natural spaces) can have positive impacts, there are also negative impacts to consider. For example, when Horseshoe Bend in Arizona became Instagram famous in 2010, its annual visitor numbers went from a few thousand to 100,000 and to 750,000 by 2015; 2 million were expected in 2020 (Simmonds et al., 2018). The crowds have caused traffic congestion and disturbed the peace and quiet. Some people argue that social media notoriety can cause us to love our parks and natural spaces to death. Being able to successfully research and weigh these pros and cons (usually done via a gap analysis) may be a useful skill in your career as agencies search for viable ways to implement digital technologies to effect positive change (this may look like more participants, educating the public, new digital leisure programs, new ways for participants to stay connected posttrip, etc.).

---

it at a high price to marketing companies looking to track popular trends of populations. The second form of immaterial labor is social and cultural labor and will be discussed in the next section.

The Role of Digital Technologies in Shaping Identity

I (Callie Spencer Schultz) once had a student say to me, "If you aren't on Insta or Snapchat, you don't exist." Often, when we think about our identities, we think about who we are in real life, which often equates to offline. However, many researchers (e.g., boyd, 2014) assert that our online profiles have a real and important impact in shaping our identities. The person we perform as online is actually the person we are becoming in real life as we discipline ourselves and others into performing as certain acceptable versions of self. Theorist Judith Butler (1990) echoed this idea when speaking specifically about one aspect of our identity—gender—noting that gender is not something that we are, but something that we do through everyday acts, practices, and performances. And because gender is learned and inscribed in everyday practices, we produce and thus become our gender daily when we make

choices about what to wear, how to cut our hair, how to act, etc. Many of these things are inscribed with traditional masculinity or femininity written by culture (e.g., pink and shaved legs = feminine). So, when we are online, the way we present ourselves is also creating us as gendered humans (among other identities).

This brings us back to Rose and Spencer's (2016) second form of immaterial labor produced using social media: our own identities and our culture. Rose and Spencer asserted that the act of creating online content such as profiles, posts, and comments on others' posts is immaterial labor because it works to shape our identities. We try on certain identities and receive feedback on those identities and then make modifications. "Through time spent on Facebook surveilling friends' pages and reading the Facebook news page, users learn how to act in a society, how to be an acceptable member. Users learn what is acceptable to discuss and what is taboo. Users are disciplined by others when they step out of line" (Rose & Spencer, 2016, p. 813). This disciplining happens through votes, emojis, negative comments, and so on. In sum, your time spent curating your social media pages can have a real-world personal and cultural impacts. When you couple this idea with the first form of immaterial labor (Facebook collecting your data to sell), there is an eerie realization of the intersection of surveillance and self. Through surveillance, social media sites are selling you to you (collecting data on what you like and then using algorithms to sell that identity to you). While this idea can seem a bit big brothery (government watching you à la Orwell's *Nineteen Eighty-Four*), it is important to note that digital technologies can also afford us unique opportunities, ways, and venues to perform our identities in meaningful and powerful ways.

Kumm and colleagues (2016) outlined several case studies that illustrate the ways technology can positively contribute to human development, including identity development. Drawing on research that explored lived experiences of leisure through songwriting (see Kumm, 2013; Kumm & Johnson, 2014), they described how one participant, Tenzing, used digital technologies (e.g., Pro Tools recording and editing software) to write songs that resulted in a shift in his identity during a period of unemployment. More specifically, technology mediated this leisure activity for Tenzing in two ways. First, the technology he used to write songs "became the raw material from which he could reshape his identity" (p. 169). Second, through engaging with these new technologies and using them to write songs, he was able to develop an ongoing "commitment and enduring passion to continually grow personally as an artist, as well as adding to his repertoire of potentially employable skills" (p. 169). In this way, a technologically mediated form of song writing (as leisure) was key to shifting his identity away from considering himself as unemployed to considering himself as a Sherpa working with a mountain of data and recognizing what his meaningful life's work should be (Kumm et al., 2016). Kumm and colleagues noted the relevance of technology to his identity shift, explaining "his experience suggested that when it comes to personal growth, development, and actualization, the challenge of learning new skills, even with technology, is quite often instrumental in how identities are transformed in positive ways" (p. 170).

Digital Technologies Are Ubiquitous

Digital technologies, in many ways, have merged with the human body (some literally, such as cloud-connected pacemakers); they have become integrated into the fabric of people's lives. Let us consider a few examples. Think about the move from the desktop computer to the laptop—the device name literally indicates it should be touching your body. Think about the transfer of the telephone from the wall or desk to the smartphone carried on your person wherever you go and then to the smartwatch that lets you wear your phone. In this section, we explore our own personal relationships (physical and affective) with these technologies and the implications for leisure, given that we believe it is necessary to first question your own relationship with digital technology before you can understand how digital technology is shaping other relationships in your life.

Digital technologies, such as iPhones and other smartphones, are often described by consumers in affective or sentimental ways (Lupton, 2015). The sense of intimacy consumers experience toward their smartphones is not surprising, given that advertising for these phones is often focused on showing their magical capabilities. Why is this? Because the affective response is essential to making that device hold meaning for the consumer. When people develop an affective or a sentimental response to their mobile phone, over time, they no longer see their mobile phones as simply mass-produced objects but rather as intimate objects that hold meanings (Lupton, 2015).

Self-Exploration

To visually depict the ways our smartphones have become extensions of our bodies, look at your phone. If it is not on, do not turn it on. First, where was your phone? Did you even have to stand up to see it? What do you see? Fingerprints? A phone grip device? How do you feel about it? Notice your urge to touch it (or not).

What words would you use to describe your phone? What words would you use to describe your relationship with your phone? What benefits to your health and well-being do you experience because of your relationship with your phone? Do you think this relationship can have negative implications for your health and well-being? If yes, what are some examples of these implications?

Mobile devices have become extensions of our bodies. We see imprints or markers of our bodies on our phones (Lupton, 2015). Lupton noted, "We are entangled with the digital through our waking (and sometimes sleeping) hours" (p. 165). For instance, many people sleep with their phones, use their phones in private spaces, ask their phones questions, and talk to their phones, sometimes like they are a friend. But in what ways can the intimate relationships people have with digital devices influence their health and well-being?

Nomophobia is a phobia that stems from the relationship people have with digital technologies, particularly smartphones. Yildrim and Correia (2015) defined nomophobia as "the fear of not being able to use a smartphone or a mobile phone and/or the services it offers" (p. 136). They identified four dimensions of nomophobia from interviews with college and university students in the United States. These include (1) not being able to communicate, (2) losing connectedness, (3) not being able to access information, and (4) giving up convenience. The researchers then took these dimensions and developed a 20-item questionnaire that can be used to assess the degree of nomophobia college students experience.

Similarly, a study by Clayton, Leshner, and Almond (2015) looked at the physiological and cognitive effects of iPhone separation. They recruited college students who owned iPhones, but they did not disclose the actual purpose of the study. Rather, researchers told participants the study was to test a new blood pressure cuff. They initially asked participants to complete a word search puzzle while testing their ability to complete the puzzle and monitoring their heart rate and blood pressure levels. The researchers then told participants their smartphones were creating signal interference with the Bluetooth technology in the blood pressure cuff and needed to be moved farther away from them in the room. Again, they asked participants to complete a word search puzzle and monitored their ability to complete the puzzle and their heart rate and blood pressure while doing so. But while participants were completing the word search, researchers called the participants' phones and let them ring. They found when participants were not able to access their smartphones, participants had lower cognitive performance, higher physiological anxiety (blood pressure, heart rate), and higher self-reported anxiety and unpleasantness.

Self-Exploration

Complete the nomophobia questionnaire on the Huffington Post website (www.huffingtonpost.ca/entry/nomophobia-smartphone-sep_n_7266468?ri18n=true).

What was your score? If you received a 61 or above, noting a moderate or high level of nomophobia, take some time to explore ideas of digital detox (linked in the article) and see if you are inspired by any of them.

Related to these ideas, another topic that is important to consider when thinking about relationships between technologies and ourselves and our bodies is how we can use digital technologies to self-track. Also known as life logging and quantifying the self, **self-tracking** refers to the practice of "gathering data about oneself on a regular basis and then recording and analyzing the data to produce statistics and other data (such as images) relating to one's bodily functions and everyday habits" (Lupton, 2015, p. 181). Self-tracking is not a new practice. Humans have been self-tracking their habits for centuries. What is new is how people are using digital technologies to do so. People can wear forms of smart tech on their bodies (e.g., wristbands, watches, eyewear, clothing). These are also examples of digital technologies that are placed inside a person's body to track data that is sent wirelessly to health-care professionals. Digital gaming can also track a person's body and activities (Lupton, 2015). With the growing number of wearable devices available (there are even smart tech devices for your pets now), these technologies play a significant role in configuring our understandings of health and well-being. But why do people self-track?

There are many reasons why people self-track; however, in many Western societies, where there is a focus on individualism, people self-track because of a desire for self-improvement. Lupton (2015) explained:

Generating detailed data about oneself using digital devices is represented as an undeniable good part of the ethos of working upon the self. Part of engaging in data collection using self-tracking devices is the idea that the self-knowledge that will eventuate will allow users to exert greater control over their destinies. (p. 182)

However, digital technologies do not just affect people's personal lives; they also affect their social lives, which is where we turn next.

The Impact of Digital Technologies on Our Social Lives

Digital leisure does not necessarily have an interactive and social component; however, a large proportion of digital leisure does involve connecting and interacting with others (Valtchanov & Parry, 2016). But what does digital leisure's emphasis on interactivity mean for how people connect with and relate to others in society? This is complicated. Part of why it is complicated is because we get a lot of conflicting messages about how technologies are influencing or affecting our relationships with other people. If you do a Google search, you will find copious articles that talk about how technologies are negatively affecting how we relate and connect to one another. However, you will also find numerous articles that discuss how technologies can support relationships and provide pathways and opportunities to establish and maintain social connections. In this section, we touch on some of the negative impacts of digital technology use before we highlight findings from a few studies in the leisure research that report positive connections between digital leisure and social connections.

Negative Impacts of Digital Technology Use as Leisure

There tends to be a strong focus on the negative impacts of digital technology use as leisure, particularly from an antitechnology or technophobic perspective. The following are some arguments made against digital leisure. If you would like to know more, Brown (2018) presents an excellent review of recent studies surrounding impacts of social media use, more specifically.

- *Social isolation and loneliness.* The more time we spend on our phones, the less we spend socializing face-to-face with one another. This can lead to social isolation regardless of how many virtual friends a person has. Glover (2018) noted how it is ironic that in a time where we are connected to one another in so many ways digitally, that social isolation is a pressing social problem.

- *Decrease in face-to-face social skills.* Studies on teens and youth in particular have noted a decrease in traditional socialization skills in correlation with increased smartphone use. However, it is important to note that some new research is challenging this idea (see Price-Michelle, 2020).

- *Depression.* Several studies have reported links between social media use and depression (Brown, 2018). Lin and colleagues (2016) suggested that reasons for this can include cyberbullying and feeling like you are wasting time on social media.

- *Overuse and addiction.* We can become addicted to digital technologies, causing us to neglect other aspects of our life for technology (Jabr, 2019).

- *Superficial, less meaningful relationships.* Some scholars have found that while a person may have a great number of friends on social media, the relationships with those people are superficial and less meaningful than with friends they spend time with face to face.

Self-Exploration

There are dating apps for almost every flavor of sex, romance, and identity imaginable. A key term in understanding how some of these apps work is geosocial networking. A **geosocial networking application** uses both social networking and a user's geographical location to connect users who are close to one another geographically. There is a growing body of research in the leisure field focused on the role of digital technologies in people's sex lives. Many scholars argue that the dating apps have gamified the dating world, which has both benefits and detriments. To consider the implications of digital technologies on dating and sex lives, please listen to the "Dating in the Digital Age" episode of Lauren Laverne's 2015 radio show titled *Late Night Woman's Hour*, which you can find at www.bbc.co.uk (Mulhall, 2015).

Ibnjaafar/E+/Getty Images

A large proportion of digital leisure involves connecting with others, which is shown to have both negative and positive impacts on people.

- *Social comparison.* Social media can promote jealously through social comparison as a person compares their own life with their friends' lives as depicted in their profiles, posts, and the like.

Kumm and colleagues (2016) proposed that the perception of technologies as either wholly detrimental or beneficial to social and individual development in leisure contexts is overly simplistic. They emphasized the importance of seeking virtue in the virtual while keeping a finger on the negative side of technology use and being intentional about understanding the ways we use or access technologies and how those ways can have potential beneficial outcomes in individual and collective development.

Positive Impacts of Digital Technology Use as Leisure

Both Holt's (2011) ethnographic research of online inhabitants of *World of Warcraft*, as well as Nimrod's (2014) study of seniors' online communities stressed the importance of technologies for enhancing sociability and intergenerational connections in a digital age. For example, Holt discussed how online gaming can lead to stronger relationships both for people who live together and also for people who are at a geographic distance. In comparison, Nimrod's study illustrated how seniors can experience joy, stimulation, and companionship from participating in an online community with other seniors. These ideas are also reflected in the documentary *Cyber-Seniors* (you can find this on YouTube), in which seniors are paired with adolescents and young adults to learn how to use technologies.

In addition to the possibilities for social development during leisure time that can stem from engagement with digital technologies, several other leisure studies have highlighted the ways digital leisure practices and spaces can foster social connections. Valtchanov and Parry (2016) explored the digital leisure experiences of nine immigrant adolescent girls living in Ontario, Canada. Findings from their research highlighted the ways adolescent

Ozgurdonmaz/E+/Getty Images

Seniors are a growing group of digital technology users. Many report finding social connections through digital technology use.

immigrant girls can use digital leisure to negotiate interpersonal leisure constraints and promote social connections. More specifically, they found the girls in their study used digital leisure to maintain connections with family and friends from their home countries, to establish social connections with friends in Canada, and to form social connections with groups of people with shared interests in online communities.

Similarly, Parry, Glover, and Mulcahy (2013) explored how mothers used Momstown (a social networking site) to develop social support. They found that several mothers spoke about feeling isolated and lonely when they first became mothers. Not surprisingly, many of the mothers in their study also talked about a desire to connect with other mothers. Mothers spoke about feeling like it was awkward to make friends in person and said it was often difficult to carry on meaningful conversations in person because they were dealing with sleep deprivation or trying to manage their children at the same time. In response to these challenges, Moms-

town helped mothers forge connections with other mothers. According to Parry and colleagues (2013), it provided women with the opportunity to "court other moms before meeting face-to-face" and "such actions facilitated the development of momances that provide the women with the peer support they clearly desire" (p. 40). As these examples illustrate, digital leisure can play an important role in helping people (and girls and women in particular) negotiate leisure constraints to foster social connections with others. However, it is important to note that digital leisure is not always equitable.

Equitability of Digital Leisure Spaces

At first, you might think digital leisure spaces are equitable. Digital leisure spaces have been touted by some as social levelers, meaning that the power structures that exist in analogue leisure spaces do not exist in digital spaces, offering folks from a wide variety of identities the chance to participate equitably. There are certainly niche cases where this is true. For example, a person who uses a wheelchair may be able to participate in some forms of online leisure more equitably than in analogue leisure activities. However, it is important to note that digital technologies are created by coders and manufacturers who are steeped in culture, disciplined by stereotypes, and who live with and operate by some of the rules and regulations of existing oppressive systems. Therefore, as Lupton (2015) explained,

> Digital technologies are not neutral objects: they are invested with meanings relating to such aspects as gender, social class, race/ethnicity and age. It can be difficult to resist or overcome these meanings even when people have an overt political agenda in attempting to do so. (p. 124)

Pinckney and colleagues (2018) echoed these ideas noting that "racial neutrality does not exist within digital and virtual spaces. Our racialized identities are imported into these spaces, as are the ideologies of our respective societies" (p. 267). In their study of Black Internet users using digital leisure spaces to "counter and disrupt messages that perpetuate inaccurate stereotypes and social inequalities" (p. 267), they noted that the "White racial frame" normalizes White social and political ideals in digital leisure spaces. Indeed, digital leisure can be used by marginalized individuals and communities to confront power relations, have their voices and perspectives heard, reclaim power and control, and work toward making social change. Outley, Bowen, and Pinckney's 2020 article "Laughing While Black: Resistance, Coping and the Use of Humor as a Pandemic Pastime Among Blacks" explores how Black Twitter users use humor as resistance, to reclaim power and cultivate collective identities in perilous times.

While digital leisure can be used in emancipatory ways to counter or disrupt stereotypes and call attention to oppressive systems (e.g., #BlackLives Matter, #metoo, #WomensMarch), it is also important to recognize and reflect on the ways digital leisure can be oppressive, replicating offline power relations online (Spracklen, 2015). For example, Soucie, Parry, and Cousineau (2018) illustrated the ways online activism, and hashtag activism more specifically, can be appropriated by mainstream (White) feminism in ways that erase Black feminist work. As an example, they described how Alyssa Milano was originally credited for starting the #MeToo movement, although it originated from the

grassroots work of Tarana Burke in 2006. Watch the video "Tarana Burke on How the #MeToo Movement Started and Where It's Headed" on YouTube to learn more about how #MeToo started. With this example in mind, Soucie and colleagues (2018) noted leisure scholars need to be more "intentional about taking up a feminist praxis based on intersectionality" (p. 158) to ensure they are not erasing and appropriating the work and activism of Black women as well as women with diverse identities.

Moreover, participation in digital leisure practices and spaces is not always rooted in equity. Not everyone can contribute and participate in digital leisure in the same ways. Jenkins, Ito, and boyd (2016) explained that

> true participation requires many qualities: agency, the ability to understand a social situation well enough to engage constructively, the skills to contribute effectively, connections with others to help build an audience, emotional resilience to handle negative feedback, and enough social status to speak without consequences. (p. 22)

Indeed, social, cultural, and political factors make it easier for some people to participate in digital leisure than others. In turn, while digital leisure can be important for activism and open up space for marginalized individuals to have their voices heard, it is also important to think about "who is being denied existence or being silenced" (Berbary & Richmond, 2011, p. 206) through digital leisure. Another example of this was found in a study about the augmented reality game *Pokémon Go*. Layland, Stone, Mueller, and Hodge (2018) discovered that players who identified as White women, Black men, or Black women experienced specific race- and gender-related constraints to playing the game. These constraints had to do with the physical locations of the poke stops built into the game (they were often in wealthy White neighborhoods where Black bodies would be seen as a threat). Black men and women were arrested, interrogated, shunned, or assaulted while playing the game in predominantly White spaces. Women (regardless of color) experienced constraints based on gender such as sexual harassment. While these constraints are certainly the result of social ideologies and oppressive systems, they were also built into the game with the physical location of the stops. The authors urged leisure scholars, game designers, marketers, and advocates to work together to fight injustice in digital leisure spaces.

OLI SCARFF/AFP via Getty Images

Both physical and digital protests work to bring awareness and change.

Big Brother Watching During Our Leisure Time

Let's consider the Netflix science fiction anthology series *Black Mirror*, which "explores a twisted, high-tech near-future where humanity's greatest innovations and darkest instincts collide" ("Black Mirror," 2011) and provides us with several interesting intersections with ideas in this chapter. In particular, in "Nosedive," the opening episode of season 3, we are invited to imagine a world where every single encounter with another person is rated on a scale of one to five. From a conversation in an elevator to lunch with a friend to a maid of honor speech, everything is rated and averaged into a cumulative personal rating. In this society, these ratings are public knowledge. A person with a score of 4.0 or above is considered good quality and anyone with a score less than 4.0 is looked down upon and ostracized, resulting in negative impacts on socioeconomic status and lifestyle. For example, the main character, Lacie, starts off at a 4.2 and has her heart set on a luxury apartment, but a 4.2 isn't quite high enough to get her into that level of apartment; she

needs at least a 4.5 social prowess for entry. Lacie then spends an inordinate amount of time, money, and energy disciplining herself and her body (body image plays a role in the rating system) into trying to be a 4.5-type of person. She thinks about what she should post, who she should be seen with, what she should look like, and how she should act in order to curate a 4.5 Lacie.

While this episode may seem far-fetched—a distant dystopia—there are some parallels that point to this reality as a not-so-distant future. Think of the prominent position the likes rating system has on your own personal and professional identity and sense of self-worth. We are increasingly becoming obsessed with all things data driven. Take note, for example, of how many times you are asked to rate, rank, like, or review something or someone on a daily basis. From ratemyprofessor.com to Instagram, to the little smiley- and frowny-face buttons in public restrooms, to follow-up rate-your-experience emails after you receive any service. On the flip side, how often do you consume ratings, thus perpetuating a system where rating one another is the norm? When you buy something on Amazon? When you choose an Uber driver? When you pick a restaurant? For example, an app called Peeple allows users to rate and recommend people based on relationships (professional and personal) and interactions with them. A board game called Nosedive and based off the *Black Mirror* episode allows players—through play—to practice creating a perfect life while avoiding getting dings for falling out of the metaphorical socially acceptable line. The Chinese government has been testing a mandatory social credit system since 2014 (see Kobie, 2019), with the goal of making it a unified nation-wide system mandatory for everyone. The social credit system will reinforce the idea that "keeping trust is glorious and breaking trust is disgraceful" (Creemers, 2015, para. 14). But what does all this surveillance do? Should we care?

Michel Foucault (1975/1977) would argue that surveillance can work to discipline us into behaving as acceptable members of a society. In his book, *Discipline and Punish*, he describes the history of the prison system and how discipline has become hidden and centralized through surveillance mechanisms. Prisons evolved so that all cells were organized in a circle and a tall guard tower was in the middle of the circle. All cells and prisoners were visible by the guard, but the prisoners could not see the guards in the tower. Therefore, prisoners disciplined themselves, behaving as if they were being watched whether they were or not. It can also be argued that social media acts as a similar type of panopticon. People censor and carefully curate posts *as if* someone will be reading them (whether or not someone actually does). In this way, we are disciplining ourselves to perform in a specific acceptable way in these digital spaces.

Echoing Foucault's ideas, Andrejevic (2002) also asserts that we should and must care about the surveillance we are submitting ourselves to when we use digital technologies. He believes that we are being exploited by providing free labor that makes the rich richer while we toil away for free and asserts that we should be paid for our labor. Our labor produces both social and cultural capital and that data, in the hands of the few, has dangerous implications.

Summary

In this chapter, we have addressed positive and negative impacts of digital technologies surrounding our identities, social lives, sex lives, bodies, social equity, and privacy. The assumption has been that we have all chosen to opt in to using digital technologies. We conclude this chapter by exploring the important questions: What real options do we have if we want to opt out of using social media and other digital technologies? Can someone live a connected, healthy, and happy life without having any form of social media? Can they do so without participating in digital leisure in some way? These are very personal questions. We would like you to think back on the results of your digital time use activity and reflect on the knowledge you have gained while reading this chapter, while contemplating these questions and the learning activities that follow.

Learning Activities

1. Your data for social media sites like Instagram are stored on large server farms. Look into the option of owning your own server to store your own data. How do you do it? What does it cost?

2. Think about options to keep social media accounts but increase your own privacy and control over your own data (search for "all the social media opt-outs you need to activate right now" on mashable.com).

3. How can you resist social media sites altogether? Can you create a certain content that doesn't play into traditional content? Can you think of a political way to gain control over what you produce?

Review Questions

1. What designates a technology as a digital technology?

2. What is self-tracking? Do you see this as a positive or negative thing? Why?

3. In what ways are digital technologies practically merging with human bodies? Can you think of an example of this that the authors did not mention?

4. The media, our parents, and our grandparents often make digital technologies and the use of them by millennials and Generation Z seem wholly negative. Make a convincing argument for the positive impacts of digital technology use.

5. Why aren't digital leisure spaces equitable? What can be done to make them more equitable?

6. How might you perform your identity in digital leisure spaces? Give a concrete example.

7. What, according to the authors (and Michel Foucault), does surveillance do to a person and to a society? Do you agree or disagree?

Go to HK*Propel* to access additional learning content.

Leisure, Natural Landscapes, and Sustainability

Leah Joyner
University of Utah

N. Qwynne Lackey
SUNY Cortland

Kelly Bricker
Arizona State University

Nathan Bricker
Arizona State University

Daniel L. Dustin
University of Utah

VOCABULARY TERMS

Antiquities Act of 1906
built environment
Bureau of Land
  Management
Civilian Conservation
  Corps
climate change
environment

environmental justice
gateway communities
global positioning systems
Leave No Trace
leisure landscapes
manifest destiny
National Outdoor
  Leadership School

natural environment
nongovernmental
  organizations
Organic Act of 1916
Outdoor Foundation
Proposition 13
social justice
sustainability

Tennessee Valley Authority

traditional ecological knowledge

U.S. Department of the Interior

U.S. Fish and Wildlife Service

U.S. Forest Service

U.S. National Park Service

wilderness

Works Progress Administration

After reading this chapter, you will

- understand the historical foundations of leisure as it relates to natural landscapes and sustainability;
- understand the impacts of leisure pursuits on our landscapes;
- understand the ways in which leisure landscapes are managed for quality experiences; and
- understand the connections between leisure, environment, society, and sustainability as guiding principles in managing leisure landscapes.

To begin, we acknowledge that we write this chapter while situated on the traditional and ancestral lands of the Shoshone, Paiute, Goshute, and Ute nations, as well as other Indigenous Peoples who have traditionally been and continue to be the original peoples and stewards of this land. We acknowledge the existing sovereignty of Indigenous groups, including those in Utah: the Confederated Tribes of the Goshute Reservation, Navajo Nation, Northwestern Band of Shoshone Nation, Paiute Indian Tribe of Utah, San Juan Southern Paiute, Skull Valley Band of Goshute, Ute Mountain Ute Tribe, and Ute Indian Tribe. We invite readers of this chapter to join us in reflecting upon the ongoing manifestations of both colonization and survivance in the landscapes around each of us. As visitors upon this land, we respect Indigenous communities, past, present, and future, and recognize them as the original stewards of this land. In learning about the historical connections between leisure, **environment**, society, and sustainability, we should also commit ourselves to the contemporary pursuit of more reciprocal and decolonized leisure landscapes.

Imagine you are driving down a lonely highway late at night. Suddenly, on the road in front of you, is a small animal, frozen by your headlights. What do you do? Do you barge ahead in some sort of Darwinian fit? Do you apply the brakes out of a sense of altruism, endangering yourself for the sake of the other? Or do you stop because you really believe that if you destroy that creature you will be destroying a part of yourself? Therein lies the crux of this chapter. How do we see ourselves in relation to the larger living world?

Nature is the wellspring of our existence, a place for testing our mettle in the name of leisure, a place that gives increased meaning to our lives. Nature also provides us with the opportunity to extend ethical consideration to people and creatures and to the Earth in its entirety through the leisure choices we make. In the end, leisure is a critical context for exploring our own ethical commitments as well as a pleasant reminder of our essential grounding in the natural world.

This chapter begins with the assumption that leisure pursuits, at their best, contribute to the growth and development of social and environmental responsibility. Leisure provides a context within which we participate in personally and socially rewarding activities that help us better understand our place in the world and our obligations to our fellow people and living beings. Leisure is fundamentally about human aspiration and quest.

The chapter focuses on the interactions between human beings and the natural environment within a leisure context. Framed within the possibility of seeing ourselves as members and citizens of a larger community of life, we examine the evolution of leisure in the United States. In the end, informed by ecology, we characterize the need for personal, social, economic, political, and environmental relationships that benefit and sustain generations to come.

Changing Landscapes in North America

When the first Western Europeans immigrated to the North American continent, they brought with them a Judeo-Christian tradition that viewed nature as a storehouse of raw materials that became valuable only when employed for human use. Unlike Indigenous Peoples of North America, who have lived with and stewarded the land for centuries, these settlers saw no intrinsic value in wild lands, and they set about cutting back and reaping from nature to tap its instrumental value.

Buoyed in their colonial endeavors by the logic in Adam Smith's *The Wealth of Nations* (1776), the settlers plowed westward, fortified by the belief that if they looked out for their own individual best interests they would be led by an "invisible hand" to promote the public interest. This perspective drove their aims to slash and burn and otherwise convert the **natural environment** into domesticated farmland, and they went about their business imbued with the settler goals of accumulating wealth and property for themselves and their fledgling nation.

There were so few settlers scattered about North America that little thought was given to the possibility of exhausting the country's natural resources. Settlers sought to eradicate almost anything in the path of the rapidly expanding population. Native peoples were subjected to widespread genocide and pushed from their ancestral lands, causing rippling injustice that continues to affect contemporary Native Americans. As westward colonization unfolded (Limerick, 1987), settlers felled trees, destroyed forests, and ravaged plant and animal species; and much of the landscape was denuded of its primeval character. This was carried out in the name of **manifest destiny**, and the young nation boasted its ability to subdue and convert wilderness into capital to support its growing population.

It was not until the middle of the 19th century that settler attitudes toward the American landscape began to change. Three forces, in particular, accounted for this turn of events (Nash, 1967).

Natural beauty inspires inner reflection. Humans are merely a part of nature.

Photo courtesy of N.K. Bricker

First, romanticism as a way of thought worked its way into the hearts and minds of America's East Coast literati. Romanticists believed that pristine nature was God's best handiwork and humankind could not improve on it. Henry David Thoreau, Ralph Waldo Emerson, John James Audubon, and George Perkins Marsh were of this tradition, as was John Muir in the twilight of the 19th century. It was during this period that the idea of **wilderness** materialized as something markedly separate from the **built environment** of North American Anglo-Saxon civilization. Romanticism elicited both a sense of reverence and fear for the uncivilized wild (Stankey, 1989). The work of the Romanticists has instilled a deep love for the natural environment in many avid readers and conservationists, yet it was also based upon an erasure of Indigenous Peoples for whom a symbiotic relationship with land had long been a part of social fabric and culture.

Second, nationalism emerged as a powerful influence. European settlers of the United States

Self-Exploration

In what ways does nature serve as a mirror? Why does a walk in the woods, along the shore, or in the mountains lend itself to introspection and self-reflection? What factors do you think might influence your own relationship with the natural world?

of America held a cultural inferiority complex and yearned for something to distinguish itself from its Old World, or European, roots. Although Europe had its share of mountains, they were not a romanticized wilderness. Indeed, the Alps had been settled and cultivated for centuries. An idea began to take form that America should cherish its wild lands and protect and preserve parts of them as parks in perpetuity. The establishment of Yellowstone National Park in 1872 was the first manifestation of the U.S. federal government's commitment to this ideal.

Third, and perhaps most important, by the end of the 19th century, the United States had been transformed into an urban society. In the early 1800s, only 20 percent of the populace resided in towns and cities, whereas 80 percent resided in rural areas. By the end of the 1800s, the percentages were reversed. Now 80 percent of the citizenry lived in towns and cities and only 20 percent lived in rural areas. The most famous expression of this reversal was an essay published by historian Frederick Jackson Turner in 1893, in which he pronounced the end of the frontier (Turner, 1921). North America was settled from the Atlantic coast to the Pacific coast. There was no more uncolonized territory, and thus the nation turned its sights to setting aside tracts of land for conservation and recreation.

Progressive Movement

The collective effect of these three 19th-century forces resulted in a new appeal to safeguard natural landscapes that heretofore had been thought to have little intrinsic value. The 20th century was ushered in by what was termed *progressive thinking*, led by President Theodore Roosevelt. The country's leaders championed setting aside the nation's "crown jewels" as national parks, and other large tracts of public lands were set aside as national forests. The former were managed as "museums" (look but don't touch) by the U.S. **National Park Service** (NPS),

established in 1916 and housed in the U.S. Department of the Interior. The latter were managed for multiple uses (timber, watershed, mining, grazing) by the U.S. **Forest Service** (USFS), established in 1891 and housed in the Department of Agriculture. Large parcels of less desirable land west of the 100th meridian were turned over to the Interior Department's **Bureau of Land Management** (BLM) for custodianship. Other public lands were assigned to the U.S. **Fish and Wildlife Service** (USFWS), also housed in the Department of the Interior, to care for wildlife habitats. Together, these four federal agencies were entrusted with the stewardship of the lion's share of the United States' public domain.

Throughout the first half of the 20th century, recreation lands at the federal, state, and local levels were expanded dramatically, and the roles of large land-managing agencies solidified. The USFS, under the early leadership of Gifford Pinchot, adopted a utilitarian philosophy toward land management, whereas the NPS, under the early leadership of Stephen Mather, adopted a preservationist philosophy. To this day, the differences in land management practices between these two federal agencies can be explained by those philosophical differences. The USFS's emphasis is on using nature. The NPS's emphasis is on appreciating nature.

Other forces of progressivist thinking were equally hard at work. The American Antiquities Act of 1906 made it possible for presidents to single-handedly protect pockets of the public domain from exploitation by private interests by designating these areas as national monuments. Every president of the United States since 1906—Republican and Democrat alike—has used the Antiquities Act to his advantage (Dustin, McAvoy, & Ogden, 2005). During the Great Depression, many of President Franklin Roosevelt's New Deal initiatives were devoted to recreational development. The **Civilian Conservation Corps**, the **Tennessee Valley Authority**, and the **Works Progress Administration** all contributed to growing the public recreation estate. While these initiatives were widely touted by some for their contributions to recreational infrastructure development, much of which is still in use today, it is important to note the controversial tactics employed by these agencies. For instance, the Tennessee Valley Authority displaced thousands of families from their homes using compulsory relocation through a process known as eminent domain (Kitchens, 2014).

Despite this development, there was little demand for these public pleasuring grounds in the first half of the 20th century because the American public was largely homebound.

Post–World War II

World War II changed everything. Prior to the Second World War, few Americans had the wherewithal to travel about their country. But when the engines of industry resumed operation at full throttle upon the war's conclusion, masses of Americans outfitted with more free time, more discretionary income, more knowledge about available opportunities, and more mobility set out to enjoy their public lands. These factors resulted in an explosion of demand for outdoor recreation in the 1950s and 1960s.

This upswell of interest in outdoor recreation was welcomed at first as a boon. Recreation was not viewed as inherently problematic. Everything about it was deemed good. People were beginning to enjoy nature and each other in a leisure context. They were learning about their cultural and natural heritage in a way that led to countless individual, social, cultural, economic, and environmental benefits. Measures were taken to sustain this growing interest in the outdoors, and projects like the NPS's Mission 66 (initiated in 1956 to construct park facilities in preparation for the 50th anniversary of the NPS in 1966, including the construction of over 100 visitor centers) were undertaken to make sure a sufficient infrastructure was in place to accommodate the growing enthusiasm for exploring America's cultural, historic, and scenic treasures.

Recreational Limits

Skyrocketing demand for outdoor recreation eventually ushered in a variety of management problems. The problems were rooted in the limited nature of the nation's store of outdoor recreation resources in the face of a seemingly unlimited demand for them (Dustin & McAvoy, 1980; Shelby & Heberlein, 1986). Heavy recreational use resulted in unwelcome impacts on the quality of recreation experiences as well as the quality of the environment itself. Recreation congestion, crowding, conflict, and constraints became part of the managerial lexicon. How best to manage for outdoor recreation? How best to manage recreation settings that were now in danger of being *loved to death*?

These issues, occurring in the late 1960s and during all of the 1970s, led to the development of a variety of management strategies, such as attempts to determine recreation-carrying capacity, assess limits of acceptable change, and develop elaborate organizational frameworks like the recreation opportunity spectrum, within which to accommodate the public's wide-ranging recreational tastes (Manning, 1999). Essentially, the management challenge was how best to satisfy those tastes while safeguarding the quality of the recreation settings themselves. The inherent contradiction in this challenge—making all kinds of recreation available to all kinds of people while simultaneously protecting the environment—has been at the center of the recreation debate since the Organic Act of 1916 charged the NPS with meeting that challenge. Serving these two masters has been daunting.

Financial Limits

Exacerbating the managerial challenge has been a fundamental change in the way outdoor recreation is funded. For much of the 20th century, the nation's parks and open spaces were treated as public goods. Their existence was subsidized through taxes, and admission was otherwise free of charge. Then, in 1979, a taxpayer revolt in California culminated in **Proposition 13**, a referendum that put a lid on property taxes. Because public parks and recreation, museums, libraries, and other public goods relied on property taxes for their lifeblood, they had to look elsewhere for financial support. The thinking behind Proposition 13 spread like wildfire across the country, and the last quarter-century saw an uphill battle for money to support what used to be paid for by taxes. What formerly was treated as a public good (tax supported) is now treated as a merit good (a combination of tax and private support) and soon may be treated merely as a private good (fees and charges). This could eventually result in public parks and recreation being available only to those who are willing and able to pay for them. This raises serious questions about fairness and equity as well as what ought to be the role of public parks and recreation in a democracy. In the meantime, the stewards of access and custodians of choice do what they must do to sustain the services and settings for which they are responsible.

The decline in tax support for public parks and recreation also has forced the profession to become

The Impact of Taxes on Parks and Recreation

Imagine that you work for a public parks and recreation agency, such as the U.S. National Park Service. If your role is to create and manage recreation opportunities for visitors, how would funding influence your decisions? If your park were treated as a public good and funded entirely through taxes, what services would you provide? If your park were treated as a merit or private good funded partially or entirely through visitor fees, what changes would you make to the services you offer and why? What are the implications of your thinking for issues of access, fairness, equity, and **social justice**?

more creative and innovative in its service delivery. Before Proposition 13, little thought was given to marketing leisure services, and little thought was given to leisure services outside the traditional public parks and recreation mainstream. Marketing is now a cornerstone of professional preparation, and the field has broadened its focus dramatically. Specializations in therapeutic recreation, commercial recreation, hospitality management, event planning, convention and visitor bureaus, festivals, sport management, outdoor adventure, outdoor leadership, organized camping, tourism, ecotourism, and sustainable tourism are all now considered to be important parts of the service delivery mix (Bricker, 2016; Winter, Selin, Cerveney, & Bricker, 2019).

Widening the Circle of Ethical Consideration

Adding to the complexity is a slowly evolving idea that there is more to parks and recreation than looking out for human interests. Proponents of this line of thought argue that nature is much more than a backdrop for the unfolding of our human drama. Conservationists, Indigenous Peoples, spiritual leaders, and many others speak of the rights of nature. They advocate for extending ethical consideration outward from people to other species to the Earth in its entirety. They urge us to become less anthropocentric, be less human centered, and consider the possibility that the Earth was made for more than human beings alone.

There are many obstacles to finding our way toward such a symbiotic relationship with nature. Chief among them is an increasing human separation from nature and increasing detachment from our biological moorings. Per capita visits to national parks are on the decline, and we seem to be more and more likely to stay inside and live highly technological, sedentary, urban lives.

Our continued separation of ourselves from nature and the ideological separation of the natural environment from the built environment also uncovers yet another obstacle to building a more harmonious relationship with the world around us. Continued ways of thinking that couch the natural environment as wilderness imply that the environment is indeed something separate from humans and denies the inextricability of the relationship of people with all of Earth's inhabitants (Cronon, 1996). This separation can distract us from the connections between the built environment and the natural environment, pulling our attention away from the ways in which our leisure and lifestyle choices affect planetary health as a whole.

In sum, our adaptable human nature makes it possible for the world around us to change for the worse without our even being aware of it (think about **climate change**). Therein lies a much more nuanced, but perhaps more dangerous, by-product of our increasing separation from the natural world: We may well adapt to living without close association to it. We may not miss what we do not know.

The 21st Century

The gargantuan task before us is to figure out how to live, and how to recreate, in ways that recognize and honor our embeddedness in a larger community of life. Our charge is to learn how to practice leisure in a manner that does not harm our fellow people, living creatures, or the Earth in biological wholeness. This requires a basic understanding of ecology. It also requires a willingness to conduct our lives with a conscious appreciation of the condition of the rest of the world. This is not an easy thing to do. It demands the will to restrain ourselves when restraint is called for out of a concern for others. More than anything else, it requires understanding the consequences of our actions before we act and then conducting our lives accordingly.

Self-Exploration

Consider your own existence on this planet. Where do you live? What is the air quality in the area you currently call home? Do you have easy access to fresh water? What is access to fresh air and water like for Indigenous Peoples in the areas where you live? Consider this: Almost one fifth of the world's population (about 2.2 billion people) live in areas where access to a safely managed water supply is scarce. One quarter of the global population also lives in developing countries that face water shortages due to a lack of infrastructure to fetch water from rivers and aquifers (World Health Organization, 2020). How much water do you use daily? Could you adapt to one third of your use today? How would this affect your life?

Ultimately, what we are talking about is sustaining health—the health of people and the health of the larger world of which we humans are but a small part. Health, in turn, is a function of living in the light of ecologic interrelationships and interdependencies. As the renowned ecologist Dr. Robin Wall Kimmerer writes,

> We need acts of restoration, not only for polluted waters and degraded lands but also for our relationship to the world. We need to restore honor to the way we live so that when we walk through the world we don't have to avert our eyes with shame, so that we can hold our heads up high and receive the respectful acknowledgment of the rest of the earth's beings. (2014, p. 195)

Managerial Challenges

The leisure landscape has changed significantly since the U.S. federal government seized and then set aside large tracts of the public domain for the so-called common good. Many historically famous accounts of this period focus on the influences of President Teddy Roosevelt; the educational writings of Gifford Pinchot, Aldo Leopold, and Rachel Carson; prose and philosophical insights of Henry David Thoreau, Walt Whitman, and John Muir; and the artistic influence of Thomas Moran, George Catlin, and Ansel Adams, which all reflected a colonized perspective of the United States and have shaped much of the philosophical discussion surrounding primarily White America's relationships with the natural world. The very problems that worried these conservationists (i.e., exploitation and loss of connection with nature) stemmed from European colonization of North America and the genocide against Indigenous Peoples, long-time stewards of the environment (Dunbar-Ortiz, 2014). Current issues in conservation management echo

this dynamic. For example, as wildfires consume the Western United States, some land management agencies are employing prescribed burns to better manage fires in ways that are in keeping with Indigenous traditions (Sommer, 2020). Prescribed, or controlled burns, have long been a part of the **traditional ecological knowledge (TEK)** of Indigenous Peoples who practice symbiotic stewardship ethics (Eisenberg et al., 2019; Berkes, Colding, & Folk, 2000). Contemporary conservationists are, unfortunately, following in the footsteps of their predecessors who gained recognition by effectively advocating for the employment of Indigenous land stewardship without allocating any credit or leadership within the conservation movement to Native Americans (The Wilderness Society, 2020, p. 25).

Today, a host of new forces are influencing our leisure choices and relationship with public lands. Characterized by a growing population and increasing pressure on public lands, today's management challenges are daunting. Here, we examine these through three categories: volume, activity diversity, and access. Now more than ever before, the sheer volume of interest, diversity of use and perspective, and unprecedented and unequal access confront and confound recreation planners, resource managers, and the recreating public. This presents a series of complex questions about how best to manage parks and protected areas, advance the aims of conservation, and balance our understandings of the leisure landscape within a framework of not only environmentalism but also **environmental justice**.

Volume

In 1900, the population of the United States was 76 million. By 2000, the population had climbed to 281 million, more than tripling in size (U.S. Census Bureau, 2010). By 2100, the population is expected to more than double again to 571 million (U.S. Census

Bureau, 2010). The impact of this exponential population growth on the public recreation estate is amplified when we consider the urbanization of the country and the burgeoning number of communities now located adjacent to our public lands. The buffer zones that once protected outdoor recreation settings from anthropogenic impacts—such as air and water pollution, invasive species, and excessive use—are shrinking as larger numbers of people are living in close proximity to parks and protected areas. Isolation is no longer the frugal land manager's insurance policy, and the quality of the recreational lands that the majority of people can most easily access is threatened (Zajchowski, Desocio, & Lackey, 2019). New ways of thinking about the volume and type of use are required to address the evolving challenges associated with massive access to outdoor recreation.

When we speak of volume, it is helpful to consider both the economics of visitor use and the number of visitors themselves. From an economic standpoint, access to disposable income and the willingness to apply it to outdoor recreation interests are alive and well. This is demonstrated clearly by annual reports of the **Outdoor Foundation**, which help us quantify the volume of use in dollars and cents. The last census on outdoor recreation (2019) revealed the following:

- Americans embarked on a collective 10.2 billion outdoor outings—an average of 67.2 annual outings per outdoor participant.
- Based on the year before, outings actually declined by an average of 7.4 trips per participant.

The declining recreational use of the outdoors is reflective of long-term trends. The Outdoor Foundation found that from 2017 to 2019, overall outings dropped by 4.5 percent (Outdoor Industry Association [OIA], 2020, p. 6). This historical downward trend indicates that Americans will likely continue spending less time outdoors, especially with intensifying external barriers, such as work and family demands as well as technology and cost of entry. Yet, the outdoor economy remains strong. Nationally, outdoor recreationists contribute $887 billion annually to the economy, which in turn provides 7.6 million jobs, $65.3 billion in federal tax revenue, and $59.2 billion in state and local tax revenues (OIA, 2019). There are also indications that people increasingly turned to the outdoors as a means of

social distancing to combat the impacts of COVID-19 and, in some cases, due to limitations on travel. All in all, as an industry, outdoor recreation ranks as one of the economic and political heavyweights of our time.

Outdoor recreation is big business, and the resulting political clout has been demonstrated across the country, where environmentalists and recreationists regularly join forces in disputes over how public lands are managed for leisure. As of 2020, 16 states have created

———

offices of outdoor recreation, task forces, or policy advisors to serve as the state lead in bolstering economic development and the outdoor recreation economy; promoting health and wellness; ensuring conservation and stewardship of public lands and waters; educating and engaging children in the outdoors; and serving as a point of contact [for multi-stakeholders, various levels of government, and businesses, in care of the widespread outdoor recreation sector of society]. (OIA, 2020, p. 1)

Consider the following as well:

- Many more Americans camp than play basketball or hike than play soccer or watch football.
- The number of Americans who run, bicycle, hike, fish, or camp is nearly 1.5 times the total population of Canada (37.5 million, 2019).
- The number of annual participants in outdoor recreation in the South Atlantic region alone (Eastern Seaboard and West Virginia; 27.7 million) is higher than the population each of our U.S. states, with the exception of California and Texas.

In sum, the sheer numbers of outdoor recreationists and the economic benefits they generate have a tremendous effect on the environment. They influence how our public lands are managed, and, for better or worse, they shape the nature of outdoor recreation experiences. If managing volume were the only issue, we might be inclined to think that the custodial challenge is not that complex. However, several other issues affect our public lands.

Activity Diversity

Because of the multiple-use missions of many large public land–managing agencies (e.g., the USFS and BLM), space is commonly allocated for a vast array of recreational activities. The diversity of these activities and the unique management challenges they present complicate our love affair with outdoor recreation in manifold ways. For example, accommodations are typically made for mountain biking, dog sledding, rafting, kayaking, hot air ballooning, snowmobiling, hang gliding, heli-skiing, scuba diving, and an assortment of off-road motorized, water-based motorized, and nonmotorized leisure pursuits. Accommodation is also made for a cornucopia of extreme sports, wherein adventure-loving, thrill-seeking participants tumble down hillsides in inflated, see-through bouncing balls (called *zorbing*); jump from bridges, natural arches, and overhangs on what amounts to nothing more than industrialized rubber bands (bungee jumping); ski and inline skate using a kite wing (called *skimbating*); or wear wetsuits, body armor, and flippers while boogie boarding (called *river sledging*). Other adventure sports include paragliding, shark diving, ski paragliding, kiteboarding, and BASE (building, antenna, span, earth) jumping. Then there are all the iterations of motorized use, including cross-country flying in ultralights (called *aero-trekking*) and rock crawling in machines that defy gravity as they claw at the rock and earth in an effort to go where no human or machine has gone before.

Stretching the imagination even more are organized events like Burning Man, where several thousand event goers from every imaginable subculture converge on Nevada's Black Rock country to burn a 40-foot stick figure. It has been said that "Burning Man enables all the black sheep of the world to graze together" (Rough Guides, 2007, p. 184). Burning Man has also become increasingly commercialized; what began with small roots as a desert arts festival has grown into a burgeoning hub of capital, replete with amenities such as private lounges, bars, private showers, and Wi-Fi (Gillette, 2015). This type of festival provides an interesting lens through which we may reflect on the amenities that accompany outdoor recreation and the implications these have for user groups. Who is able to procure access to outdoor recreation? How does this change with access to luxury amenities and increasingly expensive gear?

Mix together the volume of use, the economics of the industry, the diversity of activities, and

Nature offers a range of opportunities to push yourself beyond your comfort zone.

increasing multiculturalism, and you can see why managing leisure landscapes becomes even more daunting. Understanding changing demographics and how to manage to ensure quality leisure experiences is no mean feat. Different values drive different recreational choices, including how, when, and where recreationists will interact with the outdoor recreation environment. What historically may have been a one-dimensional, traditional-use landscape has quickly become a multidimensional, nontraditional-use landscape.

Adding to this managerial task is the changing face of America's populace. The Pew Research Center estimates large changes within various ethnic groups by 2050 (table 10.1) (Passel & Cohn, 2008, p. 1). As table 10.1 illustrates, the largest changes may be within the Latino and White communities. How might these changes affect the management of leisure landscapes? For instance, research has shown that Latinos primarily recreate in large family groups and often place high value on the social qualities of participating in outdoor recreation that promotes family cohesiveness (Chavez, 2000; Gobster, 2002; Shaull & Gramann, 1998; Virden & Walker, 1999). Latino Americans are more likely to recreate with immediate and extended family than with friends, frequently in groups of three or more (Sasidharan, Willits, & Godbey, 2005; Virden & Walker, 1999). Because of these cultural differences, recreation land managers need to plan for diversity in outdoor recreation opportunities, for example, accommodating a range of group sizes (Gobster, 2002), providing for a greater variety of activities, and creating facilities to accommodate divergent interests (Sasidharan et al., 2005). While the American populace is increasingly diverse, visitors to national parks remain predominantly White, which indicates a need for the NPS and other federal land management agencies to increase representation of diversity across visitor and employee groups (Schultz et al., 2019). Enjoyment of the outdoors by an increasingly diverse population heightens the complexity of the managerial challenge. There is every indication that these demographic profiles will become increasingly varied, requiring more creativity and innovation from those charged with managing public lands for all citizens. But once again, it is not only increasing volume and activity diversity that shape recreationists' choices and associated management challenges. The next factor we discuss is access to leisure landscapes.

TABLE 10.1 Changing Populations in the United States From 2005 to 2050

2005	2050
5% Asian	9% Asian
14% Hispanic	29% Hispanic
13% Black	13% Black
67% White	47% White

Data from Passel & Cohn (2008).

Access

Today there is unprecedented access to public lands created through increased population, road access, creative technology, urban sprawl, and the combined effects they have on leisure landscapes. Access plays a critical role in the types and volume of use taking place. Lands once protected by their remoteness or difficult terrain are now being affected by the growth in mechanized outdoor recreation. From snowmobiles to rock crawlers, ultralight aircraft to hovercrafts, the outdoors is being accessed in ways once unimagined. Rock crawlers, motorcyclists, and electric cyclists are exploring the front country and backcountry like never before, whereas aero-trekkers and hovercrafts are going places once thought impossible.

This type of unprecedented access is complicated not only by advances in transportation but also by the technological birth of cell and satellite phones and **global positioning systems**, which now empower recreationists to go farther afield than ever before. Perhaps with the reassurance of help being only a phone call away and the mystery of direction and location virtually eliminated, outdoor spaces have become more broadly accessible to an expanded population of outdoor users. Access to the outdoors is also influenced by the growth of population centers, creating a wildland–urban interface. As more and more Americans find their way out of cities, the resulting sprawl affects lands once considered more backcountry than front country. This has increased the potential for pollution, human–wildlife interactions, and the spread of wildland fires to neighborhoods and decreased buffer zones between front-country and backcountry access.

Another consideration is that all people ought to have fair and equitable access to parks in their communities. Because many physiological and psychological health benefits are associated with outdoor recreation (Kaplan, 2001; Kaplan, 1995; Ulrich, 1981), community parks that are accessible have numerous benefits. However, not all citizens have safe and equal access to outdoor places for recreation (Garcia, 2006; Neighbors, Marquez, & Marcus, 2007; Parks, Housemann, & Brownson, 2003). Access to parks is unevenly distributed throughout the United States, and important reasons for this disparity include influences such as racism, socioeconomic disparities, and different access levels for urban or rural communities (Garcia, 2006; Neighbors et al., 2007; Parks et al., 2003).

The American population is also changing; the U.S. Census Bureau projects that one in five Americans will be 65 or older by 2030. Due to this aging, it is also projected that immigration will outpace births as the largest source of population increase in the country by 2030 (U.S. Census Bureau, 2020). This means that the types of demands placed on leisure landscapes are likely to change because many users will have decreased physical ability, and many more users will seek out new types of recreation outlets. The desire to explore, commune with nature, and enjoy outdoor recreation is not likely to subside with age. Rather, the nature of involvement will likely gravitate toward types of recreation more suitable to an aging power train. This could mean increased use of off-road and all-terrain vehicles and an increased dependency on other forms of technologically assisted recreation.

As previously discussed in this chapter, the development of the American Conservation movement was largely driven by a small number of leaders in a limited demographic. In the mission to increase access to nature, we will need to take into consideration the structure of parks and protected area management in the United States. The history of the conservation movement coupled with the increasingly changing and diversifying American population indicates that the movement itself must seek to increase justice and equity-oriented work. Through engaging with a wider audience, outdoor recreation and parks and protected areas will have broader levels of support (Bonta & Jordan, 2007) and ultimately increase the possibilities for enjoyment of nature by all.

The love affair with the outdoors has evolved in ways we could never have imagined and will continue to do so as technology advances and the demographics of our society change. The increased use of social media and the exponential growth in popularity of platforms like Facebook and Instagram have presented new considerations for growth and access regarding outdoor recreation activities. The practice of geotagging allows social media users to check in to specific locations and share beautiful images of the environments in which they recreate. This has led to some debate amongst outdoor recreationists, with some arguing that the location of such prized sites should be kept secret or passed on only by word of mouth. Others argue that geotagging increases knowledge and access for people who may not otherwise have access to resources on how and where to recreate outdoors. How does the increasing use of social media contribute to diversity in outdoor recreation? How do you think this will shape recreation in the future?

Moving Toward a Sustainable Future

What will it take to continue to move toward a sustainable future? The encouraging news is that many programs are working on this through education, guidelines, and certification (e.g., the Global Sustainable Tourism Council, #WildSanctuaries, PADI AWARE's responsible shark and ray tourism guide, to name a few). Increased education and establishing industry standards to assist in the problems faced by planet and people living in and around protected areas, as well as communicating and engaging with the next generation of leaders, can make a difference.

Programs and Initiatives in Sustainable Recreation

Several initiatives and programs support concepts of **sustainability** and promotion of responsible use of the outdoors and related areas. More and more programs are being implemented to help our current and future generations adopt a responsible use ethic, which will assist in conserving the natural capital we all depend upon. We share examples of programs in the next section.

Leave No Trace

To address the challenges associated with the sheer number of recreationists, the diversity of their pastimes, and types of access they use when visiting their public lands, the NPS, USFS, BLM, and other federal and state land managing agencies have implemented an educational approach to visitor management known as **Leave No Trace** (LNT). LNT is founded on the principle that education can help reduce the impacts of recreational use to create a more sustainable relationship with the outdoors we depend on for quality experiences. LNT's mission is "to promote and inspire responsible outdoor recreation through education, research, and partnership" (Leave No Trace, 2021, p. 1). The fundamental goal is to instill responsibility in outdoor recreationists by providing them with the knowledge to make informed decisions about their outdoor recreation choices and practice the skills necessary to reduce their impacts.

The ideas underpinning LNT grew out of Paul Petzoldt's work with the **National Outdoor Leadership School** (NOLS) in the mid-1960s (Marion & Reid, 2001). Petzoldt had witnessed firsthand the negative impacts outdoor recreation programs were having on the natural environment, and he began exploring and experimenting with new techniques and teaching approaches to reduce those impacts. By the 1970s and 1980s, reducing impacts on wild lands

Photo courtesy of N.K. Bricker

We must learn to live in harmony with nature by minimizing our impact on the environment.

from recreational use was gaining popular support within the USFS as well (Marion & Reid, 2001).

The phrase *leave no trace* was first used by the forest service in an effort to reduce visitor impacts on popular recreation sites located in Utah's Uinta Mountains to the east of Salt Lake City (Tilton, 2003). The concept spread gradually through other forest service districts and other outdoor education programs across the United States, including NOLS, Outward Bound, and the Wilderness Education Association. In 1993, the Forest Service, Bureau of Land Management, National Park Service, Fish and Wildlife Service, and NOLS signed a memorandum of understanding establishing Leave No Trace as the officially recognized national outdoor ethics education program in the United States. The guiding principles LNT instills through its training programs and materials include these:

- Plan ahead and prepare.
- Travel and camp on durable surfaces.
- Dispose of waste properly.
- Leave what you find.
- Minimize campfire impacts.
- Respect wildlife.
- Be considerate of other visitors (www.lnt.org).

Programs for Diverse Populations

Many other organizations, including schools, university outing clubs, and recreation providers (commercial and nonprofit), are addressing environmental issues through information, voluntary certification, and educational programs. In fact, it is hard to find outdoor organizations, schools, and clubs that don't promote a reduced-impact message or provide training to educate their constituents. There is also an increasing number of organizations dedicated to diverse populations in the outdoors. As one example, Outdoor Afro

has become the nation's leading, cutting edge network that celebrates and inspires Black connections and leadership in nature. . . . With nearly 90 leaders in 30 states from around the country, we connect thousands of people to outdoor experiences, who are changing the face of conservation. (Outdoor Afro, 2020)

There are also many LGBTQ+ organizations across the United States, such as LGBT Outdoors, which seeks to "encourage and enable members of the

LGBTQ+ community to get outdoors and connect with nature and the world around them while breaking down stereotypes towards LGBTQ+ people" (LGBT Outdoors, 2020, p. 1). Social media has also provided prolific platforms for the work of groups such as Indigenous Women Hike, a collective of Indigenous women reconnecting with ancestral homelands with more than 78,000 followers at the time of this publication. Other particularly noteworthy activists and groups that represent diversity in the outdoors across social media include @FatGirlsHiking, @Disabledhikers, @Browngirls climb, @Unlikelyhikers, @Melaninbasecamp, and @QueerNature.

Moving Beyond Islands of Hope

Now, more than ever before in history, sustainability is a critical consideration. From the impacts of climate change to the impacts of millions of travelers exploring the globe, the health of our planet is threatened by human conduct. Encouraging people to recreate in the outdoors—to romp the far reaches of the Earth in pursuit of new experiences, cultures, and ecosystems—must be undertaken responsibly and sustainably, so that when we write about leisure and the environment in the future, we can extol their same qualities that we do today.

The value of natural landscapes is incalculable. They provide inspiration to a nation of dreamers, artists, inventors, politicians, engineers, musicians, scientists, and citizens. These places are storehouses of baseline biological data, providing insight into a natural world that is deteriorating at an alarming rate. They are religious sanctuaries, burial grounds, homes, wellsprings of medicines and foods, and sites of survivance to native peoples. Many of us treat these islands of hope (Brown, 1971) as hideaways from the trappings of modern technology and the hustle and bustle of our fast-paced lives. However, despite the distinctions often drawn between the natural and built environment within Westernized colonial thought, the environmental, socioeconomic, and cultural connections between the two are becoming more widely recognized and understood. Ultimately, in one way or another, the well-being of our public lands is linked to our own well-being.

While the tradition of U.S. federal land managers has been to manage public lands as isolated islands of nature, a relatively new movement toward managing public lands as part of larger landscapes inclusive of public and private lands has begun. Some federal land management agencies are now collaborating with partners on cross-boundary conservation and sustainable tourism development projects (Lackey & Bricker, 2020; Joyner, Lackey, & Bricker, 2019). Existing partnerships take many forms, including a variety of partnerships between different federal agencies, local governments, native peoples, **nongovernmental organizations**, and private entities (Bricker, Black, & Cottrell, 2012; Bushell & Bricker, 2016; Snyman & Bricker, 2019).

As an example, The Bears Ears Inter-Tribal Coalition is a historic consortium of sovereign tribal nations, including the Hopi Tribe, Navajo Nation, Ute Mountain Ute Tribe, Pueblo of Zuni, and Ute Indian Tribe, who have united in an effort to conserve and potentially comanage the Bears Ears cultural landscape through partnerships with federal agencies (Bears Ears, 2020). The coalition collectively advocated to protect 1.35 million acres of sacred mesas, canyons, mountains, rivers, and red rock outcroppings in southern Utah (Wilkinson, 2018), which culminated in President Barack Obama's use of the Antiquities Act to designate the Bears Ears National Monument in 2016. In 2017, President Donald Trump moved to reduce the monument's size by 85 percent, effectively opening much of the original monument area for leasing by energy developers and ranchers. The fight over the boundary of Bears Ears National Monument continues, and a new generation of outdoor recreationists and advocates are being called upon to support the work of partnerships like the Bears Ears Inter-Tribal Coalition and new approaches to public land management.

Other examples of cross-boundary conservation can be found in increasing collaborations between U.S. national park managers with communities that lie just beyond the borders of national parks (Lackey & Bricker, 2020). The decisions of those living and working in these communities, which are often referred to as **gateway communities**, can have both positive and negative impacts on neighboring public lands. Likewise, the land management decisions of federal agencies can have profound effects on those in gateway communities. In recognition of these connections, some gateway communities and national parks are working together to identify and pool their resources to accomplished shared management and community development goals (Snyman & Bricker, 2019; Winter et al., 2019).

Collaboration may very well be the future of public land management. Yet, even though collaboration promises an abundance of opportunity, it comes with challenges. Establishing shared goals and action items may be difficult as potential partners face a multitude of resource, political, and institutional barriers. We are just beginning the journey of learning to overcome these obstacles, and many opportunities exist for those engaged in the parks, recreation, and tourism field to contribute to this endeavor as we move toward managing our public lands as part of larger landscapes that we are all a part of.

Our future lies not only in what we create but in what value we can preserve from the past. Our future lies not only in technological advancement but in how we use those advances to safeguard nature. The future of the United States will be etched in the designs of our built environments and heard in the whisperings of our natural landscapes. Our achievements are not merely measured in the grandeur of our nation's mountains and deserts but also through the ways in which we seek to redress injustice and to embed equity and equality across all our pursuits in leisure and life. If we cannot see our future, we should at least strive to protect the giant trees from which we hope to gain a better perspective on it, the clear lakes from which we attempt to glimpse a reflection of it, the deep canyons in which we strain to hear its echoes, the wild rivers upon which we pursue it, and the mountain meadows from which we contemplate it.

Self-Exploration

Consider where you are today and your dreams for tomorrow. How will you make a difference in the world you live in? What will you contribute? How should you contribute? What are you passionate about? What motivates or inspires you to action or inaction in your life?

Natural landscapes are not something we can create or re-create. We may never be able to experience the same places and walk the same trails that helped inspire those today and those who came before us. Still, the burden to conserve our natural environment rests not solely on the shoulders of management agencies and others, but on our own individual shoulders as well. Our obligation is not simply to enjoy the land but to protect it for those who follow us, including nonhuman inhabitants. What will inspire future generations, and what will they build upon, if we do not practice equitable stewardship of our natural landscapes? How can all people of this country relate to and believe in the importance of these natural areas?

Summary

Many people who inhabited these landscapes before you have changed the way we think about the environment, the out of doors, and responsible relationships with Earth's inhabitants. We understand that through nature, we can learn a lot about ourselves and the way in which we as human beings fit in the larger picture of life. We also note the importance and challenges of a large outdoor industry and how decisions we make today in managing natural landscapes will ultimately affect future generations. As a society, we interact without environmental landscapes in many ways, and one important use is for renewal, recreation, and the health of all beings who inhabit these places. A sustainable and healthy future rests on the shoulders of today's generations, and as we have learned from our historical roots, decisions made today affect tomorrow (Schwab, Dustin, Bricker, 2017). Many programs and initiatives support the conservation of these landscapes, yet how we individually decide to live on the planet affects not only these decisions but also decisions of policy makers and those who take the responsibility to value these places. Will you be a changemaker? How will you contribute to the future? What will your impact be on future generations?

Learning Activities

1. Managing agencies, private users, commercial operators, and outdoor retailers are reaching out more than ever to the general public in an attempt to educate outdoor recreationists in the reduction of their impacts and preservation of the experiences they seek to enjoy. One of the more widely known programs is Leave No Trace. For this activity:
   • Go to www.lnt.org and review the resources the organization provides.
   • Get to know the seven principles, located here: https://lnt.org/why/7-principles.
   • Go to this website to complete the awareness training course.

2. Discuss the following questions in pairs, and then bring your findings to the entire group and share your thoughts:
   • What kinds of impacts do you think forced removal and assimilation might have on Indigenous Peoples? How do you think this relates to the management of national parks and public lands today?
   • What kinds of impacts do you think slavery and racism had, and continue to have, on the relationships to the land and outdoor spaces of African Americans and people of color?
   • How might the inability to vote have affected everyone but EuroAmerican men? How might this have prevented people from participating as decision makers in the birth of the public lands movement?
   • How would the history of public lands be different if everyone had been allowed to participate in shaping the movement from the beginning? What are some of the impacts of these events and concerns on public lands management today? (For additional activities, please visit: www.wilderness.org.)

Review Questions

1. What key events shaped our current use of the outdoors?
2. What challenges are present in managing leisure landscapes for future generations?
3. Why is sustainability important, and how does it affect our leisure natural landscapes?
4. Considering the present-day use of our leisure landscapes. What influences will shape how these places are managed 25 years from now?
5. What influences does a pandemic such as COVID-19 have on outdoor recreation use?

Go to HK*Propel* to access additional learning content.

Leisure Economics

Brent Beggs
Illinois State University

Michael Mulvaney
Illinois State University

VOCABULARY TERMS

direct expenditure

discretionary income

economic multiplier

indirect expenditure

leakage

LEARNING OUTCOMES

After reading this chapter, you will be able to

- define key economic principles related to leisure services, such as discretionary income, direct expenditure, indirect expenditure, and economic multiplier;
- recognize the interconnectedness between economics and leisure;
- describe the significant economic impact that different sectors of the leisure service industry have on society; and
- review the economic implications of current leisure trends.

Leisure Economics: An Illustration

Tomas and four of his friends are making plans to attend a summer music festival this weekend. The festival is a free event featuring a mix of local and national artists. Tomas and his friends have been looking forward to this festival all year. It's free and should be a low-cost weekend of great music and memories. The festival is a three-hour drive from their hometown, and they leave early Saturday morning. As a college student, Tomas is on a limited budget and has decided to keep costs to a minimum. Rather than staying in a hotel that evening, Tomas and his friends have made plans to stay with his cousin who lives in the area. On their way out of town Saturday morning, they stop at a convenience store and spend $30 on gas and $25 on coffee and snacks. They arrive at the festival, pay $10 for parking and search for their favorite food truck for lunch and beverages, which costs them another $45. After they eat, they enjoy the musical performances, buy souvenir T-shirts ($60), and visit with some of

their friends from out of town who also made the trip. The weather, performances, and atmosphere are amazing; there are over 30,000 people attending this year's festival. It is perfect. At the end of the festival, Tomas and his friends head to his cousin's apartment. When they get to the apartment, they hang out and decide to order pizza, which costs them another $40. They sleep in the next morning before heading home. On their way home, they spend $40 for lunch and drinks.

In total, Tomas and his friends spent $250, or $50 per person, to attend a free music festival and really didn't have any large expenditures associated with the event (hotel room, concert tickets, etc.) as they were trying to be frugal with their expenses. While $50 per person to attend a free music festival may or may not seem that significant, consider the overall impact of 30,000 people spending about $50 to attend the festival. That adds up to $1.5 million in spending! Also, consider that Tomas and his friends were deliberately trying to keep their costs to a minimum. It is likely that several of the festival attendees spent more on souvenirs, food, lodging,

Attending a free music festival creates a ripple effect of economic activity.

FilmMagic/Getty Images

and so on. Thus, the economic impact is likely to be much larger. Furthermore, consider the ripple effect of this festival. For instance, think about the food vendors at the festival. During the weekend, they generate revenue for their business and additional compensation for their employees. In turn, these employees reinvest some of this extra money they earned back into the economy through their own spending. These food trucks also had to order additional supplies and food to support the increased demand from the one-day music festival and the money they spent to purchase these items also had an impact on their suppliers and their employees. Many special events also include sponsorship opportunities that create additional economic impact. For instance, in 2017, over $1.5 billion dollars was spent on the sponsorship of music festivals alone (IEG, 2017). These sponsorship dollars are often used to fund operational expenses associated with the specific event and hiring workers to run the event.

The economic impact one modest festival can have on society is surprising. The leisure service industry is often regarded as an industry of service. However, the economic impact of leisure services cannot be ignored. All people participate in some type of leisure activity, and for many of those activities, there is a financial cost.

This chapter looks at the relationship of economics and leisure and the impact that the leisure service industry has on the economy. The relationship of economics to leisure is discussed first by examining the role that economic status once played in determining one's leisure and social status. Although the role that economics plays in determining one's leisure can be debated, it cannot be debated that leisure has a significant economic impact on society. The chapter also introduces some key economic terms and demonstrates the significant economic impact that different sectors of the leisure service industry have on society. Societal trends and their impacts on leisure and the economy are also examined.

Economic Foundations

Before diving deeper into the economics of leisure, it is important to review some of the relevant terminology used when discussing this topic. These concepts include

- discretionary income,
- direct and indirect expenditures,

- economic multiplier, and
- leakage

Discretionary income refers to the money an individual earns after taxes have been taken out and life's necessities (food, shelter, etc.) have been addressed. To illustrate, consider the following example. Mary has an income of $50,000, and her income tax rate is 30 percent, or $15,000. Mary spends $23,000 per year on rent, insurance, food, transportation, and clothing. After paying $15,000 in income taxes and $23,000 for necessities, Mary is left with $12,000 in discretionary income (i.e., $50,000 – $38,000 = $12,000) for the year.

Expenditures represent money spent for a leisure pursuit. **Direct expenditures** are the monies spent to purchase the primary leisure service or product. For instance, a direct expenditure for an avid golfer might be the cost of a round of golf at the local course. While direct expenses are directly linked to the actual leisure service, **indirect expenditures** represent the money spent on leisure services or products that *support* the primary leisure service or product. Returning to our golfer, an indirect expenditure might be the fuel purchased to drive to the course.

The final two concepts, **economic multiplier** and **leakage**, are often examined at a more macro level such as the community or leisure service agency. Economic multiplier is a numerical value that represents the degree that money spent on leisure services in a community is respent in that same community. Consider a professional baseball game as an example. Fans buy tickets to attend the game. Many of these fans also purchase food from the concessionaires. In turn, these concessionaires receive compensation for their work during the game and will likely spend a portion of their compensation on goods or services within the community. Thus, the money originally spent by a family to buy food from the concession vendor had a ripple, or multiplied, effect as the vendor reinvested some of the money they earned from the family back into the community through the purchasing of goods and services. While some of the money originally spent to attend the baseball game is respent into the community, some of it is not. Rather, some of this respent money is spent in other communities. This is referred to as leakage, which is defined as the money spent in a community that is then respent outside the community.

Leisure Economics and Its Importance

Leisure services are designed to provide quality experiences for all people. However, leisure service agencies also operate as businesses. Being such, the agencies typically incur costs by providing services and products. Because of this, consumers must pay to participate in activities or obtain products from leisure service agencies. In some instances, these costs may be minimal; however, costs associated with leisure activities and products can be significant. These costs frequently create barriers to participation in leisure activities. If people do not have the money to participate in an activity, they will probably find something else to do.

It has long been argued that leisure participation is designed for those who can afford it, and, in fact, having leisure is a symbol of status (memberships in country clubs, eating at ritzy restaurants, or owning an expensive car or boat are examples of social status being defined by leisure). The theory of the leisure class (a theory as well as a book by the same title; Veblen, 1899), although economic in nature, had strong social implications for the United States and suggested that only the wealthy could afford and were entitled to leisure. This idea is based on the principle that people spend their discretionary income on leisure services. Discretionary income is usually higher for people who make more money. So, the argument is that if you make more money, then you have more money to spend on leisure. The theory of the leisure class suggested that if you were in a high social class and had a high income, then you could afford leisure. The theory also stated that those who only had enough money for the necessities of life and were in a low social and economic class could not afford leisure and that this was reflected in their status in society.

We have come a long way in understanding leisure since the theory of the leisure class was proposed in 1899. We now understand that leisure isn't only about money but is more about time for leisure and meaning of activities that take place during leisure time. In fact, you could argue that those who have high incomes and work many hours

Ken Murray/Icon Sportswire via Getty Images

Do luxury suites at a sporting event convey a sign of social class?

during the week do not have as much leisure as those who make less money, because the people with high incomes have less time for leisure. This is a paradox of leisure: Money allows us the opportunity for leisure, but the time required to earn that money limits opportunities for leisure.

Whether you agree with the theory of the leisure class, you cannot ignore the fact that participation in leisure services can be limited by money. A typical college student cannot afford to travel every weekend or purchase high-end leisure products. In fact, lack of money is a significant barrier to leisure participation (Reichert, Barros, Domingues, & Hallal, 2007). However, if our activities are limited because of money, we still find other leisure outlets. Regardless of how much discretionary income we have, we still manage to spend money on leisure services.

Economic Impact Within the Predominant Leisure Service Delivery Models

Economic impact occurs in all sectors of leisure services. Typically, the commercial, or for-profit, recreation sector is the first that comes to mind when discussing the economic impact of leisure. However, public and not-for-profit leisure service agencies significantly affect the economy as well. The following sections discuss the economic impact of different sectors of leisure services. Some of the numbers in the upcoming snippets are staggering, and these are only some of the types of leisure service organizations; there are many others.

For-Profit Recreation

For-profit recreation agencies are primarily funded through money collected by the resale of their products or services. The primary goal, or motive, of these agencies is to make a profit. Also referred to as the commercial recreation sector, these agencies rely extensively on revenue generated from their services, membership fees, and products or merchandise sold. Because of their enterprise focus, they typically charge more money for their programs and services than do municipal and not-for-profit agencies. Thus, the impact of the many different types of for-profit recreation agencies on the economy is significant. For-profit recreation can include things such as amusement and entertainment venues, health clubs, travel and tourism, food services, professional sporting events, golf courses, and entertainment. Following is a glimpse of the economic impact of these for-profit recreation industries.

Amusement and Entertainment Venues

Businesses within the amusement and entertainment venue subsector include theme parks, carnivals, museums, water parks, and observational experiences. Millions of people visit these popular destinations each year. For instance, in 2018, worldwide attendance across all of the Disney facilities, Six Flags, and SeaWorld exceeded half a billion visits combined; the Skytree in Tokyo, Japan, had 6.4 million visitors; and the Willis Tower Skydeck in Chicago, Illinois, welcomed 1.6 million visitors (Theme Index, 2018). In addition, over 80 million people visited the more than 1,000 water parks in the United States in 2018, with these parks generating over $5 billion in revenue (World Waterpark Association, 2020). Taken collectively, these numbers represent approximately 12 percent of the world's population! The economic impact is also staggering, with worldwide spending at these theme park venues exceeding $45 billion in 2017 (Sylt, 2018).

Health Clubs

The health club industry includes agencies that typically require memberships and offer a variety of fitness opportunities. Some health clubs may also offer various aquatic, sport, child care, food, and entertainment options for members. A majority of the more than 210,000 health clubs that served more than 183 million members in the United States during 2019 were enterprise facilities that operated on a for-profit basis (Rodriguez, 2019). In 2019, the global industry revenue for health clubs was $94 billion, with projections to reach more than 230 million members by 2030 (Rodriguez). Millennials and Gen Xers represent the majority of health club members with memberships from the baby boomer generation continuing to grow. Health club memberships for an individual can be as little as $35 per month, but most are much more expensive. Many clubs have membership categories for families, older adults, or other specialty groups.

Travel and Tourism

Travel and tourism include the movement of people to leisure destinations around the world. This industry has grown considerably as modes of travel have improved. According to the World

Tourism Organization (2018), this sector supports 319 million jobs, which translates to nearly 10 percent of the jobs around the world. Over 1.4 billion international tourists explored various worldwide destinations, resulting in more than $1.45 trillion in receipts each year (World Tourism Organization). Prior to the COVID-19 pandemic, the number of tourists continued to increase at a rate of 5 to 7 percent each year. While the pandemic will likely have a lasting effect on the travel and tourism industry, the sheer numbers and economic activity in this area are significant.

Food Services

The food service industry is a large part of the recreation industry. Many recreation facilities provide vending and concession services to patrons. Facilities that host special events and sporting events rely heavily on concessions as a major source of revenue. However, the main source of revenue from food services is generated through the restaurant industry. Visiting a restaurant for a meal is a popular leisure activity and has a major impact on the economy. In the United States, restaurant sales have continued to experience year-to-year revenue growth, ranging from 5.5 percent to 7.5 percent. Nearly 150 million people go to a restaurant or order takeout each year. The number of jobs within this sector is also significant, with an average of nearly 20,000 jobs added each month (National Restaurant Association, 2020). The restaurant industry generates more than $1.5 billion in sales in one day and $566 billion in sales in a year. Similar to the travel and tourism industries, restaurants experienced a great deal of volatility during the COVID-19 pandemic, with millions of jobs cut during that time. While the industry did see a significant employment bounce following the initial phase of the pandemic, this industry will likely experience a long road back to the previous employment levels (National Restaurant Association, 2020).

Self-Exploration

Think about your last trip. How much money did you spend on travel? How much was spent on lodging? How much was spent on food and beverage? How much was spent on souvenirs, shopping, or attending an event? Estimate the total cost for the trip.

Professional Sporting Events

Another leisure service industry that makes a significant contribution to the economy is professional sporting events. Sporting events that take place before a paying audience generate direct and indirect revenue that can have a major impact on a local or regional economy. As of 2019, there were 963 professional or semiprofessional sport organizations in the United States, and the sporting event industry employed more than 85,000 people and generated more than $22 billion in revenue (U.S. Census, 2019).

The National Football League (NFL) is one of the most well-known leagues of professional sports in the United States. Although attendance varies from city to city, the impact that the NFL has on the economy is worth noting. In 2019, the NFL generated over $16 billion in revenue (Colangelo, 2019). Individual NFL teams, over a season, can also have an economic impact of more than $100 million in their host cities (Gruenhagen, 2010). The culminating event of the NFL, the Super Bowl, has an even greater impact. It is estimated that the 2020 Super Bowl generated nearly $17.2 billion in nationwide spending on items such as food, beverages, decorations, parties, and other merchandise (Mitchell, 2020).

Golf Courses

Golf is an industry that saw incredible growth in the 1990s and a steady decline since the turn of the century. Despite its recent decline in popularity, it still remains a popular leisure pursuit as nearly 33.5 million people in the United States played an average of 18.2 rounds of golf in 2019 (National Golf Foundation, 2019). Furthermore, over 108 million people in the United States, or 1 out of every 3 people, played golf or watched it during 2019 (National Golf Foundation). Approximately 16,300 golf courses exist in the United States, with nearly 1,300 major golf course renovations being completed since 2006, totaling nearly $3.75 billion (National Golf Foundation). Consumer spending on golf equipment and green fees is also significant with nearly $25 billion being spent in the United States per year.

Entertainment

Movies, television, video streaming, and gambling continue to be popular leisure pursuits in the United States. These consumption-based activities also spur a great deal of economic activity. For instance, box office earnings from movies in North America were over $11 billion while television and video streaming companies generated over $70 billion in 2019. According to the American Gaming Association, casino gaming is another billion-dollar industry, supporting 1.8 million jobs, generating $41 billion in annual revenue, and creating an economic impact of $261 billion across 43 U.S. states (American Gaming Association, 2019).

Public Recreation

Public recreation agencies exist at local, state, and federal levels in the United States. These agencies are funded by the government to provide leisure services for their citizens. While the primary source of revenue for these agencies is taxes, the agencies are becoming increasingly reliant on membership, program, and service fees to keep pace with the public's demand for their services. Fifty years ago, taxes might have accounted for over 90 percent of local agencies' annual revenue. Today, that number is around 50 percent, as many agencies rely more and more on membership, program, and service fees to support their operations. Despite this shift, these agencies still typically charge lower fees for programs and services because of the support these agencies continue to receive from citizens' taxes. This blend of public support from taxes combined with an enterprise-focused approach within specific aspects of their operations creates an organizational environment for these agencies that still has a significant impact on the economy.

Local Level

The economic impact local, or municipal, recreation has on communities is significant. Oftentimes accounting for a majority of the community's travel and tourism activity, these agencies manage a number of special events, festivals, programs, facilities, and parklands. The activities and spending of local park and recreation agencies in the United States generate nearly $170 billion in revenue each year (Clower & Nguyen, 2020). These activities boost the U.S. gross domestic product by almost $90 billion and support over 1.1 million jobs that pay over $50 billion in salaries, wages, and benefits (Clower & Nguyen, 2020). Obviously, local parks and recreation are much more than simply parks, programs, and facilities for local residents. These agencies are key economic engines for communities

through the tourism dollars they bring to the area, the role they play in attracting new residents, and the jobs they support.

State and Federal Level

There are over 10,200 state park areas within the United States. These parks host nearly 1 billion visitors each year and employ more than 51,000 full-time, part-time, and seasonal personnel (National Association of State Park Directors, 2020). At the federal level, the National Park Service consists of 419 parks and recreational sites across the United States. These sites have experienced significant growth in interest and popularity in recent years. For instance, in 2019, more than 327 million people visited a national park, which was an increase of more than 9 million visits from the previous year (National Park Service, 2020). Estimates indicate these visitors contributed $40 billion to the U.S. economy.

Not-for-Profit Recreation

Despite the term *not-for-profit*, that sector of leisure services has a significant impact on the economy. Not-for-profit organizations create considerable economic activity; however, unlike agencies in the for-profit sector, not-for-profit organizations put their revenue back into the organization and its programs. In the for-profit sector, revenue generated often goes toward employee bonuses or dividends to stockholders. The majority of not-for-profit organizations in the United States are in the fields of health care and education. The not-for-profit sector in leisure services includes many organizations that are advocates for the environment, such as Greenpeace, Rainforest Action Network, Sierra Club, Nature Conservancy, and Rainforest Alliance. Most not-for-profit organizations operate with a mission to serve a cause. Not-for-profit organizations employ more than 11.4 million people in the United States (Independent Sector, 2016). Two of the most well-known not-for-profit organizations in leisure services are the YMCA and the Boys & Girls Clubs of America. With nearly 2,700 facilities in the United States, YMCAs employ nearly 20,000 full-time workers and more than 60,000 volunteers while serving over 9 million youth and 13 billion adults each year (YMCA, 2020). Like most not-for-profit agencies, YMCAs generate their nearly $6 billion in revenue through program fees, memberships, and financial supporters. The Boys & Girls Clubs of America serve

4.7 million boys and girls and have 4,645 locations. These clubs employ more than 67,000 people and in 2007 generated over $2 billion in revenue (Boys & Girls Clubs of America, 2020).

Many museums within the United States operate within a non-profit business model and represent a popular leisure outlet for individuals and families. In 2020, there were nearly 40,000 museums in the United States that supported over 726,000 jobs and contributed $50 billion to the economy (American Alliance of Museums, 2020). Three out of every four U.S. travelers visited a museum or participated in cultural or heritage-based activities (Mandala Research, 2013). Museums create a significant economic impact in their communities, generating more than $4 billion in tax revenue for state and local governments, and each direct job at a museum supports the creation of an additional job elsewhere in the community (American Alliance of Museums).

Similar to the food services sector, museums were significantly impacted by the COVID-19 pandemic. Many of these sites were forced to close during the pandemic only to reopen with reduced staff and higher costs to support safety. In 2020, the American Alliance of Museums projected the pandemic could lead to the permanent closure of nearly one third of museums in the United States without assistance from governments and private donors. Clearly, the future of museums in a postpandemic world will be heavily influenced by the levels of financial support received from these public and private sources.

Undoubtedly, the not-for-profit sector of leisure services serves many people. It also employs a considerable number of leisure services professionals and generates billions of dollars in economic activity.

Leisure Trends: Economic Implications

In recent years, our consumption and interaction with leisure is evolving. In our technology-driven world, new leisure trends such as esports (electronic gaming); increased interest in public health and wellness initiatives; recreational drugs; and increased screen time associated with binge watching TV shows, streaming, and online shop-

Esports have become some of the fastest growing leisure pursuits in the world.

Adamkaz/E+/Getty Images

ping through various social media platforms have emerged.

Esports

According to Forbes, the esports industry is worth more than $10 billion and is projected to reach almost $25 billion by 2024 (LeVoir-Barry, 2020). Esports have a rapidly increasing following of nearly 400 million people worldwide. In response to the industry's growth, more than 80 colleges and universities in the United States offer esports as a varsity sport with athletic scholarships to talented esport athletes. More and more media networks are broadcasting the esport competitions and drawing audiences that are larger than those on HBO, Netflix, and ESPN combined (LeVoir-Barry, 2020). In addition to the economic impact associated with the marketing and entertainment aspects of esports, these sports also support growth in the data economy. Existing entirely in the digital realm, esport events require significant real-time networking; cloud computing; sophisticated data security; and the fans' consumption and creation of their own streams of content, tracking of esport players, social media posts, and competition monitoring (LeVoir-Barry, 2020). States such as Georgia and Kansas have also invested millions of dollars and other resources to support the growth of esports and have seen these investments generate hundreds of millions of dollars of economic activity and job growth in their states.

Public Health

An aspect of public health that continues to experience growth can be found in the area of self-care leisure. Self-care leisure comes in many forms, but at its core is a focus on ownership and prioritization of an individual's mental and physical well-being. Self-care, particularly in the area of mental health, has become one of the biggest wellness-related trends in recent years. In 2018, self-care was the most popular app theme, and a report released in the same year by the Barnes and Noble company found that more people invested in self-care books to improve mental health than dieting and physical fitness (Ali, 2019). The economic impact of the self-care movement is also staggering; it has become a $10 billion industry (Conlin, 2019).

The COVID-19 pandemic created ripple effects for individuals and leisure service industries. While large gatherings, resorts, lodging, and entertainment venues experienced significant drops in revenue, other leisure pursuits, particularly those in outdoor or small-group settings (i.e., boating, golfing, fishing, hiking, etc.) experienced significant increases in spending and participation (Dwyer, 2020). Public health outbreaks can also spur new growth and the transformation of existing businesses to capitalize on the conditions created by these pandemic-type environments (Dwyer). With gyms, parks, theaters, restaurants, sporting events, concerts, and any other large social gatherings all being canceled or closed, professionals had to be creative in how they could deliver and serve their customers. Many organizations launched virtual services such as group workouts, home-based family activities, recipes for cooking or baking, curbside pickup, promotions, free concerts, game nights that people could watch or participate in via Facebook Live, Zoom Houseparty, and virtual conferencing platforms. The lasting impact of the pandemic is unknown;

On the Job

Planning Festivals and Special Events

Ranging from sporting events and concerts to historical and holiday celebrations, festivals and special events can be enjoyed in nearly every metropolitan area and rural community alike. Behind every festival or special event are professionals who are responsible for creating, planning, organizing, coordinating, and supervising these impactful experiences. Employment opportunities in this industry are diverse, ranging from community event planners, coordinators, and managers to positions within convention centers, expos, and special event planning companies. The employment outlook in this area is also bright; the U.S. Bureau of Labor Statistics projects the industry to grow much faster than other professions over the next 10 years. If you're interested in a fast-paced and growing industry, festival and event planning could be for you. Consider researching festivals in your area to learn more about the types of opportunities that exist in this industry.

however, people found ways to interact and discover new leisure hobbies.

Shopping

Products purchased for use during leisure activities affect the economy significantly. For instance, the amount of money spent on fitness-related equipment alone is staggering. A 2018 study found that Americans spend more money on fitness than college tuition (Settembre, 2018). Americans spend nearly $4.5 billion spent annually on sporting goods equipment. More than $17 billion is spent annually on athletic footwear and nearly $11 billion is spent on sporting goods clothing. Retail product purchases are not limited to sporting goods. It is estimated that Americans spent more than $43 billion on video games in 2018, with more than 10 percent growth projected each year through the next decade (Gera, 2019).

Streaming Services

Streaming services for movies and television programs such as Netflix, Hulu, Disney+, and YouTube have become increasingly popular in recent years. For instance, Netflix has nearly 200 million paid subscribers worldwide, with over 70 million in the United States alone. During the COVID-19 pandemic, these streaming services become increasingly popular as people spent more time in their homes. The economic impact associated with these services is also notable. In 2019, Netflix generated nearly $6 billion in revenue from its services. Future projections suggest streaming services will continue to increase in popularity and use as people spend more time in screen-based experiences.

Self-Exploration

Identify a leisure activity you enjoy. Describe the process required to get started in this leisure pursuit. What is needed to participate in this activity (i.e., equipment, space needs, training, etc.)? Estimate the costs associated with participating in this activity on a regular basis. How was your participation in this activity affected by the COVID-19 pandemic?

Gambling

The gambling industry includes various forms of gambling. With a growing number of states and organizations legalizing gambling, the industry is growing rapidly. Casino gaming has an annual economic impact of $261 billion, supports nearly 2 million jobs, and generates over $50 billion in annual revenue (American Gaming Association, 2019). Most of that revenue was generated through gambling; however, the gambling industry also generates revenue by providing casino visitors with amenities such as hotels, restaurants, and retail shopping. The casino experience is more than just gambling for many guests. According to the American Gaming Association, more than two thirds of casino visitors reported eating at a fine-dining restaurant in 2007 as part of their visit to the casino.

Summary

All sectors of leisure services have a significant impact on the economy. For years, for-profit recreation has been the sector that has followed a business model with its focus on revenue generation. Not-for-profit and public leisure service agencies have operated on a service model, focusing on the customer and providing the best experience possible. In an effort to do this, not-for-profit agencies and public agencies have worked to keep costs down. With the battle for tax and grant money in society today, these agencies are not supported by government, as they once were. The call to action for future leaders in the field is to embrace the quality of the service model and to incorporate the concepts of the business model. Revenue generation in all sectors of leisure services will only become more important over the years, and administrators and professionals in these areas must develop agencies that can be self-sustaining, as are for-profit agencies. If this happens, you can expect the economic impact of leisure services to be even greater than it is today.

Regardless of our economic situation, we will spend money on leisure activities. Society has moved beyond the idea that leisure is a status symbol. Leisure is for everyone, and everyone spends money on leisure services and products. The economic impact of leisure is tremendous and continues to grow in all sectors of leisure services.

Learning Activities

1. Select a leisure pursuit. Research the leisure pursuit and determine how much revenue is generated from that pursuit over a 10-year period. Has the revenue increased or decreased during this 10-year period? See if you can determine the reasons for this change in revenue. What are the businesses that support this leisure pursuit doing to manage this revenue shift?

2. Monitor your leisure spending and the amount of leisure time you have for a week. Project this cost and your leisure time across a month and an entire year. Are your projected yearly leisure expenses more or less than you thought they would be? Can you calculate how much, on average, you spend on leisure per hour? What, if anything, does this hourly leisure expense tell you?

Review Questions

1. Is Veblen's theory of the leisure class still relevant today? Explain.

2. Describe the links between leisure and the economy. Provide examples to support your position.

3. In what ways has the public sector (local, state, or federal) become more enterprise-focused in its operations?

4. How are trends and issues in public health related to leisure and the economy?

5. What is a direct expenditure? An indirect expenditure?

6. Provide an example to illustrate the economic multiplier concept.

Go to HK*Propel* to access additional learning content.

Leisure, Politics, and Public Policy

Andrew Mauldin

Lipscomb University

H. Joey Gray

California Polytechnic State University

VOCABULARY TERMS

blue laws

city manager–council model

commons

efficiency

eminent domain

enabling legislation

federalism

life politics

morale, welfare, and recreation

parliamentary system

pluralist politics

public goods

public policy

separation of powers

special district

strong mayor–council model

Supremacy Clause

LEARNING OUTCOMES

After reading this chapter, you will

- understand the concept of politics and its connection with leisure behavior;
- recognize the role that the three branches of government play in creating leisure regulations;
- understand the government's role in leisure services provision;
- understand how politics influences the development of public policy; and
- become familiar with key public policy areas affecting leisure behavior.

Have you ever been to a local, state, or national park or recreation area? How did the experience affect you? Maybe you had the chance to learn something about the history of your country, or perhaps you had the chance to renew yourself physically, emotionally, or spiritually. Maybe you had the opportunity to marvel at a unique natural wonder, like the geysers in Yellowstone, the waterfalls in Yosemite, or the swamps in the Everglades. As you reflect on these experiences, have you ever considered what would happen if these places were not protected or available to the public to visit? Think about recreation opportunities closer to home, perhaps even those offered at your college or university. What if there were no leisure spaces, places, activities, or opportunities available to you? Or what if the opportunities that were available did not meet your needs or you believed that you had no say in what was available to you? These questions highlight the political nature of leisure services delivery, and in this chapter, we examine its implications for our leisure lifestyles as well as for the management of leisure programs and resources.

In 2009, a very popular TV sitcom changed the way many view politics and the impact that policy has on leisure. *Parks and Recreation* illustrated in a comedic way the political ramifications that policy can have on leisure. One episode, entitled "How a Bill Becomes a Law," walks the viewer through the process of getting a park built in the fictional city of Pawnee, Indiana. Though this show does not depict every aspect of how policy affects leisure, it does give an accurate and brief introduction.

Leisure is experienced socially as well as individually, and much of our leisure takes place in public spaces, such as parks, playgrounds, schools, recreation centers, athletic fields, arts centers, museums, and concert halls. Being public spaces, all of these venues have been developed and are managed by some external body with the authority to make decisions that influence the way leisure is experienced in these places. For example, someone must decide where to locate a new playground, how much public money will be spent to build it, who will be eligible to use it, how it will be used, and who will be responsible for management and upkeep. The

Danny Lehman/The Image Bank/Getty Images

Publicly accessible leisure spaces such as national parks provide benefits to both individuals and society.

same is true with any number of public spaces used for leisure and recreation activity.

All of these decisions are political—they involve issues of power, control, and influence. All of these decisions affect the way you experience leisure, including what you do and when, where, and how you do it. Because of this, it is important to view leisure through a political lens to better understand how these decisions are made, how they affect your life, and how you might be able to influence their outcomes. This chapter focuses on the political aspect of leisure, including the concept of politics, the government's role in leisure, how public policy is formed, and how it affects leisure behavior.

Governmental Role in Leisure

When you think about politics, you tend to think about the governing of society. Government is a good starting point in thinking about the political process. Recalling the formal levels of the U.S. government's power—the executive, legislature, and judiciary—is useful, because it is through these mechanisms that priorities are set, compromises are brokered, and decisions are made that affect the citizenry.

Western democracies, such as the United States and Canada, most often have three branches of government—the executive, legislative, and judicial branches. Although the actual form of these branches of government differs from system to system, the basic framework holds true. In the classic sense, the legislative branch makes and debates laws and other forms of legislation, the executive branch helps to set policy and carry out the work of the legislature, and the judiciary ensures that laws and policies created by the other branches meet constitutional muster.

Legislative Branch

In the United States, the legislature is truly a law-making body (Grant, 2004). The major function of the U.S. Congress—the House of Representatives and the Senate—is to introduce bills and make laws. This is similar at the state level. Although it is true that law and public policy are often formulated elsewhere, both inside and outside of government, by a variety of executive agencies and public interest and advocacy groups, it usually takes an active and supportive member of the legislative branch to help turn public policy ideas into law (Peters, 1996).

Hundreds of laws have been passed by federal and state legislatures dealing with parks and recreation provision and leisure behavior. Every time you visit a U.S. national park, you experience the influence of the legislative branch because Congress passed the National Park Service Organic Act of 1916, which created the National Park Service. Other laws, such as the Multiple-Use Sustained-Yield Act, the Wilderness Act, the Federal Water Project Recreation Act, the Wild and Scenic Rivers Act, and the National Trails Systems Act, help provide opportunities for recreation delivery and regulate visitor behavior and land use. At the federal and state levels, legislatures pass **enabling legislation** that provides the authority for appropriate administrative bodies or officials to carry out mandates or enforce the laws. Eminent domain is one example of this. **Eminent domain** is when a governing body can seize private land for public use by compensating the owner of the land (Block, 2019). Enabling legislation at the federal level is used to provide guidance in managing specific national parks and provides authority to manage aspects of armed forces **morale, welfare, and recreation** programs. At the state level, enabling legislation might create special parks and recreation districts or empower county and municipal governments to provide parks and recreation services or create conservation commissions.

Federal and state legislatures also make laws that regulate and control certain types of leisure behavior. For example, federal drug laws establish the legal status of controlled substances. Some drugs, such as codeine, are legal to possess with a valid prescription, whereas others, such as heroin, are illegal in all circumstances. Federal and state laws limit or prohibit prostitution, pornography, and sex trafficking. Even alcohol use and tobacco use are regulated by state laws, including the legal age of purchase and possession. In some states, laws restrict alcohol purchases to special state-run liquor stores. Local legislatures sometimes pass laws prohibiting the sale of alcohol at certain times and days, such as prohibitions on the sale of alcohol on Sundays. Laws that are enacted to protect the Sabbath, ordinarily defined as Sunday, from commercial or other forms of activity are sometimes referred to as **blue laws**. These laws are sometimes broadened to restrict other types of activities primarily because of concerns with moral or ethical standards. For example, there may be laws dictating where adult-only clubs can be located or where adult media or products (e.g., magazines, videos, paraphernalia) can be sold and purchased.

In addition to making laws, the legislature serves as an important check on the executive branch of government through its oversight function, represents the interests of the American people, and, perhaps most important for leisure services provision, controls the budget and allocates scarce tax dollars. In fact, most of the National Recreation and Park Association's major legislative priorities deal with funding and resource allocation (see figure 12.1).

The legislative branch in the United States is a separate and independent branch of government. This idea of a **separation of powers** was developed by the founders of the United States to avoid an accumulation of power within one branch of government. The U.S. Congress may coordinate with the president on legislative matters, but the responsibility for making and passing laws rests primarily with the members of Congress. This often makes for a slow and deliberate legislative process that has been described as an obstacle race (Grant, 2004). The legislative process in other Western democracies with strong parliamentary forms of government, such as Great Britain or Canada, is different. Governments under the **parliamentary system** have the ability to both make and execute laws. The executive in a parliamentary system is the head of the government. The government is the political party with the most members or largest coalition in the legislature. The primary function of the parliamentary legislature in these countries is to debate and pass laws introduced by the government. This makes for a less cumbersome legislative process but one that is less responsive to checks and balances.

Executive Branch

The executive branch in the United States consists of the president, vice president, Executive Office of the President, and the cabinet (see figure 12.2). Although the president, and, to some extent, the vice president, are the most visible members of the executive branch, more than 2.1 million civilians are employed in positions representing 15 executive departments as well as the Executive Office of the President. The number of citizens employed by the executive branch swells to more than 4 million when including active-duty personnel in the U.S. armed forces and the National Guard and Reserve (White House, 2009).

At first glance, it might appear that leisure and recreation services are absent from the executive branch and agenda. However, many of the public policy priorities related to recreation and leisure can be found in the executive branch. For example, the Office of Management and Budget is where the president forms the budget priorities that are then sent to Congress for debate and approval. In President Barack Obama's fiscal year 2010 budget, for example, the president proposed to increase the National Park Service's budget for park operations by $100 million to better maintain facilities and natural resources (Office of Management and Budget, 2009). This proposed increase in the National Park Service budget is in addition to the $750 million allocated to the National Park Service by Congress in the American Recovery and Reinvestment Act of 2009 (Recovery.gov, 2009). Compare that to President Donald J. Trump's 2021 proposed budget. The allocation for the National Park Service proposed by Trump consisted of a total cut of $587 million, a 17% decrease from the previous fiscal year's budget (National Park Conservation Association, 2020). These two scenarios show how the executive office determines the priorities for budget allocation. Notably, there are several factors that influence these presidential decisions. For example, The COVID-19 pandemic potentially could have a

1. Fund the Land and Water Conservation Fund state assistance program at $140 million
2. Fund the 21st Century Community Learning Center Program (21st CCLC), the only federal funding stream to support summer and after-school learning programs, at $1.322 billion
3. Fund the Youth Mentoring Grant managed by the Office of Juvenile Justice and Delinquency Prevention at the Department of Justice at $100 million
4. Fund the Centers for Disease Control and Prevention's arthritis program at $12 million to begin rebuilding the lost funding from the previous 3 years and to begin expanding the reach of the program

FIGURE 12.1 Legislative priorities: National Recreation and Park Association (2019).

President

EXECUTIVE OFFICE OF THE PRESIDENT
Council of Economic Advisors
Council on Environmental Quality
Council on Women and Girls
Domestic Policy Council
National Economic Council
National Security Council
Office of Administration
Office of Management and Budget

THE CABINET
In order of succession to the presidency:

Vice President of the United States
Secretary of State (www.state.gov)
Secretary of the Treasury (www.treasury.gov)
Secretary of Defense (www.defenselink.mil)
Secretary of Justice (www.justice.gov)
Secretary of the Interior (www.doi.gov)
Secretary of Agriculture (www.usda.gov)
Secretary of Commerce (www.commerce.gov)
Secretary of Labor (www.dol.gov)

CABINET-RANK POSITIONS
Council of Economic Advisers
 (www.whitehouse.gov/administration/eop/cea/)
Environmental Protection Agency
 (www.epa.gov)
Office of Management and Budget
 (www.whitehouse.gov/omb/)

Vice President

Office of National AIDS Policy
Office of National Drug Control Policy
Office of Science and Technology Policy
Office of the U.S. Trade Representative
President's Intelligence Advisory Board
 and Intelligence Oversight Board
Privacy and Civil Liberties Oversight Board
White House Military Office

Secretary of Health and Human Services
 (www.hhs.gov)
Secretary of Housing and Urban Development
 (www.hud.gov)
Secretary of Transportation (www.dot.gov)
Secretary of Energy (www.energy.gov)
Secretary of Education (www.ed.gov)
Secretary of Veterans Affairs (www.va.gov)
Secretary of Homeland Security (www.dhs.gov)

U.S. Trade Representative (www.ustr.gov)
U.S. Ambassador to the United Nations
White House Chief of Staff

FIGURE 12.2 U.S. executive branch.

significant influence on future budget allocations for our industry. Other executive-level priorities related to leisure and recreation can be found in the various executive departments, including the Departments of Agriculture, Defense, Education, Health and Human Services, Housing and Urban Development, and Interior, among others. Although the priorities of the executive branch with respect to leisure and recreation (as well as other areas) are subject to frequent changes and revisions, selected leisure and recreation priorities that are covered within executive branch agencies at the time of this writing are listed in figure 12.3. In addition to these priorities, the day-to-day administrative functions related to leisure services provision are carried out in the executive branch. Although the legislature makes the laws that provide legal authority and mandates, approves the budget, and allocates funding, executive branch agencies carry out the actual duties of service provision.

DEPARTMENT OF AGRICULTURE

- Activities of the U.S. Forest Service
- Conservation easements
- Nutrition assistance
- 4-H and extension services at land grant institutions
- Rural broadband infrastructure
- Wildfire management

DEPARTMENT OF DEFENSE

- Morale, welfare, and recreation programs
- Base funding for family support initiatives

DEPARTMENT OF EDUCATION

- Early childhood education programs
- After-school programs and activities

DEPARTMENT OF HEALTH AND HUMAN SERVICES

- Research funding for health promotion and disease prevention
- Expansion of Head Start programs

DEPARTMENT OF HOUSING AND URBAN DEVELOPMENT

- Funding for the Community Development Block Grant program
- Community improvement funding for concentrated poverty neighborhoods

DEPARTMENT OF THE INTERIOR

- Funding activities of the National Park Service
- Conservation of federal and state land through the Land and Water Conservation Fund (LWCF)
- Environmental education initiatives for youth
- Wildfire management on National Park Service lands

CORPS OF ENGINEERS AND CIVIL WORKS

- Maintenance of infrastructure supporting land- and water-based recreation

ENVIRONMENTAL PROTECTION AGENCY

- Restoration of the Great Lakes

CORPORATION FOR NATIONAL AND COMMUNITY SERVICE

- Expand funding and opportunities for AmeriCorps volunteers
- Expand opportunities for service-learning opportunities in schools, higher education, and community-based organizations

FIGURE 12.3 2021 Executive budget.

Judicial Branch

The judicial branch in the United States government consists of two separate systems—the state system and the federal system—set up to try both civil and criminal cases. In cases where state and federal laws come into conflict, the federal system takes precedence based on the **Supremacy Clause** in the U.S. Constitution (Garvey, 2012). In the United States, the federal judiciary consists of three tiers—district courts, circuit courts of appeals, and the Supreme Court. District courts make up the first tier. They are primarily trial courts and hear federal cases that arise within the states themselves. There are 94 federal district courts operating in the United States and its territories. The second tier consists of 12 circuit courts that span the boundaries of several states. The 12 circuit courts of appeals hear cases that are appealed from the district courts in their circuit or appeals of decisions made by federal administrative agencies. The vast majority of federal cases are heard in either district courts or circuit courts of appeals. In matters of extreme importance to federal law or on serious constitutional questions, the U.S. Supreme Court may elect to hear a few select cases each year from the state or federal court system (U.S. Courts, 2009).

Most federal cases involving parks and recreation are likely to be heard in the district courts or circuit courts of appeal. For example, the District Court of the District of Columbia has been involved in the ongoing snowmobile ban controversy in Yellowstone National Park, and the District Court of the Northern District of California has adjudicated a case involving restricted access of off-road vehicles in the Bureau of Land Management's California Imperial Sand Dunes. Other high-profile cases heard by federal courts involving parks and recreation issues include the rights of boaters using the Colorado River in Grand Canyon National Park and recreation uses of the White River National Forest (Haas, 2003).

Federalism

Many Western democracies, most notably Australia, Canada, and the United States, have federal political systems. **Federalism** refers to the constitutional arrangement of balancing and sharing rights and powers between different levels of government. Federal systems in general have five main characteristics (Smith, 2004):

1. The combination of shared rule (central government) and local self-rule
2. The constitutionally protected autonomy of each unit of government
3. A written constitution and courts that are empowered to settle disputes
4. A constitution-amendment process designed to prevent any unit of government from changing the constitution on its own
5. A central government that, in part, represents the various units of government of the federation

Although most federal systems share these five characteristics, not all federal systems are the same in practice. Closer examination of federalism in Canada and the United States, for example, reveals differences both in structure and practice. Examples include the structural differences in the nature of both countries' constitutional governments, including Canada's historical ties to the British Crown and its parliamentary system, which differs substantially from the U.S. system of checks and balances and strong separation of powers (Thomas, 2008).

Government has a significant responsibility in managing recreation resources and in the delivery of leisure services and programs. Because of this, students of recreation and leisure behavior should understand the basic concepts of federalism, because the nature of political units such as the federal government, state and provincial governments, and local governments dictates the type of services offered through public-sector leisure services provision. Particularly in the United States, where there is no coordinated national policy for leisure services provision, knowing the differences between federal, state, and local levels of government is important in understanding the nature and scope of leisure services delivery.

Federal Government

In the United States, federal agencies provide a range of functions related to leisure services provision and delivery. Perhaps one of the largest federal functions is land and natural resources management for recreation and conservation purposes. Dozens of federal agencies, including the National Park Service, the National Forest Service, the Bureau of Land Management, the U.S. Fish and Wildlife Service, and the Army Corps of Engineers, are responsible for managing thousands of acres of land available to the public for recreation and leisure uses. Outdoor recreation spaces such as the properties managed by the National Park Service provide opportunities for millions of Americans and non-Americans to engage in numerous recreation activities. In addition to the benefits to individual users of these outdoor recreation areas, significant economic benefits accrue to the larger community as well. For example, money that tourists spend while vacationing on land managed by federal agencies can help to create business and stimulate local economies. The sale of timber and other natural resources from federal land such as national forests provides an important funding source for the federal government.

The federal government leverages its financial resources to support local priorities by distributing funding to the states for projects that are often related to leisure and recreation services provision. Programs such as the LWCF, the Community Development Block Grant Program, and the 21st Century Community Learning Centers Program are important funding mechanisms for state and local recreation provision. For example, the LWCF provides funding to state and local governments through the provision of matching grants—grants that are given contingent on the recipient's raising money for the project from other sources. These grants provide funding "to acquire lands, waters, and interests therein necessary to achieve the natural, cultural, wildlife, and recreation management objectives of federal land management agencies" (Land Water Conservation Fund, 2020). One of the advantageous features of LWCF projects is the requirement that they be developed for use by the public for recreation purposes in perpetuity—that is, that they always be available for public recreation with no definitive end.

Although the main responsibility of the federal government in recreation and leisure services provision is land and resource management and development, program delivery can also be found in federal agencies. For example, each of the six branches of the U.S. armed forces—the air force, army, coast guard, marine corps, space force, and

State parks, forests, historical sites, and trail systems help to make outdoor recreation opportunities accessible to local populations.

AnnaStills/iStock/Getty Images

navy—provides recreation programs and services for military personnel and their families. Referred to as morale, welfare (or well-being), and recreation programs, these services provide a comprehensive set of recreational, social, and community support services, including sports, physical fitness, youth and child development programs, entertainment, and food and beverage services. Other recreation programs offered through the federal government include therapeutic recreation services offered through the U.S. Department of Veterans Affairs.

State Government

In many ways, the system of recreation delivery at the state government level parallels that of the federal government. State governments often manage large outdoor recreation areas, such as state parks, forests, nature areas, historical sites, and trail systems, among other recreation resources. In most states, these recreation areas are funded through some combination of taxes and user fees, supplemented by other public and private funding sources. As mentioned previously, the federal government often assists states in the acquisition and development of outdoor recreation resources through matching grant programs like the LWCF.

States are often in a position to influence recreation and leisure services through regulation and oversight functions. In 2014, Colorado became one of the first states to legalize recreational marijuana at a statewide level. One of the primary arguments in favor of the legalization of marijuana is the economic impact that the taxation of cannabis can bring for the state. Forbes predicts that the legalization of marijuana in the United States could result in 1.6 billion jobs and $128 billion in tax revenue (Krane, 2020).

Local Government

Local government represents the level of government closest to the citizenry. Local government generally encompasses municipalities (cities, towns, villages), counties, and special districts. Municipalities are the smallest unit of government and are typically governed by a democratically elected mayor and city council. In some municipalities, the mayor plays a strong administrative role in municipal governance. In this strong mayor–council model of governance, the mayor has broad administrative duties, including hiring and firing, budgeting, and setting the strategic direction of the city. In other municipalities, a professional public administrator or city manager is hired to carry out the day-to-day governance of the municipality. The public administrator or city manager often works with the elected city council and, in many cases, an elected mayor to provide governance, hire employees, approve budgets, and make administrative decisions. This form of municipal governance is referred to as the **city manager–council model** (Hurd, Barcelona, & Meldrum, 2008).

Municipal governments often provide a broad range of services for their citizens. Many municipalities have police and fire departments, maintain local roads, provide schools, manage public housing units, enforce planning and zoning rules, assess and collect taxes, handle judicial cases, engage in environmental conservation and protection, and promote economic development. Municipalities often have responsibility for providing parks and recreation services to their community. In particular, municipal parks and recreation agencies are responsible for developing and maintaining a diverse range of public recreation facilities that meet the leisure needs in their communities. These facilities may include parks, playgrounds, athletic fields, community centers, aquatics facilities, beaches, pet or dog parks, community gardens, fitness facilities, golf courses, boat launches, multiple-use trail systems, skateboard parks, ice arenas, and even downhill ski hills! Municipal parks and recreation agencies are generally responsible for providing recreation programs as well. Like facilities, recreation programs vary from community to community, depending on the need of the citizenry. Programs offered by the municipal parks and recreation agency may include youth and adult sport leagues, instructional lessons, fitness classes, camps, after-school programs, historical and cultural activities, therapeutic recreation services, senior activities, and performing arts. Parks and recreation departments are often funded by some combination of appropriated tax money from the municipal government as well as user fees and other forms of public and nonpublic financing.

Many county governments offer parks and recreation services that are generally focused on rural or unincorporated areas within their jurisdiction. Many of the services found in municipal parks and recreation agencies can be found at the county level as well. This reflects a shift in the original mandate for county services, because counties were traditionally seen as administrative arms of state government, helping to provide state level services locally (Todd, 1996). Today, many county governments are involved in a vast range of service provision, including parks and recreation, and often work with local municipalities to coordinate services and to avoid duplication.

Another form of local government that has applicability to parks and recreation is the **special district**. Special districts are created by enabling legislation. Special districts are separate, independent forms of government that have the authority to tax and administer specific services (Hurd et al., 2008). Not all special districts are set up to administer parks and recreation services, although many special districts are set up specifically for this purpose. For example, the Greenville County Recreation District was created by enabling legislation passed by the South Carolina legislature in 1968.

Pluralism and Public Policy

Focusing on just the formal branches of government is an incomplete view of the political system. In liberal democracies like the United States and Canada, political activity can be found working outside the boundaries of formal government structures. Individuals and groups organize to build support for their interests and then use this support to influence the political decision-making process.

Politics in liberal democracies happens at multiple levels, by multiple factions—both inside and outside the formal structures of government. As such, any definition of politics needs to focus on the pluralistic nature of the United States and Canada and must take into account the role that the citizen plays in the political process. **Pluralist politics** can be seen as the process of various interest groups working, and sometimes competing, to influence the institutions of government to advance ideas and policies that reflect their goals (Grant, 2004). The importance of citizen action in influencing the political process is described in the research liter-

ature related to leisure, politics, and public policy as published in the major research journals in this field. Politics, as the research literature has come to define it within the leisure sciences literature, is both formal and informal—occurring at the highest levels of government and at the most basic level of individuals, families, and communities.

The political process is a social construction and as such reflects the individuals who work within it. The process may at times be overly partisan and influenced by corruption, and other times it may lead to outcomes that result in the greatest good for the greatest number. The pluralistic and competitive nature of politics in liberal democracies will almost always lead to winners and losers. As such, it is virtually impossible to find unanimous agreement on any particular political decision. Yet in the end, politics should be seen as a means to an end—a tool that is used to advocate for the issues and policies that are most important to a particular interest group.

Political influence is not directed only toward government institutions. Interest groups might organize to advocate for specific causes and to influence policy outcomes associated with nongovernmental organizations as well. Some scholars have noted that the traditional political system is not the center of political action any longer. Citizens are no longer as dependent on the political party apparatus to organize and advocate for a particular cause. This is due to a general feeling of alienation from political parties and political life as well as to new forms of political organization, such as online communities. This new political activism has been termed *life politics* (Rojek, 2001). **Life politics** is defined as "a nonparty form of social and cultural orientation focusing on issues of lifestyle, environment, and globalization" (Rojek, 2001, p. 115). Leisure is, in many ways, at the center of this new kind of politics, as citizens begin to define the kind of world that

On the Job

Legalization of Marijuana

The legalization of marijuana certainly falls within the categories of both political influence and life politics. Consider your personal point of view and then those of your parents and grandparents. Are your views different or the same? Now, consider what political interest groups might be supportive or unsupportive regarding the legalization of marijuana. What impact could the legalization of marijuana have on a public recreation organization both financially and regarding policy? What about a private organization? Would the legalization of marijuana affect your opinion regarding personal or public use? If so, what would you do? As a director of an organization, you may be frequently faced with these types of personal and political issues regarding policy and funding. Thus, it is paramount that you know your policy at the agency, local, state, and federal levels. Equally important is to know who the political players are in your community as they can heavily influence funding and policy. You job is to figure out how to work with them, regardless of the issue.

they want to live in and organize to draw attention to the issues and causes that are most important to them and their communities.

As a citizen, you might put politics into practice through the formal political process, such as voting or working on a political campaign. You might get involved by volunteering on behalf of a moral cause that is important to you outside of the formal political process, or you can volunteer for service projects focused solely on the betterment of your community. One way to understand this more expansive view of the political landscape in communities is to see a civic engagement continuum, with formal political involvement on the one side, political or moral advocacy at the center, and community service involvement on the other side (see figure 12.4). Oftentimes, formal participation in the political process will emerge from basic participation in the life of a community (Youniss et al., 2002).

Consider this: A group of young adults become involved in a community service project to help build a system of walking trails within the community. As they begin to research community issues,

they might become more aware of the need for public places to be physically active, the need to preserve land for public use instead of commercial development, or the need to encourage nonmotorized transportation to reduce carbon emissions. In the process, the group might organize to advocate for a more livable, walkable community, raising funds and awareness for their cause. Perhaps at some point, some of the members might align with a political party or candidate that supports their active living agenda. Through the process, the participants begin to develop a common identity as they share ideologies and values (Youniss et al., 2002). This simple example draws attention to the civic engagement process and how involvement in one particular community issue may spur a more deepened sense of political involvement along the way.

Public policy, much like the politics that helps to shape it, is a complex process. A basic definition of **public policy** is the activities of government, working directly or through its agents, that influence the lives of citizens. Three levels of policy affect citizens: policy choices, policy outputs, and policy

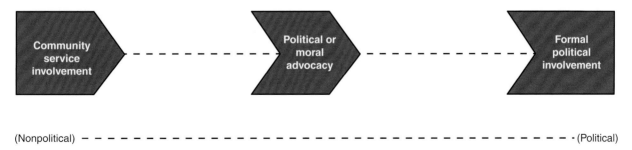

(Nonpolitical) – · (Political)

FIGURE 12.4 Civic engagement continuum.

impacts (Peters, 1996). To demonstrate these levels as they relate to leisure and recreation, consider the following quotation regarding the political position of parks and recreation:

> It has been noted that the provision of park, recreation opportunities for their own sake still lacks political clout. They have to be shown to solve community problems before politicians see them as being worthy of additional funding. The present position of parks and recreation services that has existed in the minds of most stakeholders for several decades is that they are relatively discretionary, non-essential services. They are nice to have if they can be afforded after the important, essential services have been funded. (Crompton, 2000, p. 68)

Consider how each of the following levels of public policy is reflected in the quotation.

Policy Choices

Policy choices refer to the decisions made by people who have an influence over the formation of public policy. Oftentimes, these are elected officials at the local, county, state, or national level, or they may be political appointees serving in administrative roles. The people who wield the power and authority to make public policy must choose among a variety of competing priorities. According to the preceding quotation, those with the power to make policy choices include elected officials as well as stakeholders—those individuals or groups who have a vested interest in the decisions of government because of the effect the decisions have (or might have) on them. Stakeholders may influence policy choices through their votes for elected officials, votes on public ballot measures, or political organization and advocacy.

Policy Outputs

Although policy choices refer to the key policy priorities of a particular government, the outputs of policy refer to what governments actually do. In the previous example, the policy output refers specifically to funding—how much money should be allocated to the provision of parks and recreation opportunities within the community. Political decision makers may give lip service to a particular set of policy choices. But to really see where their priorities lie, it is important to examine how the policy choices are put into action. Most of the time, this refers to the money that is appropriated for

particular programs and services. Other types of policy outputs could be the people who are hired or the infrastructure that needs to be provided for the policy to be enacted.

Policy Impacts

The policy impact refers to how public policy actually affects people. How do the support and funding of parks and recreation programs, facilities, and services affect the broader population? Recreation professionals need to do a better job articulating and demonstrating that parks and recreation services positively affect society beyond just providing a place for fun and games. To gain political (and policy) clout, parks and recreation must show that they have a significant impact on other broad public policy agendas in order to be worthy of additional funding (Crompton, 2016). These agendas will differ depending on the local community. For example, depending on the community, alleviating juvenile crime, stimulating economic activity, preserving scarce land resources, or improving health and physical well-being of citizens may be more or less important. This means that for parks and recreation agencies to be seen as viable public priorities worthy of funding and public support, they need to be seen as contributing in some way to these broader policy impacts. Otherwise, public resources may be allocated to other community services, like police departments (juvenile crime), chambers of commerce (economic stimulation), conservation commissions (preservation of natural resources), or local hospitals and public health facilities (health and well-being). In the eyes of stakeholders, these organizations may be more worthy of public support because they are more easily associated with the desired ends of public policy.

Justification for Public Recreation and Leisure

Historically, the justification for public involvement in parks and recreation services came about as a means of social reform in response to the social conditions that were created in the mid- to late-19th century as a result of the growing industrialization and urbanization of the United States.

The movement toward public funding and resource support for parks and recreation was exemplified at the federal level by the conservation and setting aside of land by the federal government that would eventually be used to form the National Park Service; the creation of public spaces within cities, such as Central Park in New York, and Golden Gate Park in San Francisco; and the public funding of neighborhood playgrounds in cities such as Boston, Massachusetts, and Chicago. Public infrastructure support for parks and recreation was accelerated through the "make work" programs associated with Franklin Delano Roosevelt's New Deal. In fact, much of the state park infrastructure was built through the efforts of Depression-era organizations such as the Civilian Conservation Corps.

Historically, support for public recreation was rooted in the notion that such services helped to alleviate many of the distressed social conditions that arose from the industrialization and urbanization of America. The general philosophy underlying public (government) support of parks and recreation is that they are considered to be a public good—that there is broad public value that accrues for both users and nonusers of these services. As with any public good, such as fire protection, police, education, and transportation, the service is assumed to have value regardless of whether a citizen is using it, and it also is assumed that the service should be available to the public regardless of their ability to pay full market value for its use.

We can think about these same questions or examples when considering the role of government in the provision of parks and recreation services. There are at least three major justifications for public recreation (National Parks & Recreation Association, n.d.):

1. Efficiency
2. Equity
3. Preservation of resources

All three of these justifications are explained in further detail next.

Efficiency

Consider how much it might cost an individual property owner to install a private, backyard swimming pool. Although the price of equipment and installation will vary from place to place, let's assume that it will cost the homeowners $20,000 to install their swimming pool. Of course, this price does not include accessories, chemicals, energy to operate the pool, and yearly maintenance, which increase the financial burden on the individual consumer. However, by paying 100 percent of the price for the swimming pool, the homeowner gets to enjoy 100 percent of its benefits—convenience, privacy, and unlimited use. To determine whether this is the most efficient use of a homeowner's financial resources, one needs to do a cost–benefit analysis related to the purchase. How often does the family use the pool? How important is the pool to the family's quality of life? Can the family afford the expense, given its other needs? If the family is not using the pool frequently enough to justify its annual cost and impact on the household budget, then the purchase of the pool might be an inefficient use of the family's financial resources. In addition, think of the potential waste of scarce resources (e.g., water, energy, raw materials, human effort) that are needed to build, install, and maintain the pool. Multiply these factors by all of the private swimming pools in the community, and you can see how this system of service delivery is inefficient.

Imagine another community—one with a municipal parks and recreation department. In this community, the average household pays approximately $25 per year as part of its property taxes to

---

Self-Exploration

Think about your most cherished memory on a public playground. As a child, the simple thought or mention of going to the playground brings excitement. We can still remember that feeling as adults. Free play with other children along with equipment and space to explore are key components of our childhood. Now, think about never having access to these public recreational facilities and what impact that would have on your childhood. These spaces and facilities are paid for by our tax dollars. What would life be like if the government completely unfunded these resources? This is why it is vital that you, the professionals in our field, are aware of public policy and the impact our tax dollars have on public access to recreational spaces. If your local board wanted to defund public parks in your city, as the local parks and recreation director, how would you defend the importance of government funding of public recreational spaces?

Allen J. Schaben / Los Angeles Times via Getty Images

Public recreation facilities that are accessible to the public, such as swimming pools, provide opportunities for communities to share recreation costs and use.

support a full range of parks and recreation services, including a public swimming pool. In addition, the average household pays $25 per year in fees to the city for a pool membership, which includes a bundle of other services such as swimming lessons and water aerobics classes. In this case, the household is only paying for a fraction of the total cost of the swimming pool and reaps many of the other benefits of a full-service parks and recreation department (e.g., parks, athletic facilities, playgrounds, community centers). Given the physical, human, and fiscal resources involved with installing an outdoor swimming pool, it makes sense to spread the resource burden, especially if there is an expressed need for the service and it has value to the broader community (a public good).

This example refers to what is known as a **commons**—an opportunity for the entire community to share recreation costs and use (Kelly & Freysinger, 1999). This allows community members to pool their collective resources to develop and preserve

recreation spaces that everyone in the community can use. If we define **efficiency** as the effective allocation of scarce resources to produce the most benefit for the most people, then there is another efficiency argument for government involvement in parks and recreation (More, 1999). Government agencies are generally thought of as being responsible for the common good, and as such they play a pivotal role in planning and ensuring that scarce space is allocated to promote that public good. For example, government entities can ensure through effective planning and zoning processes that there is enough space for public recreation and commercial interests.

Equity

One of the major roles of government in public recreation is to provide equity in the distribution of leisure services and programs. Some have argued that given their mandate, government provision of parks and recreation services should be primarily concerned with issues of equity before considering other issues such as effectiveness and efficiency (Crompton & Lamb, 1986). Returning to our swimming pool example, if access to a swimming pool is truly considered to be a public good, then some provision must be made to ensure that everyone in a community, regardless of their background, has access to the resource. For example, cities don't, as a rule, have income requirements for the use of city parks. In general terms, and as we see in our swimming pool example, the cost of many public recreation resources is subsidized through some system of taxation or differential pricing method that spreads the cost burden throughout the community as a whole. This allows access to the park for a diverse range of users from different financial means.

However, the issues about what constitutes a public good, who should pay, and how much should be paid are rife for debate in public policy circles. In the 1970s and 1980s, a number of state and municipal governments began to respond to the political shifts against government provision of public services by passing legislation to reduce the tax burdens on citizens. California led the way with Proposition 13 in 1978, which placed a limit on state property taxes, reducing property tax rates and at the same affecting the public services that could be provided to citizens. By 1980, approximately 13 other states followed California's lead. The debate about whether parks and recreation services are **public goods** is still active today.

Since the tax revolts of the 1970s and 1980s, government agencies have been asked to continue to provide the same (or increased) levels of service with less appropriated (tax) funds. One financial response has been to charge user fees for the use of certain parks and recreation services, as is evidenced in the swimming pool example. Some argue that charging fees for certain parks and recreation services creates equity in that these fees place a greater proportion of the financial burden on the citizens who use the service directly. Others argue that fees lead to greater efficiency as well, because they allow administrators to direct user behavior through various pricing schemes. For example, the fee for access to a popular public park during peak demand times might be higher than the fee for access to a less popular park during the same time period. In this case, efficiency may be created by shifting demand and spreading out use. This could also have

a positive impact on resource preservation as well (discussed subsequently) by controlling the overuse of a particular natural resource (Crompton, 2016).

Although there may be good reasons for user fees, public recreation managers must take issues of equitable access into account. Who owns public lands? Should only those with the ability to pay be allowed access to places like Yellowstone National Park or the Grand Canyon? Should only those who have the ability to pay be able to access the swimming lessons offered at the local community pool? Should only those who have the ability to pay have access to an after-school playground program? Questions about resource allocation and equity—who gets what and who pays—are political questions that public recreation managers must contend with.

Preservation of Resources

Theodore Roosevelt, the 26th president of the United States, is widely considered to be one of the great conservationist presidents and an important figure in the development of public outdoor recreation in the United States. In his book, *Outdoor Pastimes of an American Hunter,* Roosevelt summed up his conservation ethic:

> There can be nothing in the world more beautiful than the Yosemite, the groves of giant sequoias and redwoods, the Canyon of the Colorado, the Canyon of the Yellowstone, the Three Tetons; and our people should see to it that they are preserved for their children and their children's children forever, with their majestic beauty all unmarred. (Roosevelt, 1908, p. 317)

This statement reveals another justification for government involvement in leisure provision—the conservation, preservation, and management of natural resources for the public good.

This principle goes beyond efficiency and equity arguments. It speaks to the government's role as a protector or steward of public treasures that need to be preserved for both the good of the citizenry today and for future generations. The idea here is that government is in the best position to manage historical, cultural, and sensitive natural resources for the long term and to avoid making decisions that sacrifice long-term preservation for short-term benefits. This speaks to the understanding that such resources are not infinite. We have only one Old Faithful, one Grand Canyon, and one Washington Monument. Federal, state, and local government agencies are tasked with the responsibility of balancing present use of sensitive natural, historical, and cultural resources with the need to preserve them for future generations and protect the interests of local stakeholders.

Summary

Leisure is experienced both individually and collectively. Due to the collective aspect of leisure, it is necessary for many aspects of leisure to be political in nature. Decisions are made both within and outside the formal political process. The formal political process includes the major structures of government, particularly the executive, legislative, and judicial branches. The government's role in leisure services provision is to ensure efficiency, equity, and preservation of resources. Politics and public policy formation in a federal system takes place at various levels of government. In the United States and Canada, public policy related to leisure behavior and service delivery takes place at the federal, state or provincial, and local levels of government. Public policy is also influenced by the pluralist nature of liberal democracies, giving voice to people through organized advocacy and special interest groups. Leisure policy is often driven directly by the expressed needs, desires, and interests of the citizenry through organized political action.

Learning Activities

1. Consider the following fictional scenario: Imagine that a legislative proposal to reform the federal government of the United States would have the government sell off its 88 million acres (more than 3.5 million square kilometers) of land to private entrepreneurs at fair market value, allowing them to manage sensitive, historical, or cultural areas as private enterprises by charging users and keeping profits. All nonsensitive areas or areas that do not have historical or cultural significance could be developed as the private entrepreneurs see fit. The federal government would save $1.7 billion annually, would gain the revenue from the sales of the real estate, and would be out of the business of land and recreation program management.

   - What do you think about this proposal?
   - Would this solution work?
   - Is there anything you like about the proposal?
   - Is there anything that you don't like about it?

2. Consider the following questions about the potential benefits and drawbacks of leisure for both individuals and society:

   - Leisure and recreation activities have the potential to play a role of fundamental importance for both individuals and society at large. In groups, brainstorm and discuss the potential benefits of leisure experiences and recreation activities on our lives from both an individual and a social perspective.
   - Leisure experiences and recreation activities can produce negative impacts for individuals, societies, and the environment. Can you think of some of the potential negative impacts of leisure and recreation?
   - What role should government play (if any) in the promotion and delivery of leisure services or in the regulation of leisure behavior? What is your justification for this position?

3. Consider this scenario: Citizens concerned with traffic congestion and the physical and environmental health of Anytown, USA, propose that the downtown business district be closed to all automobile traffic in order to create a walkable community. This group says that walkable downtowns increase business for shops, restaurants, and entertainment businesses in the downtown district. The business community vehemently disagrees, claiming that people do not want to walk and that they will instead drive to, park, and shop in the suburban megamall outside of town. What arguments could you make to the mayor, city council, and planning department that might support walkable downtowns? Take a look at your argument. Is it persuasive? Is it more persuasive than the argument from the downtown business community? What evidence might you cite to support your position?

4. If you were given the responsibility to draft a philosophy statement for a public recreation department in your hometown, what key points would you include?

5. Look at your philosophy statement. Does it resonate politically? Do you think politicians and community leaders would see public recreation as worthy of receiving additional public funds (i.e., money from taxes) based on what you believe the emphasis should be? Think about this from both sides of the issue.

Review Questions

1. Why is leisure political?

2. What are the five characteristics of a federalist society?

3. Explain how each of the three branches of government in Western democracies is involved in creating leisure policy.

4. What are the three branches of government in Western democracies?

5. How can citizens become involved in the political process to influence policies affecting leisure behavior?

Go to HK*Propel* to access additional learning content.

Leisure in Your World

Campus and Community

H. Joey Gray

California Polytechnic State University

Danielle Lauber

Middle Tennessee State University

VOCABULARY TERMS

campus community

campus recreation

casual leisure

community

community recreation

esports

exergaming

microcosm

recreational sport

serious leisure

theory of student involvement

third place

virtual fitness

LEARNING OUTCOMES

After reading this chapter, you will

- be able to define and identify microcosms within the campus and community settings;
- better understand recreational activities and associations offered in campus and community settings;
- know the benefits associated with leisure participation;
- understand the importance of getting involved in campus and community activities; and
- be familiar with some of the leisure theories associated with microcosms, campus recreation, and community recreation.

If someone on the street stopped you to ask what a Hoosier was, would you know what they meant? If you attended or were a fan of Indiana University, you certainly would! The mascot for Indiana University is a Hoosier, and those who attend the university identify closely with their mascot. Ironically, there is much debate what the word *Hoosier* means. But just say the word *Hoosier* and Indiana students, faculty, and fans alike fill with pride because of their association with Indiana University; they have made themselves a part of the Hoosier community—a microcosm. Can you think of a microcosm that you belong to? Most college students are loyal fans of their sports teams. Perhaps you are one of the legendary Toronto Maple Leafs hockey fans who are well known for their loyalty despite the fact they have not won a championship since 1967. Or maybe you have discovered a new world of friends through geocaching, by frequenting your local Jewish Community Center, or by using social media like TikTok, Twitter, Instagram, or Snapchat.

What makes people have pride for an organization? Often it is a sense of belonging or community. Community can be created in a variety of ways, such as through shared enjoyment from time spent in leisure activities. Various organizations offer a variety of recreation opportunities. Do you know all of the recreation opportunities offered on your campus? What recreational activities are available within your community? Do you have a say in what is offered? In this chapter we explore the facets of microcosms within campus and community recreation. We discuss the leisure opportunities and benefits associated with participation in the campus and community settings. Last, we examine leisure theories as they relate to our topics.

College campuses and residential communities are filled with microcosms, small worlds within one or more larger worlds. For instance, a family is a microcosm living within a neighborhood microcosm within a community microcosm, and so on. A sense of belonging is an important aspect of defining a microcosm and an integral part of campus and community recreation. Like those who are a part of the Hoosier community, we all share a sense of value, individualism, and acceptance within our campus and community recreational activities. These affiliations allow us to develop unique relationships that form into microcosms.

What Is a Microcosm?

Did you know you live in a community microcosm? A **microcosm** is often referred to as a miniature world; therefore, a community microcosm refers to the little worlds in which we live our daily lives. This tiny world might consist of our friends, social groups, clubs, and recreational groups. Who do you choose to spend time with? Your answer reveals your own community microcosm. You may be a part of several community microcosms (a sorority or fraternity, club sports, religious groups, a circle of close friends). The theory of serious leisure is closely related to the concept of microcosms. **Serious leisure** is the methodical pursuit of an amateur, a hobbyist, or a volunteer activity so substantial and interesting that the participant centers their life on special skills, knowledge, and experience associated with the leisure pursuit (Stebbins, 1997). Those who participate in serious leisure gain a sense of belonging within their community, which becomes a microcosm. An example would be marathon runners. Those on campus might train together for marathon events, thus forming their own circle of friends and running community. At times, serious leisure joins people together from various backgrounds and ages based on a common leisure interest, resulting in a microcosm.

How Is Your Campus Community a Microcosm?

Consider the meaning of *microcosm*. How might a campus community be considered a microcosm? Sports teams, club sports, special interest groups,

Self-Exploration

Your community microcosm will probably change over time as you develop and grow. Think about the time before you started college: Who were your friends? Are they the same people now, or have you added new affiliations? Other changes in your community microcosms may include starting a new job, beginning a new romantic relationship, or moving to a new place. Give some thought to your life: What small worlds do you participate in?

fraternities, sororities, and individual colleges are examples of campus community microcosms. Each has its own formal and informal rules in addition to identity and values.

Student life is more than just going to class and learning from a textbook; an important part of the collegiate experience is learning life lessons and being a part of community. One's sense of campus community is associated with being valued as an individual, gaining acceptance within the community, and improving individual quality of campus social life (Cheng, 2004). Fraternities and sororities are prime examples of community microcosms, because students affiliated with these organizations sometimes spend a great deal of their collegiate life participating in events or socializing with their fellow members in the organization. A key component of Greek life is to establish its own miniature world with unique rituals, rules, and social activities. The theory of student involvement refers to "the quantity and quality of the physical and psychological energy that students invest in the college experience" (Astin, 1984, p. 307). The theory proposes that the more involved students are in extracurricular and academic activities, the more they will experience enhanced socioemotional development, particularly through sport and recreation. The most important aspect of the theory of student involvement is that the more involved students are, the more likely they are to have positive developmental experiences. Students who are active in student recreation centers have a better likelihood of experiencing a sense of social belonging in both the recreation centers themselves and the university, which in turn increases their changes of staying at that university (Miller, 2011). Students involved in Greek life are also less likely to drop out of college (Astin, 1975). Social participation (Cicognani et al., 2008) and participation in campus recreational sports (Elkins, Forrester, & Noël-Elkins, 2011) are both linked to the positive development of a sense of community for college students. One could conclude that increased involvement in chosen microcosms increases feelings of cohesion to the campus community, increasing the likelihood that students will want to stay long enough to graduate.

Collegiate campuses are full of opportunities to become involved in microcosms. Are you a member of a social group, sports club, academic club, or fitness class? Do you attend scheduled campus events like movies, concerts, and plays? Do you have classmates and friends whom you hang out with frequently who also attend your university? All of these groups establish their own community relationships with rules, social norms, and expectations. Think about the little world that only you and your close college friends experience. Consider all the inside jokes, spring break vacations, social situations, and recreational activities that you and your cohorts have shared together. Within your own little world, you share good times, recreate, and enjoy your time together. You are a part of your own campus community, a microcosm, and these community ties are likely to help you have a better college experience than people who are less socially engaged. Recreational activities enrich life in so many ways.

How Is Community Recreation a Microcosm?

As previously mentioned, microcosms are worlds that fit within larger worlds. The campus microcosm exists as a world unto itself, but it also exists within a larger community, city, and state. Each of the larger systems is capable of exerting pressures on the smaller systems; thus, the systems can never be fully separated. Similar to the campus community, community recreation consists of microcosms. Sports clubs, social groups, family, neighbors, friends, and other recreational groups all consist of microcosms. Have you ever seen those soccer ball stickers on windows of minivans or cars that say things like "Go Rockets" or "Seth, #16, is #1?" Youth sport microcosms are common within communities. Parents, youth, families, and neighbors all join in and participate in their own worlds of soccer, baseball, basketball, gymnastics, and other sports. Of course, community microcosms are not limited to sport. One can find microcosms in all aspects of community recreation and activities. For instance, Nashville, Tennessee, is well known for its musical endeavors. Musically inclined people often want to be a part of the music community in Nashville. They form bands, play music, and listen to other musicians almost every weekend. Other activities from gardening clubs to religious organizations are also part of community recreation. All have their own individual microcosms.

Self-Exploration

What does this discussion mean for you? Be aware of your surroundings and the microcosms you join. Are these activities you enjoy? Do the people you recreate with share your beliefs and values? Do you enjoy the time you spend with your friends? Is there some activity or a group you have always wanted to learn about or be a part of? Explore your campus and community recreational opportunities now. Seize the opportunities that you have. Explore opportunities you might find interesting. Take chances and join activities you always wanted to attempt. You never know what doors campus and community involvement might open for you in the future.

Have you ever moved to a new place and wondered how to make new friends who shared your interests and values? A great way to make new friends is to explore and join recreational opportunities offered in your area. Community recreation helps us find microcosms to which we may comfortably belong.

Explore Your Campus and Campus Recreation

A large number of students graduate from college without fully exploring the recreation opportunities available on campus. Are you aware of the numerous recreational opportunities and student organizations that are offered on your campus? Did you know that many campus recreation centers offer low-cost massages and personal training sessions? What other unique opportunities are offered on your college campus? If you do not know, you must explore your campus! It is unlikely that you will ever have unrestricted access to so many free recreation opportunities ever again.

How can you find out all that your campus recreation center has to offer? The most efficient way to explore your campus is by using the Internet. The key to useful exploration is knowing where to look. Most students are aware of the campus recreation center. Campus recreation centers usually disseminate information about their activities on a website, through flyers, and by posting schedules around campus. Facebook is another way to capitalize on activities. But do not stop there! The student affairs department often has a list of activities as well; these offerings may be listed under student life or student programs on your college's website. Check with the student government association and with individual academic departments for clubs that you might be interested in joining. Explore all interesting opportunities, because many academic clubs are not restricted to majors. You may need to keep your eyes open to find all the opportunities campus

recreation has to offer. In fact, some feel that campus recreation centers need to do a better job of publicizing program information to students (Schneider et al., 2007). Research has shown that some of the top reasons students do not participate in campus recreation programs are lack of awareness, lack of time, lack of a partner, and beliefs that their skills are inadequate (Young, Ross, & Barcelona, 2003). In an effort to better understand why students do not participate in campus recreation activities more, one researcher found that freshmen believed they had less access to campus recreation facilities than did students in upper classes (Reed, 2007). Do not let any of these obstacles stand in your way. Campus recreation is a great way to meet people who share similar interests and to try new activities. At no other time in your life will you have this many recreational opportunities for such little cost. Do not make the mistake and think you will have time later—do not wait. *Carpe diem* (seize the day)! When exploring your campus, look for five major opportunities for involvement: campus recreation, student programs, student organizations and clubs, Greek life, and learning environments.

Discover Opportunities: Components of Campus Recreation

The purpose of campus recreation is to provide a wide variety of recreational experiences and opportunities for students, faculty, and staff. According to Dr. Ray Wiley, the most popular activities offered by the campus recreation centers he directs are (1) intramurals; (2) fitness programs (weight room, fitness classes); (3) club sports; (4) outdoor trips, often referred to as outdoor pursuits; and (5) aquatics. This list is similar to results at other universities. Campus recreation centers are exploring new programming directions with virtual opportunities such as esports and online fitness programs. With all of these activities, one might think that all college students would use their campus recreation centers several times per week. However, research shows that students participate at differing rates, and not all students are aware of activity choices. One study found that men tend to participate in campus recreation activities more than women (Zizzi, Ayers, Watson, & Keeler, 2004). Another study revealed that freshmen were less aware of recreational offerings on campus and that men and women had different understandings of their campus choices (Reed, 2007). These results suggest that students participate more in campus recreation activities as they learn about their options. Centers are continuing to incorporate technology to communicate opportunities as well as provide innovative activities.

Technology and Campus Recreation

Cell phones now function as minicomputers that most of us depend on to function in everyday life. Social media accelerates information distribution, connectivity, and trends. Campus recreation, like the rest of the world, must adapt to the growing technologies and demands of users, from online registration to communication of program offerings to virtual activities. Technology offers an avenue to reach those who may prefer or require virtual participation and open the door to new activities. Leabo and Ostendorf (2018) describe four key technologies used to increase participation: exergaming, wearable technology, virtual fitness on demand, and esports. **Exergaming** is using technologically driven activities, such as video games, that require the participant to exercise or be physically active (e.g., dancing, running) to play the game. A key feature that attracts participants to exergaming is that they can choose the level of difficulty, pace, or play mode on an individual basis. Universities are also exploring using wearable technology, such as FitMetrix and Fitbit, to track fitness progress so students can compete on their own schedule. **Virtual fitness** encompasses livestreaming and technology to allow participation in workouts via virtual reality. The appeal of virtual fitness is the freedom of choice and increased opportunities to

Many recreational sport opportunities build lifelong friendships, skills, and love for the sport.

Pixelfit/E+/Getty Images

deliver high-quality programs to the masses as opposed to the limited time and space of in-person fitness programs. Esports comprise both amateur and professional players participating in video game events or tournaments that include championships at both regional and international levels.

Campus recreation's primary goal is to serve students; thus, many of the activities and much of the programming revolves around student interests. Students, faculty, and staff participate in campus recreation activates to have fun, maintain healthy lifestyles, and socialize. Leisure activities assist with life stress, enhancing both mental and physical health (Iwasaki & Mannell, 2000). Leisure activities also promote self-efficacy and achievement motivation for college students (Jdaitawi et al., 2020). Now a major marketing and recruiting tool for many universities, campus recreation has become a vital component to universities and their students, faculty, and staff. In fact, the National Intramural–Recreational Sports Association provides several awards to campus recreation programs and professionals for outstanding programs and innovations. Among the most prestigious are the Creative Excellence Award for innovation and creativity in marketing programs and the Outstanding Facilities Award.

The benefits associated with participation in campus recreation activities are endless and range from stress management to social engagement. Areas that many campus recreation centers address are recreational sport, fitness, outdoor opportunities, and student program opportunities.

Recreational Sport

The term recreational sport was coined because of the popularity of informal sports programs: It is an umbrella term that refers to intramurals, extramurals, club sports, informal sports, and instructional sports (Mull, Bayless, & Jamieson, 2005). Numerous benefits are associated with recreational sports involvement, including decreased stress, improved social integration, enhancement of self-esteem, improved grades, and student development (Belch, Gebel, & Mass, 2001; Bryant, Bradley, & Milborne, 1994; Haines, 2001; Kanters, 2000; Nesbitt, 1998). The most popular of all recreational sports activities are intramurals (Artinger, Clapham, Meigs, Sampson, & Forrester, 2006). Intramurals are structured sports programs within the campus. They offer a wide range of sport opportunities with various levels of competition (beginner, intermediate, advanced). Typical examples of intramurals include softball, basketball, rugby, disc golf, hockey, badminton, volleyball, Wiffle ball, and flag football.

Fitness

Although sports are a large part of campus recreation, there are numerous recreational opportunities in addition to recreational sports. Most universities offer fitness programs, often in state-of-the-art fitness centers. Universities began incorporating fitness programs around the 1970s, although at the time such programs were considered a passing fad. Fitness programs are one of the top recreational activities on college campuses today, and it is predicted that fitness programming will remain essential as our country continues to struggle with obesity. Programs of interest tend to be group fitness classes such as tai chi, swim classes, water aerobics, Spinning classes, yoga, kickboxing, Pilates, and Zumba (a type of dance fitness). Research has revealed a significant decrease in depression and anxiety in those who exercise regularly (Goodwin, 2003). Fitness activities also offer a stress-free way to meet people who share the common interest of fitness. The benefits from fitness opportunities, such as regular exercise and stress management, are key components to a healthy life.

Outdoor Trips

Outdoor trips are another unique opportunity offered by campus recreation programs. The trips range from short day hikes to longer international trips. Students can also learn skills such as canoeing, rock climbing, and scuba, and campus recreation often incorporates these skills into outdoor trips. One such example might be a spring break trip to Hawaii for scuba diving. Equipment for personal or major-related camping or kayaking trips is often available for rent through the campus recreation center. You are unlikely to ever find equipment rental as inexpensive as that offered by the campus recreation center: Rental can be as little as $5 a day! Whether students are skilled outdoor enthusiasts or simply would like to learn to kayak, the campus recreation center offers a variety of outdoor recreation opportunities.

Student Programs

Recreational opportunities also exist outside of campus recreation facilities. Some are called student programs or student activities, and some are sponsored by the office of student affairs. Regardless of the name, universities are filled with various

When your life depends on those with whom you dive, engaging in the activity often fosters deep respect for and kinship with fellow divers.

microcosms outside of campus recreation and most are created, programmed, and delivered by students. Examples include inexpensive movies, concerts, comedians, lectures, variety shows, and fine arts. Student fees usually cover the majority of the expenses for these events, and therefore they are provided for students either free of charge or for a minimal cost. A variety of leisure pursuits have been classified as **casual leisure**, intrinsically rewarding activities requiring little skill or training to enjoy (Stebbins, 1997). Some believe that casual leisure activities are just as important as serious leisure because people highly value casual leisure opportunities. Everyone participates in casual leisure, and most appreciate the opportunity to relax and emotionally recharge (Stebbins, 1997). Examples of casual leisure within campus recreation include going to movies or hanging out with friends. Campus recreation activities can also require specialized skills and time commitment, considered as serious leisure. Student programs for serious leisure activities include concert or theater productions or active participation in committee work. More than

Self-Exploration

Take a moment to reflect on your own casual leisure. What simple leisure activities give you the most enjoyment? How about a playing a game on your phone as a reward for finishing a paper? Or perhaps spending quality time with your dog at the park on a nice sunny day?

just an opportunity to participate in inexpensive, fun social activities, student programs offer great leadership and experiential opportunities.

Clubs and Student Organizations

Your campus offers a host of other student program opportunities such as student organizations and clubs, Greek life, religious organizations, and cultural opportunities. Additionally, student unions and other venues on campus are filled with social learning environments such as cyber cafes, study spaces, and open green spaces. One can never overlook the importance of informal collegiate experiences that occur as people gather to study or simply to hang out.

Clubs and student organizations are a major part of campus recreation and can range from the Rock Paper Scissors Club, like the one at the University of Florida, to the Young Republicans club, such as that at Wellesley College in Wellesley, Massachusetts. The Rock Paper Scissors Club has grown nationally and even has a college tournament, which is broadcast on ESPN. Of course, there are the typical clubs; for example, each major on campus usually has a club (math club, theater club, Spanish club). Notably, the recreation major's club should be having the most fun! Special interest clubs and organizations are plentiful on campus. Every collegiate campus has student government organizations, and most have Greek organizations. Other clubs or organizations may range from a 24-hour movie club to a gardening club. If you are not in at least two clubs, it may be fair to say you are missing out. There are collegiate clubs for just about every leisure interest one could imagine. And if one does not exist on your campus, you could start one tomorrow. On second thought, why wait until tomorrow? You could start a mustache club just like the one at Carleton College in Northfield, Minnesota. (This Carleton College club does include women, as long as they agree to shave their faces except their upper lip!) Club and student organizations are derived from common leisure interests and frequently include philanthropic pursuits: The Carleton College Mustache Club raises money for a domestic abuse shelter. However, some clubs are purely for casual leisure experiences, like the Harvard Tiddlywinks Society or the University of Minnesota Campus People Watchers. Do not wait: Join or start a club or student organization today!

Have a Voice and Get Involved: Volunteer and Job Opportunities on Campus

There is no need to wait until after graduation to seek experience. Let your voice be heard and get involved in both planning and providing feedback regarding campus programs. Volunteer for committees. Serve on student boards. Participate in service learning and seek employment opportunities in campus recreation and on campus. Some available positions include trip leader, referee or official, student director, program chair, events coordinator, fitness instructor, and student program specialist. Internships, practicum learning, and field experiences are also excellent ways to gain valuable life skills that will serve you in both your personal and professional careers. Another way to make your voice heard is through evaluations. Comprehensive evaluations of campus recreation programs are vital for their success (Cooper & Faircloth, 2006). When you have the opportunity, make sure to provide feedback. Directors, program managers, and instructors really do care about what you have to say, and they want to hear from you! If leisure constraints are interfering with your ability to participate (e.g., hours of operations) or if you would like to see changes in campus activities, providing feedback is an important place to start.

Explore Your Community

Students hear the word *community* almost daily while participating in college life, but what does the term really mean? Most agree that community can refer to a group of people living in close proximity to one another; a group of people sharing common interests, like the scientific community; people comprising a distinct segment of the population, like the gay community; or people sharing a common identity, like the Irish community. Given these definitions, it is easy to see how a university can be considered a community containing many smaller communities, such as dorms, fraternities, majors, and campus organizations. But beyond the borders of the university is a larger community, city, township, neighborhood, or area.

Community recreation providers and centers strive to provide recreation and leisure opportunities to people living nearby (much like the opportunities offered by the campus recreation center), but community recreation organizers must cater their offerings to a larger range of age groups. Activities are likely to vary widely, such as holiday events for toddlers, league sports for youth and teens, tournaments for adults, and water aerobics targeted for senior citizens. With the diverse selection of age groups, ability levels, and interests that community recreation centers seek to serve, building a sense of community is a task that must be carefully managed. Recreation professionals want participants not only to participate but also to feel connected,

On the Job

Exploring Recreation-Based Jobs on Campus and in the Community

Almost everyone has participated in some type of campus or community recreation. But have you stopped to think about all the components that had to take place to provide you with that experience? Someone had to hire and train the staff, schedule the facility, referees, or instructor, or block the schedule to ensure there was open gym time so you could have access to free play or to work out. Think about the many opportunities offered at your campus recreation center. All of the various programs, special events, and facilities are carefully planned, organized, and delivered by numerous recreational staff, interns, and volunteers who you never see but who are paramount to all participants' recreational experiences. Both campus and community recreation organizations and private business provide a plethora of job opportunities. Some examples of recreation jobs include the following:

- Directors of campus recreation are often responsible for directing university recreation programs, including student activities. This position is a higher-level position that will require administrative leadership and often is also in charge of facility management.
- Recreation directors and coordinators are similar to activities directors. Recreation directors and coordinators typically work in activity centers, senior centers, correctional facilities, recreation facilities, parks and recreation, or other community-based facilities.
- Special events coordinators and event planners plan, organize, and promote events for a wide variety of organizations. Events could include corporate retreats, concerts, weddings, professional development workshops, sporting events, and many others. These positions require logistical knowledge and good organizational planning skills.
- A youth sport director is similar to that of the campus recreation director but obviously focuses on sport. This could be isolated to one sport or a multisport organization. The organization could be public, like parks and recreation, or a private nonprofit or for-profit organization. Depending on the size of the organization, the director is either directly in charge of or oversees all staff, practice and game scheduling, registration, team rosters, facilities, equipment, budget, and policy; serves as liaison to the public or the board; and much more.

These positions require leadership and human resource skills and public relations and budgeting knowledge.

which increases the likelihood that community members will return and benefit from other leisure offerings as well.

Community is created in many ways. Living physically near others is one way community is built and might be the most easily recognized meaning of community. However, simply being near others is not enough for people to call themselves a community: We do not normally consider ourselves the community of moviegoers as we wait in line! A sense of community also requires a level of shared identity. Sometimes a sense of community is gained through being near others and participating in activities together, as in being teammates or classmates. Community may be gained even when people are not near one another, as with online organizations: People may be separated by continents but may be connected through their shared commitment to a

task or belief system. People may be committed to beliefs such as fighting global warming, supporting adoption, or seeking equal rights. People may become a community through participating in adult and youth athletics, special interest clubs, online gaming, and cultural events. These shared desires and beliefs can unite people, helping virtual strangers feel like next-door neighbors.

So what is this sense of community we have been discussing? Cohesiveness is fundamental. People bond through a shared purpose or shared interests. As people feel emotionally connected, this creates a shared sense of identity, which reduces feelings of isolation. Community recreation is "a means for improving and maintaining societal cohesion and the quality of life; its development is dependent on social participation" (Torkildsen, 2005, p. 53). Thus, community recreation activities facilitate opportunities for community members to participate and create emotional attachments to the activity, to the recreation facility, and to one another, which builds a shared sense of community. Both serious and casual leisure can be found in community recreation activities. Serious leisure may be undertaken by avid motorcycle riders, NASCAR race fans, or members of local community theater. Casual leisure examples include attending movies, watching television, surfing the Internet, or having dinner with friends.

Discover Opportunities in Community Recreation

Community recreation provides numerous opportunities for participation. Activities may be organized by local recreation departments, which usually maintain facilities and plan, organize, and deliver programs. Some of the most common community activities include adult and youth sports, cultural arts, senior centers, educational and instructional courses, aquatics facilities, wellness programs, and special events. Amenities include pavilions, parks, playgrounds, lakes, walking trails, greenways, bike paths, dog parks, and skate parks. Although many of the activities offered by parks and recreation departments are organized, free play opportunities are an important component of parks and recreation as well. Lakes, greenways, bike paths, walking trails, and open access to facilities and spaces are an integral part of the services offered and an important part of building community.

Community centers may be owned and operated by the local parks and recreation department or they may be privately owned. Local YMCA centers, Jewish community centers, Boys & Girls Clubs, and fitness centers are examples of privately owned community centers. Although not government funded or operated, these centers play a valuable role in community recreation. Private community centers sometimes offer a wider variety of opportunities, and a competitive market tends to work in favor of the participant.

Many communities and even small towns offer unique activities for their populations. For example, Nashville, Tennessee, holds a variety of musical festivals, concerts, and programs given the resources and common interests of the people

Visiting a dog park is a great way to meet and recreate with people who share your love for animals! Members of the dog park community (usually) follow common rules of play as well as social responsibility: Leave no trace!

FluxFactory/E+/Getty Images

within the community. In a much smaller area, Smithfield, North Carolina, the annual Ham & Yam Festival attracts hundreds of community members. Many community activities are not hosted by or even affiliated with the local parks and recreation department but are spearheaded by community members themselves. In rural communities, common Halloween events are haunted forests, hayrides, and corn mazes. Many farmers will organize hayrides and transform their cornfields with great detail for the community. Often those who share a common interest organize activities. Other examples of activities created around shared interests include quilting, knitting, and garden clubs and block parties. Still other community members may open horseback trail rides for members of the public.

The term third place was coined by psychologist Ray Oldenburg to describe the places where we spend our time outside the home (first place) and work (second place). Third place, as defined by Oldenburg (1999), is a welcoming community space where people spend their free time with friends, colleagues, or neighbors. Third places can comprise various types of places to gather and socialize, including local bars and community churches. While many of these places are physical, we are now seeing virtual third places emerge as well. Third places can play an important role in communities as they often bring people together.

Summary

Campus recreation activities (recreational sport programs, fitness programs, outdoor trips, and aquatics) play a major role in student leisure, and numerous campus recreation opportunities are available on campus: student programs, student organizations and clubs, Greek life, religious organizations, cultural arts opportunities, cyber cafes, and student unions. Serious leisure and casual leisure can be found in all aspects of campus activities and community recreation, although leisure constraints can impede participation in either arena. An important task for college students is to become aware of the leisure opportunities and get involved! Capitalize on the benefits that your campus and community recreation opportunities offer. Getting involved allows participants to stay healthy, reduce stress, meet new people who share common leisure interests, learn new skills, gain new experiences, and rejuvenate. After having experienced campus and community recreation offerings, participants are able to use their knowledge to improve service delivery. Use your voice: Volunteer to serve on advisory boards, committees, and event delivery. Understanding how communities fit one inside the other to create a sense of belongingness, experiencing campus and community recreation activities, and then using lessons learned to become an activist will give you a fuller appreciation for the time you spend in leisure activities.

Learning Activities

1. Explore your campus. Your mission is to find and provide details (costs, dates, instructions) for the following:

   • An individual class that you could take alone to become more physically fit
   • A team sport that is offered this semester that everyone in class could register for
   • A club sport developed in the past five years
   • A new leisure activity you have never participated in
   • An aquatics program offered in the mornings
   • A spring break trip
   • Hours of operation for the recreation center
   • The name of the recreation center's director
   • The recreation center schedule of events
   • Web address for the recreation center
   • Web address for student programs
   • Schedule of events for student programs
   • Contact information for becoming a member of student programs
   • Name of the movie playing next Friday at the student union, if any

- One student organization you could join
- Two clubs you could join
- The next concert on campus
- Two sororities or fraternities you could join
- Six different pieces of equipment you can rent from campus recreation
- Other programs or events specific to your campus

Add any details, restrictions, time constraints, and parameters specific to your campus.

2. Select a leisure activity that you have never done before (but perhaps always wanted to) and try it! Write a summary of your experience. Include a description of the activity and explain what you liked or did not like about it. Will you continue to participate? Why or why not? What did you learn about yourself through this experience?

3. Explore the opportunities for community recreation where you currently live. Find out how many community recreation centers there are and what programs they offer. Identify some of the local festivals, craft shows, or other events that are hosted by your local town or city and how these are experienced. What opportunities are there for community sport or outdoor recreation? What are some online clubs or social resources that are specific to events in your local area? Go out into your community and find information about all of these or go online to get your start. Make a resource packet with information that includes the who, what, when, where, why, and how for each of these. While making this packet, think about how each of these can build a sense of community for those involved.

Review Questions

1. What are the ways you can get involved in your campus activities? Community activities?
2. What is a microcosm?
3. What are three community microcosms on your campus, in your hometown community, and in the world?
4. What are the major categories of campus recreation?
5. What is the purpose of campus recreation?
6. What are some of the common activities on your campus that are provided by campus recreation and by student programs?
7. What are some of the top reasons students do not participate in campus recreation programs?
8. How does a sense of community bring people together?
9. How can you learn about campus recreation programs?
10. How can you find out about student programs, clubs, or organizations?
11. What are some ways to learn about programs offered in the community?
12. What are some of the benefits of participating in campus activities? Community activities?
13. How can you become more active and effective on campus? In the community?
14. How can you become an activist on campus? In your community?
15. How can leisure constraints (interpersonal, intrapersonal, structural) hinder a person's participation in campus or community activities?
16. Describe what third place is and how it can affect the lives of people within a community.
17. What are esports and why are they so popular?
18. Describe the role of technology in campus recreation.

14

Leisure for All

Linda Oakleaf
Missouri State University

LEARNING OUTCOMES

After reading this chapter, you will

- be able to identify at least two constraints to recreation participation for people with disabilities, people with different gender identities, and ethnic and racial groups;

- understand the importance of inclusion in the provision of recreation, sport, and leisure services;

- understand the challenges and benefits of leisure service provision to those experiencing homelessness;

- be able to explain how gender identity might affect one's experience of recreation, sport, and leisure; and

- be able to explain three different ways that recreation, sport, and leisure practitioners could ensure that their programming, policies, and facilities are inclusive.

Does everyone have the same access to leisure? The research tells us that they do not. For many, societal rules and social roles limit their opportunities for leisure. This chapter discusses the benefits that leisure provides for all people, as well as the constraints that some populations face while trying to access and enjoy leisure.

People With Disabilities

The U.S. Census Bureau reports that 17.6 percent of the nation's citizens have a severe disability (Taylor, 2018). People of all ages, ethnicities, and socioeconomic statuses have impairments related to their sight, hearing, physical abilities, cognitive abilities, and emotional functioning. An **impairment** is an organic or functional condition that may be temporary or permanent (Dattilo, 2002). Impairments range from mild to severe and may or may not be visible to an observer.

We use the term *people with disabilities* as part of **person-first language**. When using person-first language, the goal is to spotlight the human being that is being discussed. It's important not to define someone by their disability, and this should be reflected in the language we use. For example, rather than describing someone as an epileptic, it's better to say "a person with epilepsy." If someone has an impairment, it should not define them.

Some people with disabilities are born with the conditions and others acquire their impairments through injury, disease, and age. Those who are born with impairments typically learn to adapt to barriers at an early age. Those who acquire impairments later in life may have more difficulty accepting their conditions and adjusting to resulting changes (Mackelprang & Salsgiver, 1999). People with disabilities, whether they are born with the conditions or the conditions are acquired, have a range of feelings about that part of themselves, just as various attitudes are connected to the physical, emotional, and cognitive features we are born with or acquire.

Only a small percentage of people with disabilities, even those with severe impairments, live in an institutional setting. According to the ADA Participatory Action Research Consortium (n.d.), 5.1 percent of people with disabilities in the United States live in an institution like a nursing home, hospital, or group home. Thus, most people with disabilities, even with severe impairments, live, work, and play as our neighbors in every corner of the country.

Self-Exploration

Consider the people in your life. Do you know someone with a disability? If so, in what ways do that person's leisure interests differ from your own? Are those differences based on personal preferences, or are they influenced by the person's life experience as a person with a disability? What modifications (if any) make their leisure activities more accessible to them?

In 1990, the Americans With Disabilities Act (ADA) was signed into law. This civil rights act was passed to ensure equal opportunities in employment, housing, and access to goods and services (including recreation) for individuals with disabilities. In the decades before the passing of the ADA, people with disabilities were often relegated to recreation programs for special populations, separate from the services provided to those without disabilities. Program choice and availability were often sparse. The passing of the ADA, however, spurred a growing trend toward inclusive recreation programming. In **inclusive recreation** programs, everyone, regardless of ability, participates together in the same programs. Adaptations, if needed, are provided so that the person with a disability is an equal participant. The concept of inclusion enables people the freedom to choose programs and services based on their interests and to engage in activities with friends and family.

The benefits of recreation for people with disabilities are the same as the benefits for those without disabilities (American Academy of Pediatrics, 2008). Whether it's a child gaining social skills from participating in a team sport or an adult joining a tennis league to meet people, the benefits are the same for all, such as better mental health, a better quality of life, or increased physical activity.

Some people with disabilities may also engage in recreation as part of a prescribed treatment program when receiving **recreation therapy** services, which is an allied health field that uses recreation as a tool to treat individuals with physical, emotional, or cognitive impairments. Recreation therapists work with clients to identify specific goals that aim to enhance their clients' quality of life. They frequently accomplish this as part of a treatment team that is managing multiple aspects of the clients' needs (Kinney, 2020). Clients participate in individual or group treatment to achieve their goals under the

Thomas Barwick/DigitalVision/Getty Images

Physical activity and social connections are important benefits of many leisure activities.

guidance of the recreation therapist. People with disabilities may encounter a recreation therapist in various settings, depending on their impairment. A child with a learning disability may work with a recreation therapist at their school, while an adult who has had a stroke may receive recreation therapy services while in a rehabilitation hospital.

Older Adults

The nation's older adult population is growing. Between 2010 and 2020, the number of adults over the age of 65 in the United States grew by one third (United States Census Bureau, 2020a). The Census Bureau predicts that by 2034, there will be more older adults than children in the United States for the first time (United States Census Bureau, 2020b). While most older adults do have health problems related to their age, medical advances and health education have allowed many older adults to remain active well into their retirement. As noted by Epstein (1994), the conditions that are often accepted as signs of aging are "now understood to be hypokinesia, a disease of *disuse*, the degeneration and functional loss of muscle and bone tissue" (p. 65).

Older adults can prevent much of the degeneration that results from sedentary lifestyles through physical activity. It is important to note that the health conditions that underlie many disabilities are not distributed evenly across the population of older adults. Black and Hispanic people who are 65 and older are more likely to be living with a disability (Taylor, 2018).

The notion of older adults and their recreation interests has changed in recent decades. Traditional programming for older adults at community or senior centers often consisted of activities such as bingo, card clubs, and other sedentary activities. Programmers recognized this group's need for socialization and focused on large-group activities that required little mobility. Over the years, the need for socialization has not changed. Leisure still serves as the primary social outlet for many older adults, especially those who are retired, single, or widowed. What has changed are the types of programs people in this age group desire. A lifestyle survey (Kluge, 2005) reports active recreation as the leading leisure interest for older adults. Older adults are now engaged in activities such as casino trips, hikes, biking tours, and wine clubs.

Anchiy/E+/Getty Images

Age should never be a limitation. You're never too old to get involved and have some fun.

Although the legislation is now in place to ensure equal access to recreation programs and services, not all constraints have been removed. The numbers of inclusive recreation programs and services have increased, but people with disabilities continue to report difficulty in accessing services. In a Harris survey, 69 percent of adults with disabilities reported their disability prevented them in some way from attending cultural or sporting events, participating in recreation, or socializing with friends outside their home (Taylor, 2018). Barriers include negative attitudes of staff and participants, refusal to provide services, and lack of physical access. People with disabilities also report lower income, which limits many opportunities for leisure (Pagán-Rodríguez, 2014). Recreation professionals need to continue their efforts to increase awareness, train staff, and retrofit facilities to provide truly inclusive recreation.

Sports

People with disabilities and older adults benefit from all areas of recreation, including outdoor adventure, art, and volunteering. One particular area of recreation warranting notice is sport participation. Some people with disabilities choose to participate in league sports that are not aimed specifically at people with disabilities. Others participate in one of several sport leagues or associations developed for specific disabilities.

The United Cerebral Palsy Athletic Association, the Dwarf Athletic Association of America, the Veterans Golden Age Games, and Special Olympics International are all examples of associations that sponsor various sport leagues or events for individuals with disabilities. Other associations, such as the National Wheelchair Basketball Association and the International Wheelchair Rugby Federation, provide opportunities in particular sports for individuals with various disabling conditions (in these cases, for those who use wheelchairs).

Most of these associations create competitions on local, state, national, and sometimes international levels; requisite skill levels increase as the level of competition increases. Players range from casual participants to those who compete nationally and internationally at a very high level.

The highest level of sport for people with disabilities is the Paralympics. What originated as a way to help World War II veterans rehabilitate in 1948 has now become the international Paralympic movement, hosting the world's elite athletes with disabilities. The Paralympic Games are held during the same years as the Olympics, and since the Seoul games in 1988, both Games have been held at the same venues. The International Olympic Committee and the International Paralympic Committee now work together to host both the Paralympic Games and the Olympic Games (International Paralympic Committee, n.d.).

Location and Income

Where a person lives has a strong influence on their leisure choices. Easy access is one reason why a person who lives in a rural area may be more likely to engage in fishing, whereas a person who lives in a city may be more likely to visit a museum. Of course, the person in the rural area may enjoy museums but not have the same access as the person in the city.

Both rural areas and large urban areas create constraints to leisure involvement. Lack of organized programs, facilities, and transportation are common constraints in rural communities (Perry & Kendall, 2008). Without an official recreation department, schools, not-for-profit organizations, and other community organizations fill in the gaps of recreation service by sponsoring sport leagues and craft clubs and organizing social events. Rural recreation initiatives, such as the Illinois Rural Recreation Development Project, are focused on developing sustainable recreation opportunities through the promotion of partnerships among community organizations. Nonprofit organizations, churches, schools, and county and state agencies work together to maximize offerings and minimize duplication of services.

Many urban neighborhoods face some of the same constraints as those encountered in rural areas. Lack of facilities, organized programming, and transportation can be just as prevalent in these areas. Neighborhoods in most cities in the United States are highly segregated. Black neighborhoods in particular suffer from a lack of open recreational space. Since such spaces promote physical activity, this inequity may lead to adverse health outcomes (Duncan, Kawachi, White, & Williams, 2013). Even when parks are present in Black neighborhoods, they are less likely to be well maintained or have attractive amenities (Bruton & Floyd, 2014).

Closely connected to where a person lives is their socioeconomic status, which refers to "the status one retains in society as a consequence of three individual attributes: income, occupation, and education" (Dawson, 2000, p. 100). If recreation programs are indeed to be available to all, then public recreation facilities should provide programs at little or no cost. This was the case in the late 1900s as public and not-for-profit recreation agencies provided programs aimed at improving quality of life for those of lower socioeconomic status. Budget cuts over the past several decades, however, have reversed those efforts. Currently, most recreation opportunities are fee based, and even those offered by municipal recreation departments require ever-increasing registration fees as other funding sources are reduced. Since leisure funds are typically pulled from citizens' expendable income, those with lower socioeconomic status have limited funds to dedicate to leisure interests, limiting their leisure opportunities.

One population recreation professionals may overlook is those who are experiencing homelessness. Nickasch and Marnocha define a person who is homeless as someone who is unhoused and "who lacks a fixed, regular, and adequate nighttime residence" (2009, p. 40). To use person-first language, avoid using terms such as *the homeless* or *a homeless person*. People who are unhoused may be living with friends, in shelters, in their cars, or on the streets. Estimates for the number of people experiencing homelessness in the United States vary based on the definition used but range from 500,000 to 2.5 million. While White males make up the largest number of people who are unhoused, a growing number of families, especially single-mother families, fall into this category. Recreation providers are in a unique position to provide services for this population through drop-in centers or outreach services at shelters; they can collaborate with other community service agencies, becoming part of a referral network. Recreation programs provide opportunities to decrease social isolation, increase self-awareness, and offer a sense of community to those who are experiencing homelessness. This may require organizations to reconsider how they view the population. Some parks, for instance, consider the presence of people experiencing homelessness to be a nuisance, and they respond with hostile architecture such as adding spikes to potential seating areas, installing benches with armrests, or even removing benches altogether (Hu, 2019).

Leisure and Segments of Society

Like other important elements of American culture, access to resources for leisure and recreation is regarded as a right of citizenship. However, not all segments of society participate equally, as has been demonstrated for various activities in relation to socioeconomic background (Burch, 2009). There are various dimensions that may be viewed as a constraint to leisure. **Leisure constraints** theory explains that leisure impediments may interfere with participation; these are referred to as interpersonal, intrapersonal, and structural constraints (Crawford & Jackson, 2005). **Interpersonal constraints** are barriers to participation that deal with social relationships with others. For instance, a backpacking enthusiast may go backpacking much less if they start dating someone who hates backpacking. **Intrapersonal constraints** are individual psychological factors that get in the way of leisure participation. These may be ability level, personality needs, prior experiences, or personal preferences. For instance, a person may find chess to be too difficult to be a satisfying leisure activity. **Structural constraints**, such as cost, intervene with participation even though a particular form of leisure may be preferred.

Gender and Leisure

When considering gender and leisure, participants are affected by both their gender as they experience it and how others respond to their gender expression. The people around us police gender norms, typically without even thinking about it. Gender policing can take the form of teasing someone gently or informing them that "real men don't do that." Cultural ideas about gender dictate many forms of social expression, and they run very deep. There are even gender expectations about how to sit or stand. It's not surprising, then, that we have gendered ideas

Self-Exploration

Have you ever wanted to participate in a leisure activity but did not? Think about why you did not participate. Can you identify what type of leisure constraint might have prevented your participation? Was it an interpersonal, intrapersonal, or structural constraint?

about what leisure is suitable for men or women and that these ideas likely affect participation rates in activities such as sports and physical activity.

For many of us, gender represents one of the most important parts of our identity. Our society is largely organized around the idea that gender is fixed, binary, and unchanging. Another term for this is **cisnormativity**. Most people are largely comfortable with the gender that they were assigned at birth, but this is not universally true. **Transgender** is a term for people who identify with a gender that differs from their assigned birth gender. People who are **nonbinary** do not identify strictly as either male or female, either considering themselves to be on the spectrum between those or else outside of the gender binary altogether. People who identify with the gender that they were assigned at birth are **cisgender**. Almost all of the research about gender and leisure has been done from a cisnormative perspective that assumes that gender is a fixed and unchanging binary. However, some research moves beyond that. Meyer and Borrie (2013) recruited lesbian, gay, bisexual, transgender, and queer (LGBTQ) individuals who had at some point identified as female and asked them about their experiences in the outdoors. The participants expressed that being in the wilderness allowed them be more free from gender constraints and expectations.

Gender has been shown to substantially affect quantity and quality of leisure practices, opportunities, and experiences (Shaw & Henderson, 2005). Girls often stop playing sports because the stigma is intimidating if playing sports is viewed as contradicting their gender role (Guillet, Sarrazin, & Fontayne, 2000). Despite advances in equality, such as Title IX and the corporate and societal sense of equality of the sexes, questions still remain regarding diversity in background, marital conditions, and degrees of power (Henderson & Shaw, 2006). However, leisure also allows for women to resist societal ideas about gender. Until recently, most of this research has been concerned with the gendered nature of women's leisure, but there are beginning to be more studies about men's leisure (Henderson & Gibson, 2013). Issues surrounding gender and leisure constraints should address people of all gender identities.

Women, regardless of ethnicity, indicate that family obligations are the main constraint on their leisure. Traditional power relationships in society have proscribed women's leisure activities and emphasized that women should be at home to take

On the Job

Ensuring That Parks Are for Everyone

Dr. Tiffany Johnson is deputy director of parks, recreation and tourism for Prince William County, Virginia. Dr. Johnson was the first person of color ever hired to be in executive leadership within the Prince William County Department of Parks. Her dissertation was about increasing **implicit bias** awareness in city government officials. The term *implicit bias* refers to the unconscious stereotypes that we all have about different groups, which may unknowingly influence our decisions.

Dr. Johnson puts her knowledge about inclusion and diversity to work every day on the job. She says that "it's important to be open-minded, to have those uncomfortable conversations, and to educate others" (personal communication, March 17, 2021). Dr. Johnson is currently the lead for increasing awareness, education, and training for her department, and she is part of a countywide initiative to do the same. She wants to make sure that the county is helping to share its resources with everyone.

When she is hiring staff, she is looking for those who work hard "to be open minded, to listen, to ask questions, to research, to dive deep, and to understand the why." Dr. Johnson emphasizes that understanding different dimensions of diversity is an ongoing project. "I, too, am still learning about the successes and challenges of our communities. Whatever you're doing, it's important to be the change you want to see!"

care of their children. Therefore, women typically provided for the needs of others first, thus neglecting their own leisure needs (Miller & Brown, 2005). Economic factors have also been reported by both men and women as a constraint to leisure participation. Women's lack of economic power and their lower earnings compared to those of men have been shown to be particularly constraining on their leisure time as well (Bryson, 2008). Lack of opportunities, or lack of facilities or programs, may also constrain leisure. The availability of recreational opportunities (Henderson & Hickerson, 2007), particularly sport opportunities, is reflected in the continued unequal funding and unequal provisions of programs, teams, and sport leagues for men and women. Other constraints to women's leisure include stress and lack of time (Shaw & Henderson, 2005). Overall, research has documented constraints on women's leisure, and much of this research links their constraints to specific positions within a patriarchal society. While recognizing and addressing leisure constraints for women are still an important agenda, women are beginning to negotiate constraints as they cast aside social barriers (Shaw & Henderson, 2005). Once women can identify the benefits of a leisure activity, they are more apt to overcome the constraints. Men are less constrained by fear than women; however, women are more likely than men to take more precautions and preparations to overcome the fears they may have (Coble, Selin, & Erickson, 2003). Participation is the key. Whether policy changes are needed,

constraints are overcome, or women ignore social pressures to conform to a stereotype, leisure benefits can be recognized only through participation.

The lack of research on men, leisure, and gender means relatively little is known about the gendered nature of men's leisure constraints. Although much of the research on leisure has been about men, this research has rarely used gender or masculinity as an analytic concept (Shaw & Henderson, 2005). Is it possible that gender is viewed as an enabling factor for men rather than a constraint? At times, yes, it is possible because men frequently have a higher level of participation and a stronger sense of entitlement to leisure compared to most women. However, males do face problems in leisure activities. Men may feel that they do not fit the ideal image of masculinity; they might not feel competitive, tough, successful, or heterosexual. Males participating in feminine-classified sports, such as figure skating, face homophobic ridicule, which can be considered a constraint to participation (Schmalz, Kerstetter, & Anderson, 2008). Thus, males may reject leisure activities and possibilities they otherwise might enjoy because of the desire to appear masculine (Henderson & Shaw, 2006) to conform to social pressures. Nevertheless, leisure can be an important social and emotional outlet for men, including older men (Broughton, Paine, & Liechty, 2017). So how do males overcome societal or cultural constraints? They must have a strong sense of inner self, and the desire to participate must supersede what their peer group thinks.

Self-Exploration

Are you gender biased, or do you hold gender constraints? You might have said to a man, "You throw like a girl." Do you think that some activities are for boys only or girls only? If so, you have gender biases or constraints. Most people do have gender biases; it is our culture and human nature. However, it is important to recognize these biases and constraints and determine for ourselves if this is right or wrong. Think about your bias or constraint again. Should you think about changing your views? Why or why not?

Leisure for LGBTQ Individuals

As recreation providers, it is our job to ensure that we are inclusive of everyone, including members of the LGBTQ community. There is currently comparatively little research about the needs of LGBTQ people, partly because this is not a group that many recreation agencies have sought out as participants. As attitudes toward the LGBTQ community have shifted, more and more agencies are starting to serve this population. When members of this community are looking for leisure spaces, one thing they focus on is their estimation of the likely presence or absence of discriminatory attitudes (Barbosa & Liechty, 2018; Oakleaf & Richmond, 2017). One key to serving this community is to communicate to all users that you are welcoming of LGBTQ individuals. You can do this through equitable policies and inclusive staff training and by working with your local LGBTQ organizations.

There have long been leisure opportunities designed by and for LGBTQ individuals. LGBTQ-specific bars, community centers, hotels, and cruises

Robyn BECK/AFP via Getty Images

Many leisure services providers target their programs toward members of the LGBTQ community.

have provided leisure spaces for LGBTQ people and their families. However, these spaces themselves are not always equitable. White, affluent gay men are often more welcome in LGBTQ spaces than, for example, Black, homeless, transgender people (Knee, 2019). None of the groups discussed in this chapter are monolithic, and it is incumbent on us to see the multiple dimensions of diversity in any given group.

For recreation agencies to be inclusive of transgender individuals, it is necessary to address both programming and facilities. Recreation providers frequently provide programs that are just for men or boys or just for women or girls. In sports that are coed, there are frequently requirements that a certain number of people on the team be female. Agencies should think carefully about whether gender-segregated programs are really necessary. When agencies do provide these programs, they should ensure that their policies are inclusive of everyone. Agencies should have a written policy that allows participants to choose the most appropriate programs for themselves. Policies that require transgender participants to provide birth certificates, IDs, or documentation from medical providers constitute a real barrier to participation and are not inclusive practices.

Participants who are transgender should be able to use the locker room, shower, and restroom facilities that are consistent with their gender identity. Showers with curtains are safer for transgender participants than open showers, and the setup of showers and locker rooms should maximize privacy to the largest extent possible. Family showers and locker rooms should be available, but organizations should not require that they be used by all transgender patrons. It is extremely rare for providers to create programs that are aimed at transgender or intersex people, although this is changing. Some recreation departments host events like an all-bodies swim that are specifically aimed at transgender participants. Reach out to transgender groups and individuals in your community to learn about their needs and interests.

Ethnicity, Race, and Culture

Racist policies and practices have existed within our profession in the past and continue today. Recreation practitioners need to examine what this means for themselves and their organizations. Our park systems are shaped by the legacies of redlining. Redlining refers to literal red lines once drawn on maps to indicate what neighborhoods (typically Black neighborhoods) would not be considered for home mortgages. Fewer parks and swimming pools were placed in Black neighborhoods, and this disparity continues today (Wen, Zhang, Harris, Holt & Croft, 2013).

Assessing the state of current research about race in the field of leisure, Floyd and Stodolska (2019) stated that not enough research that centers on race and the problems of racism has been done. We do know, however, that there are inequitable health outcomes for people of color in the United States and that this is at least partly related to increased levels of poverty and less access to positive leisure opportunities. African Americans are often subject to inequitable policing in leisure spaces. In addition, some sports and activities happen in contexts that are racialized as White space, making it more difficult for people of color to participate (Harrison, 2013).

Leisure practitioners need to critically examine their organizations' policies and practices. In particular, practitioners should watch for policies that purport to be neutral but result in differential outcomes for people of color. Practitioners should ask themselves several questions. What are the norms in your programs, and do they have the effect of shutting people out? How does the historical legacy of racist practices (e.g., redlining policies) affect your program today? Who has the most power within your organization? Does that reflect racial and ethnic diversity? If it doesn't, what steps will the organization take to change that?

Summary

This chapter examined leisure across multiple dimensions of diversity. Recreation therapy services use recreation as a tool to treat individuals with physical, emotional, or cognitive impairments. This service is frequently offered to people with disabilities and older adults. Leisure for persons with disability reaches far beyond ADA accommodations. We must recognize that leisure pursuits provide opportunity, skills, and inclusion for persons with disabilities just as they do for those without a disabilities.

Everyone faces some leisure constraints, but those constraints are different across different groups. Specifically, we can categorize leisure constraints into three basic areas: interpersonal, intrapersonal, and structural. Leisure service providers must be aware of the constraints that affect all groups—particularly members of those groups that are disadvantaged by society—and ensure that they plan recreational opportunities to alleviate barriers. Leisure should be available to everyone, regardless of group affiliation, gender, socioeconomic status, race, or ethnicity. Thus, the most important role for any recreation professional is to ensure that they and their organizations prioritize serving all people.

Learning Activities

1. Visit a local homeless shelter. Find out what services are provided. As a class, develop and implement a recreation program for the shelter.

2. Research cultural activities both on campus and within the community. Pick two activities and attend them. Write a summary paper and reflection on what you learned about the culture. Address whether you would return and how your perspectives about the culture have changed.

3. What cultural program is *not* offered on your campus but should be? Do some research and plan your own cultural festival. You should determine a schedule of activities. Remember that the festival should be both educational and fun.

4. Reflect on a time when you experienced or witnessed discrimination within a leisure setting. How did it make you feel at the time? After reading this chapter, how might you approach the situation today?

Review Questions

1. Identify some constraints to recreation for a person with a disability.
2. How are recreation interests of older adults changing?
3. What can recreation providers do to increase opportunities for people with disabilities?
4. How does a person's socioeconomic status affect recreation choices?
5. Does everyone deserve equal access to recreation? Explain your answer.
6. What are leisure constraints? Explain and define the various types of leisure constraints.
7. Discuss gender-based constraints in terms of recreational activities.
8. How might men experience constraints in leisure pursuits?
9. What can recreation providers do to increase recreation opportunities for LGBTQ participants?
10. How can recreation providers be more equitable for transgender participants?
11. Why do leisure professionals need to examine cultural differences and values?
12. How has racism affected the provision of leisure services?
13. What can leisure professionals do to promote cultural diversity and acceptance?

Go to HK*Propel* to access additional learning content.

Leisure and Geography

Augustus W. Hallmon
James Madison University

Mariela Fernandez
Clemson University

VOCABULARY TERMS

carrying capacity	places	social impacts of tourism
cultural distance	pleasure periphery	spaces
distance decay	pull factor	staycation
greenbelt	recreation business districts	tourism destination
greenhouse effect		

LEARNING OUTCOMES

After reading this chapter, you will be able to

- discuss patterns in the spatial distribution and development of leisure places;
- understand people's movement pattern for leisure;
- discuss the influence of development of transportation on leisure; and
- understand various aspects of influences of leisure on places.

Mina, a second-generation Asian American, is a first-year college student. Before the new semester on campus started, Mina traveled to her parents' home country with her sister. She met her grandparents and relatives and toured the surrounding Asian countries before returning to the United States. It was a great opportunity for her to get to know her family members and learn about other cultures. She came back refreshed to start her new life with a broadened view of the world.

Leisure happens in places through people's encounters with different places and consumption of places. As we relate human leisure experience with geography in this chapter, we explore the interactions among people, place, and the environment in the context of recreation and tourism. Specifically, we will investigate how leisure spaces are distributed in our contemporary society and the movement patterns of people to different places for leisure. Consuming spaces for leisure and sometimes exploiting them will inevitably affect these spaces. Therefore, we also examine the impacts that human leisure behavior has in places and what can be done to protect these places to preserve them for future generations.

As seen in Mina's case, taking a trip is a way of spending leisure time and also a good way to learn about cultures. In the 17th century, a trip called the grand tour was popular among young English men. The grand tour was a long trip (taking six months to three years) to the European continent for educational purposes. The wealthy young English traveled to the "civilized world" to learn the cultural legacies and to study arts and literature. Popular destinations included France, Italy, Austria,

Germany, and Belgium (Mill & Morrison, 2006). Later on, the popularity of this itinerary spread to other parts of Europe, and the grand tour remained a trend until the late 18th century, coming to a halt with the French Revolution in 1789. Mina's trip was very similar to that of the European grand tourists. To travel to a place with a culture she was not accustomed to, Mina had to learn about each country's transportation system, culture, currency, and custom. She had to find information about which airport to use, how to greet people, and how to pay for and use the local transportation (many of these tasks were done by servants and guides for the European grand tourists). Mina also had to locate the must-see attractions and decide which routes to take for the most effective use of her resources—in this case time and money. Without noticing, she could have influenced each place in many ways during her trip, such as by participating in recreational activities, buying things, or talking to residents. These are the topics discussed in this chapter. We explore how leisure places, especially tourism-related destinations and attractions, are distributed and developed and how tourism and tourists affect the destination. In this context, the World Tourism Organization's (2002) definition of a **tourism destination**, a physical space containing tourism products and services, is used throughout the chapter.

Spatial Distribution of Leisure Places

How do you spend your leisure time? Some of you might enjoy going to the movies or playing flag football. Others entertain themselves by staying at home watching TV or surfing the Internet. A more active person will find things to do outside or take a trip. Whatever activities you choose, all leisure activities occur in places; you watch TV or talk on the phone with friends at home, play basketball at the court near your residence, watch a movie at a theater, or fish on a riverbank. Leisure time is spent in spaces that are built or managed for specific reasons. Let's look at an example of leisure travel.

The early geographical research on leisure was mostly focused on classifying scenic quality of the places and investigating people's land use patterns (Aitchison, 1999). By the late 1930s and early 1940s, the emphasis of geographic research on leisure shifted from recreation to tourism, and by the 1970s,

---

Self-Exploration

If you were to take a three-month grand tour abroad for educational purposes, which tourism destination would you choose and why? What can you get out of taking this trip? What is your goal for taking this trip? What are some of the geographical and cultural characteristics you might find in the destination that differ from your native land?

Because you don't have any guides to accompany you, you have to plan your own trip. What information do you need to plan for this long trip?

a line of research on leisure geography began to focus on how leisure places, mostly tourism attractions such as resorts, were distributed spatially. These researchers explained the concentration of a leisure space in terms of the resources it held and the capacity of the space.

Ever since the American leisure service provision system was organized, meeting the demands of domestic leisure has been an important function of local government. However, as we look at how leisure places are distributed around us, we can easily see differences and specific patterns in the distribution of leisure attractions. In some parts of a city a variety of leisure facilities are clustered close to residences, whereas residents in another area of the city do not have easy access to these leisure facilities. In fact, it is difficult to balance the provision of leisure services in different parts of a region in a highly diversified and free competitive market. Providers tend to locate their services close to large population centers that are capable of maximizing profit. Therefore, urban destinations are the center of leisure services because they offer a wide variety of culture-based leisure activities and can support tourists and residents alike.

A variety of cultural and entertainment opportunities are present in urban areas and their peripheries, such as shopping, art displays, performances, sports, night life, meetings and conventions, and exhibitions. The top 10 U.S. city destinations that attract the most international tourists are located in urban settings (Hwang, Gretzel, & Fesenmaier, 2006; NTTO, 2019). According to the study, many small cities don't have sufficient pull factor as centers of leisure to attract visitors and compete with large metropolitan areas (Butler, 2004). Small, isolated towns, even those with rich historical backgrounds and cultural resources, are restricted from becoming tourism centers because of their distance from potential visitors. Therefore, there are more recreation facilities in suburban areas and in small towns that are easily accessed, including linear trails, parks and open spaces, and youth recreation facilities. On the other hand, rural leisure is characterized as outdoor activities taking place in natural settings, because access to these environments is easier in rural regions.

In addition to being affected by cost and distance to the destination, travel decisions are influenced by the traveler's personality, available resources at the origin, the characteristics of the destination, and cultural distance (Lew & McKercher, 2006). One of the motives of people traveling is to seek novelty, and therefore travelers who are eager to learn and see new things will visit culturally distant places (places that are different than their local area in many aspects) rather than culturally proximate places. Other travelers might choose to visit places because of cultural similarities, familiarity with the place, proximity, and lower travel costs (Hwang et al., 2006). That is, the more familiar the tourist is with the location and its culture, the more they know about local activities and attractions and the easier it is to fill an entire trip schedule. Language barriers, health risks, or risks of crime and terrorist activity at the destination, as well as the spatial configuration of the destination, may affect travelers' movement patterns (Hwang et al., 2006; Lew & McKercher, 2006). Depending on their personality, a traveler might visit places that use the same language; have low risks in terms of health, safety, and security; and have well-developed transportation links. These factors all affect how tourism attractions are distributed and the pattern of people's movement to these places. This concept is further discussed later in this chapter.

Even though many factors influence a traveler's movement for leisure purposes, some places are more popular and frequently visited than other places. At an international level, movement of some types of leisure travelers is characterized by a flow of tourists from developed areas to peripheral or developing countries with lower socioeconomic status (Backman & Morais, 2001; Lin, Morais, &

Self-Exploration

To see how the distribution patterns apply to you, think about the most recent trip you took for pleasure. What was your primary destination? Was it an urban, rural, or suburban destination? What attractions did you visit during the trip? What type of attractions were they? Are they the ones that are easily found in such a destination? Can they be found in your local area? If you had to choose a tourism destination for your upcoming summer vacation, how would you decide? What factors would affect your decision?

Hou, 2003), and tourism is typically concentrated in the **pleasure periphery**, defined as regions with lower socioeconomic status away from developed centers of production and consumption (Brown & Hall, 2000). In addition, one study that examined 6 million international pleasure trips to the United States confirmed that the popularity of American city destinations differed substantially among visitors from three different continents (Hwang et al., 2006). According to the researchers, Latin American travelers to the United States favored Orlando, Florida, with 40 percent of the visitors visiting the city, followed by New York, New York; Miami, Florida; and Tampa, Florida. European tourists also favored Orlando (26 percent) as a leisure travel destination. Only about 7 percent of trips made by Asians included Orlando. The most popular city for Asian tourists was Los Angeles, California (36 percent), followed by Las Vegas, Nevada (17 percent), San Francisco, California (15 percent), and Seattle, Washington. Do you notice a particular trend from this result? The result of this study can be related to geographical proximity in choosing a destination. Asian travelers to the United States preferred cities located near the West Coast, which are closer to the Asian continent, whereas Europeans favored destinations such as Miami, which are located in the eastern United States, showing that travelers generally choose leisure places located closer to their homes for reasons of time and cost. Tourism companies such as Disney use this concept in marketing their tourism products. Disney's advertisement efforts are diversified depending on where their products are located. For example, Tokyo Disney Resort and Hong Kong Disneyland focus on marketing primarily to the Asian population, whereas Disneyland Resort Paris tries to attract European visitors. In the United States, Disneyland in Anaheim, California, focuses its marketing efforts on Asians, whereas promotional efforts for Disney World in Lake Buena Vista, Florida, are focused on Europeans and Latin Americans.

A trend in leisure geography research uses GIS (geographic information systems) to analyze spatial data to track the distribution of leisure spaces, development process, and people's travel and use patterns (Butler, 1980; Hwang et al., 2006; Lew & McKercher, 2006; Tarrant & Cordell, 1999; Vogel, 2005; Wu & Cai, 2006). Some of these researchers report that leisure often occurs in close proximity to the traveler's primary residing town or city, which includes activities such as walking in the local parks or eating out at a local restaurant (Mitchell & Smith, 1989). Think about how many times you visit a local park compared to visiting a state park or a national park that is farther from your primary residence. This can be explained through the concept of distance decay (Fotheringham, 1983). **Distance decay**, applied to leisure geography, explains the effect of distance on people's interaction with places: Demand varies inversely with the distance traveled. That is, the farther a place is located from travelers' homes, the lower the tendency for them to travel to the place; thus, they tend to travel to places closer to their residence more often. It is common for people to frequently visit easily accessible (in terms of time and cost) neighborhood parks rather than a national park that may be located 100 miles (160 kilometers) or more from their residence. People are rational consumers and will choose to use their time and resources (travel cost) most efficiently. As such, they are unlikely to travel long distances for something of equal reward that is available close to them (Lew & McKercher, 2006).

Distance decay also involves people's tendency to visit more places within the destination as they travel father, especially while taking pleasure trips (Oppermann, 1995). This is done to use resources most effectively. Instead of traveling from the United States to Korea on one occasion and later traveling from the United States to other Asian countries, Mina and her sister had combined two trips to save money on plane tickets and time on the plane.

Self-Exploration

To gain a firm understanding of the distance decay concept, count the number of trips you've made in the last five years. How many were informal day trips within your residence city or town? (These may be countless.) How many were within your state? Within neighboring states? Within the United States? How about international trips? How many times were you out of country? As you count the numbers, you will realize that the numbers for each category decrease, explaining the distance decay concept. The farther a destination is from your residence, the less you tend to visit.

Together, distance and the number of intervening opportunities influence tourism decision making. This is demonstrated by many research findings, including a study by Chinese scholars who found that Shanghai urban residents traveled to the series of belt-shaped suburban destinations (explained shortly) for leisure (Wu & Cai, 2006). Another study found that city residents participated more in recreation activities and day trips in or near their home city than in visiting remote destinations involving overnight trips (Jansen-Verbeke, 1986). The popularity of short-term, short-distance leisure increased as a consequence of the September 11, 2001, terrorist attacks and related safety issues, changes in individual time use patterns, difficulty in coordinating leisure activities among family members, and increased gasoline prices (Vogel, 2005). This led to the decline of domestic, long-stay holiday tourism and the birth of the term **staycation**. A staycation is a vacation spent at home enjoying what one's home environment has to offer. Usually, a staycation involves multiple short-term, short-distance leisure trips to suburbs and adjacent hinterlands, so travelers use less money and time for travel and enjoy more opportunities.

Many studies examine the spatial distribution of leisure spaces and movement of people for leisure purposes. One of these studies reported that convenient access enables urban residents to easily visit suburban areas for leisure purposes. The authors noticed that leisure spaces such as public and private recreational facilities and tourism attractions were distributed in a circular pattern around cities, and the movement of urban residents to the suburbs for leisure purposes was distributed along the series of belt shapes (figure 15.1). This pattern of leisure space distribution is termed *recreational belt around metropolis* (ReBAM) (Wu & Cai, 2006). The formation of a ReBAM is driven by three factors: demand for weekend recreation, suppliers' development activities associated with land use, and spatial links attributed to transportation networks. Cities, especially those with large populations, are great sources of local visitors as well as international tourists (Pearce, 1981). The potential to feed a substantial number of recreationalists along with the trend toward short-term, short-distance travel has a significant implication for the future growth of ReBAMs in the cities with this pattern. In Shanghai, the largest city in China, with a population of more than 19 million, three recreational belts surround the metropolitan city. All three are located within a radius of 45 miles (72 kilometers) from the city core, and the recreational facilities located within these ReBAMs provide great leisure opportunities for those who look for places to visit as a part of staycation. With the physical growth of metropolitan areas along with increased disposable income, the significance of ReBAMs is expected to grow in Shanghai (see figure 15.1).

Some scholars shed light on the uneven development of leisure places and argue this is due to certain demographic factors (Byrne & Jinjun, 2009; Lin et al., 2003; Nicholls & Shafer, 2001; Tarrant & Cordell, 1999; Wolch, Wilson, & Fehrenbach, 2005). Many studies have found evidence of possible inequities with regard to household income for some types of outdoor recreation sites (Vaughan et al., 2013). According to these studies, census block groups (CBGs, the smallest geographical unit used by the U.S. Census Bureau) with lower household incomes were likely to have a greater number of tourists near their residences than CBGs with higher household incomes (Lin et al., 2003; Porter & Tarrant, 2001). These studies also supported that the distribution of neighborhood parks in urban areas was inequitable with respect to income and race (Moreno-Mata, 2018; Rigolon, 2017). CBGs with a higher proportion of low-income households were significantly more likely to be situated within 1,640 yards (1,500 meters) of wilderness areas, campgrounds, or good fisheries habitats than were CBGs with higher incomes (Tarrant & Cordell, 1999). Because low-income areas are more likely to receive tourists than are higher income areas, it is important to ensure that tourism improves socioeconomic conditions.

Following President Bill Clinton's Executive Order 12898, all federal land management agencies have been required to address environmental justice for all communities regardless of their racial and economic composition. Environmental justice refers to the "fair treatment and meaningful involvement of all people regardless of race, color, national origin, or income, with respect to the development, implementation, and enforcement of environmental laws, regulations, and policies" (EPA, 2020, para. 1). Environmental justice is said to be achieved when all residents have the "same degree of protection from environmental and health hazards" and "equal access to the decision-making process to have a healthy environment in which to live, learn, and work" (EPA, 2020, para. 2). Many research studies, including those previously mentioned,

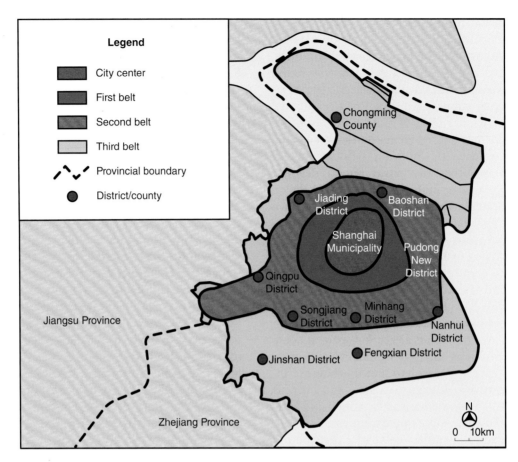

FIGURE 15.1 Spatial structure of Shanghai ReBAM (recreational belt around metropolis), which consists of the central city and three recreational belts.

Reprinted from *Shanghai. Annals of Tourism Research,* Vol 33, B. Wu and L.A. Cai, "Spatial Modeling: Suburban Leisure," pgs. 79-198, Copyright 2006, with permission from Elsevier.

report evidence of a relationship between race or income and the siting of locally unwanted land uses, including commercial hazardous waste facilities, low-income housing, homeless shelters, landfills, and recycling centers, which tend to be more frequently located in areas with predominantly Black people, Indigenous Peoples, and people of color (Tarrant & Cordell, 1999). In some communities, certain outdoor recreation sites may be considered locally unwanted land uses by virtue of the negative impacts connected to their use. Tourism development in a local area, for example, may bring increased economic revenue and job opportunities but is also associated with environmental and social costs such as increased traffic, air and noise pollution, and crime.

We can consider leisure places from two perspectives. Some scholars consider outdoor recreation sites as locally desirable land use on the belief that these sites enhance community satisfaction,

improve quality of life, increase property values, and provide leisure opportunities such as hiking and fishing (Allen, 1990; Crompton, 2008; Jeffres & Dobos, 1993; Li, 2020; Nelson, 1986). In 1986, it was reported that urban land 1,000 feet (300 meters) from a **greenbelt** was worth $1,200 less per acre than land immediately adjacent to the greenbelt boundary (Nelson, 1986). Similar findings have been reported by many scholars claiming that houses in golf course communities that face the fairway were worth 8 percent more on average than other houses in those communities and that property values increased with the amount of open space that provided recreational access and opportunities (Corwell, 1986; Gee, 1996). Some recreational facilities are considered locally unwanted land uses mainly because of perceived or actual negative impacts and poor condition associated with mismanagement and lack of resources (Tarrant & Cordell, 1999).

On the Job

Identifying Environmental Justice Issues

As a recreation professional, you should be well prepared to serve constituents who look, behave, and think just like you, but you should be *equally* prepared to serve those who don't look, behave, and think like you. You must gain and use new experiences to provide different recreation opportunities that you aren't used to providing. When you incorporate social justice ideologies into your thinking, you can provide recreation for all.

Consider the following:

- You are from an urban setting, and your boss comes to you and says they want to attract more rural constituents to their facility. What advice would you give them?
- You are from a rural setting, and your boss comes to you and states they want to attract more urban constituents to their facility. What advice would you give them?
- Think about the neighborhood where you grew up. Identify another neighborhood in your town or city that is opposite to yours in terms of race or income. In what ways do the leisure and recreational services differ in the two communities?

Development of Leisure Places

Since the early 1960s, many geographic models have been developed to describe the process of tourism destination development (Butler, 1980, 2004). One of the concepts that attracted the most attention is the life cycle model, developed by Richard W. Butler, which explained the evolutionary process of a tourist area or a resort town development (Agarwal, 2002; Butler, 1980). According to Butler, a tourism geographer, tourism destinations or resort towns go through six stages (Butler, 1980; Getz, 1992) (figure 15.2). The first is the exploration stage, the stage when the areas are not artificially developed and are visited by only a small number of tourists. Usually the attractiveness of these destinations is based on natural beauty or cultural uniqueness. A small number of adventurous tourists and active recreation participants are the major clientele of the destinations in this stage. Examples of these destinations include Antarctica and rural or peripheral regions of developing countries. Next is the involvement stage, when the number of visitors begins to increase, and local residents begin to be involved with tourism-related activities. In this stage, small tourism-related businesses that provide basic services to the tourists are started. Government also starts to develop infrastructure to support the increasing tourism volume. Nepal, a South Asian country known for its proximity to the Himalayas, experienced this stage in the 1970s accompanied by the development of an airstrip in a gateway community to the Himalayas.

This allowed easy access to the mountainous regions of Nepal, which rapidly increased the number of visitors from the Western world. The third stage is development, when the destination is settled as a tourist area and substantial numbers of tourists are attracted to destinations, making the area a mass tourism destination. These mass tourists are typically less adventurous, and the area becomes highly commercialized with their leisure activities. Fabricated attractions such as theme parks, staged festivals, and entertainment facilities replace natural or ethnic tourism resources. Because of use conflict, some areas in this stage suffer tensions between local residents and tourists. The fourth stage is called consolidation. In this stage, tourism becomes a major part of the local economy, but the area experiences slowed growth in the number of visits. Therefore, product and service providers focus on attracting new markets rather than catering to the existing market. Up to this point, destinations only experience growth, although the rate of growth may differ. The fifth stage is stagnation, and the sixth is decline and rejuvenation (see figure 15.2).

The stagnation stage occurs when the peak number of visitors and **carrying capacity** (the number of visitors who can be accommodated in a given area without degrading the natural, sociocultural, and economic environment) are reached. In accommodation facilities, occupancy rates decrease and there are frequent changes in ownership. The number of visitors will decline if the destination starts to lose existing market share because it cannot

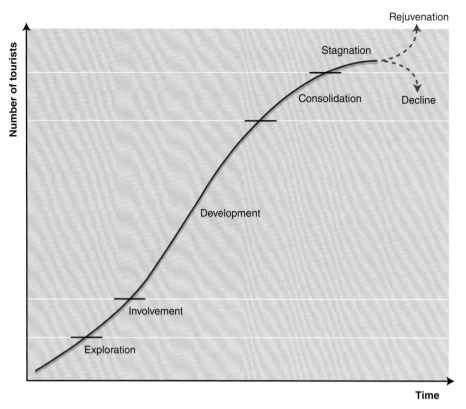

FIGURE 15.2 Destination life cycle. The number of tourists fluctuates depending on the destination's stage of development.

Reprinted by permission from R.W. Butler and L.A. Waldbrook, 1991, "A new planning tool: The tourism opportunity spectrum," *The Journal of Tourism Studies,* 2, no. 1 (1991): 1-14.

compete with newer destinations (Butler, 1980). Gradually the destination may become a slum or lose its tourism function completely. Destinations in this stage need to restructure or reorganize products and services or use new resources to avoid further decline. If the destination succeeds in reforming its products and services, there is a chance that it can be rejuvenated as a tourism destination. Until the early 1930s, Las Vegas, Nevada, had been barren land with nothing but dust and dry air. With the massive development of casinos, hotels, and associated tourism superstructure, it has now become a recreation business district and one of the world's most popular tourism destinations (ranked 34th in the world's top city destinations by Euromonitor [2019]), with more than 42.5 million visitors in 2019. If we apply Butler's model, it seems that Las Vegas is in a constant stage of rejuvenation. With new shows and performances introduced often, accompanied by new hotel and convention development projects, Las Vegas will continue to maintain its popularity as an international tourism destination for some time. To what stage of this model do you think other major tourism destinations should belong?

Leisure Travel and Transportation

Another aspect of leisure that is related to geography involves its association with transportation networks. The mass production of the Ford Model T and mass ownership of automobiles in the early 1900s significantly affected how tourism-related spaces were shaped in the United States. With the ownership of automobiles by the mass public, the government determined a need to construct roads. Acts such as the Federal Aid Road Act of 1916 and Federal Highway Act of 1921 promoted the general welfare of the citizens, and all states had their own road-related organization by 1920. Americans were able to travel for leisure purposes to farther destinations more conveniently and faster. To serve the needs of these travelers, auto camps, tourist courts, and motor hotels (motels) were built along the American road system. These amenities show cluster or linear development patterns along highways and major access roads. Suburban areas became popular locations for recreational development given the physical growth of cities accompanied by the con-

Recreation business districts offer recreation opportunities for locals and tourists.

struction of highways around urban areas to meet increasing transportation needs and to ease traffic. Clusters of businesses offering recreational activities, dining, entertainment, and shopping (called **recreation business districts**) or regional, county, or state parks can be easily found along the streets in suburban areas that are connected to major cities. These spaces provide recreational opportunities not only for local residents but also for tourists.

Impacts of Leisure on Places

Development has often been seen as a means of economic growth. In the United States and elsewhere around the world, local communities have been trying to find the right industry for their area. The public sector, especially at the local level, has turned to leisure, recreation, and tourism as its economic savior with downtown renovation schemes. Public-sector agencies have sought tourism development to satisfy their economic, social, and psychological needs and to enhance the local quality of life (Ap, 1992; Shone, 2013). Tourism is also considered to bring many more nonmonetary (social, cultural,

and environmental) benefits than any other export industries. Within the rapidly changing economic environment, many public officials seek tourism as a way to success, thinking that it is cleaner and more sustainable than industries that consume and extract natural resources. Indeed, in some parts of the country, tourism has stimulated local economies, led to modified land use and economic structure, and made a positive contribution to the community. Rural tourism development has been the trend for about two decades in small U.S. communities whose leaders wish to revitalize their communities in an alternative form (i.e., small-scale development as opposed to mass-tourism development; alternative tourism tends to lead to fewer negative impacts compared to mass-tourism development) (Gartner, 2004). Although tourism carries some negative influences, many of these communities have experienced positive economic impacts such as increased job opportunities and income, a large multiplier effect, and increased standard of living (Richards & Hall, 2000). Scholars contend that as tourism development matures, the demand for infrastructure increases, which in turn increases the demand for labor. In this way tourism development can create jobs and improve an area's economic structure. In this sense, tourism offers considerable potential for economic growth in the destination area during the early phase of development. Tourism development becomes a way of upgrading a community's economy in many areas (Doh, 2006). Some rural towns, such as Branson, Missouri, have been transformed into an urbanlike destination based on the entertainment and music industry (Gartner, 2004). Another example is the Sturgis Motorcycle Rally, held every year in Sturgis, South Dakota. With only about 6,500 residents (U.S. Census Bureau, 2000), Sturgis hosts a large-scale motorcycle rally event that attracts more than 700,000 visitors. Imagine how much economic impact these visitors will have on the community each year!

The growth of participation in outdoor recreation and tourism has fueled global concern for the environment, because tourism is likely to alter the economic and social goals of the hosts and modify the physical environment. In many parts of the world, economic motivation as a dominant theme justified tourism development as a growth strategy at the cost of environmental degradation and social and cultural disruption. Although tourism has stimulated employment and the economy and has modified land use and economic structure, the growth of tourism has raised many questions concerning the environmental desirability of encouraging further expansion (Harrill, 2004). Tourism development, within environmental contexts, provides resources and creates problems for the local community. Tourism may provide an area with a variety of outdoor recreation resources but at the same time may result in environmental degradation such as trampling, erosion, loss of wildlife habitat, and land use change, to name a few. Because tourism development may result in unexpected or negative environmental changes in a community, the terms *tourism impact* and *tourism-induced change* have gained attention in the tourism literature. Tourism impacts are defined as the net changes within the host communities, resulting from a complex process of interactions among tourists, host communities, and destination environments.

In the fall of 2019, a novel coronavirus was documented in China, and it soon affected tourism worldwide. Although the Chinese government worked to prevent the virus from spreading, the movement of people within the country spread the virus. The spread of the virus soon affected other countries as well, and in less than a year, more than 47 million people worldwide were infected (Worldometer, 2020). Governments across the world enacted preventative policies, some of which greatly affected tourism. Some countries, for example, elected to close their borders and banned international flights and cruise ships from entering, while other countries mandated an initial 14-day quarantine period to ensure visitors were not contagious.

Within countries, various national and local policies were also enacted. Some governments banned nonessential travel; residents in these places were only allowed to travel to their workplaces, medical facilities, or grocery stores. The limit on nonessential travel negatively affected many businesses, such as airlines, hotels, and restaurants, that also cater to tourists. Additionally, people were discouraged from congregating, and many establishments limited their carrying capacity. With fewer visitors, some tourist sites closed—some temporarily and others permanently. Research on many communities shows that tourism has positive and negative effects on people's lives and on the environment.

Positive Impacts of Leisure Development

Of course, new development or addition to existing tourism resources brings many advantages to the community. These include the following:

- Investment and growth
- Increased property values
- Local area improvement
- Environmental awareness

Investment and Growth

Tourism is considered to be a growth inducer (Mill & Morrison, 2006). Leisure facilities and programs attract other related businesses. World-renowned leisure destinations that demonstrate this phenomenon include Vail, Colorado; Las Vegas, Nevada; and Orlando, Florida. Vail was an unused mountainous region belonging to the U.S. Forest Service before the first ski resort was developed and opened in 1962. With deep snow cover and proximity to large population centers such as Denver, Colorado, Vail soon became the most popular ski area in the state. Followed by this success, interstate highway construction began, and the town of Vail was established at the base of the Vail Ski Resort in

1966, growing at an incredible rate (Colorado Ski History, 2008). The 1970s brought more construction to Vail, developing more trails and lifts. The town focused on infrastructure and tourism-related development, including a transit system, a library, an ice arena, parking structures, and other facilities to serve incoming skiers. With an increased supply of services due to infrastructure development (such as high-quality restaurants, cultural facilities, and shopping) in a destination, community service and facilities are improved (Brunt & Courtney, 1999; Liu & Var, 1986), as is the quality of life for residents (Coccossis, 1996; Milman & Pizam, 1988).

Increased Property Values

As mentioned in the previous section, some researchers note that the value of land is affected by the presence of leisure-related development (Corwell, 1986; Gee, 1996; Nelson, 1986). According to this research, large and well-maintained parks increase the value of adjacent properties. Houses located in golf course communities (especially houses that face the fairway) and residential property adjoining lakes, reservoirs, wildlife refuges, resorts, and other leisure sites record high values. Increased property values are not always a positive outcome because they can negatively affect some people, so this topic is discussed again in the section on negative impacts.

Local Area Improvement

Tourism development improves a community's infrastructure and appearance and provides more and better leisure facilities and parks (Green et al., 1990; Lankford, 1994). In the process of development, abandoned buildings are remodeled and used as attractions such as museums, and dilapidated or unused areas and wharves are revitalized and reborn as recreational destinations; good examples are Kemah, Texas; Navy Pier in Chicago; and Pier 39 in San Francisco. In some towns, old railroads are saved and converted to hiking trails that can be used by local residents as well as tourists; other towns engage with urban or downtown revitalization programs. The Community Heritage Development Division of the Texas Historical Commission has been involved with the Texas Main Street Program to help Texas cities revitalize their historic downtowns and neighborhood commercial districts. These regenerations may raise questions concerning undesirable impacts on the place, as discussed in the next section.

Environmental Awareness

As an area becomes a tourism destination, concern over resource use becomes an issue. Local and nonprofit organizations are created to protect the area's resources, and specific ecosystems can be protected with research and proper management schemes. Local and nonprofit organizations also provide environmental education programs for the public so that residents and tourists understand the environmental issues at play.

Negative Impacts of Leisure Development

With increasing environmental awareness, researchers have recognized the potential destructive influences of leisure development and have acknowledged the detrimental consequences. The consequences include these:

- Changes in traditional land use
- Alteration of the natural environment
- Impacts on local life
- Increased cost of living

Leisure activities such as riding horses can significantly impact the environment, including contributing to soil erosion and damaging vegetation.

Changes in Traditional Land Use

Construction of tourism attractions or leisure facilities requires space. Deforestation and loss of vegetation are associated with clearing of the area. Loss of vegetation has been a noted environmental impact due to the development of ski resorts and golf courses (Medio, Ormond, & Pearson, 1997; Terman, 1997). Croplands are converted into a "forest" of buildings, and unplanned buildings and settlements are developed in some cases. Overdevelopment, commercialization, and loss of open space are other outcomes associated with leisure development.

Alteration of the Natural Environment

The growing literature on the environmental impact of tourism emphasizes significant negative environmental impacts that leisure activities can bring to the host areas. These include soil erosion and damage to vegetation due to outdoor activities such as hiking and horse riding (Cole & Spildie, 1998). Overharvesting of native species, littering, air and water pollution, and disruption of wildlife habitats, natural sites, and entire ecological systems have been documented in a number of studies (Andereck, 1995; Brunt & Courtney, 1999; Gilbert & Clark, 1997; Rouphael & Inglis, 1997; Snaith & Haley, 1999).

Impacts on Local Life

Research on the impacts of tourism on the host population is concerned with the changes in residents' way of life brought about by tourism development and interaction with the tourists. **Social impacts of tourism** are defined as the ways in which tourism contributes to changes in social conditions. The growth of tourism and inflow of tourists inevitably modify the destination environment. Although tourism may improve the social structure of the host community and broaden cultural understanding, it also brings problems: congestion, noise, overcrowding and subsequent use conflict, degradation of air and water quality, loss of local town atmosphere, and alteration of community structure (Andereck, 1995; Brunt & Courtney, 1999; Mason & Cheyne, 2000; McCool & Martin, 1994; Snaith & Haley, 1999; Teye, Sonmez, & Sirakaya, 2002).

Tourism development can contribute to social conditions that lead to serious problems in the host society. The main impact is that the hosts modify their behavior to imitate tourists (Richards & Hall, 2000). One of the most significant and least desirable by-products of tourism development is its effects on the moral standards of the host population (Koegh, 1990).

The growth of crime and gambling has been mentioned frequently as another negative side of tourism development (Andereck, 1995; Lankford, 1994; Mason & Cheyne, 2000). Crime rates are suspected to increase with increasing tourism development. One study about gambling development of a town in Massachusetts mentioned that residents showed negative perception of the gambling development in their town in terms of loss of traditional image of town and community identity (Long, 1996). Other studies have found loss of cultural identity, changes in the size and the demographic characteristics of the host population, changes in daily rhythm of life, decline in cooperation and mutual aid between families, degradation of morality, breakdown of family, drug addiction and alcoholism, and vandalism (Andereck, 1995; Burns & Holden, 1995; Evans, 1994; Koegh, 1990; Purdue, Long, & Gustke, 1991; Richards & Hall, 2000).

Research is often undertaken to monitor the social well-being of destination areas in the presence of tourism, as the viability of an area's tourism industry can be affected negatively if deterioration is perceived to occur in the natural or social environment. Such negative perceptions can diminish residents' support for tourism development, which in turn affects visitors' experiences.

Increased Cost of Living

The renewal of low-income neighborhoods typically involves placing needed services, resources, and employment in communities. Sport stadiums and other tourist sites may also be placed in neighborhoods to attract more businesses (Gotham, 2005; Lees, Slater, & Wyly, 2008; McDonald, 2009). Government officials and private business owners attest that community renewal is necessary to increase local funding and infuse financial capital back into low-income communities (Lees et al., 2008; McDonald, 2009). Residents receiving these services may personally experience increased property values and other benefits at the beginning, but with time, residents may be negatively affected due to the rising costs of living in their neighborhood.

Glick's (2008) study on gentrification's effect on home equity in several U.S. metropolitan areas

Gambling establishments can have negative effects on the communities in which they reside.

revealed that Black and Latino households experienced an increase in "median levels of home equity" (p. 287). However, within a few years, Black and Latino residents tended to migrate to other neighborhoods due to various reasons, with the increased cost of housing being one of the major challenges (Dubin, 1993; National Environmental Justice Advisory Council, 2006). Accordingly, Betancur (1996) discussed the gentrification in Chicago, Illinois, which displaced Puerto Ricans from their neighborhoods. The development of new homes in this case attracted middle-income Whites, whereas Puerto Ricans who could not afford the increased rental fees relocated to other neighborhoods. On some occasions, residents may experience a pushback when relocating to other neighborhoods. This relocation can also be traumatic experience for families, especially to those who did not want to relocate (Atkinson & Bridge, 2005; Betancur, 2002; Curran, 2004; Fried, 1963; Newman & Wyly, 2006; Rossin-Slater, 2017), and residents may lose important community ties (NEJAC, 2006).

Although tourism often is considered a clean industry, this is not always true. Tourism can cause significant environmental changes and damages because it is often developed in attractive but fragile environments (Andereck, Valentine, Knopf, & Vogt, 2005). In addition, local development policy may focus on meeting the needs of tourists rather than the needs of the local residents and the area as a whole. Thus, tourism development has the potential to undermine itself by being insensitive to its environmental impacts on local areas (Doggart & Doggart, 1996).

Climate Change and Leisure

Global climate change and global warming have been recognized for some time. The tourism industry is one of the entities blamed for these climate changes (especially the transportation sector) as well as one of the industries most affected by such changes. Tourism is not the only industry to feel the effects of global warming, but tourism is arguably more susceptible than other industries because its attractiveness relies on the environment in many destinations, especially coastal and mountain regions. In this section we discuss how tourism is affecting the global climate, how tourism is affected by climate, and the industry responses to these issues.

The share of tourism's carbon dioxide emissions is said to be 4 to 6 percent, and transportation is the sector that least contributes to carbon dioxide emission reduction targets. Roughly 9 percent of the overall climate change is considered to be related to air traffic, and around 80 percent of international air traffic is connected to private trips (Becken, 2002).

According to the Bureau of Transportation Statistics (BTS, 2021), the total consumption of aviation fuel in the United States in 1960 was 1,954 million gallons (more than 7 billion liters), whereas in March 2021 the commercial aviation industry consumed 1 billion gallons of jet fuel (see table 15.1). Fuel consumption by private automobiles and motorcycles on highways increased more than 24 percent within 10 years; Americans used more than 112 billion gallons (425 billion liters) in 1995 and 139 billion gallons (525 billion liters) in 2005 (BTS, 2007). Despite the introduction of more fuel-efficient aircraft and automobiles, fuel consumption by the transportation industry is still increasing. There was a decrease

TABLE 15.1   Fuel Consumption by Scheduled-Service Planes From All Major Airlines

	FUEL CONSUMPTION (MILLIONS OF GALLONS)		
	Domestic	International	Total
2000	13,904	5,123	19,026
2001	13,112	4,956	18,068
2002	12,287	4,572	16,859
2003	12,417	4,451	16,868
2004	13,380	4,765	18,145
2005	13,284	5,040	18,325
2006	13,019	5,220	18,239.7
2007	12,999	5,428	18,427
2008	12,469	5,509	17,978
2009	11,147	5,087	16,234
2010	11,057	5,247	16,303
2011	10,828	5,521	16,717
2012	10,238	5,621	17,631
2013	10,156	5,749	17,164
2014	10,293	5,900	16,621
2015	10,741	5,988	11,198
2016	11,167	5,877	8,374
2017	11,340	5,955	10,002
2018	11,848	6,020	13,060
2019	12,184	6,085	12,128
2020	7,233	3,046	4,321
2021	2,558	1,085	1,794

1 gallon = 3.787 liters

Data from Bureau of Transportation Statistics (2020). www.transtats.bts.gov/fuel.asp

during the start of the COVID-19 pandemic, but fuel consumption numbers in March 2021 suggest that future numbers will be higher than before the pandemic.

Researchers report that carbon dioxide emissions from vehicles and air traffic have a tremendous impact on global climate change by contributing to destruction of the ozone layer and by reinforcing the **greenhouse effect** (Egli, 1995; Lu, Vecchi, & Reichler, 2007). What effects do these have on leisure? The possible impacts include heat waves, droughts, rising sea levels, flash floods, forest fires, and changing amounts and patterns of precipitation. These impacts may differ country by country or region by region. In cold areas, the impacts are related to warmer temperature and melting of snow. In coastal areas, the problem lies with the rising sea level. In mountainous regions, increased temperature reduces the spatial extent, depth, and persistence of snow cover (Fukushima, Kureha, Ozaki, Fujimori, & Harasawa, 2002). It is said that the amount of snowfall decreased 18 percent from 1953 to 2004. Therefore, headlines such as "Ski Industry Heading Downhill" and "It's All Downhill From Here" are only two you can find in the news. Direct impacts are especially severe to the ski industry located in the European Alps and the Rocky Mountains region in North America. Unfavorable snow conditions are blamed for shorter skiing seasons, greater demand for high-altitude resorts, and greater risk of avalanches (Abegg & Froesch, 1994). Poor snow conditions have decreased the overall demand for skiing and resulted in major declines in visits and membership, which in turn reduce the demand for accommodation, decrease income at resorts, and even lead to bankruptcies of resorts. Winter tourism is the most important source of income for countries like Switzerland, Austria, and Italy, and snow reliability is a key element of the tourist resource. It appears that many resorts in these countries, particularly the traditional lower altitude resorts of Europe, will be unable to operate as a result of lack of snow or will face additional costs, including artificial snowmaking. It is reported that some resorts already have had problems getting bank loans (De Vries, 2003). This is also happening in North America. Ski resorts in Ontario, Vermont, and New Hampshire are experiencing shorter seasons (reduced by 30-40 percent compared with 1960) and hosting fewer skiers (an average of 700,000 fewer visits in New

England), and an upward shift in the snowline has been prevalent in the Rocky Mountains (Clean Air Cool Planet, 2007). Ski resorts located in the Rocky Mountains and Pacific Northwest have experienced 30- to 50-inch reductions (75-125 centimeters) in average winter snow depth. Therefore, resorts incur costs to run snowmaking technology to smooth out inconsistent winters. Attitash, New Hampshire, spends about $750,000 per year on snowmaking to cover 97 percent of its terrain. This means that approximately 20 percent of the resort's operating costs go into making artificial snow.

Melting of glaciers is raising sea levels, which causes coastal and beach erosion, destruction of the coastal ecosystem, and, in extreme cases, total submersion of islands or coastal plains (Radford & Bennett, 2004). These events result in evacuation and resettlement of the residents and destroy the tourism industry for areas whose economy is based on tourism. Tropical islands and coastal regions are the areas most affected by the melting of glaciers associated with global warming. South Pacific islands and islands in the Indian Ocean such as Maldives, Kiribati, Tuvalu, and Papua New Guinea are experiencing decreases in tourism resources such as loss of beaches and increasing numbers of untenable beach resorts (Agnew & Viner, 2001). Some areas already have short-term and long-term evacuation or resettlement plans for their residents, and relocation of residents is already happening. To date, two islands of Kiribati have been submerged, and the Marshall Islands are under threat.

The affected industries are trying hard to adapt to the changes. Ski resorts use snow-making technology or move to higher altitudes. Eroded beaches are replenished with sand. However, these adaptive strategies may not cure the negative impacts but rather treat symptoms as they appear or even result in more negative impacts (De Vries, 2003). Snow-making machines emit carbon dioxide, consume enormous amounts of water and energy, and increase operating costs for the business. If the resort moves to a higher altitude, it will need to extend transport infrastructure higher up the mountain; the move could degrade the more fragile environment by human use, littering, and increased energy use. Importing sand to beaches to maintain their amenity value is costly and temporary and may damage the area from which the sand is drawn.

Rather than applying these short-term and symptomatic treatments, industries are now trying to adopt more comprehensive plans to address the issues related to global warming. For example, ski resorts are combining skiing with other summer and fall activities (such as alpine slides, mountain biking, water recreation, trekking, special events, scenic lift rides, and climbing walls) and developing new non–snow-related winter activity schemes to make the areas year-round tourism destinations. New leisure activities, such as grass-skiing, and residential lodging options are considered to compensate for the income decreased because of snow deterioration (Fukushima et al., 2002). The ski industry itself is committed to addressing environmental issues by creating a variety of programs such as the Sustainable Slopes program and the Keep Winter Cool public education campaign. The industry has recognized the danger of climate change and is taking steps to limit its own emissions of greenhouse gases that are responsible for climate change. Since 1998, Aspen Skiing Company, for example, has had a program to conserve energy and water and reduce greenhouse gas emissions by using wind power to run ski lifts and heat water, incorporating energy-efficient green buildings, and using alternative fuels, such as biodiesel, in resort vehicles. In 2000, more than 160 resorts signed a Sustainable Slopes charter initiated by the National Ski Areas Association that promises environmental responsibility on the issues of energy efficiency, water use, and waste production. The program was designed to voluntarily reduce the industry's environmental impacts. Of the 492 ski resorts in the United States, about 180 participate in the Sustainable Slopes program (Shaw, 2006), encouraging their guests to use mass transportation and offering free parking to guests with low-pollution hybrid vehicles. Sustainable Slopes participants achieved carbon dioxide reductions in 2005 (from energy savings, green-power purchases, waste reduction and recycling, and vehicle-miles avoided) that totaled the equivalent of 87,000 round-trip flights between New York and San Francisco (Shaw, 2006). That would be like shutting down 126,000 ski lifts for a day.

Summary

How leisure places are shaped and developed, and how they respond to these changes, are major topics for the leisure professional. Leisure places are changing because of varied participation patterns and differences in participants' perceptions of resources. These changes are sometimes for the better, but in many cases they influence the area for the worse. Leisure development must be well managed so that it does not become a tool to exploit developing areas.

Learning Activities

1. Take an inventory of your local leisure resources:
   - Find places for leisure in your community and locate them on a local map. These can include recreation sites such as parks, football and baseball fields, hiking and walking trails, or mountains, rivers, or lakes that are open for public use. The places can be related to tourism, such as accommodation facilities (hotels, motels, inns, campgrounds), cultural facilities (galleries, museums, shopping), or historic sites.
   - Which parts of the community are these places located in? Are they close to residences or commercial districts?
   - What kind of pattern do you see in the distribution of leisure places? Are they distributed in circular or linear patterns? Or are they distributed in clusters?
2. Find a magazine article about global warming and leisure or tourism. Read the article and make a list of potential positive and negative impacts of global warming on leisure. How is your leisure affected by overall climate change and global warming? Discuss with the entire class the issue of climate change and its impact on leisure.

Review Questions

1. How do you think place and space differ? How is leisure related to space?

2. How can you apply the concept of distance decay to your leisure lifestyle?

3. Do you think there is uneven distribution or development of leisure places? If yes, do you find this pattern in your local area?

4. Do you think the way you spend leisure affects the environment? If so, in what way?

5. How are your local area's natural and cultural resources affected by leisure activities and tourists?

6. How can you change your leisure lifestyle to sustain natural and cultural resources?

Go to HK*Propel* to access additional learning content.

Leisure Across the Life Span

Mary Sara Wells

University of Utah

VOCABULARY TERMS

baby boomers

cognition

cognitive development

concrete operational stage

development

empty nest syndrome

formal operational stage

learning

maturation

nature

nurture

object permanence

physical development

preoperational stage

psychosocial development

sensorimotor period

LEARNING OUTCOMES

After reading this chapter, you will be able to

- explain the terms *development, maturation,* and *learning* and give examples of these from your own life;

- describe the basic developmental theories and how they can be directly applied to leisure participation and experiences;

- explain how physical development can affect the ways in which individuals experience leisure;

- describe how cognitive development can affect the ways in which individuals experience leisure; and

- explain how psychosocial development can affect the ways in which individuals experience leisure.

At some point you have probably been curious about one or more aspects of your development or the development of others. Maybe you have wondered what the world looks like to an infant. Do babies actually think that when you play peekaboo, you have really disappeared like a magician's subject? Or maybe you have seen older adults walking in a park and have tried to imagine what the world was like when they were growing up. How was it different? Did they have more time to play? Did they have more fun? These are just a few of the thoughts surrounding this chapter, which focuses on leisure through the life span.

Life Span Concepts

To appreciate leisure through the life span, you must understand a few basic concepts. **Development** is a systematic change in a person that begins at conception and ends with death. The word *systematic* implies that the changes you go through are orderly and patterned and relatively similar to those experienced by the student sitting next you. In some cases, this is true, like the beginning of a heartbeat in a healthy embryo within a month of fertilization, or the ability to walk and utter meaningful words at one year of age. Most of these biological systematic changes unfold in a person because of **maturation**, sometimes referred to as **nature**.

A critical component is **learning**. For example, consider the ability of a five-year-old who wants to learn to ride a bike. Although the child's maturation must be at a level that will allow them to balance a bicycle, the child still needs to learn how to shift their weight to balance that bicycle. A natural progression is that a child learns to ride a bicycle on a balance bike first. The balance bike does not use pedals, so the child's feet are near the ground. Then the child learns to pedal with the assistance of training wheels, which allows for better understanding of balance without falling as often; then the child learns to ride without the training wheels. Eventually, the child may be able to ride without even using hands. What people learn in their environment is often referred to as **nurture**. Perhaps you have seen the movie *Guardians of the Galaxy: Vol. 2* (2017) in which Star-Lord meets his birth father and struggles with who he comes from genetically as opposed to who he was became as a result of his circumstances. Determining which side of us is the most crucial to who we are is relevant to everyone, and although it is not known whether nature or nurture has more influence on us, we do know that when we combine nature and nurture, or maturation and learning, we get development.

It is important to note when discussing the development of individuals that classifying people into different stages helps us to understand the big picture, but doing so may not fully explain an individual person. Each individual develops at different rates, and therefore, merely because a particular stage ends at age seven does not mean that all eight-year-olds have moved on to the next level. It simply means that a majority of people of those ages fit those descriptions. It remains crucial for leisure professionals to be able to adapt to the needs of participants who are either slightly ahead of or slightly behind the rest of the group.

Introduction to Developmental Theory

When trying to understand how we develop, it is helpful to have a basic understanding of some of the major developmental theories that exist. Among these, three in particular are commonly used to help understand how humans change over their life spans and are often connected to their leisure behavior:

1. Piaget's stages of cognitive development
2. Erikson's stages of psychosocial development
3. Kohlberg's stages of moral development

The following descriptions of each theory, while not fully comprehensive, should provide you with enough information for an understanding of the theories' primary ideas.

Self-Exploration

Think about who you are today and examine what parts of your recreation behaviors originated from nature or nurture. For example, if you are very athletic, this might come from nature from one or both of your biological parents. On the other hand, maybe your friends are into skateboarding, and although you have improved because you skate a lot, it does not come easy for you because of poor balance abilities; this might be a nurture aspect.

Piaget's Stages of Cognitive Development

Development is greatly affected by numerous other components, such as cognition. **Cognition** (Latin: *cognoscere,* to know or to recognize) is the process of applying our knowledge and information to the surroundings and situations in which we find ourselves. One of the most important cognitive developmental theories comes from Jean Piaget, a Swiss philosopher (1896-1980) who studied childhood development (see figure 16.1). Drawing on his research, Piaget concluded that there are four main stages in how people come to understand the world:

1. Sensorimotor period (birth to 2 years)
2. Preoperational stage (2-7 years)
3. Concrete operational stage (7-11 years)
4. Formal operational stage (12 years and older)

Each of these stages will be explained briefly.

Stage 1: Sensorimotor Period and Leisure Development (Birth to Two Years Old)

The period in Piaget's cognitive development theory is highlighted by the development of essential spatial abilities and learning through the senses, called the **sensorimotor period** (years zero to two). Newborn babies' main development in this stage occurs through their sense of touch, particularly through their mouths, because their vision, smell, and hearing are not completely developed at this time. Think of how often babies and toddlers grab things with their hands or put them in their mouths while playing. As their senses mature during infancy, infants begin to uncover new experiences with their other senses. For example, at eight to nine months of age, infants begin to develop **object permanence**, the awareness that objects continue to exist even when they are no longer visible, which may explain why the game peekaboo is so much fun for an infant (Piaget, 1936).

Stage 2: Preoperational Stage and Leisure Development (Two to Seven Years Old)

The second stage of Piaget's cognitive development theory is the **preoperational stage** (years two to seven). During this period, the child learns to develop language and begins representing things with words and images. As such, young children have inventive minds and primarily learn through imitation and play (Piaget, 1936). Children in this age range often pretend they are parents, doctors, teachers, cops, robbers, or pilots. Participating in this type of play helps children learn the various roles they observe so that they can begin putting together the big picture.

Stage 3: Concrete Operational Stage and Leisure Development (7 to 11 Years Old)

The **concrete operational stage** takes place when children are in elementary school. At this point, children begin to understand high-order thinking and use logic. Thus, a child in this stage is interested in formulating strategies to counter an opponent (player or team) and anticipating an opponent's tactics. This can be seen on the Little League field when the players in the infield move forward to accommodate a batter in a situation with a high probability of bunting (Piaget, 1964).

FIGURE 16.1 Piaget's stages of cognitive development theory.

Niiimage/iStock/Getty Images

Children in the preoperational stage learn through imitation and play.

Stage 4: Formal Operational Stage and Leisure Development (12 Years and Older)

The last of Piaget's stages is for children ages 12 and older who are now in the **formal operational stage**. In this period, Piaget believed a child begins to recognize and identify a problem, state numerous alternative hypotheses, carry out procedures to collect information about the problems to be studied, and test hypotheses. Children at this age are often very interested in collecting things (e.g., comic books, baseball cards, shells, postcards, stuffed animals, or dolls; Crain, 2016). While formal operations take place across this stage, it is important to note that this is a particularly long stage of development, and each part of formal operations may take place at different points within it.

Erikson's Stages of Psychosocial Development

A second commonly known stage theory of development was created by Erik Erikson to describe individuals' **psychosocial development**. Erikson described these stages as a series of conflicts or issues that are dealt with within the stage (Crain, 2016). Each of these conflicts is meant to provide an understanding of the general encounters that exist between people and the social world in which they reside.

There are eight stages of psychosocial development:

1. Trust versus mistrust (birth to age 1)
2. Autonomy versus shame and doubt (ages 1 to 3)
3. Initiative versus guilt (ages 3 to 6)
4. Industry versus inferiority (ages 6 to 11)
5. Identity versus role confusion (adolescence)
6. Intimacy versus isolation (young adulthood)
7. Generativity versus self-absorption (adulthood)
8. Ego integrity versus despair (old age)

Furthermore, in each of these stages, individuals who successfully resolve each conflict will emerge from the stage with a core ego strength to help them navigate the rest of their lives. Respectively, these strengths are hope, will, purpose, competence, fidelity, love, care, and wisdom.

Understanding psychosocial development can help leisure professionals better serve their participants in myriad ways. If, for example, you are programming for high school students, you might realize they are in the identity versus role confusion stage. They are searching to understand who they are and the direction they will take in life and ways to express their sense of self. This could lead to experimenting with different activities and learning new things or to a solid commitment to a particular sport or club to which a student has a strong attachment, such as being a swimmer, a pianist, or a future scientist.

Kohlberg's Stages of Moral Development

A final example of developmental theory is Lawrence Kohlberg's stages of moral development theory. Kohlberg believed that our moral conscience developed in ways similar to our cognitive abilities. As such, over time, we see moral decisions differently and make judgments using different reasoning (Crain, 2016).

Kohlberg separated these changes into six stages:

1. Obedience and punishment
2. Individualism and exchange
3. Good interpersonal relationships
4. Maintaining the social order
5. Social contract and individual rights
6. Universal principles

One key difference between this stage theory and others is that although most individuals proceed through the stages in order, there is no expectation that each individual will eventually move through all of the stages. Instead, some individuals may remain static at the social contract and individual rights stage for the rest of their lives rather than moving into universal principles. Furthermore, in some cases, regression occurs and people drop back into previous stages.

The key in each of the stages of moral development is the reasoning behind moral decisions (Crain, 2016).

- In the obedience and punishment stage, the belief is that individuals make a choice in order to follow a fixed set of rules or obey an authority figure. For example, a child might

not watch television because their parents disallowed it.

- In the individualism and exchange stage, people begin to understand that different people have different viewpoints and that sometimes people are allowed to follow their own interests rather than simply obey authority. This might be demonstrated by a child sneaking to the kitchen and eating ice cream even though a parent told them not to.

- In the good interpersonal relationships stage—frequently a stage that occurs at the approximate time of adolescence—children tend to believe that people should live up to expectations in order to promote positive feelings such as love, empathy, trust, and concern for others. A teenager might obey curfew because of a desire to earn parental trust rather than just because of the threat of being grounded due to staying out too late.

- In the maintaining the social order stage, the reasoning behind decisions broadens from individual relationships to respect for a larger society as a whole. There is a greater understanding at this stage that an act such as vandalism is not just bad because of the potential consequences or how you might be viewed by those you care about, but also because as a member of a community, you can view the potential impacts if all citizens did so.

The last two stages of Kohlberg's theory are less frequently attained (Crain, 2016).

- In the social contract and individual rights stage, there is an understanding that not all societies are good societies. In this stage, people share a belief in standing up for what is right regardless of what is legal. This would include protesting what are felt as unjust laws or governmental actions.

- In the universal principles stage, people are generally working toward impartially respecting the dignity of all people through an understanding of their perspectives. Thus, civil disobedience in the name of good may be more likely. It is important to note that very few people achieve this stage, and Kohlberg himself noticed that the differences between stages 5 and 6 were so minute that he stopped categorizing individuals into stage 6.

While moral development has clear impacts on how individuals engage in society, these stages can also affect how leisure professionals engage with participants in their programs. All leisure activities and experiences, for example, have rules that are expected to be followed. Convincing participants to follow those rules might differ based on the common stage of moral development within the group. For example, if you are taking a group of young children to a park, you might be able to convince them to pick up their garbage just by telling them to. At older ages, it might require you to tell them they will not get to come back unless they do so, or you might convince them based on the suggestion of how bad the park might look if everyone left their garbage. Essentially, understanding why people make moral decisions helps us to work within that reasoning in engaging with leisure participants.

While these developmental theories play an integral role in how we understand individual growth, other factors also come into play in terms of development that can affect how individuals engage in leisure. Furthermore, it is important for leisure professionals to look at concrete ways in which all of these theories and developmental features can play a role in the services they provide. This next section will look more closely at the practical impacts of development on leisure participants depending on life stage. To do so, we will discuss many of the physical development, cognitive development, and psychosocial development features of all age groups.

Developmental Aspects and Leisure Participation Across the Life Span

In looking at the development of individuals in these areas across the life span, it is important to realize there are often biological or other reasons for what is happening developmentally. Based on that, while you can challenge individuals to push themselves to a certain extent, you cannot expect them to perform beyond their developmental level. For example, just as you cannot ask a child to grow taller in order to play volleyball more effectively, you also cannot ask their brain to develop faster so they can understand

Team sports provide kids with opportunities for social interactions, leading to benefits like improved self-esteem and discipline.

abstract concepts like a zone defense in basketball earlier. This is a crucial point for leisure professionals to understand, as asking individuals to perform outside of where they are developmentally will merely lead to frustration on the part of both the leader and the participants rather than a mutually fun and fulfilling opportunity.

Development, Leisure, and Young Children (Ages Two to Seven)

Most of you have encountered young children throughout your lives, starting with the time you were one yourself. However, it is easy to forget what life is like at this age because you are so used to the skills and abilities you have gained since then. Physically, children of this age have minimal endurance and fine motor skills. They perform best in tasks that require energetic bursts and gross motor skills. Their optic nerves are still developing, which means it can be difficult to track objects and react appropriately to them. And due to their changing body structure and inner ear development, they can have troubles balancing. Sports such as T-ball are well designed for this age group as it allows them to engage in the gross motor skills of swinging their arms and running in short bursts without needing to track the ball before hitting it, and there is little focus on balance during the activity, so falling over or tripping, if it happens, is not too big of a deal (Stricker, 2006).

In terms of cognitive development, children of this age are concrete thinkers and have difficulty following rules, as anyone who has ever played Candy Land with a four-year-old would understand. They are also curious and imaginative, which can lead to playing games such as being a superhero, cowboy, dog, or whatever their current favorite movie character is (Stricker, 2006). Participants of this age group also tend to have a physical learning style. This means when you are teaching new skills it would behoove you to take them through the physical movements rather than merely explaining or demonstrating them.

Psychosocially, this age group is very egocentric, thinking primarily about their own needs and on how things affect them. Phrases like "that's not fair" are used frequently to mean "I didn't get my way" rather than a true judgment of equality among multiple parties. Young children also tend to crave approval, particularly from adults, meaning that leisure professionals should make sure they are attentive to their participants who want to hear they are doing well. Comments on performance, however, should be constructive but gentle in how they are given, as young children are particularly sensitive to feedback and often cannot differentiate between judgments of performance and judgments of worth. Focus feedback not in terms of good or bad but more in terms of specific accomplishments and specific things to work on (Stricker, 2006).

Development, Leisure, and Children (Ages 7 to 11)

Children between the ages of 7 and 11 frequently see significant change in what they are able to do physically (Stricker, 2006). They develop greater stamina, which means they are better able to be challenged with longer activities. Their coordination begins to improve at this stage, meaning they can begin to excel in activities that require more nuanced fine motor skills, such as rock climbing, or to focus on technique in certain sports, such as proper hand placement in swimming rather than merely the general movements. One particular concern for the upper levels of this age group is the onset of puberty. Some will begin to go through it, and some will be about to. In both cases, leisure professionals need to be sensitive to those changes and how they may affect a particular experience or activity.

This age group is also undergoing a number of changes in cognitive ability that affect leisure participation (Stricker, 2006). This age group is better able to handle rules and directions, but they are frequently focused on why things are the way they are. They have better ability to problem solve, and they begin to have a more visual learning style. This means you can demonstrate new skills to them rather than helping to make the movement repeatedly.

Psychosocial development in this age group has led to more awareness of others and, thus, more compassion and improved sharing (Stricker, 2006). They are still primarily adult focused and want to feel as if they are performing well in the eyes of their parents and other significant adults. Furthermore, this awareness and compassion can lead to better cooperative play, meaning they are working together to complete tasks. This could be seen in running plays in team sports such as soccer and basketball rather than everyone trying to score a goal or basket by themselves.

Thomas Barwick/DigitalVision/Getty Images

Adolescents and young adults have developed enough that they are able to more quickly learn intricately complex movements.

Self-Exploration

Reflect on your childhood experiences. What influence socially did participating in recreation and leisure activities have on who you are today? How about on your physical development?

Development, Leisure, and Adolescents (Ages 12 to 18)

Most people recognize adolescence as a time when puberty occurs. This, however, is not the only major physical change of this stage of development (Stricker, 2006). Puberty definitely has an impact on how individuals engage in leisure and with each other. Hormones change physical structure in terms of height and body shape, which can lead to a difference in activity interest. Hormones can also lead to greater flexibility due to the loosening of ligaments for growth, which can change the likelihood of injury. Growth spurts can quickly change a person's center of gravity, making those who grow quickly less balanced and more uncoordinated. Finally,

adolescents also generally experience an increase in endurance, meaning they can engage in sports that require more sustained aerobic performance.

Cognitive abilities continue to become sharper during this stage of development (Stricker, 2006). Adolescents are able to follow logic and build their own reasoning. They start to engage in abstract thought and can learn through explanation rather than merely seeing or doing an action. This means, when correcting a child, when teaching a skill, you can do so verbally rather than physically walking them through the motions. Finally, adolescents can start to engage in strategy and perspective taking, which can heighten their performance in some games, such as chess, in comparison to previous age groups.

Adolescents are also experiencing a significant shift in their psychosocial development (Stricker 2006). Whereas previous age groups were focused on approval from adults, adolescents tend to focus more on peer importance and relationships. Depending on the relationship, and in conjunction with a brain that is not fully developed, this can lead to risky behaviors in numerous ways. Some of that takes place through healthy, but somewhat

Self-Exploration

When you were in middle school or high school, did you do something that you regret today? Was there a better option that you did not choose at the time? What factors may have contributed to your making this mistake (lack of positive leisure options, boredom, poor decision-making skills)? What factors might help prevent someone else from making those same mistakes?

dangerous, activities such as cliff jumping and kite surfing. In other cases, it may lead to less healthy and still dangerous activities such as smoking, drug and alcohol use, and risky sexual behavior. Finally, this focus on peer importance can also lead to social image issues, a problem that can be heightened with the predominance of social media.

Development, Leisure, and Emerging Adults (Ages 19 to 25)

Most of you are in the stage of life referred to as emerging adulthood, which encompasses those between the ages of 19 and 25. Physically, there are few significant changes during this stage, and for many of you this could be considered your physical peak (Stricker, 2006). Activity levels for this age group are high, and there tends to be a greater emphasis on engaging in activities related to physical fitness. Part of this is because there is a greater realization of the importance of fitness, and part of it is a change in opportunity in activity type. In adolescence, there are many opportunities to engage in activities that promote physical fitness, such as team sports offered at the school level. After high school, however, the opportunities to engage in team sports are decreased and, consequently, individual sports and fitness opportunities that are more easily available, such as running, biking, and going to the gym, receive more emphasis.

Emerging adulthood is also a time of for cognitive development to reach a high level (Stricker, 2006). Most brain development is complete by the end of this stage, meaning that individuals within it are becoming better at problem solving and hypothesis testing. Each of these lead to advanced abilities to engage in strategy as well. The last section of the brain to develop is the frontal lobe, which is where our ability to control impulses resides. Because this lobe is still not fully developed until the end of this

life stage, risky behaviors and a preference for risky activities can be an issue or an interest, similar to how they are in adolescence.

Risk, while cognitively based, is also related to the psychosocial development of emerging adults. These individuals are also often searching for intimate social connections both as platonic and romantic partners, and competitiveness among individuals can be at its peak. In terms of providing leisure experiences, adapting activities for these needs could involve tournament style team events where individuals can pair up to compete against each other in any number of activities such as kayaking, esports, or trivia night at a local bar. This would provide a chance to make meaningful connections with a partner while also taking advantage of one's competitive drive.

Development, Leisure, and Middle Adulthood (Ages 26 to 40)

Physically, once you reach middle adulthood, you have already experienced a peak in most areas (Stricker, 2006). You do, however, tend to still make gains in areas such as endurance and finesse. Think about most professional athletes at this stage. Those in endurance sports tend to perform better longer, and those who are in other sports such as basketball may work on improving technique over surviving on brute strength to force their way to the basket. Individuals in this group will also likely be concerned with maintaining fitness levels as a way to minimize losses and prevent many of the physical issues that may begin to occur both in this age group and the next.

While physically those in middle adulthood may start to decline, cognitively they tend to be at their highest levels (Stricker, 2006). In middle adulthood, brains are fully developed, meaning individuals are ready to engage in creativity, logic, and perseverance. Consequently, activities that focus more on cognitive capabilities over physical strength may become more appealing to many in this age group.

Psychosocially, individuals in this stage tend to be very family and community focused (Stricker, 2006). This is the stage of life in which many individuals begin having their own children. Especially when their children are young, middle adults tend to shift toward a preference in activities that can be done all together (e.g., camping, traveling to Disneyland, board games) or those activities that support a child (e.g., becoming a meet official for a young swimmer, attending a violin recital, or volunteering to make the sets for a community theater production). Those in middle adulthood are also often beginning to help aging parents, which can further affect leisure participation by either minimizing it due to time constraints or changing it to include older family members. A community focus is also frequently connected to familial concerns. Parents typically want their children to be raised in what they would consider a good community. This might involve some sort of commitment to bettering the area by volunteering in schools, working in a community garden, or being involved in local politics such as a city council or school board.

Development, Leisure, and Older Adulthood (Ages 41 to 60)

Physical health in older adulthood is varied but overall tends to decline (Stricker, 2006). There are typically decreases in strength, flexibility, and metabolism. With significant effort, however, these can be minimized to the point where current levels are maintained. Other physical concerns include areas such as heart disease, high blood pressure, high cholesterol, and other general indicators of physical health. Physical activity is crucial in aging healthfully, and leisure professionals should promote these opportunities in appropriate formats for this population.

Cognitive ability in this age group is less concerning overall (Stricker, 2006), although there are exceptions for those individuals with diseases such as early onset dementia or Alzheimer's disease. For the most part, individuals have high cognitive functioning at this stage, and it would behoove leisure professionals to capitalize on this as they develop programs for this age group.

Psychosocially, individuals in older adulthood are in similar circumstances to those in middle adulthood. They may still have children at home and may be caring for aging parents, both of which will affect their leisure participation time and preferences. Others are experiencing **empty nest syndrome**. This is when children typically leave

their parents' houses to attend college or begin careers. This is the stage many of your parents are in today. These adults are left to deal with the newness of not having their children in the home. Because their lives had been centered around their children for so long, many adults in this stage have forgotten how to interact with one another without their children. As a result, divorce can be common for these adults. For many, however, the increasing free time and opportunity to regain independence can lead to new leisure activities.

This is also a time when beginning mentor roles are welcomed, especially at the workplace. As such, volunteerism and expertise sharing begin to increase, and involvement in social organizations and institutions is high. At this age, some may reflect on whether their life goals have been achieved and may return to placing their recreational interests as priorities. For instance, they may visit travel destinations they previously longed to visit. Planning for retirement begins to receive greater consideration, including the financial ability to retire. Perhaps in preparation for their upcoming retirement, these adults begin to participate in leisure activities that they plan to pursue upon retiring, such as fishing, walking, gardening, adventure activities (paragliding and skydiving, for instance), recreational vehicle groups, volunteer travel, riding bikes (either road bikes or motorcycles), and using Facebook, Instagram, or other forms of social media.

Currently the largest age group of Americans, **baby boomers** were born between 1946 and 1964, meaning that some of them are within this stage of life. According to census data in 2006, 4 million Americans turned 60 that year, at a rate of 7,918 each day or 330 every hour. With such a dramatic increase in the proportion of seniors within society, the entire concept of retirement has changed dramatically. This age group tends to be highly active in numerous ways including physically, socially at both a personal and community levels, and politically. The boomers' devotion to exercise and fitness is a prime example of their influence on society. These people grew up with an extensive amount of recreation and leisure opportunities. They were the first group to have Little League baseball teams; the President's Council on Physical Fitness was created during their time; and as they matured, corporate fitness centers and private health clubs became numerous. Because of this, many of these people see retirement as a midlife event; approximately half plan to launch into an entirely new job or career upon retirement. Likely due to their interests in exercise and fitness, they typically state that they feel 10 years younger than their chronological age. However, many fear aging and, as such, are health conscientious and want to live independently, out of retirement homes, for as long as possible. Given that more people in this age group are married, they may just succeed in living independently for most of the remainder of their lives. In addition to having interests in health and exercise, these seniors are especially concerned with fall prevention, as many realize that a fall is often a precursor to loss of independence.

Development, Leisure, and Seniors (Ages 61 and Older)

At the senior stage, there is perhaps the greatest variation in physical skills and abilities. Those who

are genetically lucky and have worked hard to maintain physical fitness can very often maintain a good level of fitness as they age. Others, however, become gradually more limited in strength, endurance, and cardiovascular fitness.

Individuals in this age group may not be meeting the guidelines recommended for physical activity. These state that seniors could receive substantial health benefits from participation in at least 150 minutes of moderately intense physical activity each week, with additional benefits for those who engage in up to 300 minutes per week. They should also complete muscle-strengthening exercises for all muscle groups (Centers for Disease Control and Prevention, 2018).

Research has shown that many chronic conditions facing this age group, such as arthritis, hypertension, hearing and vision loss, and heart problems, can be prevented through exercise, healthy diet, and early care (see figure 16.2). Interest in aquatic exercise activity increases for this age group as people discover that the benefits of exercise can be achieved in water without the accompanying joint pains associated with land-based exercises.

Balance is another potential issue among seniors. Many individuals in this age group have concerns of falling, which can lead to a number of serious issues such as concussions, broken bones, and even spinal cord injuries, all of which create significant complication for living healthy, independent lives. Activities that build core strength and balance, such as yoga or Pilates, can be particularly beneficial in preventing serious injury for these individuals.

Great variability also exists for seniors in cognitive ability. Most experience some slowing in cognitive functioning. Some have significant declines due to dementia or Alzheimer's disease.

On the Job

Partnerships Between Professionals and Community Groups

As a professional in parks, recreation, and leisure, it is important to be creative in how you program. One way of doing this is by developing partnerships with other professional organizations or with community groups. Doing so can lead to both parties achieving their goals. For example, in the author's hometown, there is a weekly knitting group that meets in a local restaurant each week. This agreement is mutually beneficial as the owner of the restaurant provides a discount on services, providing the restaurant with guaranteed weekly business, and the members of the group have an affordable place to meet and engage in a social recreation activity. Similar creativity and flexibility could go into engaging this population at a plethora of parks, recreation, and tourism organizations that create services for this large population while at the same time supporting local organizations and businesses. When you become a leisure professional, keep this in mind and get creative in your programming.

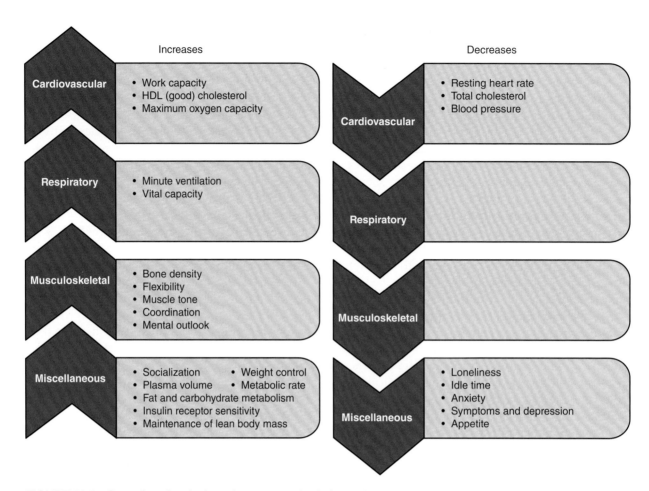

FIGURE 16.2 Some functional adaptations to exercise in frail elders.

And some appear to maintain high functioning throughout their lives. Regardless of where they are, all seniors could benefit from leisure activities that strengthen and maintain cognitive ability. Games and experiences that introduce new ideas and learning can be appealing to all who are in this stage.

Psychosocially, seniors are often in or close to retirement. This can have both positive and negative impacts. While it may create issues with a change in identity, it does provide significantly more free time for individuals to engage in the leisure experiences they choose. The senior years should be wonderful years; with a lifetime of experience and wisdom should come enjoyment and the freedom to start new hobbies, travel, and meet new people.

For many people this is the case. For others, however, these years of life are often associated with chronic illness, apathy, loss of friends and spouses, depression, fixed incomes, and, sometimes, bedside religion. As such, depression is estimated to be a significant issue among one third of the people at this age. Furthermore, this age group is at greater risk for diseases such as Alzheimer disease (Centers for Disease Control and Prevention, n.d.). Some of the best treatments for depression and memory loss are recreation, socialization, and exercise, especially mental exercises such as crossword puzzles. This may explain why public park and recreation agencies have traditionally taken the responsibility for coordinating and delivering recreation services to these adults, for whom recreation facilities are often a community focal point. Activities that are high in socialization, novelty, or familiarity, such as reading, socializing with friends, attending special events, or visiting historic or natural sites, are popular among this age group. Furthermore, it is important to realize that as seniors continue to age, there should be increasing opportunities for leisure professionals to work with this population. While many may assume this is limited to recreation directors in assisted or graduated living communities, there are many other opportunities to work with this active population. Gyms and athletic clubs should be offering classes by instructors with expertise in working with older populations to help them maintain fitness. Travel groups that specialize in the needs of seniors can offer opportunities for experiencing the cultures of the world with increased accessibility awareness, and municipal recreation departments can offer social groups of targeted activities that can help prevent feelings of isolation among the members of this population.

Summary

Leisure is an integral part of systemic change in people. Movement through different physical, cognitive, and psychosocial development stages can significantly affect the ways in which we experience leisure. Understanding these changes is, therefore, crucial to providing leisure opportunities throughout the life span. If a regimented lifestyle of activity is prescribed and adhered to beginning in early childhood, the long-term benefits into adulthood are apparent. Increases in discretionary time as one matures suggest that humans need positive leisure opportunities beyond childhood. To manage the rising numbers of older Americans and the need for leisure activities throughout the life span, steps should be taken to increase the number of qualified recreation professionals with long-term leisure education and training. This type of leadership will be necessary to ensure that appropriate leisure activities are available at every stage of one's life.

Learning Activities

1. List three of your favorite activities from each of the following life span categories: young child, child, adolescent, and emerging adult. Now explain how each of the listed activities either does or does not fit into the description of typical activity types undertaken by that age group, as described in this chapter.

2. Using your local community or school newspaper, web page, or activity calendar, identify the activities going on during any particular weekend. Now select and participate in an activity in which you would not normally participate (something brand new). Feel free to take a friend or two with you. After the activity, write a short reflection paper (one or two pages) on your new leisure experience.

3. Volunteer to work with a local youth or senior organization to host or assist with a recreation activity. Based on what you have learned from this chapter about this stage of life, how does this affect how you will design the activity and engage with the participants?

4. Interview an older member of your family or community. How has their participation in leisure changed from childhood through today? What were their limitations and unique opportunities at each stage? How does their experience differ from your own at those stages?

5. Select an age group with which you would like to work in the future and an activity you enjoy. How would you create a program of participation in this activity for a group of people in that age group that targets where they are developmentally? What specific elements would you add or adapt to meet their physical, cognitive, and psychosocial needs?

Review Questions

1. How do development and maturation work together and affect our leisure?
2. Briefly describe two major theories of development that can affect an individual's leisure participation.
3. Explain how development impacts leisure participation in each of the following major life stages:
   - Young children (ages 2-7)
   - Children (ages 7-11)
   - Adolescents (ages 12-18)
   - Emerging adults (ages 19-25)
   - Middle adults (ages 26-40)
   - Older adults (ages 41-60)
   - Seniors (ages 61 and older)

Go to HK*Propel* to access additional learning content.

Charting Your Course

Paul A. Schlag
Central State University

LEARNING OUTCOMES

After reading this chapter, you will be able to

- recognize and reflect on the physiological, sociocultural, spiritual, cognitive, and psychological influences on your development and well-being;

- recognize and challenge your perceived obstacles to intentional leisure engagement;

- learn about leisure resources that will help you make positive leisure lifestyle changes;

- discover the various career options in recreation;

- understand what it takes to prepare for a career in recreation;

- commit to an action plan of leisure that will meet your personal needs, enhance your growth, and help you achieve greater wellness and balance; and

- evaluate your leisure choices and experiences, celebrate your successes, and strategically modify your leisure plan where necessary.

The purpose of this chapter is to ignite a fire in you to be a leisure explorer, to think about all the gifts of leisure exploration and enjoyment so that you can enjoy a leisure state of mind now and forever more! Take inspiration from Nike's brilliant "Just Do It" campaign. Now is the time to embark on your leisure journey and silence the internal rationalization about why you can't do something or letting what "they" might think stop you. Today is the day to locate and activate leisure in your life.

Whose Life Is This, Anyway?

Why have free time if you are not acting freely to use it? The great thing about leisure is that it really is all about the individual. Unfortunately, far too many people do not realize what a privilege and responsibility this is.

Growing Into *You* at College

Young adults are typically engaged in **identity development**. The late teens and into the 20s is a time to look at oneself in a new and different way. At this time of life, leisure provides an important context for breaking with our personal identities associated with teen life as well as parental, family, and community expectations. College students are beginning to try out their new adult identity, which involves increasing economic, social, cognitive, financial, spiritual, and physical independence. It's a time to reflect on and learn about yourself and decide what you want to happen in this lifetime and, more important, who you want to be. College is a time for setting priorities, making personal goals, and taking the responsibility to meet those life goals because you understand what you want to gain—physically, cognitively, socially, and emotionally. Campus life provides opportunities to help a young person develop an inner **locus of control**, the extent to which individuals believe that they have control over the things that influence their lives. Our leisure is a perfect arena in which to demonstrate that we are not governed solely by external influences. We have unique interests, dreams, and needs, which we can fill through intentional leisure choices.

The Time for Action Is Now

This last chapter prepares you for the next phases in your life. In this chapter we take all the leisure theory learned, reflect on personal relevance, and marry it to action. By now you should understand the importance of a healthy choice–driven leisure lifestyle. You will engage in self-assessment, leisure education, planning, commitment, and evaluation of your own leisure lifestyle. This book's ending is the beginning for you to launch your leisure ship and commit to perhaps new and different precious leisure that meets your current social, physical, cognitive, psychoemotional, spiritual, aesthetic, environmental, civic involvement, and other needs. It also introduces you to the exciting career field that the U.S. Bureau of Labor Statistics calls "the Leisure and Hospitality supersector" (2020).

Meeting Your Developmental Needs

How are you doing in the developmental areas listed following this paragraph? Are you satisfied with the quantity and quality of these experiences in your current life? Following are some action statements to illustrate each category. Look at the list and rank your level of interest in **personal growth** or progress needed in each of the categories. If you were to commit today to improving your leisure lifestyle, where would you begin?

Socially

- Meet new people and forge new relationships
- Improve old relationships
- Spend time with family in new ways
- Enjoy dating in the hopes of meeting someone special

Physically

- Reengage in a familiar fitness-related activity
- Try a new sport like fencing, bicycle motocross racing, snorkeling, or bubble soccer just for kicks
- Change your physical appearance by toning and tightening
- Take a dance class offered at the university

Cognitively

- Immerse yourself in enjoyable literature
- Keep up with the latest news
- Do mental gymnastics with old or new forms of wordplays and puzzles (word searches, sudoku, multilevel Scrabble)

Psychoemotionally

- Actively chose to be with positive influences
- Participate in a 12-step program to overcome addictions (e.g., Alcoholics Anonymous)
- Read self-improvement books or join campus clubs
- Meditate or try yoga

Spiritually

- Take time to reflect
- Join a spiritual or religious community
- Show devotion through service to others
- Share an attitude of gratitude

Aesthetically

- Renew interest in a craft
- Change the look of your dorm, apartment, or home
- Visit an art gallery or museum
- Enjoy a spa day
- Purchase and care for a plant

Environmentally

- Sit in a park to study
- Ride a mountain bike
- Ski down a black diamond ski run
- Join a global warming action group
- Go camping with new friends

Civic Engagement

- Give back to the community by volunteering
- Find opportunities for leadership in student organizations
- Get involved in nonprofit organizations
- Canvass for a political candidate or cause

Later in this chapter, you will be called upon to make an action plan for self-improvement and leisure goal attainment. Your top two prioritized areas will lend themselves beautifully to this activity. Some people like to assess their well-being visually in the form of a **wellness** wheel.

Core Values

Core values are principles or qualities that are specific to an individual and intrinsically desirable.

Your values represent what is most important to you. Ideally, in adulthood we know and believe in our core values so completely that we are willing to speak of them and take a stand to support them. Most people feel best when their actions and core values are in alignment. For example, if you value fitness, you feel best when engaged in a plan of steady physical activity, not only for the endorphins generated, but also because of the positive psychological affect that occurs when we act in accordance with our values.

An important core value to contribute to an elevated sense of well-being is following **wellness practices**. These practices are routines or habits that help you to live your healthiest life. Habits and practices could be formed around adding probiotics to your diet, working on your flexibility, working out, taking regular breaks, having morning and nighttime routines, and eating real food. As you think about this list, what stands out to you? How can you live a healthier life? Start today to implement healthier practices into your daily life.

Two other core values are vital to wellness: **conservation** and **social equity**. These values are about thinking outside of ourselves and recognizing our interdependence on nature and on others. Human beings are completely dependent on nature, so when we seek to conserve nature, we are actually saving ourselves. Conservation is about the careful preservation and protection and planned management of a natural resource to prevent exploitation, destruction, or neglect. How do your actions affect the world around you? What actions would you take in your life if conservation were one of your core values? Making a commitment today to limit the harm you do to the environment will increase your feeling of control, help you feel good about the impact you are having on this earth, and humble you about your place in the universe.

Social equity has its roots in the teachings of Aristotle and Plato and is founded upon the ideals of justice and fairness. The Declaration of Independence, the women's suffrage movement, the Civil Rights Movement, and recent movements involving gender, sexuality, and religious freedom all began with a group of individuals actively advocating for fundamental rights, justice, and fairness. These advocates seek to make change through activism, awareness, legal methods, and policy adjustments. Where do you see injustice and unfairness in the world? What could you do with your leisure to fight for fairness and justice? Helping to move toward a more fair and just society will not only help others, but it provides you with a sense of satisfaction from making a worthwhile contribution to the world.

What Is Missing in Your Life?

To feel satisfied, many people crave some or all of the elements that follow. Does this list represent any of your current needs? What is relatable, and what's missing for you?

- New experiences: competition, adventure, learning, travel, creative expression
- Safety and security: spiritual pursuits, religious community, home-based recreation, family time
- Connection: friendship, social groups, dating and experiencing the response of others
- Recognition: advocating a cause, political involvement, receiving praise for a job well done
- Aesthetics: exposure to natural or artistic beauty, cultural involvement, experience with the visual and performing arts

When you pause to assess your current life, what needs do you notice are not being met to your satisfaction? Do you feel happy? Leisure is an area where you can meet those needs.

Holistic Leisure and Balance

Although this chapter acts as a springboard to action, our ultimate goal in writing this text is to help you achieve greater balance and well-being. Balanced people tend to reflect, take a deep breath, and evaluate the way they juggle work, school, activities of daily life, and leisure. Such people are interested in leisure enjoyment and believe that doing too much can cause stress and doing too little causes boredom or apathy. They have learned to say no to things that could throw their timing out of whack and to say yes to things that make them more balanced.

We feel balanced when we are achieving the following:

- Living in alignment with our core values
- Giving our developmental needs the attention they require
- Making time to be alone
- Making time for old and new friends
- Including a variety of experiences in our days
- Organizing our lives for efficiency
- Making time for daily recreation
- Choosing activities that promote health and wellness

- Allowing a leisure state of mind to make our chores and work more enjoyable
- Allowing ourselves to be singularly focused without outside distractions sometimes

Changing Obstacles Into Opportunities

Although we profess that we are on a quest for greater leisure satisfaction, most of us fight two kinds of obstacles on our journey to joy: external and internal obstacles. External obstacles are those circumstances that are imposed from the outside. We say we will meet our friends at an amusement park, but external obstacles such as the weather, the price, nasty traffic, the boss' demands, and family obligations keep us from going. Internal obstacles are self-imposed deterrents that constrain us just as powerfully as if we wore shackles on our wrists and ankles. Guilt, perfectionism, fear, poor self-image, shyness, lethargy, and many other internal obstacles can prevent leisure participation or distract us from enjoyment. We want to go to the aquarium, but we should be doing homework, or our roommate can't afford the admission price, so it doesn't seem fair to go without her. We are invited to a dance, but we don't know all the people who are going, so we are uncomfortable and unable to take the next step. Everyone is going to the beach, but you see yourself as overweight and are too self-conscious to wear shorts or a bathing suit. Does any of this ring true for you? We all must acknowledge our internal and external leisure opportunity thieves and take action to create the leisure lifestyles we want.

What Obstacles Hold You Back?

If you are like most people, there are many exciting leisure activities on your to-do list. These may be activities you once did and enjoyed but haven't gotten back to in a while. Perhaps there are activities you have not gotten to yet due to some perceived or real obstacles. Or maybe you have no idea what your leisure options are now. What would you do if you weren't doing what you habitually do?

Ideal Versus Habitual Leisure

Do these answers sound familiar or desirable to you? There are so many fun activities to imagine. Some are expensive. Some cost nothing in terms of money or time but take a commitment to action. There are amazing places to travel and fascinating people to meet. What would you do if you had the chance to do whatever you wanted? Wouldn't it be sad if you never were able to do most of those things? If we don't have a plan, many ideal leisure activities go unrealized. One reason for this is that we are too busy participating in our ordinary patterned habitual leisure to embark on the extraordinary ideal leisure pursuits we desire.

When students discuss what they generally do for leisure, many typical answers are given:

- Hang out with friends
- Play video games
- Hang out with family at home
- Work out
- Go to coffee shops
- Listen to music
- Communicate with friends using technology

What are your top five habitual leisure activities? What might you be doing if you were not doing the same old thing?

Live Like You Are Dying

A common theme in folklore, music, and literature is the idea of living today how you would live if you knew you were dying soon. How you would live today if tomorrow were not guaranteed? What would you do with your time? Guess what? Tomorrow is a gift and not a guarantee, so how shall we live today with the knowledge that this day may be our last? Do you find this idea sobering or invigorating? Some people enliven their time here by living with the end in mind. More simply, what do you want people to say about you at your funeral? How do you want to be remembered, and what would you like to accomplish? These powerful questions may transform your actions and inform the ways you choose to fill your leisure time.

Common Obstacles

For most of us, there is a gap between our ideal and our real leisure. We say we are going skiing, to a major concert, or even for a walk, but often we do not do what we say. What we notice about the difference between what we might do and what we actually do is a cavernous valley of risk, cost, knowledge, and routine. We get in a leisure rut because our regular leisure is familiar, easy, pleasurable, and comfortable, and we are confident engaging in it. However, sometimes this regularity is boring! When we think about our routine, we know that it isn't meeting our current identity development requirements. We are aware that greater joy, meaning, and pleasure exist if we stir it up a bit! We hope that this realization will be a wake-up call to action and that you will realize that you have many areas of interest but have actually experienced few of them.

Self-Exploration

If you only had one year to live, what would you do? What leisure pursuits would be on your bucket list? These major activities are your ideal leisure pursuits. How can you make your ideal leisure a reality?

Gremlins

We all have gremlins in our minds—gremlins are little nasty creatures whose sole job it is to convince you that the path you are on is wrong, risky, selfish, or stupid or requires too much effort. Gremlins are committed to squelching your fun and development and will do whatever it takes to get you from taking good care of yourself. The nasty thoughts feed upon themselves and multiply if we do not conquer them with their great enemies: pleasure, optimism, joy, fulfillment, and an attitude of gratitude.

Cycle of the Blues

Another reason we sometimes do not engage in ideal leisure is we are just not feeling up to it physically or emotionally. Pulling yourself up when you are down can be a difficult mountain to climb. Ironically, when you are emotionally and physically healthy and relaxed, you are more likely to make time for leisure. Making time for leisure promotes positive emotions, physical well-being, and balance, so it is a positive cycle. Lepp (2018) describes happiness as "an internal condition achieved when an individual reflects on his or her life experience and judges it as good." Engaging in meaningful leisure activities was found to be related to increased feelings of happiness. Leisure pursuits such as taking a walk, spending time with friends, and changing your environment can get your endorphins going to enhance your mood. On your down days, is there something that you do in your leisure time that helps to bring you around? How do you get motivated to do something when you are just not in the mood? It is important to make yourself do something, or your blues may very well continue longer than necessary.

Leisure Ruts and Great Excuses

Why do we do the same leisure over and over? A long list of reasons explains our leisure paralysis. When students are asked why they do not change things up for the better, the answers often come in rapid succession:

- No time
- Don't know what to try—too risky
- Unaware of local resources
- Boredom, which leads to repeated leisure
- Don't like change
- Sheer laziness
- Too much planning involved

Sometimes you need to shake up your usual leisure habits to get out of a rut. Try exploring other areas of interest—you may discover a new favorite leisure activity!

- Too far out of my self-image
- Friends will think it is weird
- It costs too much
- I believe all of my lame excuses!

Overcoming Obstacles

Now is the time to bridge the gap between leisure opportunities and pesky obstacles. Write yourself a prescription for vibrancy and joy by engaging in the following suggestions.

Prioritize Leisure and Personal Balance

Make time for leisure: "I have no time" is one of the most frequent excuses for leisure nonparticipation. Macchia and Whillans (2019, p. 1) found that "countries whose citizens value leisure more than work report higher subjective well-being at the country and individual level."

In consumer societies, we thoughtlessly spend not only our time but also our money on things that do not provide satisfaction. Regrettably, we invest in the inanimate when investing in the animate—others, ourselves, culture, community, nature—would offer more meaningful and lasting rewards. Take time from habitual time thieves such as texting, binge watching, or endless social media scrolling. Notice what leisure we do out of routine or obligation to others. Notice how much time we spend doing nonurgent, nonimportant things. It is time to put fulfilling leisure on our daily, weekly, or even monthly to-do list!

Put Aside Money

Make a designated bank account just for fun expenses. As an experiment, put all your daily loose change in a huge jar and vow to use it for leisure when it is full. When the jar is filled, you may be shocked to find it contains hundreds of dollars, and with that money you can, for example, take a road trip.

Invite a Friend or Join a Team

If getting up and going when the time arrives is challenging, invite a positive and adventurous person to join you. Allow the commitment you have made

Chatuporn Sornlampoo / EyeEm/Getty Images

to each other to keep you on track. For example, if you row crew and have to be on the water early in the morning, there are seven teammates relying on you to get out of your warm bed and onto the cold water so the team can practice.

Try Things That Will Likely Work Well for You

In elementary and high school you're expected to be equally good in all subject areas, but in adulthood that's not the case. As independent adults, we tend to move toward our preferences and strengths and engage in activities because we feel competent. Sometimes, we engage in something just for the fun of it, because life is short and we think "why not give it a try?" We also participate in activities just to share a memory with friends. Whether you show skill or not, you may create a memorable experience.

Take a Risk

In leisure, we generally use the term *high risk* in relation to leisure activities like bungee jumping and swimming with sharks. *Low risk* usually refers to passive leisure like watching a sporting or theatrical event or quiet leisure such as gardening or reading.

We encourage you to challenge this definition by participating in new leisure or entering a situation where you know no one. Trying something new is a high risk to you! And yet, without taking that risk, we are blindly repeating leisure patterns that are not meeting our current needs and expecting a different outcome. Doesn't the possibility of inviting greater joy and satisfaction make taking a leisure risk sound desirable? Go for it! Ask someone out on a date. Attend a school opera. Go to the juggling club's beginner lessons. Life is short—what is on your list that you have not dared to do? Commit to one high-risk-to-you activity and share your success with the teacher and the class. Enjoy the pride you feel just for having done the deed!

Silence Your Inner Critic

We need to trust ourselves to make safe forays into the unknown. Change the soundtrack that's always playing in your mind. Instead of listening to negative messages, give yourself pep talks again and again before you begin exploring possibilities. Ask yourself, "What is the worst thing that could happen?" and then realistically assess the likelihood of that event. The best way to beat a gremlin is to move forward and engage in joyful and positive experiences.

You are a leisure explorer and not the couch potato the gremlin would have you think that you are.

Recruit Leisure Cheerleaders

Only tell your plans to people who will support your new leisure choices. Leisure explorers need cheerleaders. Our gremlins are loud and active enough trying to convince us that our plan is unworkable. Invite your friends to support you in expanding your leisure. If you find that they are negative, then next time only tell friends who prove themselves as presidents of your leisure growth fan club!

Plan Ahead for Unexpected Obstacles

A friend's cancellation, the weather, or a change of plans should not stop you from brightening your day. Plan for the unexpected and always have an alternate plan should the obstacles arise—because they often do. Don't be a person who sees obstacles in every opportunity. Be someone who sees opportunities in every obstacle.

Oliver Weber/fotolia.com

Be adventurous—you can go ice climbing and live to tell the tale!

Schedule Unscheduled Time

How can it be so difficult to find and hold onto unstructured time? We all need some downtime to maintain balance and serenity, but sometimes, as crazy as it may sound, we need to block it out on our calendars to get it!

Today's children seem to be busier than ever. With longer school days, homework, sports, music, dance, tutoring, and clubs, it seems like today's children have less unstructured time than ever. According to a study published in *Pediatrics* (Ginsburg, 2007), free time is decreasing for many children. It is probable that adult leisure is facing the same trend as those children grow. How can you preserve opportunities for regeneration of your mind, body, and spirit through the opportunities of unstructured recreation? There is a different quality in the spontaneity of play than in structured recreation, and we need both. One possible solution could be to block out evenings or days and literally schedule unscheduled time, just letting the evening unfold as it may. If a friend calls to invite you to an activity that conflicts with your unscheduled time, you could decline it, saying, "I have other plans on my calendar." You may find those times to be wonderful escapes for your overprogrammed life.

Invite Yourself and Tag Along

Three is not always a crowd! When you overhear friends discussing a leisure opportunity that's new to you, ask whether you can join them to be a leisure explorer. Invite yourself along to a friend's very different activity—a dulcimer club, a badminton tournament, a kayaking trip, or a tai chi workshop. Go and enjoy it! Fake it until you make it: Be pleasant to all participants, including yourself. Only negativity on your part will make you a third wheel and an undesirable future companion.

Unplug

Shut down all technology with an on–off switch. Pretend an entire evening is the first 15 minutes of an airplane ride. Consciously decide to trade a bit of technology time for time with people face to face. Get off the superhighway of modern leisure called the Internet and invest in social capital like a pet therapy program with your dog, a cultural group meeting, a hunger project, or political activism. You might be surprised how great it feels to put yourself out there with real people who are acting for the common good.

Be a Lifelong Learner

Take a class just for fun. College campuses and communities are chock full of learning activities that may interest you. In college and in the community, you might take courses like ceramics, rock climbing, American Sign Language, digital photography, scuba diving, scrapbooking, karate, and much more. Some of those activities could develop into lifelong leisure pursuits. Be sure to also consider informal learning—visit a museum, a library, or a performing or cultural event that gets you interested in new things and can lead to new leisure opportunities.

Cultivate a Positive Attitude

The difference between those who live colorful, interesting lives and those who don't more often than not depends on the attitude they bring to every situation. People who choose a positive, open attitude are far more likely to enjoy their leisure, work, and home lives than those who meet life with a chip on their shoulder. Beware of the nasty gremlins whose sole job is to invite negativity into your life and ruin your leisure. Again, nasty gremlin thoughts feed upon themselves and multiply if we do not conquer them with their great enemies: pleasure, optimism, joy, fulfillment, and an attitude of gratitude.

Finding Resources

If you don't know that a form of leisure exists, then essentially for you it doesn't. A person committed to a leisure lifestyle values discovery and does what it takes to educate themself about leisure. Earlier,

---

Self-Exploration

List your top 10 leisure pursuits. Are these pursuits doing any harm to you and others, or are they enhancing your life and the lives of others? List your top five ideal leisure pursuits. How would these activities affect your life and the lives of others? If your pursuits and ideal pursuits could do harm, what is keeping you from replacing them with more healthy ones? What are the fruits of positive leisure choices? How does a positive leisure choice affect your life and the lives of others?

you prioritized which of your developmental needs could use the most attention. Say you want to improve your social life. Where would you look for resources? Where would you go to work on your cognitive, physical, or spiritual development? Might there be overlap in where the leisure opportunities are found?

Finding Leisure That Meets Your Individual Needs

Sometimes leisure opportunities are right in front of us, but we fail to see them. They await us quietly, but we are wearing blinders, looking only to consume loud, boisterous, or expensive sports, entertainment, or special events. Perhaps we are missing quieter leisure such as enjoying a picnic in nature, auditioning for a play, throwing a disc in the park, volunteering at a summer camp, or reading for pleasure. Speak with friends and leisure role models about how they find and commit to interesting and fulfilling leisure. There is wisdom all around waiting to be tapped.

College Opportunities

College is the great opportunity to explore. Whether your college serves 4,000 or 40,000 students, there are countless opportunities, many for free, to meet your developmental needs and create a meaningful life. Additionally, you are aware of some academic opportunities like degrees in nursing or business, but did you know there are degrees for people who want to take recreation so seriously they get a degree, or two or three, in it? Many of the authors of this textbook joyously took that route! On all campuses, there is plentiful intellectual, physical, social, and spiritual stimulation in traditional and nontraditional venues.

Campuses offer political lectures, art shows, cultural organizations, adventure leisure opportunities, health care, shops, restaurants, financial institutions, fitness facilities, vocational opportunities, and so much more. Some of these services are free, some cost money, and some were prepaid with student fees. Campus organizations provide opportunities to try out new experiences, rework old passions, and find what you are seeking as you leave your old life and step into this new one with an open mind. How can you locate campus activities that might be worth trying? Obviously, university websites, posters and flyers, student activity offices, resident advisors, other students, and information desks may guide

you. On campus, it is very easy to start with your desires and then see whether the new thing you want to try is on the menu. A sophomore named Sophie recently expressed a desire to try fencing, just for the fun of it. After one day of searching, she learned that fencing was offered for credit as a course at the university, as a drop-in recreational sport in the student union, and as an eight-week class at the local community center. Matt, a freshman, wanted to join a longboarding club when he arrived on campus. On finding there wasn't such a club at the university, he and a friend learned what it took to create an official club on campus and made it happen. Now the club has regular attendance by 15 participants. Matt has gotten a lot of exercise, made new friends, and is very much enjoying his first semester on and off his board.

Community Opportunities

On-campus activities are generally easy to locate, but some students yearn to go off campus to mix with nonstudents, children, or seniors. Sometimes a political cause, service learning project, or environmental, civic, or cultural involvement can best be served off campus. Amusement parks; city, state, and national parks; restaurants; racket clubs; and more are available. To find recreational opportunities off campus, perhaps even within walking distance, widen your search by searching online, asking a local resident, finding the visitors bureau, speaking to a travel agent, tapping into Yelp, or visiting a parks and recreation department.

Creative Leisure Planning

What if you don't know what you want to try? Creativity and play experts suggest warming up the mind by brainstorming so that good ideas can flow. Brainstorming is a method of allowing all ideas to be validated and added to a written list without judgment from self or others. For example, you can make an ABC list of leisure by simply free-associating whatever recreational activity comes to mind with the letters of the alphabet. *A* could be for airplane (flying, models, or whatever); *B* might be for boxing; and so on. A sample list follows.

- African dance
- Bicycle motocross racing
- Cardiopulmonary resuscitation class
- Dominos

- Engaging in civic activities
- Family time
- Growing a plant
- Hockey game
- Ice skating
- Journal article
- Karate
- Line dancing
- Marathon and then a massage
- Nap
- Off-road boarding
- Poetry night
- Quiet time
- Raku pottery
- Sailing
- Tchoukball
- Ukulele (learn to play it!)
- Volunteering
- Water skiing and water rafting
- Xbox
- Yoga
- Zip line

Form an Action Plan

Creating the life you want begins with reflection on your mission and goals. After reflection, you need to embark on a focused action plan. Creating

> ### Self-Exploration
>
> Make your own ABCs of leisure activities that are appealing to you. Pull out five of the activities that interest you most. Are these activities something that can be done where you live? Would your friends and family support your pursuit of these activities? What planning would need to be done to participate in your list?

a meaningful life does not happen accidentally. It requires thoughtful strategic planning and committed, faithful execution. Perhaps it sounds like a lot of work, but realizing that the internal locus of control allows for you to chart your future is one of the most satisfying human experiences.

You Can Major in That?

Consider all of the recreational activities listed in this chapter and throughout this book. Did you know that there are entire industries to support all of these pursuits? Behind the scenes, there are large numbers of people providing the support, equipment, facilities, transportation, lodging, food, and programming for the recreation industry. In the United States, this industry is booming. The number of employees in the leisure and hospitality supersector has grown from fewer than 12 million employees at the turn of the century to around 17 million employees in early 2020 (see figure 17.1). There was a significant downturn later in 2020

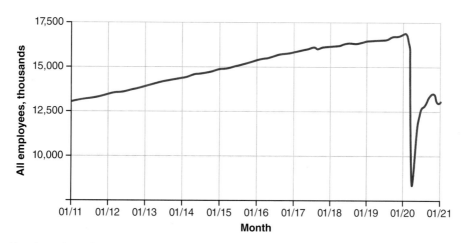

FIGURE 17.1 Number of employees in the leisure and hospitality supersector.

Reprinted from U.S. Bureau of Labor Statistics, *Databases, Tables, & Calculators by Subject* (Washington, DC, 2021).

due to the COVID-19 pandemic, which resulted in quarantines that temporarily halted programs and services.

To support rapid employment growth, universities offer degrees in recreation to help prepare professionals and researchers for this exciting, dynamic, and expanding field. A degree in recreation can prepare you for any number of fulfilling careers such as those shown in figure 17.2.

Careers in any of these areas are competitive, and people tend to stay in their positions for a long time since their jobs are so fulfilling. Therefore, now is the time to prepare yourself for success in the field. Think of ways you can learn about each area of the career map and how you can determine the area in which you would like to work. What can you do to learn about the areas, gain experience, and position yourself for entry into the field?

Volunteer

Interested in becoming a park ranger? You can volunteer with your local forest preserve or state park. Interested in youth recreation programing? Volunteer as a coach at the local Y. One of the best, low-risk ways to learn about each area of the career map is to volunteer and see if you enjoy it. It will also give you experience in the field that will help as you apply for jobs.

Practicums and Experiential Learning

Universities offer practicums and experiential learning opportunities to give you exposure to the field. These learning opportunities are often embedded in a course and allow you to participate in the field in a limited way under the supervision of practitioners and professors. Seek out these types of learning experiences because they expose you to different jobs in the field, provide you with supervised experience, and help you to develop networks with professionals.

Internships

Internships are different than practicums in that they mimic real-world jobs more closely. Employers

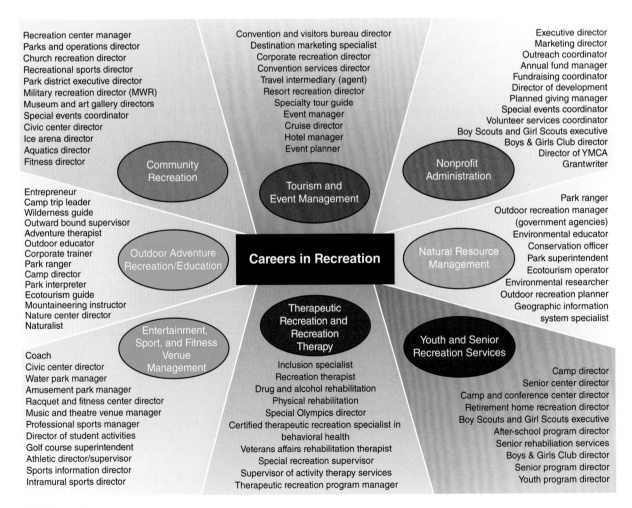

FIGURE 17.2 Recreation career map.

Anthony Killion

Anthony Killion is an excellent example of someone who majored in recreation and took the steps necessary to begin a successful career. His interest in working in the field of recreation began in high school as he worked at a Boy Scout summer camp. He had a desire to connect youth with the natural world, and his coworkers assured him that he could major in recreation and fulfill his desire through a career in recreation. He now holds the highly competitive position of park guide with the National Park Service. Here is how he gained experience and positioned himself for entry and advancement in the field.

Volunteering

As an undergrad seeking to bolster his experience in the field, Anthony volunteered at Horn Field Campus, Western Illinois University's outdoor environmental education campus, which is in a forested area with trails, a teams challenge course, and a high ropes course. He also volunteered in his hometown with the fall festival.

Practicums and Experiential Learning

While majoring in recreation, Anthony enrolled in a series of courses called the Environmental, Conservation, and Outdoor Education Expedition program, which culminates in a semester-long field studies program. He and his classmates planned and traveled across the United States, to Canada, and to Mexico to visit national parks and historic sites. He learned more about the field of interpretation and observed interpreters at work in the field as they explored natural and cultural resources and their meanings with the public. Interacting with professionals at various sites and learning different interpretive techniques helped him to develop professional tools. Learning from experts and practicing the requisite skills in front of his peers proved to be well worth the time spent away from campus in order to prepare him for entering the workforce as a well-rounded professional. This practical experience also proved essential in landing a highly competitive internship.

Internships

The next step in Anthony's journey from student to park guide occurred at the end of his undergraduate career as he completed a 13-week internship at Mount Rushmore National Memorial. Over the course of the internship, he was exposed to and learned about daily park operations. He opened and closed visitor centers, led a variety of interpretive programs, roved the grounds of the memorial, and staffed visitor center desks to serve as a resource for visitors from around the world. Most importantly, he gained experience in the field and networked with professionals.

Finding Mentors

Anthony would have never found this internship opportunity without the mentorship of his undergraduate internship coordinator. He shared his career aspirations with her, and she forwarded information about the Mount Rushmore internship when she received it and remembered their conversation about his career goals.

Following his internship, Anthony's first seasonal position as a full-time employee of the National Park Service was in part due to being hired by an alumna of his alma mater. This mentor took great personal interest in all of her employees and reached out to them in the off-season to keep them abreast of job opportunities, even when they weren't technically her employees anymore.

Another mentor—someone who interviewed Anthony for his internship—subsequently offered him his first winter seasonal position at Mount Rushmore National Memorial. That mentor took interest in the various jobs Anthony held and recommended him to hiring officials at other parks. Having someone recommend him to the interviewer was invaluable because lists of qualified candidates for jobs in national parks often include several hundred individuals.

Other mentors helped Anthony develop skills, provided feedback and guidance regarding professional development, and served as professional references for him. One of these mentors helped coach Anthony through the USA Jobs hiring process and helped him refine his résumé. Her mentorship and advice regarding best practices for applying for jobs have given him confidence in looking for his next position to continue moving up in the National Park Service hierarchy.

Anthony Killion, personal communication, February 7, 2020.

hire students to work under the supervision of professionals and oversee them like bosses or administrators. Professors often visit the internship site, but these visits are rare; they provide opportunities to assess the site and learning progress. Internships may be full-time jobs or less and they are either paid or unpaid. Although internships may occur any time during a student's studies, they are typically the final requirement for obtaining a degree in recreation. These culminating experiences help students to determine if they like or have an affinity for a particular job in the field, provide them with real-world experience, and help them to develop professional references and networks to help them advance to a full-time job. A list of recreation internships may be found on the recreation internship website (Schlag, 2020).

Find Mentors

You need people who care about you and can help you get to where you want to be in life. Don't be afraid to reach out to a potential mentor, ask for their help, and build a relationship with them. As a mentee, make yourself valuable to your mentor by helping with projects and goals. In turn, mentors can give you advice, direction, suggestions, motivation, and support. They can help you to plan for the future, apprise you of opportunities for growth and development, and connect you with other people who can help you in the field.

There are many opportunities waiting for budding recreational professionals out there. Opportunities come when who you know intersects with what you know. You can choose to prepare yourself for these opportunities by taking the right courses, volunteering, taking advantage of practicums and experiential learning programs, fulfilling an internship, and forging relationships with mentors who can help you.

Your Personal Leisure Plan

In addition to charting your course by considering a major and career in recreation, you also now know what leisure is calling to you in your personal life. Through leisure education you have found resources to meet your leisure desires. Undoubtedly, there will be obstacles, but you are willing and able to deal maturely with those obstacles to engage in a fulfilling life. Similar for planning for success in your career field, you need a plan of action to help actualize your leisure and to keep you "on the ship" when the going gets rough.

Your Personal Life Mission

Meaning making begins with a personal mission statement. A personal mission statement includes central personal themes including your life philosophy, leisure philosophy, and core values.

A personal mission statement addresses the following questions:

- What actions are you taking to live out your life's purpose and what you stand for?
- What character strengths do you wish to possess?
- Who do you want to be?

This personal mission statement should reflect what you want to accomplish within your lifetime. This is the general statement that governs your goals and objectives.

Some sample personal mission statements are:

- I live a vibrant, abundant, and authentic life.
- My work makes a positive difference in the world.
- I live a healthy, balanced life full of leisure and love and positive people.

Sample sentences that may be included in a mission statement are these:

- I travel to foreign lands and converse with the locals.
- I am physically fit.
- I give generously to my spiritual community in terms of my time, talents, and financial support.
- I spend time regularly in nature.
- Family is central to my life.

Goals

Goals relate directly to the mission statement but are more specific and measurable. If you want to live a healthy life of fitness, some goals might be to work out three times per week for 45 minutes per workout. Goals state what behaviors are needed to achieve the lifestyle detailed in the mission statement. Vague goals are of little benefit. The mnemonic *SMART* is used to assist people in creating effective goals.

S = Specific: detailed, particular, focused

M = Measurable: quantifiable; a standard of comparison

A = Attainable: can be performed and can produce results

R = Realistic: practical, achievable, accurate, possible

T = Time and resource constrained: scheduled, regulated by time, a definite duration of activity, accompanied by a deadline

Here are examples of three SMART goal statements. These goals relate to the first sample mission statement in the list provided earlier.

Mission statement: I travel to foreign lands and converse with the locals.

Goal 1: The summer following graduation, I will travel in Peru for a month.

Goal 2: I will converse with natives in Spanish while in traveling in Peru.

Goal 3: The cost for language classes and materials will not exceed $700.

Take a moment and assess these goals. Are they specific? Can you measure the results? Are they attainable and realistic? Is it clear in what time frame and with what resources the goals will be accomplished? How would you improve these goals so they are of the most benefit to a prospective world traveler? The person who wrote these goals wants to be a world traveler, so goals are of the utmost importance to get to Peru right after graduation. Without goals, this person may remain an armchair tourist, only experiencing foreign lands through video.

Action Plans

The next step in the leisure commitment process requires you to detail the activities and actions necessary to accomplish the goal. Revisit the prioritization you did of your developmental needs earlier in the chapter. Focus on your top two improvement areas and create a goal from that list that will bring you closer to your life mission. Write out your action plan. It may seem tedious to give a leisure idea this much thought and attention, but well-thought-out, written goals and tactics to reach those goals are far more likely to be reached. Don't just think it—ink it!

Monitor, Evaluate, and Modify Your Leisure Experience

Now that you are in the leisure experience, it is important to monitor progress made at specific intervals. Monitoring confirms that the time and effort pay off in achieving the intended results. Midcourse evaluation allows for needed adjustments to ensure success. Ask yourself how it's working out for you. Are you going to the gym, saving for

piola666/E+/Getty Images

Exploring a new place with your best friend can be an exhilarating experience. This sort of leisure materializes when you create an action plan and painstakingly follow the steps through to dream fulfillment.

your trip, asking people on dates, or meditating three days a week if you stated you would in your plan? No? Then stay flexible. Revisit and revise the plan—it's your plan after all. Circumstances change and so should your plans, objectives, and tactics. However, stay as true as possible to your mission and goals. If the goal is important, it should not be easily changed just because something isn't working. Instead, revisit your tactics for achieving the goal. Your creative ideas can enhance your chances for success, so bask in the possibility of this leisure experience and figure out how to make it happen. Staying motivated is a common leisure challenge, but focusing on your mission, goals, action plan, and techniques for overcoming obstacles may be just what you need to get yourself in gear once again.

When you keep the commitment to goals and rework the tactic to actualize your plan, you are being honest and true to yourself. Research suggests that if you make your commitment known to yourself as well as to others, you are more likely to keep it. Being able to report success to those you shared your dream with adds to your feeling of self-worth and joy. Let's face it—the cheering crowd at the end

of the marathon or the applause when the curtains fall after a performance are wonderful, even if they are not the primary motivators.

Beware of obstacles and have a plan to manage them. Review the many tips in this chapter to help you think creatively about staying on track, and you will go far. If you are engaging in a new activity, you are more likely to stay committed if a friend signs up, too. You are also more likely to stay committed if an economic commitment is involved. By foreseeing challenges, you can solve the challenge before it begins.

Summary

Balanced people reflect, affirm themselves, and celebrate their successes. You can become a leisure explorer and also serve as a leisure advocate and role model for others. You can even major in recreation and enjoy a career helping others to recreate. You can chart your course and live life at the helm of your leisure ship. May your leisure journey surpass your greatest expectations.

Learning Activities

1. For each area of development (social, physical, cognitive, psychoemotional, spiritual, aesthetic, environmental, and civic engagement), list two recreational activities that would help you grow.

2. Using the list you created from question 1, discuss what obstacles might prevent you from participating in those activities. Develop strategies for overcoming those obstacles.

3. Locate five websites that list recreational opportunities in your area. Choose two events or activities from each website that interest you and list them. Rank the 10 events and activities you listed with your most desirable being first. Commit to participating in at least two of the events or activities you listed. Be prepared to discuss during class which events and activities you participated in.

4. Select one of the careers listed on the career map. Research job openings for that position and be prepared to tell the class about the jobs and the qualifications needed to apply for them.

5. Develop a personal mission statement following the principles set forth in this chapter. Formulate six SMART goals related to your mission statement and leisure choices. Develop a leisure action plan to help you achieve those goals and come to class prepared to share your plan.

Review Questions

1. What physiological, sociocultural, spiritual, cognitive, psychological, and additional factors influence your development and well-being?

2. What are some perceived obstacles that get in the way of intentional leisure engagement?

3. What have you learned about leisure resources that affect positive leisure lifestyle change?

4. What is your action plan of leisure, and how will it meet personal needs and enhance growth while accessing greater wellness and balance?

Go to HK*Propel* to access additional learning content.

Glossary

activity factors—The physical and social elements of an activity known as activity environment and social interaction, respectively.

anthropology—Study of humankind including everything in culture and society: traditions, values, leisure, language, beliefs, and economics.

Antiquities Act of 1906—Federal policy act designed to protect natural, cultural, historical, and scientific resources on U.S. federal lands. The act authorizes U.S. presidents to designate national monuments that are managed by the National Park Service, the Bureau of Land Management, and the U.S. Fish and Wildlife service (www.doi.gov/ocl/antiquities-act).

arête—Greek ideal suggesting that all pursuits, including recreational activities, be performed excellently, with complete mastery; the pursuit of perfection. *Arête* combined noble actions with noble thoughts.

autonomy—An inner endorsement of one's action; personal choice.

baby boomers—People born between 1946 and 1964.

balance—A stable, calm state of the emotions. A satisfying arrangement marked by even distribution of elements and characterized by the display of symmetry.

balance activities—Family activities occurring in leisure that are unfamiliar, novel, and infrequent and tend to take more resources (like time or money) to accomplish.

benefits—Positive outcomes associated with something.

blood sports—Roman competitions that resulted in injury and often death that were enjoyed by most Romans until the introduction of Christianity.

blue laws—Laws that are enacted to protect the Sabbath, ordinarily defined as Sunday, from commercial or other forms of activity.

bread and circuses—Weekly distribution of bread to the citizens of Rome, which, combined with the free access to Roman games and competition, was used to placate the population of Rome. In this manner, leisure was manipulated for political purposes.

built environment—The human-made surroundings that provide the setting for human activity, ranging in scale from buildings and parks or green space to neighborhoods and cities and their supporting infrastructure, such as water supply or energy networks. The built environment is a material, spatial, and cultural product of human labor that combines physical elements and energy in forms for living, working, and playing (www.definitions.net).

Bureau of Land Management—U.S. federal land agency that manages 1 in every 10 acres of land in the United States and approximately 30 percent of the nation's minerals (www.blm.gov).

campus community—Associated with valuing people as individuals, accepting people within the community, and improving individual quality of campus social life.

campus recreation—Campus agency that provides a wide variety of recreational experiences and opportunities for students, faculty, and staff.

carrying capacity—The number of visitors who can be accommodated in a given area without degrading the natural, sociocultural, and economic environments.

casual leisure—Intrinsically rewarding activities requiring little skill or training to enjoy.

cisgender—People who identify with the gender that they were assigned at birth.

cisnormativity—A set of underlying assumptions that gender is fixed, binary, and unchanging.

city manager–council model—A system of local governance where a professional public administrator or city manager works with the elected city council and, in many cases, an elected mayor to provide governance, hire employees, approve budgets, and make administrative decisions.

Civilian Conservation Corps—Depression-era U.S. government program for unemployed men who performed infrastructural improvement projects in federally managed forests and parks (www.nps.gov/articles/the-civilian-conservation-corps.htm).

civilization—State brought about by invention and sustained by the need for organization, cooperation, and communication. All civilizations have institutional forms of government, economics, religion, and symbolic devices for language.

climate change—Significant variations in the average state and fluctuations of the climate that persist for an extended time (typically decades or longer). Climate change can be caused by natural Earth processes or external forces such as persistent anthropogenic changes in the composition of the atmosphere related to increased carbon dioxide emissions that lead to or change land use models (www.ipcc.ch).

cognition—Process of applying our knowledge and information to the surroundings and situations in which we find ourselves.

cognitive development—Changes in a person's ability to acquire intelligence, advanced thought, and problem-solving ability across the life span.

commercial recreation—Market-driven, private-sector recreation activities for which a profit-oriented enterprise charges participants a fee.

commons—Resources that are collectively owned or opportunities for all members of a community to share in the costs, use, and benefits of public goods.

community—A group of people living in close proximity to one another; a group of people sharing common interests, like the scientific community; a group of people comprising a distinct segment of the population, like the gay community; or a group of people sharing a common identity, like the Irish community.

community recreation—A means for improving and maintaining societal cohesion and the quality of life; its development is dependent on social participation.

competence—Feeling of capability.

concrete operational stage—Stage when children begin to understand high-order thinking and use logic; usually occurs between ages 7 and 11.

conservation—The careful preservation and protection and planned management of a natural resource to prevent exploitation, destruction, or neglect.

contemporary leisure—The meanings, types, or forms of leisure activities, experiences, and relations that are current or happening now.

coping—Process of managing difficult circumstances.

core activities—Family activities occurring in leisure that are familiar, common, and frequent and tend to not require many resources to accomplish.

creation—Process of human history based in life created and controlled by an intelligent and, some would say, benevolent supreme being.

critical theory—A set of ideas that aims to understand how dominant ruling ideologies (the ideas of those in power) conceal oppressive social relations and inequalities in order to preserve the status quo.

cross-cultural—Refers to any idea, tradition, or social norm that spans more than one culture.

cultural distance—The difference between two cultures.

cultural hegemony—The processes of negotiation over cultural values, norms, ideas, and behaviors in which dominant groups attempt to gain the consent of subordinate groups to remain in power.

culture wars—The polarization of societal views on change, values, morality, social equity, and lifestyles that play out through debates in popular culture.

Dark Ages—Period of approximately 1,000 years during which life was influenced by war, disease, migration, and a decided lack of cultural development due to the threats to survival that arose during this time.

development—Systematic change in a person that begins from conception and ends with death.

deviance—Actions or behaviors that differ from cultural or social norms.

digital leisure—Free time spent engaging with digital technologies.

digital technology—A type of technology that involves data (e.g., tracking, sharing, processing).

direct expenditure—Money spent to purchase the primary leisure service or product.

discretionary income—Money that is left after taxes have been taken out and necessities such as food and shelter have been accounted for.

distance decay—The effect of distance on people's interaction with places.

distress—Physiological response resulting from perception or appraisal of threat.

economic multiplier—The degree to which money spent on leisure services in a community is respent in the same community.

economics—Study of the production, distribution, and consumption of goods and services.

efficiency—The effective allocation of scarce leisure resources to produce the most benefit for the most people.

eminent domain—Legislation that allows a governing body to seize private land for public use by compensating the owner of the land.

emotion-focused coping—Strategies that target the thoughts and feelings associated with distress.

empty nest syndrome—Phenomenon that occurs in late adulthood, when people's children have left home.

enabling legislation—Legislation that provides the authority for appropriate administrative bodies or officials to carry out mandates or enforce the laws.

enjoyment—The experience of satisfaction and achieving something important.

Enlightenment—An 18th-century philosophical movement that freed people's minds from dependence on the supernatural and otherworldly rewards.

environment—Surroundings in which an organism lives. *Natural environment* denotes aspects of the environment that are not human made. *Built environment* denotes aspects of the environment that are human made.

environmental justice—The fair treatment and meaningful involvement of all people, regardless of race, color, national origin, or income, with respect to the development, implementation and enforcement of environmental laws, regulations, and policies (www.epa.gov).

epistemology—A person's belief about how to get information or how things should be put together.

esports—Amateur and professional players participating in video game events or tournaments that include championships at both regional and international levels.

ethnography—Field of study that relies on learning from people rather than studying people.

eudemonic or psychological well-being—Positive personal functioning and growth, including fulfillment and realization of potential, finding meaning in life, and living a life of virtue.

evolution—A process of successful existence through natural selection, environmental adaptation, mutation, and survival.

exergaming—Technology-driven activities, such as video games, that require the participant to exercise or be physically active (e.g., dancing, running) to play the game.

families—Social relationships between or among at least two individuals related by birth, marriage, adoption, or ties of affection.

family circumstances—The life conditions, traditions, cultures, or situations of families that are likely to affect daily family life and family leisure.

family connection experiences—Shared activities that sustain and maintain the bond between two or more family members and activities that establish, augment, alter, or grow the bond between two or more family members.

family factors—The descriptive characteristics of a person or subgroup within a family and the family as a whole; some characteristics are both shared between family members and not shared between family members, just as some characteristics are both shared by different families and not shared by different families.

family relationships—The named associations or connections between two or more people; individuals likely have multiple family relationships, and the number of their family relationships may change across the life span.

family structure—The organization of members of a household, including marital status, living arrangements, and whether household members are biologically related.

federalism—The constitutional arrangement of balancing and sharing rights and powers between different levels of government.

festivals—Events that mark the cessation of normal daily activities to allow access to something extraordinary, even otherworldly.

flow—State when a person's skill level and challenge are exactly matched and the person loses a sense of time and is "in the zone."

formal operational stage—Stage when a person can recognize and identify a problem, state numerous alternative hypotheses, carry out procedures to collect information about the problems to be studied, and test hypotheses; usually begins at age 12.

functionalism—A sociological paradigm that perceives leisure as part of social institutions (like organs in a body) that produce shared values and must work together in order to have a healthy, cohesive society.

gateway communities—Communities located near a park or protected area. They are also referred to as natural-amenity and park-proximal communities. They typically provide visitor services for those who recreate in parks or protected areas.

generations—People born within a defined time frame who thereby form an age cohort and experience similar life events.

geosocial networking applications—Applications that use both social networking and geographical location to connect users.

gig economy—A labor market characterized by the prevalence of short-term contracts or freelance work as opposed to permanent jobs.

global positioning systems—Devices used to geographically identify your position on the Earth.

gratifications—Immersive experiences that result in personal growth.

greenbelt—Land use designation to protect undeveloped, wild, or agricultural lands surrounding or neighboring urban areas from building or development.

greenhouse effect—The effect produced as greenhouse gases allow incoming solar radiation to pass through the Earth's atmosphere but prevent part of the outgoing infrared radiation from the Earth's surface and lower atmosphere from escaping into outer space (EPA, 2009).

gremlins—Loud, vigilant, negative monsters in our minds that try to convince us that our plans are unworkable and that we are not adequate.

growth connection experiences—Shared activities that establish, augment, alter, or grow the bond between two or more family members.

habituation—Becoming accustomed to or adapting to experiences.

health—The state of complete physical, mental, and social well-being and not merely the absence of disease.

hedonic or subjective well-being—Emotional or cognitive evaluation of the overall goodness of one's life, including frequent positive emotion, infrequent negative emotion, and evaluation of overall life satisfaction.

hedonists—People who pursue pleasure as life's primary goal.

homeless—A state of lacking a fixed, regular, and adequate nighttime residence.

identity—Individuality, distinct personal uniqueness.

immaterial labor—Labor or work that produces products that are not material such as knowledge, relationships, feelings; for example, most everything you do on Facebook is immaterial labor.

impairment—An organic or functional condition that may be temporary or permanent.

implicit bias—Unconscious stereotypes that may unknowingly influence decisions.

inclusive recreation—Recreation in which everyone, regardless of ability, participates together in the same programs.

indirect expenditure—Money spent on leisure services or products that support the primary leisure service or product.

Industrial Revolution—The movement toward centralized workplaces—factories that brought together large numbers of skilled and unskilled workers and great technological innovations in the production of goods.

intentional activity—Effortful, goal-directed endeavors.

interpersonal constraints—Barriers to participation that deal with social relationships with others.

interpretivism—Paradigm that all knowledge is a matter of interpretation; in social science, the participant rather than the researcher is viewed as the expert.

intrapersonal constraints—Individual psychological factors that interfere with leisure participation. These may be ability level, personality needs, prior experiences, or supposed attitudes of peer groups.

intrinsic motivation—Participation in an activity based on anticipation of rewards that come from within the person.

joint activities—Shared activities that require social interaction between family members to be successful.

leakage—Money spent in a community that is respent outside the community.

learning—Obtaining new knowledge, behaviors, skills, values, or preferences.

Leave No Trace—A national and international program designed to assist outdoor enthusiasts with their decisions about how to reduce the impacts of outdoor recreation (www.lnt.org).

leisure—Meanings that people attach to enjoyable activities undertaken during their unobligated time.

leisure constraints—Impediments to participation; referred to as interpersonal, intrapersonal, and structural constraints.

leisure education—Field of study that aims to help individuals, families, communities, and societies achieve a suitable quality of life and good health by using leisure time intelligently and by developing and cultivating physical, emotional, spiritual, mental, and social aspects related to the aims of education in the country and its cultural heritage.

leisure industry—The agencies, organizations, and businesses that provide facilities, programs, services, or areas for people to enjoy in their free time.

leisure landscapes—Spaces and places where people recreate, restore, and have the freedom to choose to be.

leisure-time physical activity—Exercise, sports, recreation, or hobbies that are not associated with activities as part of one's regular job duties, household, or transportation.

life politics—A nonparty social and cultural orientation that focuses on issues of lifestyle, environment, and globalization.

locus of control—The perception of the source of control in one's life.

macroeconomics—Study of the total of economic activity (growth, inflation, and unemployment) of a national or regional economy as a whole.

maintenance connection experiences—Shared activities that sustain or maintain the bond between two or more family members.

manifest destiny—An 1800s era European American settler belief that the United States was ordained by God to expand westward through colonization and territorial acquisition across the whole of North America.

maturation—Systematic biological changes that occur in a person, sometimes referred to as *nature*.

mental health—A person's condition with regard to their psychological and emotional state; an absence of mental illness.

methodology—Procedures and techniques that are used to collect information.

microcosm—A world within a world; a miniature world.

microeconomics—Study of how individuals, families, organizations, and some states make decisions to spend their money.

morale, welfare, and recreation—Programs offered to military personnel and their families, often including a comprehensive set of recreational, social, and community support services, including sports, physical fitness, youth and child development programs, entertainment, and food and beverage services.

National Outdoor Leadership School—A 501(c)(3) not-for-profit educational institution founded in 1965 by legendary mountaineer Paul Petzoldt. The institution takes people of all ages on remote wilderness expeditions, teaching technical outdoor skills, leadership, and environmental ethics in some of the world's wildest and most awe-inspiring classrooms (www.nols.edu/about).

natural environment—All living and nonliving things that occur naturally on Earth.

nature—*See* maturation.

neighborhood—The area immediately adjacent to a residential dwelling.

nomophobia—A fear of being without your mobile phone; this stems from the dependent relationship many people have with digital technologies such as smartphones.

nonbinary—People who do not identify strictly as either male or female, either considering themselves to be on the spectrum between those or else outside of the gender binary altogether.

nongovernmental organizations—Nonprofit organizations that work to promote human good while operating separately from any national government. The definition varies slightly from nation to nation, but most nongovernmental organizations fall within this framework.

not-for-profit organizations—Voluntary associations that usually focus on a particular issue, activity, or population and are limited in their scope based on the mission of the particular organization; also called *nonprofit, voluntary, third sector, independent sector,* or *nongovernmental organizations.*

novelty—The level of complexity of an activity resulting from unfamiliar physical or social elements of the activity.

nurture—What people learn in their environment (i.e., the effect that people and experiences in your life have on you).

object permanence—Awareness that objects continue to exist even when they are no longer visible.

ontology—What is known about reality and existence; the study of being and existence.

Organic Act of 1916—Act by U.S. Congress to establish the U.S. National Park Service (www.nps.gov/grba/learn/management/organic-act-of-1916.htm).

Outdoor Foundation—A not-for-profit foundation established by the Outdoor Industry Association to inspire future generations of outdoor enthusiasts. Its vision is to be a driving force behind a massive increase in active outdoor recreation in America (www.outdoorfoundation.org/about.html).

paradigm—A worldview or way of seeing that shapes what is considered meaningful, the kinds of questions we are able to ask, and dominant and alternative approaches to knowledge production (e.g., theories).

parallel activities—Shared activities that do not require social interaction between family members to be successful.

park—A natural or near-natural green or open space that is bounded in some way and has the purpose of natural resource conservation and preservation, human use, or both.

parks and natural resources—Outdoor nature-based opportunities for recreation activity.

parliamentary system—A type of governmental system, such as that found in Great Britain, in which the legislature has the power to make and execute laws.

Pax Romana—The approximately 200 years of peace begun by Caesar Augustus.

person–activity fit—Finding the activities that are congruent with the person's interests, capabilities, and needs.

personal growth—The process of increasing one's self-knowledge.

person-first language—Avoiding labels to define someone and instead leading with their personhood; examples include *people experiencing homelessness* instead of *the homeless* or *person with a disability* instead of *disabled person*.

physical development—Changes in an individual's physical capabilities throughout the life span.

physical health—State of a person's body, including presence or absence of disease.

places—Physical environments or locations that have special or value-added meaning (such as culture).

play—Activity undertaken by children and adults that includes characteristics of spontaneity, purposelessness, and the creation of an imaginary world. Play is almost always pleasurable and self-expressive and can range from disorganized activity to structured involvements.

playground movement—A philanthropic church-based effort begun in the late 1800s to provide safe places for urban children to recreate.

pleasure periphery—Regions with low socioeconomic status away from developed centers of production and consumption.

pleasures—Emotionally positive, momentary, often sensory experiences.

pluralist politics—Process of various and multiple interest groups working, and sometimes competing, to influence the institutions of government to advance ideas and policies that reflect their goals (Grant, 2004).

positive mental health—A combination of feeling good and being fully functional.

positivism—Paradigm that posits that knowledge is based on natural phenomena and their properties and relations as verified by the empirical sciences.

postmodernism—Paradigm that is skeptical of explanations that claim to be valid for all groups; postmodernists focus instead on the relative truths of each group.

postpositivism—Paradigm in which the knower (researcher) and known cannot be separated, emphasizing the importance of multiple measures and observations in social science.

preoperational stage—Stage when a child learns to develop language and begins representing things with words and images; usually occurs between ages two and seven years.

prevention—Any activity that reduces the chances of poor health or other risk factors.

problem-focused coping—Active strategies to address directly the problems that create a given distress.

Proposition 13—A precedent established by California voters that added Article XIII A to the California constitution that limits property tax rates to no more than 1 percent of full cash value (https://lao.ca.gov/Publications/Report/3497).

psychology—Study of the way the human mind works and how it influences behavior.

psychosocial development—Changes in an individual's emotional, moral, social, and other abilities across the life span.

public goods—Services provided through the public sector that produce and accrue value for both users and nonusers.

public policy—Activities of government, working directly or through its agents, that have an influence on the lives of citizens.

pull factor—Force that draws people from one place to another.

quality of life—The degree to which a person enjoys the important possibilities of life that reflect the interaction of personal and environmental factors.

quality of life—The personal determination of the worth or value of some aspect of a person's life.

recreation—Activities undertaken because of conscious or unconscious enjoyable end results.

recreational sport—Intramurals, extramurals, club sports, informal sports, and instructional sports.

recreation business districts—Clusters of recreational businesses offering recreational activities, dining, entertainment, and shopping.

recreation therapy—An allied health field that uses recreation as a tool to treat individuals with physical, emotional, or cognitive impairments.

relatedness—The desire to feel connected to others; to feel a sense of belonging.

Renaissance—An intellectual and artistic period that sought to resurrect the values and styles of ancient Greece and Rome.

sacralization—State of being sensitized to one's spiritual self.

savoring—Paying attention to the positive aspects of, and emotions associated with, an experience.

schole—The Greek word for *leisure,* meaning "free time."

self-tracking—Monitoring oneself (mind, body, or both) to track, analyze, and report data for the purpose of self-improvement.

sensation seeking—Need for varied, novel, and complex experiences; willingness to take physical and social risks for the sake of such experiences.

sensorimotor period—Essential spatial abilities and learning through the senses; usually occurs between ages zero and two years.

separation of powers—A system where each branch of government is considered separate and independent in order to avoid an accumulation of power within any one branch of government.

serious leisure—The methodical pursuit of an amateur, a hobbyist, or a volunteer activity so substantial and interesting that the participant centers their life on special skills, knowledge, and experiences associated with the leisure pursuit.

social capital—Features of community life that include interpersonal networks, clubs for public good, and volunteering.

social climate—Atmosphere resulting from the personalities of people in a social network.

social connection—Feeling close to other people, having more than one close relationship with another person, and having meaningful relationships with other people.

social embeddedness—The connectedness people have to others within their social network.

social equity—The principle that individual members of society have a right to fair, just, and equitable treatment by societal systems and people in terms of laws, policies, and services.

social impacts of tourism—The ways in which tourism contributes to changes in social conditions. The growth of tourism and inflow of tourists inevitably modify the destination environment.

social interaction—The verbal and nonverbal communications between family members during a recreation activity.

social isolation—Feeling of isolation or disconnectedness from others; having no or very few relationships with other people or having relationships with other people that are not meaningful.

social justice—Equal rights, equal opportunities, and equal treatment for all people.

social media—An application, service, or website with a social purpose framework for which content is primarily user-generated.

social network—The set of relationships between people.

social sciences—Sciences that focus on people and how they act individually and in a group.

social support—The assistance and protection given to others, especially to individual people.

socioeconomic status—The status one retains in society as a consequence of three distinct attributes: income, occupation, and education.

sociology—Systematic study of social behavior and human groups.

spaces—Boundless extents without special meaning that can be represented by distance, area, and volume.

special district—A separate, independent form of government that has the authority to tax and administer specific services, such as parks and recreation.

spiritual health—State of a person's faith, hope, and commitment in relation to a well-defined worldview or belief system that provides a sense of meaning and purpose to existence.

sports—A range of recreational and entertainment activities that involve rules, physical prowess, and contests between individuals or teams, generally with an uncertain outcome.

sport tourism—Traveling for the purpose of participating in or watching sport activities or visiting places of sports nostalgia.

state of being or state of mind—A psychological experience whereby leisure is perceived as being freely chosen, not compulsory, and done for its own sake.

staycation—Vacation spent at home enjoying what one's home environment has to offer.

strong mayor–council model—A system of local governance where the elected mayor has a strong administrative role in government, including hiring and firing, budgeting, and setting the strategic direction of the city.

structural constraints—Factors that interfere with leisure preference and participation.

Supremacy Clause—A U.S. constitutional provision that establishes the federal system's precedence in cases where federal and state laws come into conflict.

sustainability—A systematic approach in which factors including environment, culture, economics, and justice are considered holistically and together. Also, the effective management of resources for continued healthy and prosperous communities and vibrant ecosystems.

technology—The practical application of new or innovative knowledge, skills, and methods in science or industry.

Tennessee Valley Authority—A program of the U.S. federal government organized in 1933 to generate electric power, flood control, and irrigation through the extensive construction of dams and reservoirs throughout the Tennessee River basin (www.TVA.com).

theory of student involvement—The quantity and quality of the physical and psychological energy that students invest in the college experience.

third place— A welcoming community space where people spend their free time with friends, colleagues, or neighbors.

threats to survival—Natural and human events that increase risk to human existence, including natural disasters, climatic conditions, war, terrorism, and military occupation.

time—In a leisure experience, it constitutes the five chronological stages of an experience.

tourism destination—A physical space containing tourism products and services such as attractions, activities, and infrastructure.

tourists—People who travel to and stay in places for leisure outside their usual environment with the travel not associated with permanent residence or remuneration.

traditional ecological knowledge—A collection of traditional knowledge and stewardship practices that have been culturally adapted and generationally transmitted. Also known as TEK, it refers to indigenous knowledge relating to ecology and the relationships between all living inhabitants of the Earth (www.bia.gov/bia/ots/dfwfm/bwfm/fuels-management/traditional-ecological-knowledge).

transcendence—The ability of leisure to help a person overcome a traumatic life event.

transgender—People whose gender identity differs from that assigned at birth.

U.S. Department of the Interior—The executive department of the U.S. government responsible for the management and conservation of most federal land and the administration of programs relating to Native Americans, Alaska Natives, and Native Hawaiians and to insular areas of the United States. The department is administered by the U.S. Secretary of the Interior, who is a member of the cabinet of the president. The department includes several bureaus: the National Park Service, the Bureau of Land Management, the U.S. Geological Survey, the U.S. Fish and Wildlife Service, the Office of Surface Mining, the U.S. Minerals Management Service, the Bureau of Indian Affairs, and the U.S. Bureau of Reclamation (www.doi.gov).

U.S. Fish and Wildlife Service—A bureau of the Department of the Interior that was established in 1871 as a government agency dedicated to the conservation, protection, and enhancement of fish, wildlife, and plants and their habitats. This is the only agency in the federal government whose primary responsibility is the conservation and management of these important natural resources for the American public (www.fws.gov).

U.S. Forest Service—An agency of the U.S. Department of Agriculture established in 1905 that manages public lands in national forests and grasslands with an effort to achieve utilitarian use and benefits from forest resources (www.fs.fed.us).

U.S. National Park Service—A bureau of the Department of the Interior. Directly overseeing its operation is the department's assistant secretary for fish and wildlife and parks. The national park system comprises 391 areas covering more than 84 million acres in every state (except Delaware), the District of Columbia, American Samoa, Guam, Puerto Rico, and the Virgin Islands. These areas include national parks, monuments, battlefields, military parks, historical parks, historic sites, lakeshores, seashores, recreation areas, scenic rivers and trails, and the White House (www.nps.gov/faqs.htm).

virtual fitness—Encompasses livestreaming and technology to allow participation in workouts via virtual reality.

virtues—Characteristics that are viewed as universally good and that support individual and collective well-being.

well-being—The degree to which a person experiences positive emotion and fulfillment.

wellness—A state of health, balance, vigor, and energy.

wellness practices—Practices, habits, and routines that aid in living your healthiest life.

wilderness—An area that is uninhabited and undisturbed by human beings. Some wilderness areas are federally protected and managed to preserve natural conditions.

work—Activity undertaken for economic gain or social redeeming vitality.

work ethic—The valuing of activities that result in economic gain.

Works Progress Administration—A United States program established in 1935 under the New Deal designed to create jobs and stimulate the economy during the Great Depression.

References

Chapter 1

Braubach, M., Egorov, A., Mudu, P., Wolf, T., Ward Thompson, C., & Martuzzi, M. (2017). Effects of urban green space on environmental health, equity and resilience. In N. Kabisch, H. Korn, J. Stadler, & A. Bonn (Eds.), *Nature-based solutions to climate change adaptation in urban areas: Theory and practice of urban sustainability transitions* (pp. 187-206). Cham, Switzerland: Springer Open.

Brock, T. (2017). Roger Caillois and e-sports: On the problems of treating play as work. *Games and Culture, 12*(4), 321-339.

Bureau of Labor Statistics. (2020). American Time Use Survey—2019 results USDL-20-1275. Washington, DC: Author.

Crossley, J., Rood, S., Brayley, R., Price-Howard, K., & Holdnak, A. (2018). *Introduction to commercial recreation and tourism: An entrepreneurial approach* (7th ed.). Champaign, IL: Sagamore-Venture.

Ellis, J.J. (1973). *Why people play*. Englewood Cliffs, NJ: Prentice Hall.

Gallup. (2018). *The gig economy and alternative work arrangements* [Data set]. Gallup World Headquarters [Distributor].

Global Development Research Center. (n.d.). *Notes on "quality of life."* Retrieved from www.gdrc.org/uem/qol-define.html

Hallmon, A., Anaza, E., Sandoval, A., & Fernandez, M. (2020). Black mothers' recreational choices for their children: A critical race theory story. *Annals of Leisure Research, 21*(3). Retrieved from https://doi.org/10.1080/11745398.2020.1769487

Henderson, K.A., Bialeschki, M.D., Hemingway, J.L., Hodges, J.S., Kivel, B.D., & Sessoms, H.D. (2001). *Introduction to recreation and leisure services* (8th ed.). State College, PA: Venture.

Iwasaki, Y., & Hopper, T. (2017). Leisure, engagement, and meaning-making among high-risk youth. *Loisir et Société/Society and Leisure, 40*, 324-339. doi:10.1080/07053436.2017.1378504

Jennings, V., Larson, L., & Yun, J. (2016). Advancing sustainability through urban green space: Cultural ecosystem services, equity, and social determinants of health. *International Journal of Environmental Research and Public Health, 13*(2), 196. doi:103390/ijerph13020196

Kim, J., & Brown, S. L. (2018). The associations between leisure, stress, and health behaviors among university students. *American Journal of Health Education, 46*(6), 375-383. doi:10.1080/19325037.2018.1516583

Mannell, R., & Kleiber, D.A. (1997). *A social psychology of leisure*. State College, PA: Venture.

Moiseichik, M., & Moss, J. (2016). Law and jurisdiction. In M. Moiseichik, (Ed.), *Management of park and recreation agencies* (4th ed., pp. 27-53). Ashburn, VA: National Recreation and Park Association.

National Recreation and Park Association. (2020, April 23). *New report: Local parks generate more than $166 billion in U.S. economic activity.* Retrieved from www.nrpa.org/about-national-recreation-and-park-association/press-room/new-report-local-parks-generate-more-than-166-billion-dollars-in-u-s-economic-activity

National Recreation and Park Association. (n.d.). *About NRPA.* Retrieved from www.nrpa.org/about-national-recreation-and-park-association

Neulinger, J. (1981). *The psychology of leisure* (2nd ed.). Springfield, IL: Charles C. Thomas.

Pieper, J. (1963). *Leisure: The basis of culture* (A. Dru, Trans.). New York, NY: New American Library.

Pluss, M.A, Bennett, K.J, Novak, A.R., Panchuk, D., Coutts, A.J., & Fransen, J. (2019). Esports: The chess of the 21st century. *Frontiers in Psychology, 10*(1), 1-5.

Seo, Y. (2016). Professionalized consumption and identity transformations in the field of eSports. *Journal of Business Research, 69*, 264-272.

Sivan, A. (2019). World leisure organization special interest group on leisure education. *World Leisure Journal, 61*, 315. doi:10.1080/16078055.2019.1661108

Sports Events Media Group. (2019, August 5). *Youth sports boom continues; SFA says millions in facilities yet to be developed.* Retrieved from https://sportseventsmediagroup.com/youth-sports-boom-continues-sfa-says-millions-in-facilities-yet-to-be-developed

Stewart, W.P. (1998). Leisure as multiphase experiences: Challenging traditions. *Journal of Leisure Research, 30*(4), 391-400.

U.S. Department of Health and Human Services. (2018). *Physical activity guidelines for Americans* (2nd ed.). Washington, DC: Author.

Chapter 2

Babbie, E. (2002). *The basics of social research*. Belmont, CA: Wadsworth Thompson Learning.

Bartlett, E. (2018, February 18). *Tourism: A strong pillar for economic growth.* Retrieved from www.jamaicaobserver.com/news/tourism-a-strong-pillar-for-economic-growth_125467

Bonilla-Silva, E. (2003). *Racism without racists: Color-blind racism and the persistence of racial inequality in the United States*. Lanham, MD: Rowman & Littlefield.

Bureau of Labor Statistics. (2018). *American time use survey—2018 results*. Washington, DC: Author. Retrieved from www.bls.gov/charts/american-time-use/activity-leisure.htm and www.bls.gov/charts/american-time-use/activity-by-emp.htm

Burton, L.M. (1981). A critical analysis and review of the research on Outward Bound and related programs. *Dissertation Abstracts International, 42,* 158-B.

Chick, G. (1998). Leisure and culture: Issues for an anthropology of leisure. *Leisure Sciences, 20,* 111-133.

Crotty, M. (1997). *The foundations of social research: Meaning and perspective in the research process.* London, UK: Sage.

Driver, B.L., Brown, P.J., & Peterson, G.L. (Eds.). (1991). *Benefits of leisure.* State College, PA: Venture.

Ewert, A. (1982). *Outdoor adventure and self-concept: A research analysis.* Eugene: University of Oregon, Department of Recreation and Park Management.

Friere, P. (2010). *Pedagogy of the oppressed.* New York, NY: Continuum.

Henderson, K.A. (1991). *Dimensions of choice: A qualitative approach to recreation, parks and leisure research.* State College, PA: Venture.

Holland, W.H., Powell, R.B., Thomsen, J.M., & Monz, C.A. (2018). A systematic review of the psychological, social, and educational outcomes associated with participation in wildland recreational activities. *Journal of Outdoor Recreation, Education and Leadership, 10*(3), 197-225.

hooks, b. (2001). *Salvation: Black people and love.* New York, NY: HarperCollins.

Kaplan, R. (1984). Wilderness perception and psychological benefits: An analysis of a continuing program. *Leisure Sciences, 6*(3), 271-290.

Little League of America. (2003). *Little League to mark 30th anniversary of decision allowing girls to play.* Retrieved from www.littleleague.org/media/newsarchive/06_2003/03_30thgirls.htm

Lussier, R.N. (2005). *Human relations in organizations: Applications and skill building.* Boston, MA: McGraw-Hill Irwin.

McLaughlin, T. (2008). *Give and go: Basketball as a cultural practice.* New York: State University of New York Press.

Moote, G.T., & Wodarski, J. S. (1997). The acquisition of life skills through adventure-based activities and programs: A review of the literature. *Adolescence, 32,* 125.

North Dakota Department of Commerce Tourism Division. (2018). *North Dakota tourism industry.* Retrieved from www.ndtourism.com/tourism-industry

Nye, R., Jr. (1976). *The influence of an Outward Bound program on the self-concept of the participants* (Unpublished doctoral dissertation). Temple University, Philadelphia, PA.

O'Sullivan, E. (2013). Power, promise, potential and possibilities of parks, recreation, and leisure. In Human Kinetics (Ed.), *Introduction to recreation and leisure* (2nd ed.). Champaign, IL: Human Kinetics.

Root, A. (2008). *Science, math, checkmate: 32 chess activities for inquiry and problem solving.* Westport, CT: Libraries Unlimited/Teacher Ideas Press.

Samdahl, D.M. (1999). Epistemological and methodological issues in leisure research. In E.L. Jackson & T.L. Burton (Eds.), *Leisure studies: Prospects for the twenty-first century* (pp. 119-134). State College, PA: Venture.

Smith, V.H. (1998, July). *Impact assessment discussion paper no. 2: Measuring the benefits of social science research.* Washington, DC: Director General's Office International Food Policy Research Institute.

Spradley, J.P. (1980). *Participant observation.* Fort Worth, TX: Harcourt.

Steinbach, P. (2013, January). *Intramural coed basketball playing rules vary greatly.* Retrieved from www.athleticbusiness.com/intramural-coed-basketball-playing-rules-vary-greatly.html

World Tourism Organization. (2020, May). *Impact assessment of the COVID-19 outbreak on international tourism.* Retrieved June 14, 2020, from www.unwto.org/impact-assessment-of-the-covid-19-outbreak-on-international-tourism

Zuckerman, M. (Ed.). (1983). *Biological bases of sensation-seeking, impulsivity, and anxiety.* Hillsdale, NJ: Lawrence Erlbaum.

Chapter 3

Allen, L.R. (1990). Benefits of leisure attributes to community satisfaction. *Journal of Leisure Research, 22*(2), 183-196.

Baker, D.A., & Palmer, R.J. (2006). Examining the effects of perceptions of community and recreation participation on quality of life. *Social Indicators Research, 75,* 395-418.

Biddle, S.J.H., Fox, K.R., Boutcher, S.H., & Faulkner, G.E. (2000). The way forward for physical activity and the promotion of psychological well-being. In S.J.H. Biddle, K.R. Fox, & S.H. Boutcher (Eds.), *Physical activity and psychological well-being* (pp. 154-168). New York, NY: Routledge.

Bovier, P.A., Chamot, E., & Perneger, T.V. (2004). Perceived stress, internal resources, and social support as determinants of mental health among young adults. *Quality of Life Research, 13,* 161-170.

Brajša-Žganec, A., Merkaš, M., & Šverko, I. (2011). Quality of life and leisure activities: How do leisure activities contribute to subjective well-being? *Social Indicators Research, 102,* 81-91.

Caldwell, L.L. (2005). Leisure and health: Why is leisure therapeutic? *British Journal of Guidance & Counseling, 33*(1), 7-26.

Cassie, L.T., & Halpenny, E. (2003). Volunteering for nature: Leisure motivations and benefits associated with a biodiversity conservation volunteer program. *World Leisure Journal, 45*(2), 38-50.

CNN. (2009). *Obama's inaugural speech.* Retrieved from www.cnn.com/2009/POLITICS/01/20/obama.politics/index.html

Coleman, D. (1993). Leisure based social support, leisure dispositions, and health. *Journal of Leisure Research, 25*(4), 350-361.

Coleman, D., & Iso-Ahola, S.E. (1993). Leisure and health: The role of social support and self-determination. *Journal of Leisure Research, 25*(2), 111-128.

Csikszentmihalyi, M. (1990). *Flow: The psychology of optimal experience.* New York, NY: Harper & Row.

Cummins, R.A. (1996). The domains of life satisfaction: An attempt to order chaos. *Social Indicators Research, 38,* 303-328.

Deci, E.L., & Ryan, R.M. (2000). The "what" and "why" of goal pursuits: Human needs and the self-determination of behavior. *Psychological Inquiry, 11*(4), 227-268.

Diener, E., & Seligman, M.E.P. (2002). Very happy people. *Psychological Science, 13*(1), 81-84.

Finley, E. (2020). Solidarity flourishes under lockdown in Italy. In M. Sitrin & C. Sembrar (Eds.), *Pandemic solidarity* (pp. 138-153). London, UK: Pluto Press.

Fox, K.R., Boutcher, S.H., Faulkner, G.E., & Biddle, S.J.H. (2000). The case for exercise in the promotion of mental health and psychological well-being. In S.J.H. Biddle, K.R. Fox, & S.H. Boutcher (Eds.), *Physical activity and psychological well-being* (pp. 1-9). New York, NY: Routledge.

Godbey, G., Caldwell, L.L., Floyd, M., & Payne, L. (2005). Contributions of leisure studies and recreation and park management research to the active living agenda. *American Journal of Preventive Medicine, 28,* 150-158.

Hawks, S. (1994). Spiritual health: Definition and theory. *Wellness Perspectives, 10,* 3-13.

Haworth, J.T., & Ducker, J. (1991). Psychological well-being and access to categories of experience in unemployed young adults. *Leisure Sciences, 10,* 265-274.

Heintzman, P. (2002). A conceptual model of leisure and spiritual well-being. *Journal of Park and Recreation Administration, 20*(4), 147-169.

Heintzman, P. (2015). *Leisure and spirituality: Biblical, historical, and contemporary perspectives.* Grand Rapids, MI: Baker Academic.

Hudders, L., & Pandelaere, M. (2012). The silver lining of materialism: The impact of luxury consumption on subjective well-being. *Journal of Happiness Studies, 13,* 411-437.

Iso-Ahola, S.E., & Park, C.J. (1996). Leisure-related social support and self-determination as buffers of stress-illness relationship. *Journal of Leisure Research, 28*(3), 169-187.

Iwasaki, Y. (2001). Contributions of leisure to coping with daily hassles in university students' lives. *Canadian Journal of Behavioral Science, 33*(2), 128-141.

Iwasaki, Y. (2003). The impact of leisure coping beliefs and strategies on adaptive outcomes. *Leisure Studies, 22,* 93-108.

Iwasaki, Y. (2007). Leisure and quality of life in an international and multicultural context: What are major pathways linking leisure to quality of life. *Social Indicators Research, 82,* 233-264.

Kahn, E.B., Ramsey, L.T., Brownson, R.C., Heath, G.W., Howze, E.H., Powell, K.E., . . . Corso, P. (2002). The effectiveness of interventions to increase physical activity: A systematic review. *American Journal of Preventive Medicine, 22*(4 Suppl. 1), 73-107.

Kilpatrick, R., & Trew, K. (1985). Lifestyles and psychological well-being among unemployed men in Northern Ireland. *Journal of Occupational Psychology, 58,* 207-216.

Kim, J., Heo, J., Lee, I.H., & Kim, J. (2015). Predicting personal growth and happiness by using serious leisure model. *Social Indicators Research, 122,* 147-157.

Kleiber, D.A., Hutchinson, S.L., & Williams, R. (2002). Leisure as a resource in transcending negative life events: Self-protection, self-restoration, and personal transformation. *Leisure Sciences, 24*(2), 219-235.

Kochhar, R. (2020). *Unemployment rose higher in three months of COVID-19 than it did in two years of the Great Recession.* Retrieved from www.pewresearch.org/fact-tank/2020/06/11/unemployment-rose-higher-in-three-months-of-covid-19-than-it-did-in-two-years-of-the-great-recession

Langford, C.P.H., Bowsher, J., Maloney, J.P., & Lillis, P.P. (1997). Social support: A conceptual analysis. *Journal of Advanced Nursing, 25,* 95-100.

Larson, J.S. (1991). *The measurement of health: Concepts and indicators.* New York, NY: Greenwood Press.

Liu, H., & Yu, B. (2015). Serious leisure, leisure satisfaction and subjective well-being of Chinese university students. *Social Indicators Research, 122,* 159-174.

Mannell, R.C., & Reid, D.G. (1999). Work and leisure. In E.L. Jackson & T.L. Burton (Eds.), *Leisure studies: Prospects for the twenty-first century* (pp. 151-165). State College, PA: Venture.

Melamed, S., Meir, E.I., & Samson, A. (1995). The benefits of personality-leisure congruence: Evidence and implications. *Journal of Leisure Research, 27,* 25-40.

Miilunpalo, S. (2001). Evidence and theory based promotion of health-enhancing physical activity. *Public Health Nutrition, 4*(2B), 725-728.

Misener, K., Doherty, A., & Hamm-Kerwin, S. (2010). Learning from the experiences of older adult volunteers in sports: A serious leisure perspective. *Journal of Leisure Research, 42*(2), 267-289.

Mutrie, N. (2000). The relationship between physical activity and clinically defined depression. In S.J.H. Biddle, K.R. Fox, & S.H. Boutcher (Eds.), *Physical activity and psychological well-being* (pp. 46-62). New York, NY: Routledge.

National Park Service. (2020). *Frequently asked questions.* Retrieved from www.nps.gov/faqs.htm

Pedersen, B.K., & Clemmensen, I.H. (1997). Exercise and cancer. In B.K. Pedersen (Ed.), *Exercise immunology* (pp. 171-201). Austin, TX: Landes.

Reis, J.P., & Gibbs, B.B. (2012). Physical activity in chronic disease prevention. In B.E. Ainsworth & C.A. Macera (Eds.), *Physical activity and public health practice* (pp. 53-74). New York, NY: Taylor & Francis Group.

Ryan, R.M., & Deci, E.L. (2000). Self-determination theory and the facilitation of intrinsic motivation, social development, and well-being. *American Psychologist, 55*(1), 68-78.

Schnohr, P., Scharling, H., & Jensen, J.S. (2003). Changes in leisure-time physical activity and risk of death: An observational study of 7,000 men and women. *American Journal of Epidemiology, 158*(7), 639-644.

Sirgy, J.M., & Cornwell, T. (2002). How neighborhood features affect quality of life. *Social Indicators Research, 59,* 79-114.

Stebbins, R.A. (1999). Serious leisure. In E.L. Jackson & T.L. Burton (Eds.), *Leisure studies: Prospects for the twenty-first century* (pp. 69-79). State College, PA: Venture.

Wankel, L.M., & Berger, B.G. (1991). The personal and social benefits of sport and physical activity. In B.L. Driver, P.J. Brown, & G.L. Peterson (Eds.), *Benefits of leisure* (pp. 121-144). State College, PA: Venture.

World Health Organization. (n.d.). *WHOQOL: Measuring quality of life.* Retrieved from www.who.int/healthinfo/survey/whoqol-qualityoflife/en/

Chapter 4

American Academy of Pediatrics. (2006, January). *Promoting physical activity: Basic recommendations for promoting activity.* Retrieved from www.aap.org/family/physicalactivity/physicalactivity.htm

Barr-Anderson, D.J., Young, D.R., Sallis, J.F., Neumark-Sztainer, D., Gittelsohn, J., Webber, L., . . . Jobe, J.B. (2007). Structured physical activity and psychosocial correlates in middle school girls. *Preventive Medicine, 44*(5), 404-409.

Birnbaum, A.S., Evenson, K.R., Motl, R.W., Dishman, R.K., Voorhees, C.C., Sallis, J.F., . . . Dowda, M. (2005). Scale development for perceived school climate for girls' physical activity. *American Journal of Health Behavior, 29*(3), 250-257.

Bocarro, J.N., Casper, J., Henderson, K., Floyd, M.F., Moore, R., Kanters, M.A., . . . Edwards, M.B. (2009). Physical activity promotion in North Carolina: Perceptions of public park and recreation directors. *Journal of Park and Recreation Administration, 27*(1), 1-16.

Bocarro, J.N., Kanters, M., Casper, J., & Forrester, S. (2008). School physical education, extracurricular sports, and lifelong active living. *Journal of Teaching in Physical Education, 27*(2), 155-166.

Bunds, K.S., Kanters, M.A., Venditti, R.A., Rajagopalan, N., Casper, J.M., & Carlton, T.A. (2018). Organized youth sports and commuting behavior: The environmental impact of decentralized community sport facilities. *Transportation Research Part D: Transport and Environment, 65.*

Caldwell, L.L. (2005). Leisure and health: Why is leisure therapeutic? *British Journal of Guidance & Counselling, 33*(1), 7-26.

Calle, E.E., & Kaaks, R. (2004). Overweight, obesity and cancer: Epidemiological evidence and proposed mechanisms. *Cancer, 4,* 579-590.

Callow, D.D., Arnold-Nedimala, N.A., Jordan, L.S., Pena, G.S., Won, J., Woodard, J.L., & Smith, J.C. (2020). The mental health benefits of physical activity in older adults survive the COVID-19 pandemic. *The American Journal of Geriatric Psychiatry, 28*(10), 1046-1057.

Cardenas, D., Henderson, K.A., & Wilson, B.E. (2009). Experiences of participation in senior games among older adults. *Journal of Leisure Research, 41*(1), 41-56.

Crane, J., & Temple, V. (2015). A systematic review of dropout from organized sport among children and youth. *European Physical Education Review, 21*(1), 114-131.

Davidson, K.K., & Lawson, C. (2006). Do attributes of the physical environment influence children's level of physical activity? *International Journal of Behavioral Nutrition and Physical Activity, 3*(19), 1-17.

Dempsey, P.C., Matthews, C.E., Dashti, S.G., Doherty, A.R., Bergouignan, A., van Roekel, E.H., . . . Lynch, B.M. (2020). Sedentary behavior and chronic disease: Mechanisms and future directions. *Journal of Physical Activity and Health, 17*(1), 52-61.

Edwards, M.B., Bocarro, J.N., & Kanters, M.A. (2013). Place disparities in supportive environments for extracurricular physical activity in North Carolina middle schools. *Youth & Society, 45*(2), 265-285.

Farley, T.A., Meriwether, R.A., Baker, E.T., Watkins, L.T., Johnson, C.C., & Webber, L.S. (2007). Safe play spaces to promote physical activity in inner-city children: Results from a pilot study of an environmental intervention. *American Journal of Public Health, 97*(9), 1625-1631.

Freeman, C., & Quigg, R. (2009). Commuting lives: Children's mobility and energy use. *Journal of Environmental Planning and Management, 52*(3), 393-412.

Global Burden of Disease Collaborative Network. (2017). *Global Burden of Disease Study 2015 (GBD 2015) Obesity and Overweight Prevalence 1980-2015.* Seattle, WA: Institute for Health Metrics and Evaluation. Retrieved from http://ghdx.healthdata.org/record/ihme-data/gbd-2015-obesity-and-overweight-prevalence-1980-2015

Hardison-Moody, A., Haynes-Maslow, L., Bocarro, J., Kuhlberg, J., Schulman, M., Bowen, S., . . . Murphy, Y. (2020). Partners at play: Engaging parks and recreation departments in extension's health promotion work. *Journal of Human Sciences and Extension, 8*(3), 177-188.

Hedstrom, R., & Gould, D. (2004). *Research in youth sports: Critical issues status.* East Lansing, MI: Institute for the Study of Youth Sports.

International City/County Management Association. (2005). *Active living approaches by local governments, 2004.* Retrieved from www.icma.org/upload/library/2004-07/%7B05AB7A74-29FB-47E6-AA2B-B5497BE4E0A6%7D.pdf

Iso-Ahola, S.E., Jackson, E., & Dunn, E. (1994). Starting, ceasing, and replacing leisure activities over the life-span. *Journal of Leisure Research, 26*(3), 227-249.

Jennings, V., Browning, M.H., & Rigolon, A. (2019). Urban green space at the nexus of environmental justice and health equity. In *Urban green spaces: SpringerBriefs in geography*. Retrieved from https://doi.org/10.1007/978-3-030-10469-6_4

King, A.C. (2001). Interventions to promote physical activity by older adults. *Journals of Gerontology Series A-Biological Sciences and Medical Sciences, 56*, 36-46.

Koplan, J.P., Liverman, C.T., & Kraak, V.I. (2005). *Preventing childhood obesity: Health in the balance*. Washington, DC: National Academies Press.

Logan, K., Lloyd, R.S., Schafer-Kalkhoff, T., Khoury, J.C., Ehrlich, S., Dolan, L.M., . . . Myer, G.D. (2020). Youth sports participation and health status in early adulthood: A 12-year follow-up. *Preventive Medicine Reports*, 101-107.

Louv, R. (2005). *The last child in the woods*. Chapel Hill, NC: Algonquin.

Marques, A., Ekelund, U., & Sardinha, L.B. (2016). Associations between organized sports participation and objectively measured physical activity, sedentary time and weight status in youth. *Journal of Science and Medicine in Sport, 19*(2), 154-157.

McLeroy, K.R., Bibeau, D., Steckler, A., & Glanz, K. (1988). An ecological perspective on health promotion programs. *Heath Education Quarterly, 15*, 351-377.

Merkel, D.L. (2013). Youth sport: Positive and negative impact on young athletes. *Open Access Journal of Sports Medicine, 4*, 151-160. Retrieved from https://doi.org/10.2147/OAJSM.S33556

NRPA. (2020). *The essential need for parks*. Retrieved from www.nrpa.org/publications-research/park-pulse/the-essential-need-for-parks/

Office of Disease Prevention and Health Promotion. (n.d.). *Secretary's advisory committee on national health promotion and disease prevention objectives for 2030: Recommendations for an approach to healthy people 2030*. Retrieved from www.healthypeople.gov/sites/default/files/Full%20Committee%20Report%20to%20Secretary%205-9-2017_1.pdf

Orsega-Smith, E., Payne, L.L., & Godbey, G. (2003). Physical and psychosocial characteristics of older adults who participate in a community-based exercise program. *Journal of Aging and Physical Activity, 11*(4), 516-531.

Payne, L.L., Orsega-Smith, E., Spangler, K., & Godbey, G. (1999, October). For the health of it. *Parks and Recreation, 34*(10), 72-77.

Perkins, D.F., Jacobs, J.E., Barber, B.L., & Eccles, J.S. (2004). Childhood and adolescent sports participation as predictors of participation in sports and physical fitness activities during young adulthood. *Youth & Society, 35*(4), 495-520.

Pew Research Center. (2018). *Teens, social media & technology 2018*. Retrieved from www.pewresearch.org/internet/2018/05/31/teens-social-media-technology-2018

Pinckney, H.P., IV, Outley, C., Brown, A., & Theriault, D. (2018). Playing while black. *Leisure Sciences, 40*(7), 675-685.

Roberts, K. (1999). *Leisure in contemporary society*. Wallingford, UK: CABI.

Roberts, K., & Brodie, D. (1992). *Inner-city sport: Who plays and what are the benefits?* Culemborg, The Netherlands: Giordano Bruno.

Sallis, J.F., Adlakha, D., Oyeyemi, A., & Salvo, D. (2020). An international physical activity and public health research agenda to inform COVID-19 policies and practices. *Journal of Sport and Health Science, 9*, 328-334.

Sallis, J.F., Bauman, A., & Pratt, M. (1998). Environmental and policy interventions to promote physical activity. *American Journal of Preventive Medicine, 15*(4), 379-397.

Seefeldt, V., Ewing, M., & Walk, S. (1992). *Overview of youth sports programs in the United States*. Washington, DC: Carnegie Council on Adolescent Development.

Shores, K.A., & West, S.T. (2008). The relationship between built park environments and physical activity in four park locations. *Journal of Public Health Management and Practice, 14*(3), e9-e16.

Spengler, J.O., Young, S.J., & Linton, L.S. (2007). Schools as a community resource for physical activity: Legal considerations for decision makers. *American Journal of Health Promotion, 21*(4), 390-396.

Task Force on Community Preventive Services. (2002). Recommendations to increase physical activity in communities. *American Journal of Preventive Medicine, 22*(4S), 67-72.

Telama, R., Yang, X., Hirvensalo, M., & Raitakari, O. (2006). Participation in organized youth sport as a predictor of adult physical activity: a 21-year longitudinal study. *Pediatric Exercise Science, 18*(1), 76-88.

Trudeau, F., & Shepherd, R.J. (2005). Contribution of school programs to physical activity levels and attitudes in children and adults. *Sports Medicine, 25*(2), 89-105.

U.S. Department of Health and Human Services. (2019). *The national youth sports strategy*. Retrieved from https://health.gov/sites/default/files/2019-10/National_Youth_Sports_Strategy.pdf

U.S. Department of Health and Human Services. (n.d.). *Healthy People 2030: Building a healthier future for all*. Retrieved from https://health.gov/healthypeople

Van Hoye, A., Fenton, S., Krommidas, C., Heuzé, J.P., Quested, E., Papaioannou, A., & Duda, J.L. (2013). Physical activity and sedentary behaviours among grassroots football players: A comparison across three European countries. *International Journal of Sport and Exercise Psychology, 11*(4), 341-350.

Vanreusel, B., & Scheerder, J. (2016). Tracking and youth sport: The quest for lifelong adherence to sport and physical activity. In K. Green & A. Smith (Eds.), *Routledge Handbook of Youth Sport* (pp. 148-157). London, UK: Routledge.

Wallis, C., Mehrtens, R., & Thompson, D. (1983, June 6). Stress: Can we cope? *Time.* Retrieved from http://content.time.com/time/subscriber/article/0,33009,950883,00.html

Waters, H., & Graf, M. (2018). *America's obesity crisis: The health and economic costs of excess weight.* Santa Monica, CA: Milken Institute.

Weybright, E. H., Caldwell, L.L., & Weaver, R.H. (2019). Preventing leisure from being overlooked: Intersecting leisure and prevention sciences. *Journal of Leisure Research, 50*(5), 394-412.

Wickel, E.E., & Eisenmann, J.C. (2007). Contribution of youth sport to total daily physical activity among 6-to 12-yr-old boys. *Medicine and Science in Sports and Exercise, 39*(9), 1493.

World Health Organization (WHO). (2018a). *Mental health: Strengthening our response.* Retrieved from www.who.int/news-room/fact-sheets/detail/mental-health-strengthening-our-response

World Health Organization (WHO). (2018b). *Obesity and overweight.* Retrieved from www.who.int/news-room/fact-sheets/detail/obesity-and-overweight

Zarrett, N., Veliz, P.T., & Sabo, D. (2020). *Keeping girls in the game: Factors that influence sport participation.* New York, NY: Women's Sports Foundation.

Chapter 5

Allison, M.T., & Schneider, I.E. (Eds.). (2000). *Diversity and the recreation profession: Organizational perspectives.* State College, PA: Venture.

Allman, A. (1990). *Subjective well-being of people with disabilities: Measurement issues* (Unpublished master's thesis). University of Illinois, Urbana-Champaign.

Bao, K.J., & Lyubomirsky, S. (2014). Making happiness last: Using hedonic adaptation prevention model to extend the success of positive interventions. In A. Parks & S. Schueller (Eds.), *The Wiley Blackwell handbook of positive psychological interventions* (pp. 373-384). Oxford, UK: John Wiley & Sons.

Ben-Shahar, T. (2007). *Happier.* New York, NY: McGraw-Hill.

Borgonovi, F. (2008). Doing well by doing good: The relationship between formal volunteering and self-reported health and happiness. *Social Science and Medicine, 66,* 2321-2334.

Brickman, P., Coates, D., & Janoff-Bulman, R. (1978). Lottery winners and accident victims: Is happiness relative? *Journal of Personality and Social Psychology, 36,* 917-927.

Brown, K.W., & Ryan, R. (2003). The benefits of being present: Mindfulness and its role in psychological well-being. *Journal of Personality and Social Psychology, 84,* 822-848.

Bryant, F., & Veroff, J. (2007). *Savouring: A new model of positive experience.* Mahwah, NJ: Erlbaum.

Burns, D. (2020). *Feeling great: The revolutionary new treatment for depression and anxiety.* Eau Claire, WI: PESI Publishing and Media.

Carr, A. (2019). Savouring and flow. In A. Carr (Ed.), *Positive psychology and you: A self-development guide* (pp. 119-142). London, UK: Routledge.

Carruthers, C., & Hood, C. (2002). Coping skills for individuals with alcoholism. *Therapeutic Recreation Journal, 36,* 154-171.

Carruthers, C., & Hood, C. (2004). The power of the positive: Leisure and well-being. *Therapeutic Recreation Journal, 38,* 225-245.

Carruthers, C., & Hood, C. (2005). Research update: The power of positive psychology. *Parks and Recreation, 40,* 30-38.

Carruthers, C., & Hood, C. (2007). Building a life of meaning through therapeutic recreation: The leisure and well-being model, part I. *Therapeutic Recreation Journal, 41,* 276-297.

Carver, C., & Scheier, M. (2002). Optimism. In C. Snyder & S. Lopez (Eds.), *Handbook of positive psychology* (pp. 231-256). New York, NY: Oxford University Press.

Centers for Disease Control and Prevention. (2018). *Well-being concepts.* Retrieved from www.cdc.gov/hrqol/wellbeing.htm#three

Chiesa, A., & Serretti, A. (2009). Mindfulness-based stress reduction for stress management in healthy people: A review and meta-analysis. *The Journal of Alternative and Complementary Medicine, 15,* 593-600.

Chirkov, V., Ryan, R., & Sheldon, K. (2011). *Human autonomy in cross-cultural context: Perspectives on the psychology of agency, freedom, and well-being.* New York, NY: Springer.

Csikszentmihalyi, M. (1990). *Flow: The psychology of optimal experience.* New York, NY: Harper & Row.

Csikszentmihalyi, M. (2014). Toward a psychology of optimal experience. In *Flow and the foundations of positive psychology* (pp. 209-226). Berlin, Germany: Springer. doi:10.1007/978-94-017-9088-8_14

Curtis, J.E. (1988). Purple recreation. *Society of Park and Recreation Educators Annual on Education, 3,* 73-77.

Davis, D., & Hayes, J. (2011). What are the benefits of mindfulness? A practice review of psychotherapy-related research. *Psychotherapy, 48,* 198-185.

Davis, M., Eshelman, E., & McKay, M. (2019). *The relaxation and stress reduction workbook* (7th ed.). Oakland, CA: New Harbinger.

Disabato, D., Goodman, F., Kashdan, T., Short, J., & Jarden, A. (2016). Different types of well-being? A cross-cultural examination of hedonic and eudaimonic well-being. *Psychological Assessment, 28*(5), 471-482.

Dodge, R., Daly, A., Huyton, J., & Sanders, L. (2012). The challenges of defining well-being. *International Journal of Wellbeing, 2,* 222-235.

Duerden, M., Widmer, M., Taniguchi, S., & McCoy, K. (2009). Adventures in identity development: The impact of adventure recreation on adolescent identity development. *Identity: An International Journal of Theory and Research, 9,* 341-359.

Elkington, S. (2011). What is it to take the flow of leisure seriously. *Leisure/Loisir, 35,* 253-282.

Elkington, S., & Stebbins, R. (2014). *The serious leisure perspective: An introduction.* New York, NY: Routledge.

Fava, G., & Ruini, C. (2003). Development and characteristics of a well-being enhancing psychotherapeutic strategy: Well-being therapy. *Journal of Behavioral Therapy and Experimental Psychology, 34,* 45-63.

Fenton, L. (2018). "You can see their minds grow": Identity development of LCBTQ youth at a residential wilderness camp. *Leisure/Loisir, 42,* 347-361.

Fredrickson, B. (2000). Cultivating positive emotions to optimize health and well-being. *Prevention and Treatment, 3,* Article 0001a. Retrieved from http://journals.apa.org/prevention/volume3/pre0030001a.html

Fredrickson, B. (2009). *Positivity.* New York, NY: Crown Publishers.

Fredrickson, B. (2013). *Love 2.0: How our supreme emotion affects we feel, think, do, and become.* New York, NY: Hudson Street Press.

Fredrickson, B., Coffey, K., Pek, J., Cohn, M., & Finkel, S. (2008). Open hearts build lives: Positive emotion, induced through loving-kindness meditation, build consequential personal resources. *Journal of Personality and Social Psychology, 95,* 1045-1062.

Freire, T., Tavares, D., Silva, E., & Teixeira, A. (2016). Flow, leisure and positive youth development. In L. Harmat, F. Anderson, F. Ullen, J. Wright, & G. Sadlo (Eds.), *Flow experience: Empirical research and applications* (pp. 163-178). Dordrecht, Netherlands: Springer.

Frydenberg, E. (2002). Beyond coping: Some paradigms to consider. In E. Frydenberg (Ed.), *Beyond coping: Meeting goals, visions, and challenges* (pp. 1-18). New York, NY: Oxford University Press.

Garland, E., & Howard, M. (2013). Mindfulness-oriented recovery enhancement reduces pain attentional bias in chronic pain patients. *Psychotherapy and Psychosomatics, 82,* 311-318.

Goldstein, J. (2005). Desire, delusion, and DVD's. In S. Kaza (Ed.), *Hooked: Buddhist writings on greed, desire, and the urge to consume* (pp. 17-26). Boston, MA: Shambhala.

Gruszczynska, E. (2013). State affect and emotion-focused coping: Examining correlated change and causality. *Anxiety, Stress, & Coping, 26*(1), 103-120.

Gustavson, K., Roysamb, E., Borren, I., Torvik, F., & Karevold, E. (2016). Life satisfaction in close relationships: Findings from a longitudinal study. *Journal of Happiness Studies, 17,* 1293-1311.

Harter, S. (2002). Authenticity. In C.R. Snyder & S.J. Lopez (Eds.), *Handbook of positive psychology* (pp. 382-394). New York, NY: Oxford University Press.

Hartig, T., Mitchell, R., DeVries, S., & Frumkin, H. (2014). Nature and health. *Annual Review of Public Health, 35,* 207-228.

Hartman, C., & Anderson, D. (2018). Psychosocial identity development and perception of free time among college-attending emerging adults. *Leisure Sciences, 19,* 1-19.

Hixon, E. (2013). Developing young people's sense of self and place through sport. *Annals of Leisure Research, 16,* 3-15.

Hood, C., & Carruthers, C. (2002). Coping skills theory as an underlying framework for therapeutic recreation services. *Therapeutic Recreation Journal, 36,* 154-161.

Hood, C., & Carruthers, C. (2007). Enhancing leisure experience and developing resources: The leisure and well-being model, part II. *Therapeutic Recreation Journal, 41,* 298-325.

Hood, C., & Carruthers, C. (2012). Therapeutic recreation: Enhancing well-being through leisure. In T. Freire (Ed.), *Positive leisure science* (pp. 121-140). New York, NY: Springer.

Hutchinson, S., Bland, A., & Kleiber, D. (2008). Leisure and stress-coping: Implications for therapeutic recreation practice. *Therapeutic Recreation Journal, 42,* 9-23.

Hutchinson, S., & Kleiber, D. (2005). Gifts of the ordinary: Casual leisure's contributions to health and well-being. *World Leisure Journal, 47,* 2-16.

Iwasaki, Y. (2008). Pathways to meaning-making through leisure-like pursuits in global contexts. *Journal of Leisure Research, 40,* 231-249.

Iwasaki, Y., & Mannell, R. (2000). Hierarchical dimensions of leisure stress coping. *Leisure Sciences, 22,* 163-181.

Jongman-Sereno, K., & Leary, M. (2018). The enigma of being yourself: A critical examination of the concept of authenticity. *Review of General Psychology.* Advance online publication. http://dx.doi.org/10.1037/gpr0000157

Kabat-Zinn, J. (1990). *Full catastrophe living: Using the wisdom of your body and mind to face stress, pain, and illness.* New York, NY: Bantam Doubleday.

Kahana, E., Bhatta, T., Lovegreen, L., Kahana, B., & Midlarsky, E. (2013). Altruism, helping, and volunteering: Pathways to well-being in late life. *Journal of Aging and Health, 25,* 159-187.

Kleiber, D., Hutchinson, S., & Williams, R. (2002). Leisure as a resource in transcending negative life events: Self-protection, self-restoration, and personal transformation. *Leisure Sciences, 24,* 219-235.

Kleiber, D., & McGuire, F. (2016). *Leisure and human development.* Champaign, IL: Sagamore Venture.

Klein, S. (2006). *The science of happiness: How our brains make us happy—and what we can do to get happier.* New York, NY: Avalon.

Krygier, J., Heathers, J., Shahrestani, S., Abbott, M., Gross, J., & Kemp, A. (2013). Mindfulness meditation, well-being, and heart rate variability: A preliminary investigation into the impact of intensive Vipassana meditation. *International Journal of Psychophysiology, 89,* 305-313.

Kubzansky, L., Huffman, J., Boehm, J., Hernandez, R., Kim, E., Koga, H., . . . Labarthe, D. (2018). Positive psychological well-being and cardiovascular disease. *Journal of the American College of Cardiology, 72,* 1382-1396.

Layard, R. (2005). *Happiness: Lessons from a new science.* New York, NY: Penguin Press.

Layland, E., Hill, B., & Nelson, L. (2019). Freedom to explore the self: How emerging adults use leisure to develop identity. *The Journal of Positive Psychology, 13,* 78-91.

Lazarus, R., & Folkman, S. (1984). *Stress, appraisal, and coping.* New York, NY: McGraw-Hill.

Livingstone, K., & Srivastava, S. (2012). Up-regulating positive emotions in everyday life: Strategies, individual differences, and associations with positive emotion and well-being. *Journal of Research in Personality, 46,* 504-516.

Lykken, D. (1999). *Happiness: The nature and nurture of joy and contentment.* New York, NY: St. Martin's Griffin.

Lykken, D., & Tellegen, A. (1996). Happiness is a stochastic phenomenon. *Psychological Science, 7,* 186-189.

Lyubomirsky, S. (2008). *The how of happiness: A scientific approach to getting the life you want.* New York, NY: Penguin Press.

Lyubomirsky, S. (2012). Hedonic adaptation to positive and negative experiences. In S. Folkman (Ed.), *The Oxford handbook of stress, health, and coping.* New York, NY: Oxford University Press. doi:10.1093/oxfordhb/9780195375343.001.0001

Marcia, J. (1966). Development and validation of ego-identity status. *Journal of Personality and Social Psychology, 5,* 551-558.

Marcia, J., & Josselson, R. (2012). Eriksonian personality research and its implications for psychotherapy. *Journal of Personality, 81,* 617-629.

Morrow-Howell, N., Lee, Y., McCrary, S., McBride, A., Anderson, L., & Prohaska, T. (2014). Volunteering as a pathway to productive ad social engagement among older adults. *Health Education and Behavior, 41,* 845-902.

Nettle, D. (2005). *Happiness.* New York, NY: Oxford University Press.

Neulinger, J. (1981). *The psychology of leisure.* Springfield, IL: Charles C. Thomas.

Olson, E. (2006). *Personal development and discovery through leisure.* Dubuque, IA: Kendall/Hunt.

Parsons, H., Houge Mackenzie, S., Filep, S., & Brymer, E. (2019). Subjective well-being and leisure. In W. Leal Filho, T. Wall, A. Azul, L. Brandi, & P. Ozuyar (Eds.), *Good health and well-being.* Cham, Switzerland: Springer. doi:10.1007/978-3-319-69627-0-8-1

Phillips, C. (2017). Lifestyle modulators of neuroplasticity: How physical activity, mental engagement, and diet promote cognitive health during aging. *Neural Plasticity.* doi:10.1155/2017/3589271

Pillavin, J., & Siegl, E. (2016). Health benefits of volunteering in the Wisconsin Longitudinal Study. *Journal of Health and Social Behavior, 48,* 450-464.

Pulla, V., & Francis, A. (2014). A strengths approach to mental health. In A. Francis (Ed.), *Social work in mental health: Context and theories for practice* (pp. 165-182). New Delhi, India: Sage.

Quoidbach, J., Berry, E., Hansenne, M., & Mikolajczak, M. (2010). Positive emotion regulation and well-being: Comparing the impact of eight savoring and dampening strategies. *Personality and Individual Differences, 49,* 368-373.

Riva, E., Rainisio, N., & Boffi, M. (2014). Positive change in clinical settings: Flow experience in psychodynamic therapies. In P. Inghilleri, G. Riva, & E. Riva (Eds.), *Enabling positive change: Flow and complexity in daily experience* (pp. 74-90). Warsaw, Poland: De Gruyter.

Riva, G. (2014). Phenomenology of positive change: Personal growth. In P. Inghilleri, G. Riva, & E. Riva (Eds.), *Enabling positive change: Flow and complexity in daily experience* (pp. 18-38). Warsaw, Poland: De Gruyter.

Ruini, C. (2017). *Positive psychology in the clinical domains: Research and practice.* Cham, Switzerland: Springer Science.

Russell, R. (2020). *Pastimes: The context of contemporary leisure* (7th ed.). Champaign, IL: Sagamore Venture.

Ryan, R., & Deci, E. (2010). A self-determination perspective on social, institutional, cultural, and economic supports for autonomy and their importance for well-being. In V. Chirkov, R. Ryan, & K. Sheldon (Eds.), *Human autonomy in cross-cultural context* (pp. 45-64). New York, NY: Springer.

Salces-Cubero, I., Ramirez-Fernandez, E., & Ortega-Martinez, R. (2019). Strengths in older adults: Differential effect of savoring, gratitude and optimism on well-being. *Aging and Mental Health, 23,* 1017-1024.

Schlegel, R., & Hicks, J. (2011). The true self and psychological health: Emerging evidence and future directions. *Social and Personality Psychology Compass, 5/12,* 989-1003.

Schlegel, R., Hirsch, K., & Smith, C. (2013). The importance of who you really are: The role of the true self in eudaimonia. In A. Waterman (Ed.), *The best within us: Positive psychology perspectives on eudaimonia* (pp. 207-226). Washington, DC: APA. doi:10.1037/14092-011

Seligman, M. (2002). *Authentic happiness.* New York, NY: Free Press.

Seligman, M. (2011). *Flourish.* New York, NY: Free Press.

Seligman, M. (2019). Positive psychology: A personal history. *Annual Review of Clinical Psychology, 15,* 1-23.

Selye, H. (1975). Confusion and controversy in the stress field. *Journal of Human Stress, 1,* 37-44.

Shah, H., & Marks, N. (2004). *A well-being manifesto for a flourishing society.* London, UK: The New Economics Foundation.

Sheldon, K., & Lyubomirsky, S. (2004). Achieving sustainable new happiness: Prospects, practices, and prescriptions. In P. Linley & S. Joseph (Eds.), *Positive psychology in practice* (pp. 127-145). Hoboken, NJ: Wiley.

Sirgy, M., Uysal, M., & Kruger, S. (2017). Towards a benefits theory of leisure-being. *Applied Research Quarterly, 12,* 205-228.

Smith, J., Harrison, P., Kurtz, J., & Bryant, F. (2014). Nurturing the capacity to savor: Interventions to enhance the enjoyment of positive experiences. In A. Parks & S. Schueller (Eds.), *The Wiley Blackwell handbook of positive psychological interventions* (pp. 42-65). Oxford, UK: John Wiley & Sons.

Smith, J., & Hollinger-Smith, L. (2015). Savoring, resilience, and psychological well-being in older adults. *Aging and Mental Health, 19*, 192-200.

Srivastava, K. (2011). Positive mental health and its relationship with resilience. *Industrial Psychology Journal, 20*, 75-76.

Stebbins, R. (2015). *Leisure and positive psychology: Linking activities with positiveness.* New York, NY: Palgrave Macmillan.

Stebbins, R. (2018). Leisure and the positive psychological states. *The Journal of Positive Psychology, 13*(1), 8-17. doi: 10.1080/17439760.2017.1374444

Taylor, T.E. (2015). Towards consensus on well-being. In J. Søraker, J.W. Van der Rijt, J. de Boer, P.H. Wong, & P. Brey (Eds.), *Well-being in contemporary society* (pp. 1-16). Cham, Switzerland: Springer.

Thompson, N. (2018). *Mental health and well-being: Alternatives to the medical model.* New York, NY: Routledge.

Townsend, M., Gibbs, L., Macfarlane, S., Block, K., Staiger, P., Gold, L., . . . Long, C. (2014). Volunteering in a school kitchen garden program: Cooking up confidence, capabilities and connections. *Voluntas, 25*, 225-247.

Vaillant, G. (2012). Positive mental health: Is there a cross-cultural definition? *World Psychiatry, 11*, 93-99.

Vitterso, J. (2013). Functional well-being: Happiness as feelings, evaluations, and functioning. In I. Boniwell, S. David, & A. Ayers (Eds.), *Oxford Handbook of Happiness* (pp. 1-22). Oxford, UK: Oxford University Press.

Vollestad, J., Nielson, M., & Nielson, G. (2012). Mindfulness- and acceptance-based interventions for anxiety disorders: A systematic review and meta-analysis. *British Journal of Clinical Psychology, 51*, 239-260.

Walker, G., Kleiber, D., & Mannell, R. (2019). *A social psychology of leisure* (3rd ed.). Champaign, IL: Sagamore-Venture.

Chapter 6

Deaux, G. (1969). *The Black Death 1347.* New York, NY: Weybright and Talley.

deLisle, L. (2009). *Creating special events.* Champaign, IL: Sagamore Press.

Godbey, G. (1997). *Leisure and leisure services in the 21st century.* State College, PA: Venture.

McClean, D., Hurd, A., & Rogers, N. (2005). *Kraus' recreation and leisure in modern society.* Sudbury, MA: Jones & Bartlett Publishers.

Pieper, J. (1963). *Leisure: The basis of culture.* New York, NY: Random House.

Pieper, J. (1999). *In tune with the world: A theory of festivity.* South Bend, IN: St. Augustine Press.

Shivers, J., & deLisle, L. (1997). *The story of leisure.* Champaign, IL: Human Kinetics.

Chapter 7

Adorno, T.W. (1941). On popular music. *Studies in Philosophy and Social Science, 9*(1), 17-48.

Bailey, P. (2014). *Leisure and class in Victorian England: Rational recreation and the contest for control, 1830-1885.* London, UK: Routledge.

Barker, M., & Petley, J. (Eds.). (1997). *Ill effects: The media/violence debate.* London, UK: Routledge.

Benjamin, W. (1968). The work of art in the age of mechanical reproduction. In H. Arendt (Ed.), *Illuminations* (pp. 217-252). London, UK: Pimlico Press. (Original work published 1936)

Borden, I.M. (2001). *Skateboarding, space and the city: Architecture and the body.* Oxford, UK: Berg.

Bull, M. (2005). No dead air! The iPod and the culture of mobile listening. *Leisure Studies, 24*(4), 343-355.

Cambridge Dictionary. (2020). *Cambridge dictionary.* Retrieved from https://dictionary.cambridge.org/dictionary/english/contemporary

Coalter, F. (2000). Public and commercial leisure provision: Active citizens and passive consumers? *Leisure Studies, 19*(3), 163-181.

Comte, A. (2009). *A general view of positivism* (J. H. Bridges, Trans.). Cambridge, UK: Cambridge University Press. (Original work published 1865)

Delamere, F.M., & Shaw, S.M. (2008). "They see it as a guy's game": The politics of gender in digital games. *Leisure/Loisir, 32*(2), 279-302.

D'Orazio, D. (2020). Skateboarding's Olympic moment: The gendered contours of sportification. *Journal of Sport and Social Issues.* https://doi.org/10.1177/0193723520928595

du Gay, P., Hall, S., Janes, L., Madsen, A., Mackay, H., & Negus, K. (1997). *Doing cultural studies: The story of the Sony Walkman.* London, UK: Sage.

Durkheim, É. (1984). *The division of labour in society.* Houndmills, UK: Macmillan. (Original work published 1893)

Giddens, A. (1984). *The constitution of society: Outline of the theory of structuration.* Berkeley: University of California Press.

Giddens, A., & Sutton, P. (2017). *Essential concepts in sociology.* New York, NY: John Wiley & Sons.

Gough, C. (2020). *eSports market—statistics & facts.* Retrieved from www.statista.com/topics/3121/esports-market

Gough, C. (2021). *Worldwide esports audience size 2021.* Retrieved from www.statista.com/statistics/1109956/global-esports-audience

Grindstaff, L. (2008). Culture and popular culture: A case for sociology. *The Annals of the American Academy of Political and Social Science, 619*(1), 206-222.

Hall, S. (1997). *Representation: Cultural representations and signifying practices*. London, UK: Sage.

Hamilton, P. (1997). Representing the social: France and Frenchness in post-war humanist photography. In S. Hall (Ed.), *Representation: Cultural representations and signifying practices* (pp. 75-150). London, UK: Sage.

Hartman, A. (2019). *A war for the soul of America: A history of the culture wars*. Chicago, IL: University of Chicago Press.

Hise, B. (2010). *Swinging away: How cricket and baseball connect*. London, UK: Scala Books.

Horkheimer, M. (Ed.). (1937). *Traditional and critical theory: Selected essays* (M.J. O'Connell, Trans.). New York, NY: Herder and Herder.

Hunter, J.D. (1991). *Culture wars: The struggle to define America*. New York, NY: Basic Books.

Jenkins, H. (2012). *Textual poachers: Television fans and participatory cultures*. London, UK: Routledge.

Kemp, S. (2020). *Digital 2020; July global statshot*. Retrieved from https://datareportal.com/reports/digital-2020-july-global-statshot

Kuhn, T. (1962). *The structure of scientific revolutions*. Chicago, IL: University of Chicago Press.

Lamerichs, N. (2011). Stranger than fiction: Fan identity in cosplay. *Transformative Works and Cultures, 7*(3), 56-72.

Lashua, B. (2011). Between the devil and the deep blue sea: Music and leisure in an era of pop idols and digital pirates. In P. Bramham & S. Wagg (Eds.), *The new politics of leisure and pleasure* (pp. 225-244). Basingstoke, UK: Palgrave Macmillan.

Lashua, B. (2016). Recreation, development and youth. In E.K. Sharpe, H. Mair, & F. Yuen (Eds.), *Community development: Applications for leisure* (pp. 151-163). Urbana, IL: Sagamore Publishing.

Lashua, B. (2019). *Popular music, popular myth and cultural heritage in Cleveland: The moondog, the buzzard, and the battle for the Rock and Roll Hall of Fame*. Bingley, UK: Emerald Publishing.

Lyotard, J.F. (1984). *The postmodern condition: A report on knowledge* (G. Bennington & B. Massumi, Trans.). Minneapolis: University of Minnesota Press.

Major League Baseball (2019, September 30). *2019 MLB season generates increases in consumption and youth participation*. Retrieved form www.mlb.com/press-release/press-release-2019-mlb-season-generates-increases-in-consumption-and-youth-parti

Mitchell, C., & Reid-Walsh, J. (2002). *Researching children's popular culture: The cultural spaces of childhood*. London, UK: Routledge.

Mortensen, T.E. (2018). Anger, fear, and games: The long event of #GamerGate. *Games and Culture, 13*(8), 787-806.

Parsons, T. (1937). *The structure of social action*. New York, NY: The Free Press.

Peterson, R. A. (1990). Why 1955? Explaining the advent of rock music. *Popular Music, 9*(1), 97-116.

Rheingold, H. (1993). *The virtual community: Homesteading on the electronic frontier*. New York, NY: Addison-Wesley.

Roberts, K. (2006). *Leisure in contemporary society*. Wallingford, UK: CABI Publishing.

Sharpe, E.K. (2017). Against limits: A post-structural theorizing of resistance in leisure. In K. Spracklen, B. Lashua, E.K. Sharpe, & S. Swain (Eds.), *The Palgrave handbook of leisure theory* (pp. 911-926). Basingstoke, UK: Palgrave Macmillan.

Sharpe, E.K., & Lashua, B. (2008). Introduction to the special issue: Tuning in to popular leisure. *Leisure/Loisir, 32*(2), 245-258.

Skeldon, G. (2017). The Frankfurt School, leisure and consumption. In K. Spracklen, B. Lashua, E.K. Sharpe, & S. Swain (Eds.), *The Palgrave handbook of leisure theory* (pp. 507-522). Basingstoke, UK: Palgrave.

Stolley, K.S. (2005). *The basics of sociology*. Westport, CT: Greenwood Publishing Group.

Storey, J. (2018). *Cultural theory and popular culture: An introduction* (8th ed.). Harlow, UK: Pearson Longman.

Stormann, W. F. (1991). The ideology of the American urban parks and recreation movement: Past and future. *Leisure Sciences, 13*(2), 137-151.

Thompson, B.Y. (2019). Women covered in ink: Tattoo collecting as serious leisure. *International Journal of the Sociology of Leisure, 2*(3), 285-299.

Thorpe, H., & Wheaton, B. (2011). "Generation X Games," action sports and the Olympic movement: Understanding the cultural politics of incorporation. *Sociology, 45*(5), 830-847.

Wheaton, B. (Ed.). (2004). *Understanding lifestyle sport: Consumption, identity and difference*. London, UK: Routledge.

Williams, R. (1958). Culture is ordinary. In N. McKenzie (Ed.), *Convictions* (pp. 72-92). London, UK: MacGibbon and Kee.

Williams, R. (1960). *Culture and society: 1780-1950*. New York, NY: Anchor Books.

Williams, R. (1983). *Keywords*. Oxford, UK: Oxford University Press.

Witkin, R.W. (2000). Why did Adorno "hate" jazz? *Sociological Theory, 18*(1), 145-170.

Chapter 8

Agate, J.R., Zabriskie, R.B., Agate, S.T., & Poff, R. (2009). Family leisure satisfaction and satisfaction with family life. *Journal of Leisure Research, 41*(2), 205-223.

Aron, A., & Aron, E.N. (1986). *Love and the expansion of self: Understanding attraction and satisfaction* (pp. x, 172). New York, NY: Hemisphere Publishing Corp/Harper & Row Publishers.

Bialik, K. (2018, December 3). *Americans unhappy with family, social or financial life are more likely to say they feel lonely*. Retrieved from www.pewresearch.org/fact-tank/2018/12/03/americans-unhappy-with-family-social-or-financial-life-are-more-likely-to-say-they-feel-lonely

Bogenschneider, K., Little, O.M., Ooms, T., Benning, S., Cadigan, K., & Corbett, T. (2012). The family impact lens: A family-focused, evidence-informed approach to policy and practice. *Family Relations, 61*(3), 514-531. Retrieved from https://doi.org/10.1111/j.1741-3729.2012.00704.x

Broderick, C.B. (1993). *Understanding family process: Basics of family systems theory*. Thousand Oaks, CA: Sage Publications.

Cigna. (2018). *Cigna U.S. loneliness index: Survey of 20,000 Americans examining behaviors driving loneliness in the United States*. Retrieved from www.cigna.com/assets/docs/newsroom/loneliness-survey-2018-full-report.pdf

Csikszentmihalyi, M. (1990). *Flow: The psyhchology of optimal experience*. New York, NY: Harper & Row.

Dotti Sani, G.M., & Treas, J. (2016). Emotional gradients in parents' child-care time across countries, 1965-2012. *Journal of Marriage and Family, 78*, 1083-1096.

Genadek, K.R., Flood, S.M., & Roman, J.G. (2016). Trends in spouses' shared time in the United States, 1965-2012. *Demography, 53*(6), 1801-1820. Retrieved from https://doi.org/10.1007/s13524-016-0512-8

Grad, F.P. (2002). The preamble of the constitution of the World Health Organization. *Bulletin of the World Health Organization, 4*.

Heath, C., & Heath, D. (2017). *The power of moments*. New York, NY: Simon & Schuster.

Hill, M.S. (1988). Marital stability and spouses' shared time: A multidisciplinary hypothesis. *Journal of Family Issues, 9*(4), 427-451.

Hodge, C.J., Bocarro, J.N., Henderson, K.A., Zabriskie, R., Parcel, T.L., & Kanters, M.A. (2015). Family leisure: An integrative review of research from select journals. *Journal of Leisure Research, 47*(5), 577-600. Retrieved from https://doi.org/10.18666/jlr-2015-v47-i5-5705

Hodge, C.J., Duerden, M.D., Layland, E.K., Lacanienta, A., Goates, M.C., & Niu, X.M. (2017). The association between family leisure and family quality of life: A meta-analysis of data from parents and adolescents. *Journal of Family Theory & Review, 9*(3), 328-346. Retrieved from https://doi.org/10.1111/jftr.12202

Holt-Lunstad, J., Robles, T., & Sbarra, D.A. (2017). Advancing social connection as a public health priority in the United States. *The American Psychologist, 72*(6), 517-530. Retrieved from https://doi.org/10.1037/amp0000103

Holt-Lunstad, J., Smith, T.B., Baker, M., Harris, T., & Stephenson, D. (2015). Loneliness and social isolation as risk factors for mortality: A meta-analytic review. *Perspectives on Psychological Science, 10*(2), 227-237.

Kleiber, D.A., Walker, G.J., & Mannell, R.C. (2011). *A social psychology of leisure* (2nd ed.). State College, PA: Venture Publication.

Livingston, G., & Parker, K. (2019, June 19). *8 facts about American dads*. Retrieved from www.pewresearch.org/fact-tank/2019/06/12/fathers-day-facts

Melton, K.K. (2017). Family activity model: Crossroads of activity environment and family interactions in family leisure. *Leisure Sciences, 39*(5), 457-473. Retrieved from https://doi.org/10.1080/01490400.2017.1333056

Melton, K.K., Hodge, C.J., & Duerden, M.D. (2020). Ecology of family experiences: Contextualizing family leisure for human development & family relations. *Journal of Leisure Research*. Retrieved from https://doi.org/10.1080/00222216.2020.1802374

Melton, K.K., Hodge, C.J., McAninch, N., & Olschewski, E. (2018). Family matters: Supporting positive youth development through family programming. In P.A. Witt & L.L. Caldwell (Eds.), *Youth development: Principles and practices in out-of-school time settings* (2nd ed.). State College, PA: Sagamore Venture.

Melton, K. K., Larson, M., & Boccia, M. L. (2019). Examining couple recreation and oxytocin via the Ecology of Family Experiences Framework: Oxytocin in couple leisure. *Journal of Marriage and Family*. Retrieved from https://doi.org/10.1111/jomf.12556

Mintz, S., & Kellogg, S. (1988). *Domestic revolutions: A social history of American family life*. New York, NY: Free Press.

Moras, A., Shehan, C., & Berardo, F.M. (2018). African American families: Historical and contemporary forces shaping family life and studies. In P. Batur & J.R. Feagin (Eds.), *Handbook of the sociology of racial and ethnic relations* (pp. 91-107). New York, NY: Springer International Publishing. Retrieved from https://doi.org/10.1007/978-3-319-76757-4_6

Orthner, D.K. (1975). Leisure activity patterns and marital satisfaction over the marital career. *Journal of Marriage and the Family, 37*(1), 91-102. Retrieved from https://doi.org/10.2307/351033

Orthner, D.K., Barnett-Morris, L., & Mancini, J.A. (1994). Leisure and family over the life cycle. In L.L. Abate (Ed.), *Handbook of developmental family psychology and psychopathology* (pp. 176-201). Hoboken, NJ: Wiley.

Orthner, D.K., & Mancini, J.A. (1991). Benefits of leisure for family bonding. In B.L. Driver, P.J. Brown, & G.L. Peterson (Eds.), *Benefits of leisure* (pp. 289-301). State College, PA: Venture.

Pasley, K., & Petren, R. E. (2015). Family structure. *Encyclopedia of family studies*. Retrieved from https://doi.org/10.1002/9781119085621.wbefs016

Reiss, K.J. (2012). *Be a changemaster: 12 coaching strategies for leading professional and personal change*. New York, NY: Sage.

Spinelli, M., Lionetti, F., Pastore, M., & Fasolo, M. (2020). Parents' stress and children's psychological problems in families facing the COVID-19 outbreak in Italy. *Frontiers in Psychology, 11*. Retrieved from https://doi.org/10.3389/fpsyg.2020.01713

Waldinger, R. (2015, November). *Robert Waldinger: What makes a good life? Lessons from the longest study on happiness*. Retrieved March 11, 2020, from www.ted.com/talks/robert_waldinger_what_makes_a_good_life_lessons_from_the_longest_study_on_happiness

World Health Organization (WHO). (n.d.). Constitution. Retrieved August 18, 2021, from www.who.int/about/governance/constitution

Zabriskie, R.B., & McCormick, B.P. (2001). The influences of family leisure patterns on perceptions of family functioning. *Family Relations, 50*(3), 281-289.

Chapter 9

American Bureau of Time Use Statistics (2020). *American Time Use Survey-2019 results.* Retrieved from https://www.bls.gov/news.release/pdf/atus.pdf

Andrejevic, M. (2002). The kinder, gentler gaze of Big Brother: Reality TV in the era of digital capitalism. *New Media & Society, 4*(2), 251-270. Retrieved from https://doi.org/10.1177/14614440222226361

Berbary, L., & Richmond, L. (2011). The dangerous deconstruction of gender: Narrative inquiry of masculinities in a popular children's book. *Annals of Leisure Research, 14*(2-3), 194-208. Retrieved from http://dx.doi.org/10.1080/11745398.2011.615715

Black Mirror. (2011). Retrieved from https://www.netflix.com/title/70264888

boyd, d. (2014). *It's complicated: The social lives of networked teens.* New Haven, CT: Yale University Press.

Brown, J. (2018, January 4). *Is social media bad for you? The evidence and the unknowns.* Retrieved from www.bbc.com/future/article/20180104-is-social-media-bad-for-you-the-evidence-and-the-unknowns

Butler, J. (1990). *Gender trouble: Feminism and the subversion of identity.* London, UK: Routledge.

Clayton, R.B., Leshner, G., & Almond, A. (2015). The extended iSelf: The impact of iPhone separation on cognition, emotion, and physiology. *Journal of Computer-Mediated Communication, 20,* 119-135.

Creemers, R. (2015, April 25). *Planning outline for the creation of a social credit system (2014-2020).* Retrieved from https://chinacopyrightandmedia.wordpress.com/2014/06/14/planning-outline-for-the-construction-of-a-social-credit-system-2014-2020/

Foucault, M. (1977). *Discipline & punish: The birth of the prison* (A. Sheridan, Trans.). New York, NY: Random House Inc. (Original work published 1975)

Glover, T. (2018). All the lonely people: Social isolation and the promise and pitfalls of leisure. *Leisure Sciences, 40*(1-2) 25-35.

Hardt, M., & Negri, A. (2004). *Multitude: War and democracy in the age of empire.* New York, NY: Penguin Press.

Holt, A. (2011). *Deep involvement in the* World of Warcraft: *An "elfnography"* (Doctoral dissertation). University of Georgia, Atlanta.

Jabr, F. (2019, October 22). Can you really be addicted to video games? *The New York Times Magazine.* Retrieved from www.nytimes.com/2019/10/22/magazine/can-you-really-be-addicted-to-video-games.html

Jenkins, H., Ito, M., & boyd, d. (2016). *Participatory culture in a networked era: A conversation on youth, learning, commerce, and politics.* Cambridge, UK: Polity Press.

Kobie, N. (2019, June 7). The complicated truth about China's social credit system. *Wired.* Retrieved from www.wired.co.uk/article/china-social-credit-system-explained

Kumm, B.E. (2013). Finding healing through songwriting: A song for Nicolette. *International Journal of Community Music, 6*(2), 205-217.

Kumm, B., Holt, M., & Kleiber, D.A. (2016). Technology, leisure, and human development. In D.A. Kleiber & F.A. McGuire (Eds.), *Leisure and human development* (pp. 161-186). Champaign, IL.: Sagamore Venture.

Kumm, B.E., & Johnson, C.W. (2014). Becoming-shaman, becoming-Sherpa, becoming-healer: Leisure as becoming. *Leisure/Loisir, 38*(2), 102-118.

Layland, E.K., Stone, G.A., Mueller, J.T., & Hodge, C.J. (2018). Injustice in mobile leisure: A conceptual exploration of *Pokémon Go. Leisure Sciences, 40*(4), 288-306. Retrieved from https://doi.org/10.1080/01490400.2018.1426064

Lin, L.Y., Sidani, J.E., Shensa, A., Radovic, A., Miller, E., Colditz, J.B., . . . Primack, B.A. (2016). Association between social media use and depression among U.S. young adults. *Depression and Anxiety, 33*(4), 323-331. Retrieved from https://doi.org/10.1002/da.22466

Louv, R. (2005). *Last child in the woods.* New York, NY: Workman Publishing Company.

Lupton, D. (2015). *Digital sociology.* New York, NY: Routledge.

Media Technology Monitor. (2017, March 21). *Internet use in the home: An analysis of the English language market.* Retrieved from https://mtm-otm.ca/Download.ashx?req=2-1-1

Mulhall, L. (Producer). (2015, August 20). Dating in the digital age [Radio broadcast]. *Late night woman's hour.* London, England: BBC. Retrieved from www.bbc.co.uk/programmes/b065xchn

Nimrod, G. (2014). The benefits of and constraints to participation in seniors' online communities. *Leisure Studies, 33*(3), 247-266.

Outley, C., Bowen, S., & Pinckney, H. (2020). Laughing while Black: Resistance, coping and the use of humor as a pandemic pastime among Blacks. *Leisure Sciences.* Advance online publication. Retrieved from https://doi.org/10.1080/01490400.2020.1774449

Parry, D.C., Glover, T.D., Mulcahy, C.M. (2013). From "stroller-stalker" to "momancer:" Courting friends through a social networking site for mothers. *Journal of Leisure Research, 45*(1), 23-46.

Pinckney, H. P., Mowatt, R.A., Outley, C., Brown, A., Floyd, M.F., & Black, K.L., (2018). Black spaces/White spaces: Black lives, leisure, and life politics. *Leisure Sciences, 40*(4), 267-287.

Price-Michelle, M. (2020, April 15). Are young people's social skills declining? *Psychology Today*. Retrieved from www .psychologytoday.com/us/blog/the-moment-youth/202004/ are-young-peoples-social-skills-declining

Redhead, S. (2016). Afterword: A new digital leisure studies for theoretical times. *Leisure Sciences, 35*(6), 827-834. Retrieved from http://dx.doi.org/10.1080/02614367.2016 .1231832

Rose, J., & Spencer, C. (2016). Immaterial labour in spaces of leisure: Producing biopolitical subjectivities through Facebook. *Leisure Studies, 35*(6), 809-826. doi:10.1080/02 614367.2015.1031271

Schultz, C.S., & McKeown, J.K.L. (2018). Introduction to the special issue: Toward "digital leisure studies." *Leisure Sciences: An Interdisciplinary Journal, 40*(4), 223-238.

Silk, M., Millington, B., Rich, E., & Bush, A. (2016). (Re-) thinking digital leisure. *Leisure Studies, 35*(6), 712-723.

Simmonds, C., McGivney, A., Reilly, P., Maffly, B., Wilkinson, T., Canon, G., . . . Whaley, M. (2018, November 20). *Crisis in our national parks: How tourists are loving nature to death*. Retrieved from www.theguardian.com/environment/2018/ nov/20/national-parks-america-overcrowding-crisis-tour- ism-visitation-solutions

Soucie, S.M.A., Parry, D.C., & Cousineau, L.S. (2018). What #MeToo can teach us about millennial mobilization, inter- sectionality, and men's accountability. In D.C. Parry (Ed.), *Feminisms in leisure studies: Advancing a fourth wave* (pp. 149-164). New York, NY: Routledge.

Spracklen, K. (2015). *Digital leisure, the Internet and popular culture*. London, UK: Palgrave Macmillan.

Valtchanov, B.L., & Parry, D.C. (2016). "I like my peeps:" Diversifying the net generation's digital leisure. *Leisure Sciences, 39*(4), 336-354.

Victoria State Government Education & Training. (2019). *Teach with digital technologies*. Retrieved from www.educa- tion.vic.gov.au/school/teachers/teachingresources/digital/ Pages/teach.aspx

Yildrim, C., & Correia, A. (2015). Exploring the dimen- sions of nomophobia: Development and validation of a self-reported questionnaire. *Computers in Human Behaviour, 49*, 130-137.

Chapter 10

Bears Ears Inter-Tribal Coalition. (2020). *About the coalition*. Retrieved from https://bearsearscoalition.org/about-the- coalition/

Berkes, F., Colding, J., & Folke, C. (2000). Rediscovery of traditional ecological knowledge as adaptive management. *Ecological applications, 10*(5), 1251-1262.

Bricker, K.S. (2016). Endless opportunities to effect positive change: Perspectives on tourism & travel. In K. Vaidya (Ed.), *Travel and tourism management for the curious: Why study travel and tourism management* (chapter 6). The Curious Academic Publishing.

Bricker K.S., Black, R., & Cottrell, S. (Eds.). (2012). *Sustain- able tourism & the millennium development goals: Effecting positive change*. Burlington, MA: Jones & Bartlett Learning.

Bonta, M., & Jordan, C., (2007). Diversifying the conservation movement. In E. Enderle (Ed.), *Diversity and the future of the U.S. environmental movement* (pp. 13-34). New Haven, CT: Yale School of Forestry and Environmental Studies.

Brown, W. (1971). *Islands of hope: Parks and recreation in environmental crisis*. Arlington, VA: National Recreation and Park Association.

Bushell, R., & Bricker, K.S. (2016). *Tourism in protected areas: Developing meaningful standards*. Journal of Tourism and Hospitality Research, 17(1), 106-120.

Chavez, D. (2000). Wilderness visitors in the 21st century: Diversity, day use, perceptions and preferences. *International Journal of Wilderness, 6*(2), 10-11.

Cronon, W. (1996). The trouble with wilderness: Or, getting back to the wrong nature. *Environmental History, 1*(1), 7-28.

Dunbar-Ortiz, R. (2014). *An Indigenous Peoples' history of the United States*. Boston, MA: Beacon Press.

Dustin, D., & McAvoy, L. (1980). "Hardining" national parks. *Environmental Ethics, 2*(1), 39-44.

Dustin, D., McAvoy, L., & Ogden, L. (2005). Land as legacy. *Parks & Recreation, 40*(5), 60-65.

Eisenberg, C., Anderson, C.L., Collingwood, A., Sissons, R., Dunn, C.J., Meigs, G.W., & Hibbs, D.E. (2019). Out of the ashes: Ecological resilience to extreme wildfire, prescribed burns, and indigenous burning in ecosystems. *Frontiers in Ecology and Evolution, 7*, 11-26.

Garcia, R. (2006). *Equal justice, democracy, and livability: Les- sons from the urban park movement*. FLAC Public Interest Law Seminar Series, PILL Roundtable, 30 June 2006. Los Angeles, CA: Center for Law in the Public Interest. Retrieved from www.flac.ie/download/pdf/pill1_rgarcia_urbanpark_ rndtbl_30jun06.pdf

Gillette, F. (2015). Occupy Burning Man. *Bloomberg Busi- nessweek, 4414*, 60-63.

Gobster, P. (2002). Managing urban parks for a racially and ethnically diverse clientele. *Leisure Sciences, 24*, 143-159.

Joyner, L., Lackey, N.Q, & Bricker, K. (2019). Community engagement: An appreciative inquiry case study with Theodore Roosevelt national park gateway communities. *Sustainability (Basel, Switzerland), 11*(24), 7147.

Kaplan, R. (2001). The nature of the view from home: Psycho- logical benefits. *Environment and Behavior, 33*(4), 507-542.

Kaplan, S. (1995). The restorative benefits of nature: Toward an integrative framework. *Journal of Environmental Psychol- ogy, 15*, 169-182.

Kimmerer, R. (2014). *Braiding sweetgrass: Indigenous wisdom, scientific knowledge and the teachings of plants*. Minneapolis, MN: Milkweed Editions.

Kitchens, C. (2014). The use of eminent domain in land assembly: The case of the Tennessee Valley Authority. *Public Choice, 160*(3/4), 455-466.

Lackey, N.Q., & Bricker, K.S. (2020). The relationships between parks and protected areas and gateway communities in the United States and Canada: A scoping review. *Journal of Park and Recreation Administration*. Retrieved from https://doi.org/10.18666/JPRA-2020-10390

Leave No Trace. (2021). *About Leave No Trace*. Retrieved from www.https://lnt.org/about

LGBT Outdoors. (2020). *About us*. Retrieved from www.lgbtoutdoors.com

Limerick, P. (1987). *The legacy of conquest: The unbroken past of the American West*. New York, NY: Norton.

Manning, R. (1999). *Studies in outdoor recreation: Search and research for satisfaction* (2nd ed.). Corvallis: Oregon State University Press.

Marion, J., & Reid, S. (2001). Development of the United States Leave No Trace programme: A historical perspective. In M.B. Usher (Ed.), *Enjoyment and understanding of the natural heritage* (pp. 81-92). Edinburgh, Scotland: Scottish Natural Heritage, The Stationery Office.

Nash, R. (1967). *Wilderness and the American mind*. New Haven, CT: Yale University Press.

Neighbors, C., Marquez, D., & Marcus, B. (2007). Leisure-time physical activity disparities among Hispanic subgroups in the United States. *American Journal of Public Health First Look, 98*(8), 1460-1464.

Outdoor Afro. (2020). *About us*. Retrieved from https://outdoorafro.com/

Outdoor Industry Association. (2019). *The outdoor recreation economy*. Boulder, CO: Outdoor Industry Foundation. Retrieved from https://outdoorindustry.org/advocacy/

Outdoor Industry Association. (2020). *State outdoor recreation offices*. Boulder, CO: Outdoor Industry Foundation. Retrieved from https://outdoorindustry.org/advocacy/state-local-issues/state-offices-outdoor-recreation/

Parks, S., Housemann, R., & Brownson, R. (2003). Differential correlates of physical activity in urban and rural adults of various socioeconomic backgrounds in the United States. *Journal of Epidemiology and Community Health, 57*, 29-35.

Passel, J., & Cohn, D. (2008). *U.S. population projections: 2005-2050*. Washington, DC: Pew Research Center: Social and Demographic Trends & Pew Hispanic Center. http://pewhispanic.org/files/reports/85.pdf

Rough Guides. (2007). *World party: The rough guide to the world's best festivals*. New York, NY: Rough Guides.

Sasidharan, V., Willits, F., & Godbey, G. (2005). Cultural differences in urban recreation patterns: An examination of park usage and activity participation across six population subgroups. *Managing Leisure, 10*, 19-38.

Schultz, C., Bocarro, J., Lee, K., Sene-Harper, A., Fearn, M., & Floyd, M. (2019). Whose National Park Service? An examination of relevancy, diversity, and inclusion programs from 2005-2016. *Journal of Park and Recreation Administration, 37*(4), 51-69.

Schwab, K., Dustin, D., & Bricker, K.S. (2017). Reframing humankind's relationship with nature: Contributions from social exchange theory. *Journal of Sustainability Education, 12*, 2151-7452.

Shaull, S., & Gramann, J. (1998). The effect of cultural assimilation on the importance of family-related and nature-related recreation among Hispanic Americans. *Journal of Leisure Research, 30*(1), 47-63.

Shelby, B., & Heberlein, T.A. (1986). *Carrying capacity in recreation settings*. Corvallis: Oregon State University Press.

Smith, A. (1776). *The wealth of nations*. London, UK: Strahan and Cadell.

Snyman, S., & Bricker, K.S. (2019). Living on the edge: Benefit-sharing from protected area tourism. *Journal of Sustainable Tourism, 27*(6), 705-719.

Sommer, L. (2020). To manage wildfire, California looks to what tribes have known all along. *National Public Radio*. Retrieved September 22, 2020, from www.npr.org/2020/08/24/899422710/to-manage-wildfire-california-looks-to-what-tribes-have-known-all-along

Stankey, G.H. (1989). Beyond the campfire's light: Historical roots of the wilderness concept. *Natural Resources Journal, 29*(1), 9-24.

Tilton, B. (2003). *Master educator handbook: Leave No Trace outdoor ethics*. Boulder, CO: The Leave No Trace Center for Outdoor Ethics and Lander, WY: The National Outdoor Leadership School.

Turner, F. (1921). *The frontier in American history*. New York, NY: Holt.

Ulrich, R. (1981). Natural versus urban scenes: Some psychophysiological effects. *Environment and Behavior, 13*(5), 523-556.

U.S. Census Bureau. (2010). *Global population 2002 and beyond*. Retrieved from www.census.gov/prod/www/abs/popula.html

U.S. Census Bureau. (2020). *Demographic turning points for the United States: Population projections for 2020 to 2060*. Retrieved from www.census.gov/library/publications/2020/demo/p25-1144.html

Virden, R., & Walker, G. (1999). Ethnic/racial and gender variations among meanings given to, and preferences for, the natural environment. *Leisure Sciences, 21*, 219-239.

The Wilderness Society. (2020). *Public lands in the United States: Examining the past to build a more equitable future*. Retrieved from www.wilderness.org/articles/article/public-lands-united-states-curriculum#

Wilkinson, C. (2018). At Bears Ears we can hear the voices of our ancestors in every canyon and on every mesa top: The creation of the First Native National Monument. *Arizona State Law Journal, 50*(1), 317.

Winter, P.L., Selin, S., Cerveny, L., & Bricker, K.S. (2020). Outdoor recreation, nature-based tourism, and sustainability. *Sustainability, 12*(1), 81. Retrieved from https://doi.org/10.3390/su12010081

World Health Organization. (2020). *Fact file: Water scarcity.* Retrieved from www.who.int/news-room/fact-sheets/detail/drinking-water

Zajchowski, C., Desocio, A., & Lackey, N.Q. (2019). Second class wilderness: Separate but unequal air resources in American wilderness. *International Journal of Wilderness, 25*(3), 24-34.

Chapter 11

Ali, S. (2019, January 22). Is self-care just a trend? *Psychology Today.* Retrieved from www.psychologytoday.com/us/blog/modern-mentality/201901/is-self-care-just-trend#:~:text=Self%2Dcare%20was%20even%20the,than%20dieting%20and%20physical%20fitness

American Alliance of Museums. (2020). *Museums facts & data.* Retrieved from www.aam-us.org/programs/about-museums/museum-facts-data/

American Gaming Association. (2019). *Research report.* Retrieved from www.americangaming.org/research/

Boys & Girls Clubs of America. (2020). *Who we are: The facts.* Retrieved from www.bgca.org/whoweare/facts.asp

Clower, T.L., & Nguyen, D. (2020). *The economic impacts of local parks: An examination of the economic impacts of local and regional park agency spending on the United States economy.* Ashburn, VA: National Recreation and Park Association.

Colangelo, M. (2019, July 15). The NFL made roughly $16 billion in revenue last year. *USA Today.* Retrieved from https://touchdownwire.usatoday.com/2019/07/15/nfl-revenue-owners-players-billions/.

Conlin, J. (2019, May 10). The $10-billion business of self-care. *Los Angeles Times.* Retrieved from www.latimes.com/health/la-he-business-of-self-care-20190508-story.html

Dwyer, Z. (2020). Bait shops see sales surge amid fishing opener, COVID-19. *SC Times.* Retrieved from www.sctimes.com/story/news/local/2020/05/07/bait-shops-see-sales-surge-amid-fishing-opener-covid-19/3083558001

Gera, E. (2019). Americans spent more than $43 billion on video games in 2018. *Variety.* Retrieved from https://variety.com/2019/gaming/news/americans-spent-more-than-43-billion-on-video-games-in-2018-1203114642/

Gruenhagen, S. (2010). Taxation and public financing of stadiums. *Adelphia Law Journal, 1*(17), 1-26.

IEG. (2017). *Sponsorship spending on music to total $1.54 billion in 2017.* Retrieved from www.sponsorship.com/iegsr/2017/07/24/Sponsorship-Spending-On-Music-To-Total-$1-54-Billi.aspx

Independent Sector. (2016). *Nonprofit almanac: Facts and findings.* Retrieved from www.independentsector.org/economic_role

LeVoir-Barry, B. (2020). How esports are fueling the data economy. *Forbes.* Retrieved from www.forbes.com/sites/ibm/2020/01/08/how-esports-are-fueling-the-data-economy/#3de6da7435e1

Mandala Research. (2013). *Cultural and heritage traveler report.* Retrieved form https://mandalaresearch.com/

Mitchell, S. (2020). *Super Bowl revenue: How much does the big game generate?* Retrieved from www.thestreet.com/lifestyle/sports/super-bowl-revenue

National Association of State Park Directors. (2020). *America's state parks + America's national parks = great national system of parks.* Retrieved from www.stateparks.org/about-us

National Golf Foundation. (2019). *Gold industry facts.* Retrieved from www.ngf.org/golf-industry-research/#golfers

National Park Service. (2020). *Annual visitation highlights.* Retrieved from www.nps.gov/subjects/socialscience/annual-visitation-highlights.htm

National Restaurant Association. (2020). *Total restaurant industry jobs: Restaurants added 1.5 million jobs for the second consecutive month.* Retrieved from https://restaurant.org/research/economy/indicators/Restaurant-jobs

Reichert, F., Barros, A., Domingues, M., & Hallal, P. (2007). The role of perceived barriers to engagement in leisure-time physical activity. *American Journal of Public Health, 97*(3), 515-519.

Rodriguez, M. (2019). *Report: Health club, gym, & studio usage reach all-time high.* Boston, MA: International Health, Racquet and Sportsclub Association.

Settembre, J. (2018). This is the insane amount millennials are spending on fitness. *Marketwatch.* Retrieved from www.marketwatch.com/story/this-is-the-insane-amount-millennials-are-spending-on-fitness-2018-01-21

Sylt, C. (2018). "Experience economy" boosts theme park spending to a record $45 billion. *Forbes.* Retrieved from www.forbes.com/sites/csylt/2018/11/04/experience-economy-boosts-theme-park-spending-to-a-record-45-billion/#6f674ea129e4

Theme Index. (2018). *Theme index: Museum index 2018.* Retrieved from www.aecom.com/wp-content/uploads/2019/05/Theme-Index-2018-4.pdf

United States Census. (2019). *All sectors: County business patterns, including zip code business patterns, by legal form of organization and employment size class for the U.S., states, and selected geographies: 2019.* Retrieved from https://data.census.gov/cedsci/table?q=711211&tid=CBP2019.CB1900CBP.

Veblen, T. (1899). *The theory of the leisure class.* Whitefish, MT: Kessinger.

World Tourism Organization. (2018). *Facts and figures.* Retrieved from http://unwto.org/facts/menu.html

World Waterpark Association. (2020). Web page. Retrieved from www.waterparks.org

YMCA. (2020). *Organizational profile.* Retrieved from www.ymca.net/organizational-profile

Chapter 12

Block, W.E. (2019). Debate on eminent domain. In *Property rights* (pp. 335-363). Cham, Switzerland: Palgrave Macmillan.

Crompton, J.L. (2016). Using the benefits continuum, enterprise funds, and cost finding to implement best pricing practices. *Journal of Park and Recreation Administration, 34*(4), 82-101. Retrieved from https://doi.org/10.18666/jpra-2016-v34-i4-7358

Crompton, J.L. (2000). Repositioning leisure services. *Managing Leisure, 5*(2), 65-75.

Crompton, J., & Lamb, C. (1986). *Marketing government and social services.* New York, NY: Wiley.

Garvey, T. (2012). *Medical marijuana: The supremacy clause, federalism, and the interplay between state and federal laws.* CRS Report for Congress. Retrieved from https://fas.org/sgp/crs/misc/R42398.pdf

Grant, A. (2004). *The American political process* (7th ed.). New York, NY: Routledge.

Haas, G. (2003). Applying judicial doctrine to visitor decision making capacity. *Society and Natural Resources, 16,* 741-750.

Hurd, A.R., Barcelona, R.J., & Meldrum, J.T. (2008). *Leisure services management.* Champaign, IL: Human Kinetics.

Kelly, J.R. (1995). *Leisure* (3rd ed.). Boston, MA: Allyn & Bacon.

Kelly, J.R., & Freysinger, V.J. (1999). *Twenty-first century leisure: Current issues.* Boston, MA: Allyn & Bacon.

Krane, K. (2020, May 26). Cannabis legalization is key to economic recovery, much like ending alcohol prohibition helped us out of the great depression. *Forbes.* Retrieved from www.forbes.com/sites/kriskrane/2020/05/26/cannabis-legalization-is-key-to-economic-recovery-much-like-ending-alcohol-prohibition-helped-us-out-of-the-great-depression/?sh=140510273241

Land Water Conservation Fund. (2020). *Protecting lands and giving back to communities.* Retrieved from www.nps.gov/subjects/lwcf/index.htm

More, T.A. (1999). A functionalist approach to user fees. *Journal of Leisure Research, 31*(3), 227-244.

National Recreation and Park Association. (n.d.). *Why parks and recreation are essential public services.* Retrieved June 28, 2021, from www.nrpa.org/uploadedFiles/nrpa.org/Advocacy/Resources/Parks-Recreation-Essential-Public-Services-January-2010.pdf

National Park Service. (2020). *National Park Service land and water conservation fund.* Retrieved from https://www.nps.gov/subjects/lwcf/index.htm

Office of Management and Budget. (2009). *A new era of responsibility: Renewing America's promise.* Washington, DC: U.S. Government Printing Office.

Peters, B.G. (1996). *American public policy: Promise and performance.* Chatham, NJ: Chatham House.

Recovery.gov. (2009). *American Recovery and Reinvestment Act of 2009.* Retrieved from www.recovery.gov/Pages/home.aspx

Rojek, C. (2001). Leisure and life politics. *Leisure Sciences, 23,* 115-125.

Roosevelt, T. (1908). *Outdoor pastimes of an American hunter.* New York, NY: Scribner's.

Smith, J. (2004). *Federalism.* Vancouver, Canada: University of British Columbia Press.

Thomas, D.M. (2008). Past futures: The development and evolution of American and Canadian federalism. In D.M. Thomas & B.B. Torrey (Eds.), *Canada and the United States: Differences that count* (pp. 295-316). Buffalo, NY: Broadview Press.

Todd, B.S. (1996). *The implications of changing federalism: The county view.* Retrieved from www.farmfoundation.org/news/articlefiles/73-fedcount.pdf

U.S. Courts. (2009). *United States courts.* Retrieved from www.uscourts.gov

White House, The. (2009). *The executive branch.* Retrieved from www.whitehouse.gov/our-government/executive-branch

Youniss, J., Bales, S., Christmas-Best, V., Diversi, M., McLaughlin, M., Silbereisen, R. (2002). Youth civic engagement in the 21st century. *Journal of Research on Adolescence, 12*(1), 121-148.

Chapter 13

Artinger, L., Clapham, L., Meigs, C.H.M., Sampson, N.M.B., & Forrester, S.A. (2006). The social benefits of intramural sports. *NASPA Journal, 43*(1), 69-86.

Astin, A.W. (1975). *Preventing students from dropping out.* San Francisco, CA: Jossey-Bass.

Astin, A.W. (1984). Student involvement: A development theory for higher education. *Journal of College Student Personnel, 25*(4), 297-308.

Belch, H.A., Gebel, M., & Mass, G.M. (2001). Relationship between student recreation complex use, academic performance, and persistence of first-time freshmen. *NASPA Journal, 38*(2), 254-268.

Bryant, J., Bradley, J., & Milborne, C. (1994). Comparing student participation in campus recreation to other aspects of campus life. *NIRSA Annual Conference Review, 45,* 144-168.

Cheng, D.X. (2004). Students' sense of campus community: What it means, and what to do about it. *NASPA Journal, 41*(2), 216-234.

Cicognani, E., Pirini, C., Keyes, C., Joshanloo, M., Rostami, R., & Nosratabadi, M. (2008). Social participation, sense of community and social well being: A study on American, Italian and Iranian university students. *Social Indicators Research, 89*(1), 97-112.

Cooper, N., & Faircloth, C. (2006). Repositioning campus recreation: A case report on designing program evaluation procedures. *Recreational Sports Journal, 30,* 126-135.

Elkins, D.J., Forrester, S.A., & Noël-Elkins, A.V. (2011). The contribution of campus recreational sports participation to perceived sense of campus community. *Recreational Sports Journal, 35*(1), 24.

Goodwin, R.D. (2003). Association between physical activity and mental disorders among adults in the United States. *Preventive Medicine, 36,* 698-703.

Haines, D.J. (2001). Undergraduate student benefits from university recreation. *NIRSA Journal, 25*(1), 25-33.

Iwasaki, Y., & Mannell, R.C. (2000). The effects of leisure beliefs and coping strategies on stress-health relationships: A field study. *Leisure/Loisir, 24*(1-2), 3-57.

Jdaitawi, M., Rasheed, A., Gohari, M., Raddy, Y., Aydin, M., Abas, A., Hasan, A., & Khatiry, A. (2020). The determinants of leisure attitudes: Mediating effect of self-efficacy among students from science, engineering and medicine colleges. *Journal of Turkish Science Education (TUSED), 17*(2), 242-252.

Kanters, M.A. (2000). Recreational sport participation as a moderator of college stress. *Recreational Sports Journal, 24*(2), 11-24.

Leabo, K., & Ostendorf, S. (2018). Four technologies to bolster campus recreation participation. *Campus Recreation Magazine.* Retrieved from https://campusrecmag.com/four-technologies-to-bolster-campus-recreation-participation

Miller, J.J. (2011). Impact of a university recreation center on social belonging and student retention. *Recreational Sports Journal, 35*(2), 117.

Mull, R.F., Bayless, K.G., & Jamieson, L.M. (2005). *Recreational sports management* (4th ed.). Champaign, IL: Human Kinetics.

Nesbitt, G.M. (1998). Social-emotional development and extracurricular involvement of sport club participants. *Recreational Sports Journal, 2*(22), 6-9.

Oldenburg, R. (1999). *The great good place: Cafés, coffee shops, bookstores, bars, hair salons, and other hangouts at the heart of a community.* New York, NY: Marlowe.

Reed, J. (2007). Perceptions of the availability of recreational physical activity facilities on a university campus. *Journal of American College Health, 55*(4), 189-194.

Schneider, R.C., Stier, W.F., Jr., Kampf, S., Gregory, E., Wilding, G.E., & Haines, S.G. (2007). Perceived problems in campus recreation programs in North America. *Recreational Sports Journal, 31*(1), 51-60.

Stebbins, R.A. (1997). Casual leisure: A conceptual statement. *Leisure Studies, 16*(1), 17-25.

Torkildsen, G. (2005). *Leisure and recreation management* (5th ed.). London, UK: Routledge.

Young, S.J., Ross, C.M., & Barcelona, R.J. (2003). Perceived constraints by college students to participation in campus recreational sports programs. *Recreational Sports Journal, 27*(2), 47-62.

Zizzi, S., Ayers, S.F., Watson, J.C., II, & Keeler, L. (2004). Assessing the impact of new student campus recreation centers. *NASPA Journal, 41*(4), 588-630.

Chapter 14

ADA Participatory Action Research Consortium. (n.d.). *Percentage of people with disabilities living in an institution, 2012 to 16.* Retrieved September 5, 2021, from www.centeron disability.org/ada_parc/utils/indicators.php?id=1\

American Academy of Pediatrics. (2008). *Recreation.* Retrieved from www.medicalhomeinfo.org/health/Recreation.html

Barbosa, C., & Liechty, T. (2018). Exploring leisure constraints among lesbian women who attend a straight-friendly church. *Journal of Leisure Research, 49*(2), 91-108. doi:10.1080/00222216.2018.1477679

Broughton, K.A., Payne, L., & Liechty, T. (2017). An exploration of older men's social lives and well-being in the context of a coffee group. *Leisure Sciences, 39*(3), 261-276.

Bruton, C.M., & Floyd, M.F. (2014). Disparities in built and natural features of urban parks: Comparisons by neighborhood level race/ethnicity and income. *Journal of Urban Health: Bulletin of the New York Academy of Medicine, 91*(5), 894-907. Retrieved from https://doi.org/10.1007/s11524-014-9893-4

Bryson, V. (2008). Time-use studies. *International Feminist Journal of Politics, 10*(2), 135-153.

Burch, W., Jr. (2009). The social circles of leisure: Competing explanations. *Journal of Leisure, 41*(3), 313-335.

Coble, T.G., Selin, S.W., & Erickson, B.B. (2003). Hiking alone: Understanding fear, negotiation strategies and leisure experience. *Journal of Leisure Research, 35,* 1-21.

Crawford, D.W., & Jackson, E.L. (2005). Leisure constraints theory: Dimensions, directions, and dilemmas. In E.L. Jackson (Ed.), *Constraints to leisure* (pp. 153-167). State College, PA: Venture.

Dattilo, J. (2002). *Inclusive leisure services: Responding to the rights of people with disabilities.* State College, PA: Venture.

Dawson, D. (2000). Social class and leisure provision. In M.T. Allison & I.E. Schneider (Eds.), *Diversity and the recreation profession: Organizational perspectives* (pp. 99-114). State College, PA: Venture.

Duncan, D.T., Kawachi, I., White, K., & Williams, D.R. (2013). The geography of recreational open space: Influence of neighborhood racial composition and neighborhood poverty. *Journal of Urban Health: Bulletin of the New York Academy of Medicine, 90*(4), 618-631. Retrieved from https://doi.org/10.1007/s11524-012-9770-y

Epstein, R. (1994). How much do you know about recreation for older adults? *Parks & Recreation, 29*(3), 65-69.

Floyd, M., & Stodolska, M. (2019). Scholarship on race and ethnicity: Assessing contributions to leisure theory and practice. *Journal of Park and Recreation Administration, 37*(1). Retrieved from https://doi.org/10.18666/JPRA-2019-8339

Guillet, E., Sarrazin, P., & Fontayne, P. (2000). "If it contradicts my gender role, I'll stop": Introducing survival analysis to study the effects of gender typing on the time of withdrawal from sport practice—A 3-year study. *European Review of Applied Psychology, 50,* 417-421.

Harrison, A.K. (2013). Black skiing, everyday racism, and the racial spatiality of whiteness. *Journal of Sport and*

Social Issues, 37(4), 315-339. Retrieved from https://doi .org/10.1177/0193723513498607

Henderson, K.A., & Gibson, H.J. (2013). An integrative review of women, gender, and leisure: Increasing complexities. *Journal of Leisure Research, 45*(2), 115-135. Retrieved from http://dx.doi.org/10.18666/jlr-2013-v45-i2-3008

Henderson, K.A., & Hickerson, B. (2007). Women and leisure: Premises and performances uncovered in an integrative review. *Journal of Leisure Research, 39*(4), 591-610.

Henderson, K.A., & Shaw, S.M. (2006). Leisure and gender: Challenges and opportunities for feminist research. In C. Rojek, S.M. Shaw, & A.J. Veal (Eds.), *A handbook of leisure studies* (pp. 216-230). London, UK: Palgrave.

Hu, W. (2019, November 8). "Hostile architecture": How public spaces keep the public out. *New York Times*, p. 22.

International Paralympic Committee. (n.d.). *History of the Paralympic movement*. Retrieved September 7, 2021, from www.paralympic.org/ipc/history

Kinney, J. (2020). Analysis of services performed by recreational therapists. *Therapeutic Recreation Journal, 54*(3). Retrieved from https://doi-org.proxy195.nclive .org/10.18666/TRJ-2020-V54-I3-10248

Kluge, M.A. (2005). Active recreation grows among older adults. *Journal of Physical Education, Recreation and Dance, 76*(5), 39-46.

Knee, E. (2019). Gay, but not inclusive: Boundary maintenance in an LGBTQ space. *Leisure Sciences, 41*(6), 499-515.

Mackelprang, R.W., & Salsgiver, R.O. (1999). *Disability: A diversity model approach*. Pacific Grove, CA: Brooks/Cole.

Meyer, A.M., & Borrie, W.T. (2013). Engendering wilderness. *Journal of Leisure Research, 45*(3), 295-323. doi:10.18666/ jlr-2013-v45-i3-3153

Miller, Y.D., & Brown, W.J. (2005). Determinants of active leisure for women with young children—an "ethic of care" prevails. *Leisure Sciences, 27*, 405-420.

Nickasch, B., & Marnocha, S. (2009). Healthcare experiences of the homeless. *Journal of the American Academy of Nurse Practitioners, 21*(1), 39-46.

Oakleaf, L. & Richmond, L.P. (2017). Dreaming about access: The experiences of transgender individuals in public recreation. *Journal of Park and Recreation Administration, 35*(2), 108-119. doi:10.18666/JPRA-2017-V35-I2-7363

Pagán-Rodríguez, R. (2014). How do disabled individuals spend their leisure time? *Disability and Health Journal, 7*(2), 196-205. Retrieved from https://doi.org/https://doi .org/10.1016/j.dhjo.2014.01.001

Perry, C., & Kendall, J. (2008). Rural women walking for health. *Western Journal of Nursing Research, 30*(3), 295-316.

Schmalz, D., Kerstetter, D., & Anderson, D. (2008). Stigma consciousness as a predictor of children's participation in recreational vs. competitive sports. *Journal of Sport Behavior, 31*(3), 276-297.

Shaw, S.M., & Henderson, K.A. (2005). Gender analysis and leisure: An uneasy alliance. In E.L. Jackson (Ed.), *Constraints to leisure* (pp. 23-34). State College, PA: Venture.

Taylor, D.M. (2018). *Americans with disabilities: 2014*. Retrieved from www.census.gov/content/dam/Census/ library/publications/2018/demo/p70-152.pdf

United States Census Bureau. (2020a). *65 and older population grows rapidly as baby boomers age*. Retrieved from www.census.gov/newsroom/press-releases/2020/65-older- population-grows.html

United States Census Bureau. (2020b). *By 2030, all baby boomers will be age 65 or older*. Retrieved from www.census. gov/library/stories/2019/12/by-2030-all-baby-boomers-will- be-age-65-or-older.html

Wen, M., Zhang, X., Harris, C.D., Holt, J.B., & Croft, J.B. (2013). Spatial disparities in the distribution of parks and green spaces in the USA. *Annals of Behavioral Medicine, 45*, 18-27. Retrieved from https://doi-org.proxy195.nclive .org/10.1007/s12160-012-9426-x

Chapter 15

Abegg, B., & Froesch, R. (1994). Climate change and winter tourism. In M. Beniston (Ed.), *Mountain environments in changing climates* (pp. 328-340). London, UK: Routledge.

Agarwal, S. (2002). Restructuring seaside tourism: The resort lifecycle. *Annals of Tourism Research, 29*(1), 25-55.

Agnew, M.D., & Viner, D. (2001). Potential impacts of climate change on international tourism. *Tourism and Hospitality Research, 3*, 37-60.

Aitchison, C. (1999). New cultural geographies: The spatiality of leisure, gender and sexuality. *Leisure Studies, 18*, 19-39.

Allen, L.R. (1990). Benefits of leisure attributes to community satisfaction. In B.L. Driver, P.J. Brown, & G.L. Peterson (Eds.), *Benefits of leisure* (pp. 331-350). State College, PA: Venture.

Andereck, K.L. (1995). Environmental consequences of tourism: A review of recent research. In S.F. McCool & A.E. Watson (Eds.), *Linking tourism, the environment, and sustainability* (pp. 77-81). Ogden, UT: U.S. Department of Agriculture, Forest Service, Intermountain Forest and Range Experiment Station.

Andereck, K., Valentine, K., Knopf, R., & Vogt, C. (2005). Residents' perceptions of community tourism impacts. *Annals of Tourism Research, 32*, 1056-1078.

Ap, J. (1992). Residents' perceptions on tourism's impacts. *Annals of Tourism Research, 19*, 665-690.

Atkinson, R., & Bridge, G. (Eds.). (2005). *Gentrification in a global context*. Abingdon, UK: Routledge.

Backman, K.F., & Morais, D.B. (2001). Methodological approaches used in the literature. In D.B. Weaver (Ed.), *The encyclopedia of ecotourism* (pp. 597-609). Wallingford, UK: CAB International.

Becken, S. (2002). Analyzing international tourist flows to estimate energy use associated with air travel. *Journal of Sustainable Tourism, 10*(2), 114-131.

Betancur, J.J. (1996). The settlement experience of Latinos in Chicago: Segregation, speculation, and the ecology model. *Social Forces, 74*(4), 1299-1324.

Betancur, J.J. (2002). The politics of gentrification: The case of West Town in Chicago. *Urban Affairs Review, 37*(6), 780-814.

Brown, F., & Hall, D. (2000). Introduction: The paradox of periphery. In F. Brown & D. Hall (Eds.), *Tourism in peripheral areas* (pp. 1-6). Clevedon, UK: Channel View Publications.

Brunt, P., & Courtney, P. (1999). Host perceptions of socio-cultural impacts. *Annals of Tourism Research, 26,* 493-515.

Bureau of Transportation Statistics (BTS). (2021). *Fuel consumption by mode of transportation in physical units.* Retrieved from www.bts.gov/publications/national_transportation_statistics/html/table_04_05.html

Burns, P., & Holden, A. (1995). *Tourism: A new perspective.* London, UK: Prentice Hall.

Butler, R. (1980). The concept of a tourist area cycle of evolution: Implications for management of resources. *Canadian Geographer, 24,* 5-12.

Butler, R. (2004). Geographical research on tourism, recreation and leisure: Origins, eras and directions. *Tourism Geographies, 6*(2), 143-162.

Butler, R.W., & Waldbrook, L.A. (1991). A new planning tool: The tourism opportunity spectrum. *Journal of Tourism Studies, 2*(1), 1-14.

Byrne, J., & Jinjun, Y. (2009). Can urban greenspace combat climate change? Towards a subtropical cities research agenda. *Australian Planner, 46*(4), 36-43.

Clean Air Cool Planet. (2007). *Global warming threatens New England's ski industry.* Retrieved from www.cleanair-coolplanet.org/information/pdf/ski-factsheet.pdf

Coccossis, H. (1996). Tourism and sustainability: Perspectives and implications. In G.K. Priestley, J.A. Edwards, & H. Coccossis (Eds.), *Sustainable tourism? European experiences* (pp. 1-21). Wallingford, UK: CAB International.

Cole, D.N., & Spildie, D.R. (1998). Hiker, horse, and llama trampling effects on native vegetation in Montana, USA. *Journal of Environmental Management, 53,* 61-71.

Colorado Ski History. (2008). *Vail.* Retrieved form www.coloradoskihistory.com/areahistory/vail.html

Corwell, P. (1986). Open space on real estate values. In *Proceedings of the Governor's Conference on the Economic Significance of Recreation in Illinois.* Springfield, IL: Office of the Governor.

Crompton, J.L. (2008). Empirical evidence of the contributions of leisure services to alleviating social problems: A key to repositioning the leisure service field. *World Leisure Journal, 50*(4), 243-258.

Curran, S. (2004). *Every family in the land: Understanding prejudice and discrimination against people with mental illness.* [Review of the book *Every family in the land: Understanding prejudice and discrimination against people with mental illness. Revised edition,* by A.H. Crisp, Ed.]. *Primary Care Psychiatry, 9*(3), 112.

De Vries, L. (2003). *Ski industry facing meltdown?* Retrieved from www.cbsnews.com/stories/2003/12/03/tech/main586554.shtml

Doggart, C., & Doggart, N. (1996). Occasional studies: Environmental impacts of tourism in developing countries. *Travel and Tourism Analyst, 2,* 71-86.

Doh, M. (2006). *Change through tourism: Resident perceptions toward tourism development in the Big Bend area, Texas.* (Unpublished PhD dissertation). Texas A&M University, College Station.

Dubin, J.C. (1993). Poverty, pain, and precedent: The fifth circuit's social security jurisprudence. *St. Mary's Law Journal, 25,* 81.

Egli, R. (1995). Climatic effects of air traffic. *Environmental Conservation, 22,* 196-198.

Environmental Protection Agency (EPA). (2009). *Environmental justice home.* Retrieved from www.epa.gov/compliance/environmentaljustice/index.html

Environmental Protection Agency (EPA). (2020). *Environmental justice.* Retrieved from www.epa.gov/environmental justice

Euromonitor. (2007). *Top 150 city destinations: London leads the way.* Retrieved from www.euromonitor.com/Top_150_City_Destinations_London_Leads_the_Way

Euromonitor. (2019). *Top 100 city destinations.* Retrieved from www.hwa.uk.com/site/wp-content/uploads/2020/10/CD-20.69-EuromonitorTop100Cities19.pdf

Evans, G. (1994). Whose culture is it anyway? Tourism in Greater Mexico and the Indigena. In A.V. Seaton, C.L. Jenkins, R.C. Wood, P.U.C. Dieke, M.M. Bennett, L.R. MacLellan, & R. Smith (Eds.), *Tourism: State of the art* (pp. 836-847). Chichester, UK: Wiley.

Fotheringham, A.S. (1983). A new set of spatial-interaction models: The theory of competing destinations. *Environment and Planning A, 15*(1), 15-36.

Fried, M.H. (1963). *Anthropology and the study of politics.* Voice of America, US Information Agency.

Fukushima, T., Kureha, M., Ozaki, N., Fujimori, Y., & Harasawa, Y. (2002). Influences of air temperature change on leisure industries: Case study on ski activities. *Mitigation and Adaptation Strategies for Global Change, 7,* 173-189.

Gartner, W.C. (2004). Rural tourism development in the USA. *International Journal of Tourism Research, 6,* 151-164.

Gee, C.Y. (1996). *Resort: Development and management.* East Lansing, MI: Educational Institute of the American Hotel & Motel Association.

Getz, D. (1992). Tourism planning and destination lifecycle. *Annals of Tourism Research, 19,* 752-770.

Gilbert, D., & Clark, M. (1997). An exploratory examination of urban tourism impact, with reference to residents' attitudes, in the cities of Canterbury and Guildford. *Cities, 14*(6), 343-352.

Glick, J. (2008). Gentrification and the racialized geography of home equity. *Urban Affairs Review, 44*(2), 280-295.

Gotham, K. (2005). *Public dollars, private stadiums: The battle over building sports stadiums.* [Review of the book *Public dollars, private stadiums: The battle over building sports stadiums,* by K.J. Delaney & R. Eckstein.] *American Journal of*

Sociology, 111(3). Retrieved from www.journals.uchicago.edu/doi/10.1086/500781.

Green, H., Hunter, C., & Moore, B. (1990). Assessing the environmental impact of tourism development: Use of the Delphi technique. *Tourism Management, 11*, 111-120.

Harrill, R. (2004). Residents' attitudes toward tourism development: A literature review with implications for tourism planning. *Journal of Planning Literature, 18*(3), 251-266.

Hwang, Y., Gretzel, U., & Fesenmaier, D.R. (2006). Multicity trip patterns: Tourists to the United States. *Annals of Tourism Research, 33*(4), 1057-1078.

Jansen-Verbeke, M. (1986). Inner-city tourism: Recourses, tourists and promoters. *Annals of Tourism Research, 13*, 79-100.

Jeffres, L.W., & Dobos, J. (1993). Perceptions of leisure opportunities and the quality of life in a metropolitan area. *Journal of Leisure Research, 25*(2), 203-217.

Koegh, B. (1990). Resident recreationists' perceptions and attitudes with respect to tourism development. *Journal of Applied Recreation Research, 15*(2), 71-83.

Lankford, S. (1994). Attitudes and perceptions toward tourism and rural regional development. *Journal of Travel Research, 32*(4), 35-43.

Lees, L., Slater, T., & Wyly, E. (2013). *Gentrification.* Abingdon, UK: Routledge.

Lew, A., & McKercher, B. (2006). Modeling tourist movements: A local destination analysis. *Annals of Tourism Research, 33*(2), 403-423.

Li, C.L. (2020). Quality of life: The perspective of urban park recreation in three Asian cities. *Journal of Outdoor Recreation and Tourism, 29*, 100260.

Lin, C., Morais, D.B., & Hou, J. (2003). Case study of the relationship between socio-economic equality and spatial distribution of tourist sites in Taiwan: An application of geographic information systems. *Proceedings of the 2003 Northeastern Recreation Research Symposium*, pp. 177-184.

Liu, J., & Var, T. (1986). Resident attitudes toward tourism impacts in Hawaii. *Annals of Tourism Research, 13*, 193-214.

Long, P.T. (1996). Early impacts of limited stakes casino gambling on rural community life. *Tourism Management, 17*(5), 341-353.

Lu, J., Vecchi, G.A., & Reichler, T. (2007). Expansion of the Hadley cell under global warming. *Geophysical Research Letters.* Retrieved from www.atmos.berkeley.edu/~jchiang/Class/Spr07/Geog257/Week10/Lu_Hadley06.pdf

Mason, P., & Cheyne, J. (2000). Residents' attitudes to proposed tourism development. *Annals of Tourism Research, 27*(2), 391-411.

McCool, S.F., & Martin, S.R. (1994). Community attachment and attitudes toward tourism development. *Journal of Travel Research, 32*, 29-34.

McDonald, J.R. (2009). Complexity science: An alternative world view for understanding sustainable tourism development. *Journal of Sustainable Tourism, 17*(4), 455-471.

Medio, D., Ormond, R.F., & Pearson, M. (1997). Effect of briefings on rates of damage to crabs by scuba divers. *Biological Conservation, 79*, 91-95.

Metropolitan Pier and Exposition Authority. (2009). *About Navy Pier—history.* Retrieved from www.navypier.com/about/history.html

Mill, R.C., & Morrison, A.M. (2006). *The tourism system.* Dubuque, IA: Kendall/Hunt.

Milman, A., & Pizam, A. (1988). Social impacts of tourism on central Florida. *Annals of Tourism Research, 15*, 191-204.

Mitchell, L., & Smith, R. (1989). The geography of recreation, tourism and sport. In G. Gaile & W. Cor (Eds.), *Geography in America* (pp. 387-408). Columbus, OH: Merrill.

Moreno-Mata, A. (2018). Urban sprawl, environmental justice and equity in the access to green spaces in the metropolitan area of San Luis Potosí, Mexico. In W. Leal Filho, R. Noyola-Cherpitel, P. Medellín-Milán, & V.R. Vargas (Eds.), *Sustainable development research and practice in Mexico and selected Latin American countries* (pp. 499-516). Cham, Switzerland: Springer.

National Environmental Justice Advisory Council (NEJAC). (2006). *NEJAC meeting summary, June 2006.* Retrieved from www.epa.gov/environmentaljustice/nejac-meeting-summary-june-2006

National Travel and Tourism Office (NTTO). (2019). *Fact sheet: Top 10 U.S. city destinations.* Retrieved from https://travel.trade.gov/

Nelson, A.C. (1986, Spring). Using land markets to evaluate urban containment programs. *American Planning Association*, pp. 156-171.

Newman, K., & Wyly, E.K. (2006). The right to stay put, revisited: Gentrification and resistance to displacement in New York City. *Urban Studies, 43*(1), 23-57.

Nicholls, S., & Shafer, C.S. (2001). Measuring accessibility and equality in a local park systems: The utility of geospatial technologies to park and recreation professions. *Journal of Park and Recreation Administration, 19*(4), 102-124.

Oppermann, M. (1995). A model of travel itineraries. *Journal of Travel Research, 33*(4), 57-61.

Pearce, D.G. (1981). *Tourist development: Topics in applied geography.* New York, NY: Longman.

Porter, R., & Tarrant, M.A. (2001). A case study of environmental justice and federal tourism sites in Southern Appalachia: A GIS application. *Journal of Travel Research, 40*(1), 27-40.

Purdue, R., Long, T., & Gustke, L. (1991). The effects of tourism development on objective indicators of local quality of life. In *Travel and Tourism Association 22nd Annual Proceedings* (pp. 191-201). Salt Lake City, UT: TTRA.

Radford, J.Q., & Bennett, A.F. (2004). Thresholds in landscape parameters: Occurrence of the white-browed treecreeper *Climacteris affinis* in Victoria, Australia. *Biological Conservation, 117*, 375-391.

Richards, G., & Hall, D. (2000). *Tourism and sustainable community development.* London, UK: Routledge.

Rigolon, A. (2017). Parks and young people: An environmental justice study of park proximity, acreage, and quality in Denver, Colorado. *Landscape and Urban Planning, 165,* 73-83.

Rossin-Slater, M. (2017). *Maternity and family leave policy* (No. w23069). Cambridge, MA: National Bureau of Economic Research.

Rouphael, A.B., & Inglis, G.J. (1997). Impacts of recreational scuba diving at sites with different reef topographies. *Biological Conservation, 82,* 329-336.

Shaw, D. (2006). Ski bummer. *Daily Grist.* Retrieved from www.grist.org/article/shaw

Shone, M.C. (2013). *Local government and tourism public policy: A case of the Hurunui District, New Zealand* (Doctoral dissertation). Lincoln University, New Zealand.

Snaith, T., & Haley, A. (1999). Residents' opinions of tourism development in the historic city of York, England. *Tourism Management, 20,* 595-603.

Tarrant, M.A., & Cordell, H.K. (1999). Environmental justice and the spatial distribution of outdoor recreation sites: An application of geographic information systems. *Journal of Leisure Research, 31*(1), 18-34.

Terman, M.R. (1997). Natural links: Naturalistic golf courses as wildlife habitat. *Landscape and Urban Planning, 38,* 183-197.

Teye, V., Sonmez, S.F., & Sirakaya, E. (2002). Residents' attitudes toward tourism development. *Annals of Tourism Research, 29*(3), 668-688.

U.S. Census Bureau. (2000). *Fact sheet: Sturgis, South Dakota.* Retrieved from http://factfinder.census.gov/servlet/SAFFFacts?_event=Search&geo_id=&_geoContext=&_street=&_county=sturgis&_cityTown=sturgis&_state=04000US46&_zip=&_lang=en&_sse=on&pctxt=fph&pgsl=010&show_2003_tab=&redirect=Y

Vaughan, K.B., Kaczynski, A.T., Wilhelm Stanis, S.A., Besenyi, G.M., Bergstrom, R., & Heinrich, K.M. (2013). Exploring the distribution of park availability, features, and quality across Kansas City, Missouri by income and race/ethnicity: An environmental justice investigation. *Annals of Behavioral Medicine, 45*(suppl. 1), S28-S38.

Vogel, A. (2005). *Modeling leisure day trips between Berlin and its surrounding.* Paper presented at the 45th Congress of the European Regional Science Association. Vrije Universiteit Amsterdam.

Wolch, J., Wilson, J.P., & Fehrenbach, J. (2005). Parks and park funding in Los Angeles: An equity-mapping analysis. *Urban Geography, 26*(1), 4-35.

Worldometer. (2020). *COVID-19 coronavirus pandemic.* Retrieved from www.worldometers.info/coronavirus/

World Tourism Organization. (2002). *WTO think tank enthusiastically reaches consensus on frameworks for tourism destination success.* Madrid, Spain: World Tourism Organization.

Wu, B., & Cai, L.A. (2006). Spatial modeling: Suburban leisure in Shanghai. *Annals of Tourism Research, 33,* 179-198.

Chapter 16

Centers for Disease Control and Prevention. (n.d.). *Alzheimer's disease and healthy aging: Healthy People 2030.* Retrieved from www.cdc.gov/aging/publications/healthy-people-2030/index.html

Centers for Disease Control and Prevention. (2018). *Physical activity guidelines for Americans* (2nd ed.). Washington, DC: U.S. Department of Health and Human Services.

Crain, W. (2016). *Theories of development: Concepts and applications* (6th ed.). New York, NY: Routledge.

Piaget, J. (1936). *The construction of reality in the child* (M. Cook, Trans.). New York, NY: Ballantine Books.

Piaget, J. (1964). Development and learning. In R. Ripple & V. Rockcastle (Eds.), *Piaget rediscovered.* Ithaca, NY: Cornell University Press.

Stricker, P.R. (2006). *Sports success Rx: Your child's prescription for the best experience: How to maximize potential and minimize pressure.* Elk Grove Village, IL: American Academy of Pediatrics.

Chapter 17

Bureau of Labor Statistics. (2020). *About the leisure and hospitality supersector.* Retrieved from www.bls.gov/iag/tgs/iag70.htm

Ginsburg, K.R. (2007). The importance of play in promoting healthy child development and maintaining strong parent-child bonds. *Pediatrics, 119*(1), 182-191.

Lepp, A. (2018). Correlating leisure and happiness: The relationship between the leisure experience battery and the Satisfaction With Life Scale. *Annals of Leisure Research, 21*(2), 246-252.

Macchia, L., & Whillans, A. (2019). Leisure beliefs and the subjective well-being of nations. *The Journal of Positive Psychology.* Retrieved from www.hbs.edu/ris/Publication%20Files/Leisure%20beliefs%20and%20the%20subjective%20well%20being%20of%20nations_0fe0ed8c-5711-4d43-9894-e420a0837d38.pdf

Schlag, P. (2020). *Recreation internships.* Retrieved from http://recreationinternships.com

Index

Note: The italicized *f* and *t* following page numbers refer to figures and tables, respectively.

About the Editors

Tyler Tapps, PhD, is an associate professor and assistant director for health sciences at Northwest Missouri State University, where he currently serves as a fellow for institutional strategy. He received his PhD  in health, leisure, and human performance from Oklahoma State University in 2009. In 2015, he was certified as a park and recreation professional by the National Recreation and Park Association, from which he also received the Robert W. Crawford Young Professional Award. Dr. Tapps is a military veteran with recreation programming experience in the military. He is a past president of the leisure educators' section of the Missouri Park and Recreation Association. In 2020, he became research fellow for the Oklahoma Association for Health, Physical Education, Recreation and Dance board and council, from which he received the Betty Abercrombie Scholar Award.

Mary Sara Wells, PhD, is an associate professor in the Department of Parks, Recreation, and Tourism at the University of Utah, where she serves as the director of undergraduate studies in the Depart-  ment of Health-Kinesiology. She teaches courses in youth development, community recreation, and sport management. She has been a member of the Academy of Leisure Sciences, the National Recreation and Park Association, and Society of Park and Recreation Educators since 2004. Dr. Wells has researched sportsmanship issues in youth sport. She has published her research in numerous journals, presented at several national and international conferences, and conducted trainings and evaluations for multiple municipal youth sport agencies across the country.

Mary Parr, PhD, is a professor of recreation, park, and tourism management at Kent State University. She has received both a meritorious award in teaching and service and in research and scholarly activity.  Since 1987, Dr. Parr has been a member of the National Recreation and Park Association, where she served as chair of the education network (2017-2021). She was a member of the Society of Park and Recreation Educators for more than 25 years, where she served as a board member from 2007 to 2010. Dr. Parr is a member of the Academy of Leisure Sciences (TALS) and served as president in 2017. She also received the TALS Excellence in Teaching Award in 2017.

About the Contributors

Brent Beggs, PhD, is a professor and the director of the School of Kinesiology and Recreation at Illinois State University, where he teaches undergraduate and graduate courses in facility design, the management of sports and recreation, and research methods. Dr. Beggs coauthored the textbooks *Recreation Facility Management* and *Mastering the Job Search Process in Recreation and Leisure Services*. Before teaching at Illinois State University, he served as a lecturer and internship coordinator for the Department of Recreation, Park, and Tourism Studies at Indiana University and worked for recreation agencies in the states of Illinois and Missouri. He is an active member of the National Recreation and Park Association and the National Intramural-Recreational Sports Association and serves on multiple editorial boards. Dr. Beggs earned his bachelor's and master's degrees in recreation from Southern Illinois University and completed his PhD in leisure behavior at Indiana University.

Jason N. Bocarro, PhD, is a professor and university faculty scholar in the Department of Parks, Recreation and Tourism Management at North Carolina State University. Dr. Bocarro's research focuses on the intersection of childhood and adolescent health and inactivity and specifically examines the relationship between the built environment and public spaces and human health. His research has been funded by the Robert Wood Johnson Foundation (RWJF), the Centers for Disease Control, the National Park Service, the European Union (EU), the National Recreation and Park Association, the Aspen Institute, and sport governing bodies such as USA Hockey. In 2015, he was named Alumni Distinguished Undergraduate Professor, awarded in recognition of distinguished service in support of undergraduate teaching. Dr. Bocarro has published over 70 peer-reviewed research journal articles and book chapters spanning several disciplines, including medicine, sociology, public health, psychology, parks and recreation, exercise science and education. He is also the coeditor of the book *Legacies of Mega Events: Fact or Fairy Tales*. Before working in academia, Dr. Bocarro was involved with the devel-opment and supervision of park and recreation and sport programs in a variety of places and settings, including London, Nova Scotia, Texas, and New Hampshire.

Kelly Bricker, PhD, is a professor; director of the Hainan University-Arizona State University International Tourism College, located in ASU's Watts College of Public Service and Community Solutions; a practitioner in ecotourism; and a consultant. She completed her PhD at the Penn State University, where she specialized in sustainable tourism and protected area management. She has applied and research experience in ecotourism, visitor and protected area management, and the impacts of tourism. She has authored books on sustainability that highlight case studies in tourism meeting environmental and societal issues (*Sustainable Tourism and the Millennium Development Goals: Effecting Positive Change*), on adventure education (*Adventure Programing and Travel for the 21st Century*), and on graduate education in *De-Mystifying Theories in Tourism Research*. She serves on the board of the Global Sustainable Tourism Council as vice chair and on the Executive Committee of the Tourism and Protected Area Specialist Group of the IUCN.

Nathan Bricker, MS, is an internship coordinator in the School of Community Resources and Development at Arizona State University. Previously, he was the general manager for OARS, Inc. Bricker completed his master's degree in parks, recreation, and tourism at West Virginia University in 2003, where his educational pursuits focused on management and geography of protected areas. His master's project focused on developing a lease for conservation, the Upper Navua Conservation Area, and the Ramsar Wetland of International Importance designation in the Republic of Fiji. Together with George Wendt of OARS, Bricker and his wife, Kelly, started Rivers Fiji in 1998, and they still run whitewater rafting and sea kayaking programs in the rural highlands. Bricker started his career in commercial guiding with OARS and Sobek Expeditions in 1984. From that time, he has guided extensively for

World Heritage, Australian Himalayan Expeditions, and Sobek Expeditions, which provided firsthand experiences in the adventure and sustainable travel arenas as well as a solid background in the skills required for leading groups safely into a range of unique environments. He holds instructor certifications with the Wilderness Education Association, Leave No Trace, Special Rescue Services (in swift-water rescue), Wilderness Medical Associates, and the American Canoe Association. Bricker has developed and led adventure travel programs to Tanzania, Kenya, Ecuador, Belize, Guatemala, Honduras, Portugal, Yugoslavia, Thailand, Bali, Sumatra, Borneo, China, Fiji, New Zealand, Australia, Nepal, Galapagos, India, and Tibet.

Cynthia Carruthers, PhD, is a professor emerita in the College of Education at the University of Nevada at Las Vegas. She received her bachelor's, master's, and doctoral degrees from the University of Illinois at Urbana-Champaign in the areas of leisure behavior and therapeutic recreation. Her research interests include leisure and well-being, mindfulness, recovery from addiction, and youth development.

Lee J. deLisle, PhD, is the program director for the tourism, hospitality, and event management major at Southern Connecticut State University in New Haven. Prior to that, he was the department chair of the Human Performance Department at Western Michigan University. Dr. deLisle authored the text *Creating Special Events* for Sagamore Publications and coauthored *The Story of Leisure* for Human Kinetics. He has contributed research articles to the *World Leisure Journal*, the *Annals of Leisure Research*, the *Journal of Park and Recreation Administration*, and *SCHOLE* and to publications for the National Recreation and Park Association and the Michigan Recreation and Parks Association. Dr. deLisle served on the Society of Park and Recreation Educators Board of Directors and as Chair of the Education Section of National Recreation and Park Association. He is also a member of the Connecticut Recreation and Park Association. Previously, Dr. deLisle worked as the director of parks and recreation in Groton, Connecticut, supervising sport and cultural events, concerts, park facilities, and programs for the public. He spends his leisure at his home in Roccantica, Italy, and leading a four-piece, old-school rock-and-roll band, the *Nosmo Kings!*

Daniel L. Dustin, PhD, is professor emeritus, having recently retired from the University of Utah. He served as department chair at San Diego State University, Florida International University, and the University of Utah. He also served as president of the Society of Park and Recreation Educators and the Academy of Leisure Sciences. Among his many academic honors, he received the Cornelius Amory Pugsley Medal from the American Academy for Park and Recreation Administration in 2020 for his literary contributions to the advancement of conservation in the United States.

Mariela Fernandez, PhD, is an associate professor in the Parks, Recreation, and Tourism Management Department at Clemson University. She completed her bachelor's and master's degrees in the Department of Recreation, Parks, and Tourism Sciences at Texas A&M University, and she completed her PhD in the Department of Recreation, Sport and Tourism at the University of Illinois at Urbana-Champaign. Throughout her college career, she worked for various organizations such as the National Forest Service, the U.S. Fish and Wildlife Service, and the Champaign Park District, where she gained valuable experience in recreation programming, research, and recovering threatened species. Dr. Fernandez's doctoral dissertation examined how nonprofit organizations, alongside Latinx community residents, could mobilize against environmental injustices. As a faculty member, she has continued to research the environmental injustices affecting Latinx urban communities with a primary focus on their limited access to community-based parks. Dr. Fernandez also collaborates with other researchers on projects related to food insecurity and youth development.

H. Joey Gray, PhD, is the department head and professor in experience industry management at California Polytechnic State University (Cal Poly). She has taught numerous sport management and leisure and recreation courses. She is the editor of *SCHOLE* and has published scholarly papers and presented research findings at international, national, and regional conferences and coauthored chapters in *Recreational Sports Management*. Dr. Gray has earned numerous university teaching awards from both Indiana University and Middle Tennessee State University. Dr. Gray earned her PhD from Indiana University with a degree in leisure behavior, specializing in sport management, and a minor in educational psychology; her MS from North Carolina State University in parks, recreation, and tourism management with a concentration in sport management; and her BS from Averett University in sport management. Her teaching and research interests include sport management, youth sport, event planning, and pedagogy in leisure, sport, and tourism studies. Dr. Gray has a long history of experiential learning and dedication to student success and fully embraces Cal Poly's "Learn by Doing" motto.

Augustus W. Hallmon, PhD, is an assistant professor in the Hart School of Hospitality, Sport, and Recreation Management at James Madison University. Dr. Hallmon's research explores how perceptions and beliefs guide underprivileged and underrepresented populations' understanding, interest, and participation in recreation programming in the public and nonprofit sectors. The focus of this research is to develop and advocate for a practical application within recreation organizations to be more intentional in strategic planning, staff training, and mentorship concentrating on incorporating culturally competent perspectives into the organizational structure.

Camilla J. Hodge, PhD, is an assistant professor in the Experience Design and Management Department at Brigham Young University (BYU) in Provo, Utah. She earned her bachelor's degree in communications, with an emphasis in print journalism, and her master's degree in youth and family recreation from BYU. Dr. Hodge earned her PhD in parks, recreation, and tourism, with an emphasis on family recreation, from North Carolina State University. Her innovative research on family leisure experiences has been published in peer-reviewed interdisciplinary journals and in book chapters. She conducted the first study using sociometric badges (wearable devices that simultaneously measure multiple indicators of social interaction) to study family leisure experiences. Dr. Hodge has also published research on marginalized or overlooked family structures (e.g., single-parent families) and relationships (e.g., siblings).

Colleen Hood, PhD, is a professor in the Department of Recreation and Leisure Studies at Brock University in St. Catharines, Ontario, Canada. She received her bachelor's degree in physical education from the University of Calgary and her master's and doctoral degrees in therapeutic recreation and leisure behavior from the University of Illinois at Urbana-Champaign. She completed further studies at the Toronto Institute for Relational Psychotherapy in 2017 and is a registered psychotherapist in the province of Ontario, Canada. In addition to her academic work, she carries a small private psychotherapy practice. Her research interests include leisure and well-being, therapeutic recreation and recovery with mental illness, positive psychology and leisure, and professional practice in therapeutic recreation. She and Cynthia Carruthers have been research partners for more than 30 years and are coauthors of the Leisure and Well-Being Model, a service delivery model for therapeutic recreation practice.

J. Joy James, PhD, is a professor in recreation management at Appalachian State University. She received her doctorate in parks, recreation, and tourism management from Clemson University. She was a recipient of the 2009 and 2017 Society of Parks and Recreation Educators Innovation in Teaching Award. As a lifelong learner, Dr. James has a passion for innovation, best teaching practices, and scholarship in formal and nonformal outdoor learning environments.

Leah Joyner, is a PhD student and teaching and research assistant in the Parks, Recreation, and Tourism department at the University of Utah. She holds a master's degree in sustainable tourism from East Carolina University and bachelor's degrees in sustainable development and in technical photography from Appalachian State University. Her research focuses on food sovereignty and (in)justice and explores intersections of food systems, farming, and leisure. In Salt Lake City, much of her work examines historic and contemporary factors that shape the foodscape of the city and produce geographies of food inequity within the urban context of the Wasatch Front. Joyner has previously worked with farmers and tourism industry partners on food, farming, and agritourism development projects in the United States and internationally. She currently serves as a research fellow with the Race, Ethnicity, and Social Equity in Tourism (RESET) Initiative.

Michael A. Kanters, PhD, is a professor at North Carolina State University. He received his PhD from Indiana University. Dr. Kanters has taught at Brock University in Canada and the University of Western Illinois. Over his career, Dr. Kanters has worked to support and enhance the recreation and sports industry through teaching and research that examine factors associated with children's sport and recreational experiences. He has been the principal investigator or collaborator on numerous externally funded projects totaling more than $2 million, and much of his research has been widely disseminated through publication in high-impact journals and presentations at national and international scholarly conferences. He has also led the development of initiatives that positively impact the lives of children through sport and positive youth development. He has made notable contributions to national organizations through service on national boards and committees and through the development of a national peer-reviewed journal on the scholarship of teaching in sport management (*Sport Management Education Journal*).

N. Qwynne Lackey, PhD, is an assistant professor at SUNY Cortland in the Department of Recreation, Parks and Leisure, where she teaches courses relevant to recreation and environmental education. She earned her PhD from the University of Utah by completing her dissertation titled *Understanding Relationships and Sustainable Tourism Development in and around Parks and Protected Areas.* Her primary research interests include sustainable tourism, park and protected-area management, and community quality of life. Lackey also serves as a member of the National Parks Conservation Association's Next Generation Advisory Council.

Brett Lashua, PhD, teaches sociology at University College London. He has a bachelor's degree in history and a master's degree in recreation (both from Kent State University) and a doctorate in leisure studies from the University of Alberta (Canada). Brett has worked with schools, community centers, and arts organizations in the United States, Canada, and the United Kingdom to address questions of youth inequalities, racialized borderlands, and urban place-making. His research is underscored by creative and collaborative methods, including participatory music-making, cultural mapping, documentary filmmaking, and digital storytelling, as well as archival approaches. His most recent book is *Popular Music, Popular Myth and Cultural Heritage in Cleveland: The Moondog, The Buzzard and the Battle for the Rock and Roll Hall of Fame* (Emerald, 2019).

Danielle Lauber, PhD, is currently a lecturer in leisure and sport management at Middle Tennessee State University. For 13 years, Dr. Lauber has worked as a recreational therapist with a variety of populations in inpatient, outpatient, and community therapeutic settings. Dr. Lauber has supervised and directed therapeutic recreation and creative arts programming for the Department of Veterans Affairs and currently serves as a board member for Operation Song, a nonprofit organization that uses the process of songwriting to help military service members, veterans, and their families. Dr. Lauber earned her bachelor's degree in therapeutic recreation from Indiana University, her master's in leisure and sports management from Middle Tennessee State University, and her PhD in human performance from Middle Tennessee State University.

Andrew Mauldin, MS, is an assistant professor in the Department of Kinesiology at Lipscomb University. He is currently in his final year of his PhD program at Middle Tennessee State University. He received his master's degree at the University of North Alabama, where he concentrated in sport and recreation management. While a student at the University of North Alabama, Mauldin worked as graduate assistant on a grant with the Natchez Trace Parkway. As part of this grant, Mauldin researched the policy design of the Natchez Trace Parkway and developed additional outdoor recreation programs that would increase the appreciation of the history of the National Parkway. Mauldin also worked as a political campaign advisor for several Alabama state representatives, which has given him expertise in policies that contribute to the field of leisure and recreation.

Janet K. L. McKeown, PhD, is a faculty member in the Department of Recreation and Tourism Management at Vancouver Island University in Nanaimo, British Columbia, Canada. Her research explores the intersections between women's intimate and personal relationships and leisure; digital leisure practices, spaces, and communities; and the ways leisure can be used as a form of political practice. She completed her undergraduate degree in kinesiology at Western University, her master's degree in recreation and sport administration at the University of New Brunswick, and her doctoral degree in recreation and leisure studies at the University of Waterloo.

Karen K. Melton, PhD, is an associate professor at Baylor University. She received her PhD from Texas A&M. Her research focuses on the healthy development of adolescents through the maintenance of healthy families. Currently, she is working on identifying the behavioral and environmental mechanisms of shared leisure activities that facilitate connection experiences. These findings culminate in scholarship for practitioners and families focused on creating positive family experiences. Her work on family experiences has been featured more than 100 times in domestic and international media sources, including *Time, GQ, Good Morning America, Today Talk, MarketWatch, US News & World Report, iHeart-Media*, among many others. Practical implications from her research can be found in the family life intervention website Intentional Family.

Michael Mulvaney, PhD, CPRP, is a professor and director of the Recreation and Park Administration Program within the School of Kinesiology and Recreation at Illinois State University. Dr. Mulvaney is a member of the National Recreation and Park Association, the Illinois Park and Recreation Association, and several regional park and recreation associations. Dr. Mulvaney's areas of research include human resource management functions in public park and recreation agencies, management and organization of public park and recreation agencies, learning and the use of learning technologies in employee training, and planning processes in park and recreation agencies. Publications he has authored include two textbooks, journal articles, technical reports, and several national and international presentations. Dr. Mulvaney received his PhD from the University of Illinois at Urbana-Champaign. Prior to obtaining his PhD, Dr. Mulvaney was employed with the Decatur Park District (Illinois) in a variety of capacities, including facility management, fitness, programming, and special recreation.

Linda Oakleaf, PhD, is an assistant professor in the recreation, sport, and park administration program at Missouri State University, where she teaches undergraduate and graduate courses in inclusion, facility management, and outdoor recreation. Dr. Oakleaf's research focuses on inclusion, particularly for the LGBTQ+ community. She has seven years of experience as a camp director and has worked the Girl Scouts and the YMCA. Dr. Oakleaf serves on the board of the Academy of Leisure Sciences. She earned her BS in parks and recreation management at Western Carolina University, her MS in recreation administration at the University of North Carolina, Chapel Hill, and her PhD in parks, recreation, and tourism management at NC State.

Erik Rabinowitz, PhD, is an assistant professor of recreation management at Appalachian State University. He previously taught at Oklahoma State University and Southern Illinois University. Dr. Rabinowitz received a PhD in educational psychology and an MS in recreation from Southern Illinois University and a bachelor's degree in social science from Colorado State University. Dr. Rabinowitz previously worked as assistant to the director of university assessment at Southern Illinois University and as manager of WDBX 91.1, a community radio station with more than 100 volunteers. He also worked for Project Achieve and Brehm Preparatory School, both centers that assist individuals with learning disabilities. He is interested in research on the benefits of recreation, psychological constructs of leisure participation, and extreme sports. He spends his leisure time chasing around his two little girls. He enjoys skiing, soccer, canoeing, playing chess, playing his mandolin like David Grisman (he wishes), and going to Dead shows.

Ariel Rodríguez, PhD, CPRP, is an associate professor and the program director of recreation management at Springfield College in Massachusetts. He also currently serves as a council member on the Council on Accreditation of Parks, Recreation, Tourism and Related Professions. Dr. Rodríguez completed his PhD at Michigan State University, where he specialized in leisure and quality of life. At Springfield College, he teaches courses on the management of leisure and recreation services, recreation programming, and event management. He also provides evaluation services to municipal and nonprofit agencies. Dr. Rodríguez has contributed articles to the *Journal of Park and Recreation Administration, Leisure Sciences, Social Indicators Research*, the *Journal of School Health*, and the *American Journal of Health Education*. He has also authored numerous national and international presentations and was the keynote speaker at the 2019 Annual Leisure and Recreation Student Academic Conference at Dayeh University, Taiwan.

Paul A. Schlag, PhD, is the inaugural executive director of the Honors College at Central State University. Previously, Dr. Schlag served as the director and formerly as the associate director of the Centennial Honors College, as the inaugural chief of staff of the university, as an assistant department chair, and as a professor at Western Illinois University. Having taught and developed more than 30 different online and in-person courses over his 20-year academic career, he received the highest awards for teaching at the department, college, and university levels, culminating with the Provost's Award in Teaching. His impressive academic dossier includes a plethora of publications, including book chapters, peer reviewed journal articles, popular articles, and invited peer reviews. He has presented at conferences around the world and led a study abroad trip to Russia (he is fluent in Russian). As an engaged citizen, he has enjoyed serving as a coach and scout leader in the community and also as the vice chair and board member of the Macomb Area Convention and Visitor's Bureau.

Callie Spencer Schultz, PhD, is an assistant professor in the human services department at Western Carolina University. She is the program director of the parks and recreation management (PRM) program and teaches both in PRM and in the graduate experiential and outdoor education program. Dr. Schultz's research interests include leisure and new media, leisure and social justice, and the performance of subjectivities in transmedia leisure spaces. Utilizing qualitative methodologies that trouble notions of traditional epistemologies, her work aims to challenge us to think about what counts as leisure scholarship.

Daniel Theriault, PhD, is an assistant professor of Recreation Management at Appalachian State University. Before joining the faculty at Appalachian State, he was an assistant professor at Benedict College. Dr. Theriault has taught 18 unique recreation courses, but his primary teaching interests relate to inclusion and personnel management. Dr. Theriault's current research focuses on building narratives of leisure institutions that center African American people and perspectives. His life's work, whether in the classroom, through research, or in the recreation profession, has been devoted to building and sharing a set of tools to create more just leisure institutions. He lives in Tennessee with his beautiful wife Alexandra, his adorable son Ethan, and his dog Lucca.